OXFORD MONOGRAPHS IN INTERNATIONAL LAW

Recognition of States in International Law

OXFORD MONOGRAPHS IN INTERNATIONAL LAW

The aim of this series is to publish important and original pieces of research on all aspects of international law. Topics that are given particular prominence are those which, while of interest to the academic lawyer, also have important bearing on issues which touch the actual conduct of international relations. Nonetheless the series is wide in scope and includes monographs on the history and philosophical foundations of international law.

RECENT TITLES IN THE SERIES

Overlapping Individual and Interstate Claims in International Law
Jessica Howley

Party Status to Armed Conflict in International Law
Alexander Wentker

The Identity of Governments in International Law
Niko Pavlopoulos

Access to Courts for Asylum Seekers and Refugees
State Obligations under the 1951 Refugee Convention
Emma Dunlop

Gravity at the International Criminal Court
Admissibility and Prosecutorial Discretion
Priya Urs

International Law Obligations on Climate Change Mitigation
Benoit Mayer

Coastal State Jurisdiction over Living Resources in the Exclusive Economic Zone
Camille Goodman

International Law and Corporate Actors in Deep Seabed Mining
Joanna Dingwall

The Concept of an International Organization in International Law
Lorenzo Gasbarri

Necessity and Proportionality and the Right of Self-Defence in International Law
Chris O'Meara

Neutrality in Contemporary International Law
James Upcher

Recognition of States in International Law

PAVLE KILIBARDA

OXFORD
UNIVERSITY PRESS

OXFORD
UNIVERSITY PRESS

Great Clarendon Street, Oxford, OX2 6DP,
United Kingdom

Oxford University Press is a department of the University of Oxford. It furthers the University's objective of excellence in research, scholarship, and education by publishing worldwide. Oxford is a registered trade mark of Oxford University Press in the UK and in certain other countries

Published in the United States of America by Oxford University Press
198 Madison Avenue, New York, NY 10016, United States of America

British Library Cataloguing in Publication Data

Data available

Library of Congress Control Number: 2024939131

ISBN 978–0–19–890565–3

DOI: 10.1093/oso/9780198905653.001.0001

The manufacturer's authorised representative in the EU for product safety is Oxford University Press España S.A. of El Parque Empresarial San Fernando de Henares, Avenida de Castilla, 2 – 28830 Madrid (www.oup.es/en or product.safety@oup.com). OUP España S.A. also acts as importer into Spain of products made by the manufacturer.

For Eni, my best friend.
Always by my side,
forever in my thoughts.

General Editors' Preface

Brave is the young scholar who tackles in a first monograph a canonical topic of international law. The risk is of just enumerating old themes, in the words of Yeats, or instead of breaking so radically with received wisdom as to raise doubts as to the soundness of the argument. Yet scholarship on the international legal canon needs regular renewal, not least if it is to take account of developments in state and other relevant practice. The task calls for a discerning balance of respect for what has gone before and independence of mind. In practice-rich areas of the discipline it also demands a command of the historical record. The challenge can be daunting.

Pavle Kilibarda is clearly not easily daunted. In *Recognition of States in International Law*, he tackles as canonical a topic of international law as could be imagined. He proves more than up to the task.

The book covers most conceivable aspects of its classic theme, starting with what is meant by, and the purpose and forms of, the recognition of a state, as well as the concept and obligations of non-recognition, before moving to states, as understood in international law, and their international legal personality. Yet, perhaps naturally, the heart of the work lies in the longstanding controversy as to the legal effect of the recognition of a state. It is here that Dr Kilibarda brings to bear his emphasis from the outset on the opposability or otherwise to another state of the statehood—in the juridical, as distinct from material, sense—of a new state. He posits that the essential question 'is not whether recognition creates statehood', as debated by the constitutive and declaratory schools, 'but whether it can render it opposable and, if so, under what conditions' to an existing state. In response, he advances a 'mixed' theory of recognition. The general or fallback legal position, said to be rare in practice today, is that, all other legal things being equal, the recognition by an existing state of a new state 'is not only capable of giving rise' to the opposability of the latter's statehood to the former 'but is necessary for it', with the consequence that, in the bilateral legal relations between the two, recognition is constitutive of the new state's statehood. More commonly, however, in practice, Dr Kilibarda argues, some special rule of international law renders opposable to all existing states parties to a treaty or to all existing states the statehood of a new state, in which case recognition is unnecessary for the opposability of this statehood to any of these states and the effect of any such recognition is merely declaratory. After this the book enquires into the international legal obligations of unrecognised states and the opposability to a new state of the statehood of an existing state. It closes with an analysis of the recent practice of withdrawal of recognition in cases of contested statehood.

Recognition of States in International Law represents confident and sophisticated legal conceptualisation that strives to remain faithful to the practice of states and its motivation. It stakes its original claim without overreaching. On the way, it covers a great deal of interesting ground. Its tone is engaging, even personable. It will prove a stimulating and enjoyable read and provoke discussion, as does the best international legal scholarship.

RO'K, CR
Milan and Oxford
May 2024

Acknowledgements

This book was initially prepared as my doctoral thesis at the University of Geneva. As such, I must once again thank my thesis supervisor, Professor Robert Kolb, who not only provided priceless insight during my doctoral studies but has also remained a source of inspiration throughout my work on the modified, abridged, and updated version now before you. It is a rare privilege for any student of law to work so closely with a scholar of such magnitude and I am deeply grateful for the opportunity.

I must also thank my jury members: Professor Benedict Foëx, then dean of the Faculty of Law, who presided over the defence; Professor Gloria Gaggioli-Gasteyger, also of Geneva; and Professor John Dugard of Leiden and Pretoria. It is a singular honour to engage with individuals of such renown and expertise in matters of recognition, and their engagement and good humour have made our discussion a truly memorable experience.

I must acknowledge the willingness of the Serbian Foreign Ministry to share with me some of the *notes verbales* notifying them of the withdrawal of recognition of Kosovo by a number of States. The diplomatic correspondence provided by the ministry enabled me to conduct the first in-depth study of 'derecognition' in recent legal scholarship.

I thank most sincerely my wife, Ana, whose love, devotion, and patience surely permeate every word written in this book.

My deepest love and gratitude go to the rest of my family: Aleksandra, Branko, Olga, and Bak, who saw this one to the end; and to Ranko, Vera, Bogosav, Ružica, Vladimir, Dušan, and Eni, who did not.

Geneva, April 2024

Contents

Table of Cases

PERMANENT COURT OF INTERNATIONAL JUSTICE

INTERNATIONAL COURT OF JUSTICE

INTERNATIONAL CRIMINAL TRIBUNAL FOR THE FORMER YUGOSLAVIA

INTERNATIONAL CRIMINAL COURT

EUROPEAN COURT OF HUMAN RIGHTS

EUROPEAN COURT OF JUSTICE

AFRICAN COMMISSION ON HUMAN AND PEOPLES' RIGHTS

HUMAN RIGHTS COMMITTEE

COMMITTEE ON THE ELIMINATION OF RACIAL DISCRIMINATION

ARBITRAL AWARDS

DOMESTIC JURISPRUDENCE

Canada

Czechoslovakia

France

Japan

Serbia

South Africa

Switzerland

United Kingdom

United States

Table of Instruments

TREATIES

UN SECURITY COUNCIL RESOLUTIONS

UN GENERAL ASSEMBLY RESOLUTIONS

INTERNATIONAL LAW COMMISSION DOCUMENTS

OTHER SOURCES

Abbreviations

CIS	Commonwealth of Independent States
EU	European Union
FRG	Federal Republic of Germany
FRY	Federal Republic of Yugoslavia (Serbia and Montenegro)
GDR	German Democratic Republic
ICC	International Criminal Court
ICJ	International Court of Justice
ICTY	International Criminal Tribunal for the Former Yugoslavia
ILC	International Law Commission
OAS	Organisation of American States
OAU	Organisation of African Unity
PCIJ	Permanent Court of International Justice
PISG	Provisional Institutions of Self-Government of Kosovo
PRC	People's Republic of China
ROC	Republic of China (Taiwan)
SFRY	Socialist Federal Republic of Yugoslavia
UK	United Kingdom
UN	United Nations
UNGA	United Nations General Assembly
UNMIK	United Nations Mission in Kosovo
UNSC	United Nations Security Council
US	United States of America
USSR	Union of Soviet Socialist Republics
VCLT	Vienna Convention on the Law of Treaties

1
Introduction

1. The Problem of Recognition

The word 'recognition' has a difficult history in international law. Since the early modern period, it has been employed to designate an acceptance of another's claim and invoked most often and with the greatest vigour when coming from some higher authority as a sort of 'bill of rights'. Whether recognition was given by a religious or worldly authority, the concept was employed to denote a *title*, the validation of a claim of specific rights. Thus, Pope Alexander VI recognised Spanish and Portuguese claims to the New World in a series of bulls leading to the Treaty of Tordesillas in 1494, and later, the Spanish Empire recognised the independent Dutch Republic in Antwerp in 1609.

But the concept of recognition has long since expanded beyond territorial titles and claims. In contemporary practice, the word is used in a plethora of such widely differing situations that it is sometimes difficult to establish its link with a *legal* entitlement. It has thus become commonplace to speak of recognition of Russian 'interests' in the borders of the former USSR, or of US 'interests' in Latin America. We speak of recognition of a foreign State's judicial decisions, its high school and university degrees, or marriage concluded abroad. Various disciplinary frameworks today discuss recognition of victim status, or of one's gender identity and minority rights, or even of the legal personality of some species of animals. When the same term is employed in such dissimilar situations, it is unlikely to conserve the same meaning beyond its core significance: namely, that the seeker of recognition has a *claim* (legal, moral, political, or otherwise), and that its giver is *accepting* that claim in whatever frame of reference it is made.

Not all these phenomena are of interest to this study, which focuses on recognition in law, specifically international law and the best-known type of recognition by far—*recognition of statehood or of independence* (also often referred to as 'diplomatic recognition' as it is normally done through diplomatic channels). Such recognition is very different from 'recognition' of political interest or of individual identity for it is vested with legal meaning. It would be inappropriate to say that at least these forms of legal recognition are somehow poorly understood or unexplored: scholarship has been churning out detailed and specific analyses of diplomatic recognition for the better part of two centuries.

And yet, recognition somehow remains a mystical term, drawing controversy and scorn which have only grown since the Second World War. Unlike

Recognition of States in International Law. Pavle Kilibarda, Oxford University Press. © Pavle Kilibarda 2024.
DOI: 10.1093/oso/9780198905653.003.0001

nineteenth-century scholarly debates, contemporary discussions appear to be so deeply entrenched in political matters that any position one adopts might lead to suspicions of bias. On the very rare occasion that States publish their views of recognition, they are at once confronted by the opposing camp, then neutral observers reduce both groups' views to their perceived underlying interests: perhaps one government favours self-determination to support its kinsmen across the border; yet another fears secession and dismemberment and so espouses a different view—the criticism piles on and denigrates recognition in an attempt to remove its legal veneer and lay bare the political machinations truly at work.

There is much to criticise in relation to diplomatic recognition—its ambiguous conditions and effects, the inconsistency and even the banality with which it is made and revoked—but a black-and-white description of recognition as *only* political or some sort of fig leaf for political interests is not only prejudice, it is itself a position (however simplistic) on a complex phenomenon unlikely to soon disappear. Just as politics shapes law and law seeks to restrain politics, so too does recognition have the two faces of Janus: motivated by political interests, it produces legal results.

More disconcerting is the idea that the legal regime of recognition is too unclear to be of any use. This is a strong argument, for the 'law of recognition', if such a thing exists, is murky indeed, and not, incongruously, because it is unexplored, but rather because too much has been written about it. There is not a manual or textbook in use today that does not reflect upon recognition (if at least to dismiss it as irrelevant!), and dozens of treatises have been written on it, mainly in the mid-twentieth century: even today, when recognition has become something of a pariah in the legal vernacular, monographs and theses are regularly produced on keywords from the same family, such as statehood, self-determination, secession, and many others. To use the colloquial term, recognition has been 'done to death' in legal doctrine.

2. The Great Debate

The myriad works on recognition comprise a prickly field to traverse. Its authors all have very different views of how, when, and why recognition takes place, whether it is a legal or political act, or whether States are obliged to extend recognition to others and under what circumstances: perhaps no two writers will answer all of these questions in the same way. But it has become habitual to speak of two schools of thought depending on whether recognition confers statehood or whether it merely takes note of it.

The latter school, called 'declaratory' (its adherents 'declaratists'), is today the more influential. Although a casual review of the literature may give the impression that the declaratory view is more modern, this is incorrect: in fact, some of the oldest writings take this position either expressly or implicitly. Under the influence of Enlightenment thought, eighteenth- and early nineteenth-century writers such as Vattel or Heffter describe statehood as a simple fact: a State is, or it is not; recognition does not figure in the equation. It is however the more modern strain of declaratory thought that attaches legal consequences to this fact and describes the mechanism whereby this comes to pass. This view is often seen as flowing from natural law thinking, but this is an oversimplification: many declaratory scholars today do not subscribe to natural law philosophy.

The opposing 'constitutivist' school ascribes to recognition a key role in the achievement of statehood. It has become something of a mantra among students of law to say that constitutivists argue that recognition *creates* a State: I am not aware of any author making such a counterintuitive and disingenuous claim; they may at most argue that recognition creates a State's legal personality. Thus, the State as a political and material phenomenon exists separately from the State as a subject of international or municipal law. This doctrine arose and spread in the second half of the nineteenth century and is today usually linked, and criticised together with legal positivism. Again, there is no necessary link between constitutivism and positivism: Hersch Lauterpacht was a constitutivist who shunned positivism.

Because the two schools are seen as being at opposing poles of the recognition debate and thus mutually exclusive, it is common to overstate their differences and disregard ways in which they might be complementary. A closer look at older doctrinal works demonstrates that both schools originate as a reaction to different problems: whereas the early declaratists tried to explain the phenomena of statehood and independence (and not *solely* in a legal sense), constitutivists sought to understand the expansion of the legal system to encompass new subjects. The normative framework that we know today as international law and understand as global and all-encompassing was not always such: it first arose as a regional—European and Christian—phenomenon, and was only gradually extended to other subjects, whether these subjects had previously been regarded as States or not. An entity could thus be a State and not form part of this particular system of law: for example, it is commonly raised in nineteenth-century literature that the Ottoman Empire was admitted into the legal community through the 1856 Treaty of Paris.

This study does not seek to lay to rest age-old debates on the relationship between statehood and recognition. Today such general debates seem little else than rhetorical exercises: whether an entity is recognised because it is a State, or it is a State because it is recognised, is just another version of the chicken-and-egg dilemma. In fact, this discussion will probably never be resolved, as my research points towards the conclusion that international law simply does not regulate recognition of statehood.

The last sentence might appear to the reader an exaggeration. There exist *legal* rules on premature recognition, and on non-recognition—and there exists so much State practice almost every year that surely recognition as an indubitably legal term must come under legal regulation? The answer will depend, naturally, on one's own preconception of 'legal regulation'. As we will see, there do exist some rules on recognition (or more precisely, rules relevant to recognition), but they are all ephemeral: they proscribe when recognition cannot be made and nothing else. In vain might lawyers seek a rule stating, 'Recognition is declaratory' or 'It is constitutive'—even the scant treaty provisions and some jurisprudence in this regard are so ambiguous and contextual that they cannot be taken as proof of a norm of general scope. If such a norm were identified, then surely it would be the Holy Grail of recognition studies—but there is little indication that this is the case. Therefore, if we may speak of an 'international law of recognition', this can be little more than a poor and disorganised assortment of rules that may here and there be of local relevance.

Yet recognition is nonetheless a legal notion, for when States choose to extend or deny it, they do so using legal terminology and in the aim of producing legal consequences.[1] In a legal sense, to recognise something means to identify it as lawful and to accept its normative implications; this is so even if the legal framework is not specific to recognition and must be sought elsewhere in law. In other words, recognition may not be *specifically* regulated by law, but that does not mean it is unbound by it.

3. The Importance of Opposability

How then might we proceed with an analysis of recognition? This book assumes that any legal system is essentially a network, however intricate, of relations of rights and obligations between its various subjects: these rights and obligations may not be distributed in equal measure across the playing ground. Some norms will only bind specific subjects; others will be applicable to all individually but not between them; a third group will involve obligations owed by one subject to some others but not to all of them; yet a fourth will be owed to the community as a whole, but to no particular individual; and so on. The real question is *how* to determine whether a stakeholder has certain obligations towards another individual subject. Thus, the fundamental idea of this study is not whether recognition creates statehood, but whether it can render it opposable and, if so, under what conditions.

Opposability is a word that seldom appears in English-language literature on recognition, although the concept is often discussed. The only treatise so far to fully problematise the relationship between opposability and recognition is Jean

[1] This point has been identified and argued convincingly by John Dugard 'The Secession of States and Their Recognition in the Wake of Kosovo' (2013) 357 RCADI 9, 213ff; for a criticism of the view that international law does not regulate secession or recognition at all, see pages 26–27 of the same work.

Charpentier's doctoral thesis (published in 1956) *La reconnaissance internationale et l'évolution du droit des gens*. Charpentier finds that States do not recognise a new State or government directly: what they recognise is a legal fact, produced by the appearance of a new authority, that requires them to modify their behaviour. He defines opposability as 'the necessary reaction to a modification of the international legal order by a third State' (*la réaction nécessaire d'une modification de l'ordre juridique international sur le comportement d'un État tiers*).[2] If a State is legally bound to act in a certain way towards a fact or situation, then that fact or situation is 'opposable' to it. Although Charpentier's analysis leads him to conclude that recognition has nothing to do with the opposability of statehood (a conclusion very different from my own), I am convinced that his focus on opposability is fully justified.

To illustrate: from a purely practical perspective, is it more purposeful to ask whether A is a State in the absolute, or whether B is simply required according to the rules of international law to treat it as a State? Insisting on the former raises complex and difficult questions that law may ultimately be ill-equipped to answer, a point raised convincingly by Arrigo Cavaglieri.[3] Consider in this respect that even the oft-invoked Montevideo Convention, which contains a definition of statehood, has brought us no closer to resolving situations of contested statehood: States simply ignore some of its criteria, or invoke others, when reacting to such cases. But the law *can* pinpoint its own subjects, their relations and interactions, with a sufficient degree of clarity to work as a functional system.

This is where recognition comes into play. The first question I asked myself in preparing this study was whether State A is opposable to State B if B does not recognise A (namely, whether opposability results from recognition). The answer will of course depend on the context, namely whether a specific rule may be identified to ground opposability: if such a rule exists, then opposability could be inferred from it regardless of recognition, but if it does not, could opposability still flow from recognition?

The paucity of international law on the topic points to the conclusion that, in general, recognition is not only capable of giving rise to opposability, but is necessary for it to exist. There is no rule of general international law leading to another conclusion.[4] In its absence, every State is free to choose with whom it enters legal relations, following a principle-based approach.

But the 'in general' above does not mean that these conditions arise frequently. To the contrary, in many situations today when statehood is newly created—perhaps in most cases—rules *can* be identified to render it opposable to existing

[2] Jean Charpentier, *La reconnaissance internationale et l'évolution du droit des gens* (Pedone 1956) 9.

[3] Arrigo Cavaglieri, 'Règles générales du droit de la paix' (1929) 26 RCADI 311, 321.

[4] I understand by 'general international law' the contemporary rules of universal (and not regional or bilateral) customary law and the general principles of law binding upon all States regardless of express individual acceptance.

States. This might be the case, for example, if the new State is admitted into the United Nations (UN), or enjoys a 'right to statehood' under the principle of self-determination.[5] Because a rule-based approach is then possible, recognition is not a condition of opposability as there exist other applicable rules establishing it. Regardless of their relative frequency, circumstances where a rule-based approach is possible are normatively exceptional as the requisite rule cannot be inferred from general international law and must be drawn from the given context.

For example, a new State may arise by seceding from its Parent State, a UN member, and achieve UN membership itself. In this case, the Parent State will be required to treat the breakaway entity as a State by virtue of the provisions of the UN Charter regardless of whether it has recognised it individually: this is why Pakistan could no longer deny the statehood of Bangladesh even some time before it had recognised it. However, where the secessionists do not have the consent of their parent to create a new State, do not enjoy membership in the United Nations or a similar collective entity, and are not entitled to external self-determination, there will not exist any rule of international law requiring the parent or any other State to legally treat them as a State: only recognition could produce such a result.

Fleshing out the principle-based and rule-based approaches is my primary goal in this study. This involves describing the relationship between recognition and opposability. The issue cannot be resolved without first being broken down into a number of related questions, such as: does recognition ever lead to opposability? Can opposability exist without recognition? Are existing States opposable to a new State if it does not recognise them? What is the legal position of an unrecognised State, namely does it have obligations under international law? Is there such a thing as partial opposability? Is there an obligation to extend recognition? And, can opposability be undone if recognition is withdrawn?

To adequately digest these questions, it is first necessary to adopt an analytical view of diplomatic recognition. When State A recognises State B, it is carrying out a specific *act* (recognition) towards an *object* (State B) bringing about legal *effects* (B's rights as a State vis-à-vis A). This act–object–effects triptych seems most convenient for this study and forms the basis of its structure; a similar approach was developed by Joe Verhoeven in his seminal treatise on recognition.[6] 'Object' signifies here an occasion or fact that *as a matter of law* requires or authorises certain conduct as an 'effect'; the 'act' may be the necessary link between these two elements.

A clean-cut differentiation between the three is conceptually impossible. Thus, some points will necessarily overlap: for example, the elements of statehood are

[5] We will discuss in the coming chapters whether the principle and right of self-determination could directly establish the opposability of statehood or simply lead to an *entitlement* to create an independent State.

[6] Joe Verhoeven, *La reconnaissance internationale dans la pratique contemporaine* (Pedone 1975).

part of the object of recognition (if it is a State that is being recognised), but they may also be prerequisites for an act of recognition to produce effects. Similarly, statehood rights may result from recognition and thus be considered an effect, but it is also possible to regard them as inherent in statehood and thus part of the object of recognition (regardless of whether recognition is required for opposability). Law is not an exact science and some degree of logical inconsistency or at least uncertainty is tolerable if we want to avoid the chicken-or-egg moment, as mentioned earlier. In my view, when discussing recognition of States, it is best to treat material statehood and a State's legal personality as part of the object of recognition, whereas the only effect may be to render them opposable towards the issuer.

4. Outlook, Methodology, and Structure

I have already mentioned the 'Great Debate' between adherents of the constitutivist and declaratist schools of thought on recognition. I have no delusions of being able to finally resolve these controversies, which will doubtless continue for years to come. But if one conclusion poignantly stands out from this study it is that many constitutivists and declaratists are more closely aligned than meets the eye. Whether recognition 'creates' statehood in any fashion is a theoretical matter: whether it is needed for opposability is something else entirely. If they examine the matter at all, some unabashed declaratists might require recognition for the possession or at least the exercise of legal rights towards other States (which is, of course, opposability). Therefore, one of my main goals was to recast major doctrinal works on recognition on an opposability axis, rather than one focusing on the 'creation' of statehood or legal personality. The resulting classification is similar to what one might otherwise expect, but there may be a few surprises: for example, some have described the theories of Pradier-Fodéré, Fauchille, and Verhoeven as declaratory; I regard the former two rather as constitutivists, while the latter produces a rare example of a truly 'mixed' theory.

Regarding 'mixed' theories, which are commonly discussed in more recent works on recognition, I only discuss them briefly. Insofar as opposability is expressed in binary terms, there is no room for an intermediate approach (A is either opposable to B or it is not). Nevertheless, a few authors have ingeniously come up with ways of overcoming the dichotomy altogether. Although I ultimately disagree with their understanding, I concede that they draw attention to important aspects that the more traditional constitutive–declaratory debate has largely ignored. In truth, my own proposed 'normative theory of recognition' may be regarded as a mixed theory, bearing in mind the precarious relationship it identifies between recognition and opposability.

I have also said that this book should enable a comprehensive approach to all situations of contested statehood. An analysis of the combination of material and legal factors present in such cases (including the current and historic claims of statehood of Abkhazia, the Baltic States, Biafra, Cabinda, Donbas, the two Germanies, Israel, Northern Cyprus, Korea, Kosovo, Palestine, Rhodesia, Somaliland, South Ossetia, Taiwan, Vietnam, Western Sahara, and the Yugoslav republics) demonstrates that an alternating application of the principle- and rule-based reasoning allows sense to be made of very complex situations. This requires us to accept that statehood as a legal fact and statehood as a material fact are not the same phenomenon: failing to acknowledge the distinction will leave us in the quagmire of absolute thinking that has already plagued this field for more than two centuries.

Not even a comprehensive approach will leave all readers satisfied. This is not a work on ethics and may at times come across as unduly conservative or even reactionary. I wish to underline that the primary focus of this book is to ascertain the state of positive law (*lex lata*) in the domain of statehood and recognition; when I give recommendations for how the law should be, but is presently not (*lex ferenda*), I do so explicitly. On a few points where I found it impossible to glean whether a positive law rule exists—such as the automatic opposability of separation with the consent of the Parent State to third States—I give my own opinion as to how the problem should be tackled. My reflections in this regard were always based on the values underpinning contemporary international law.

This leads me to the problem of unknowability in law. International law in its current state does not provide answers to all possible questions, and some matters will remain *aporia*, to use the Platonic term. For example, opposability (or lack thereof) in the sense discussed in this work has meaning on a bilateral level, as expressed in the mutual legal relations of different subjects; it loses any meaning in situations where the bilateral axis becomes obscured or indirect. It is therefore impossible to know, given the current state of the law, whether unrecognised States can participate in the creation of customary international law, or how to classify an armed conflict between two States when the statehood of one of them is not opposable to the other (this is a point I examine in some detail, but I can ultimately only make assumptions and suggestions). Yet these questions are ephemeral for recognition: they depend on the state of other branches of international law, and therefore deserve separate analysis.

The rules of international law are to be found within its sources: these are largely or even exclusively a product of State practice. While practice on recognition of States and governments is abundant, it is also opaque and inconsistent. Very few States publish their views on the role and effects of recognition of other States and governments, and when they extend recognition, it is often impossible to know whether they are making a political or legal commitment (to be clear, recognition is *always* political: the question is whether, in addition to being a political act, it is also a legal one). It is likely that many, if not most, States simply do not have a clear position on this issue; to make matters worse, different governments of the same State may give the act a differing significance.

Jurisprudence is also not of much help in making sense of State practice and the shape of customary law. This work examines a large amount of international and domestic jurisprudence, but very little of it is directly relevant to recognition. When it comes to recognition of States, most international bodies seem to consciously avoid taking a position on the matter. Domestic courts tend to be less shy, but it is often difficult to determine whether their position is formed as a matter of international law or local legislation, or even if it is simply a matter of judicial policy. This leaves us with doctrine, which is sharply divided, as mentioned above. But while analysing jurisprudence and doctrine, I was mindful of the fact that a lack of consensus or explicit statements from relevant authorities may itself be significant—namely, that positive law simply does not provide an answer.

This book is split into thirteen chapters, including the introduction and concluding remarks. As I analyse recognition according to the act–object–effects formula, the initial chapters reflect on recognition as a legal act, its basis in international law, the forms and types of recognition, as well as the question of non-recognition. Chapters 5 and 6 then turn respectively to material and legal statehood, whereas the subsequent chapters evaluate the state of positive law on recognition and statehood in light of jurisprudence, State practice, and legal doctrine. Chapters 9 and 10 outline my normative theory of recognition, which distinguishes between situations where statehood may be inferred from the legal norms applicable to the case at hand (when recognition is declaratory) and those where this is not possible, giving lawful recognition a constitutive effect. These chapters synthesise findings presented in the rest of the book and may be considered the theoretical crux of the whole work. Chapter 11 considers the legal position of States regardless of recognition and Chapter 12 reflects on the phenomenon of withdrawal of recognition or 'derecognition', a matter that has not previously been subjected to serious academic scrutiny. Chapter 13 summarises the main findings and offers some concluding observations and reflections.

2
Recognition as a Legal Act

1. Recognition as Cognisance and Acceptance

Legal literature often discusses the purpose and function of recognition. The notions are sometimes used interchangeably, but it is also possible to distinguish between them. Thus, the function of any act is discernible from its intended consequences in a given system of reference. An act is then 'legal' because it is made in a system of law that determines its functions as normative, judicial, or retributive, to name a few. They are determined by the nature and workings of the legal system and cannot be understood outside its confines. At the same time, the purposes of an act may lie well beyond this system of reference, meaning that a legal act could be undertaken for political, moral, or symbolic purposes. When a national parliament enacts a statute setting new restrictions on traffic, it presumably wishes to protect commuters and pedestrians. Whether the legislation is purposeful must be asked of experts on traffic; whether parliament is entitled to pass the new legislation, and how this impacts the existing normative order, are questions for lawyers. It is therefore the legal functions of recognition, and not its purposes, that are of primary interest in the study of international law.

The function and purpose of recognition are not always easy to discern. Brownlie and Crawford write that the act of recognition involves 'the determination of statehood, a question of law', and serves as 'a condition of the establishment of formal relations, including diplomatic relations and the conclusion of bilateral treaties'.[1] From the perspective of the recognising State, recognition is strictly an expression of its views that the normative order has changed and that it will abide by the modification, but also that it wishes to establish diplomatic and commercial relations with a new State or government, foster friendship and cooperation, support its nationals in the latter's territory, and so on. The former are the functions of recognition, the latter its purposes. The purposes for which A recognises B may be multi-layered, complex, and politically significant: but law provides no yardstick with which to measure them. Conversely, if recognition is indeed a legal act, then its functions can only be determined according to law.

The first function of recognition is evident from the classical notion of this act as a mechanism whereby the author of recognition ascertains that certain material

[1] James Crawford, *Brownlie's Principles of Public International Law* (OUP 2019) 137–38.

Recognition of States in International Law. Pavle Kilibarda, Oxford University Press. © Pavle Kilibarda 2024.
DOI: 10.1093/oso/9780198905653.003.0002

-gal circumstances have come together and infers from them the appropriate legal consequences. This is how any court of law functions: in a criminal case, it must first be determined whether a crime has been committed in fact before the sanction prescribed by law can be ordered.[2]

(1) It is the same with recognition of States or governments. In the first instance, the granter of recognition takes cognisance of the fact that a new State has come into existence; when a government is recognised (a rare but persistent occurrence), the recognising State takes note of its effective control over a territory and capacity to speak for its State. What is recognised, writes Reuter, is not a legal rule but a fact from which flow legal consequences.[3] The cognitive aspect corresponds to the original meaning of the words recognise in English and *reconnaître* in French, both of which find their roots in the Latin *recognoscere*, signifying 'to acknowledge, recall to mind, know again',[4] similarly to the German *anerkennen.* No formality is required for the cognitive function to play out: it is subconscious and not based on will any more than an individual human being may 'choose' not to recognise an acquaintance, however frustrating or distasteful, when we run into them in the street. Of course, the matter is not as simple when an existing State becomes 'aware' of the existence of a new one, but the two situations do not differ in principle. Thus, recognition achieves its original meaning as an internalised act exclusive to the granter and *a priori* unknowable to any other State or any other subject of law, but as a formal act, recognition is nothing else than a public and officious proclamation of the insight which precedes it. This first function of recognition is cognitive, which we may also call juridical, because it is done in the context of a State's role as adjudicator under international law.[5] This is what I mean by 'recognition as cognisance'.

Many scholars single this out as the true purpose of recognition. For Kelsen, recognition is 'the establishment of the fact that in a given case a "state in the sense of international law" exists'.[6] Lauterpacht similarly writes, 'To recognize a community as a State is to declare that it fulfills the conditions of statehood as required by international law.'[7] This view, which is common in doctrine and may be found with scholars as diverse as Bluntschli[8] and Rivier,[9] is best summarised by Shaw: 'The act

[2] 'If a legal order attaches to a certain fact as condition a certain consequence, then it must determine in what manner and especially by whom the existence of the conditioning fact is to be established in order that the consequence provided for may be attached to it.' Hans Kelsen, 'Recognition in International Law: Theoretical Observations' (1941) 35(4) The American Journal of International Law 605, 606.

[3] Paul Reuter, *Institutions internationales* (Presses universitaires de France 1969) 120.

[4] See eg Merriam-Webster Dictionary entry for 'recognize' at <https://www.merriam-webster.com/dictionary/recognize> last accessed 30 May 2024.

[5] See Hersch Lauterpacht, *Recognition in International Law* (CUP 2013) 23–25 and Arrigo Cavaglieri, 'Règles générales du droit de la paix' (1929) 26 RCADI 311, 344.

[6] Kelsen, 'Recognition in International Law' (n 2) 606.

[7] Lauterpacht, *Recognition in International Law* (n 5) 6.

[8] Johann Caspar Bluntschli, *Das moderne Völkerrecht der civilisirten Staten als Rechtsbuch dargestellt* (Druck und Verlag der C H Beck'schen Buchhandlung 1872) 71ff.

[9] Alphonse Rivier, *Principes du droit des gens: Tome premier* (Arthur Rousseau 1896) 57.

of recognition by one state of another indicates that the former regards the latter as having conformed with the basic requirements of international law as to the creation of a state.'[10] Such recognition, construed narrowly as a legal determination of facts, is impossible to withdraw, because one cannot suddenly cease to be conscious of a fact one has previously taken cognisance of: States do not, or should not, suffer amnesia. This role of recognition is often (but not exclusively) emphasised by scholars claimed to have a 'declaratory' view of the act.[11]

In relation to the cognitive role of recognition, it is important to bear in mind that the above scholars, who properly focus on the act of recognition itself, highlight that this act nevertheless conveys an internal conviction and is thus an external act: it is typically a declaration and thus others may become aware of it. This seemingly contradicts the position taken here on the purely internal aspects of recognition as cognisance or somehow renders them meaningless; if cognisance is present but not declared, it cannot be the object of legal analysis by third parties. Yet cognisance necessarily pre-dates the act of recognition, which gives voice to it, and it may be added that, when faced with a legal fact, subjects to whom that fact is opposable need to react regardless of whether their awareness of it is expressly stated. A new legal situation may arise even if it is not specifically acknowledged by a given subject of law. It is therefore important, in my view, to understand that (from the recognising State's perspective), cognisance of a change in legal facts takes place before recognition is formally given.

(2) That recognition is not merely cognisance is attested by its other key aspect, namely recognition is not a purely cognitive or even juridical act: there is a considerable amount of political consideration involved in the decision to recognise. This does not mean that the act itself is merely political, at least not any more than it is 'political' to enter a treaty. When recognising, States are not only guided by legal criteria. Shaw recalls: 'Recognition is not merely applying the relevant legal consequences to a factual situation, for sometimes a state will not want such consequences to follow, either internationally or domestically.'[12] In such matters, there is much room for policy considerations before granting recognition.

Of course, the reason for this is that States are suspicious of new legal facts arising that might oblige them to act in a certain way, which includes situations where a new State is established: one or more existing States may not be willing to treat it as a peer. Southern Rhodesia, having proclaimed independence in 1965, did not receive any recognition from other States until its final reconstitution as

[10] Malcolm N Shaw, *International Law* (CUP 2017) 331.
[11] Alfred Verdross, 'Règles générales du droit international de la paix' (1929) 30 RCADI 271, 125–26.
[12] Shaw, *International Law* (n 10) 329–30.

Zimbabwe in 1979 even though it had functioned as a *de facto* State for more than a decade.[13] Therefore, while we cannot consciously refuse to recognise that distasteful acquaintance in the street, we can still choose to rudely (or rightly!) ignore or fail to acknowledge him. This is not a new phenomenon at the inter-state level, but older doctrine prudishly attempted to camouflage it in functionalism: thus Bluntschli wrote that recognition leads to the 'acceptance' of new States into the 'international legal community'.[14] Jellinek more realistically wrote that legal relations may only be established through mutual recognition,[15] and Cavaglieri insisted that a non-recognised State was deprived of legal personality. Existing States may decide whether they wish to be bound by law towards the new State, in which case the material elements of statehood only have value as indicators of lawful recognition.[16]

Regardless of how solemn or banal we should regard diplomatic recognition, it doubtless also has a normative function which is typically asserted by the 'constitutive' view of recognition. This normativity manifests itself in establishing the opposability of the new State towards existing ones in a manner somewhat analogous to the creation of a new rule of international law. When State A recognises State B, it does not only take note of the fact that B is factually a State but also accepts to treat it as such by law, for example by respecting the personal and functional immunities of its dignitaries. The word 'recognition' then becomes a misnomer, at least in those languages borrowing from Latin, because it is not merely a cognitive act; it draws closer to the meaning of the term employed in Slavic languages, such as the Serbo-Croatian *признање* (*priznanje*), or the Russian *признание* (*priznanie*). Rather than a cognitive act, these words signify 'social recognition, respect, reward'[17] (the root verb may also signify an 'admission [of guilt]') and are as such not value-neutral terms. In this sense, recognition also signifies acceptance.

State practice supports both a notion of recognition as a cognitive and as a normative act, wherefore it is best not to single either one of them out, but to take both as inherent in recognition as an act with a dual nature. Sometimes, recognition will be closer to cognisance, and at other times to acceptance: but both sides will be present in every instance of recognition.

[13] See more in John Dugard, *Recognition and the United Nations* (Grotius Publications Limited 1987) 97.

[14] Bluntschli, *Das moderne Völkerrecht der civilisirten Staten* (n 8) 71; cf Lassa Oppenheim, *International Law: A Treatise, Volume I: Peace* (Longmans, Green and Co 1912) 116ff.

[15] Georg Jellinek, *Allgemeine Staatslehre* (Verlag von O Häring 1914) 99.

[16] Cavaglieri, 'Règles générales du droit de la paix' (n 5) 347.

[17] See eg Milica Vujanić and others, *Rečnik srpskoga jezika* (Matica srpska 2011) 1023, for the word's meaning in Serbian.

2. Conceptualising Recognition as a Legal, Political, Domestic, and International Act

2.1 Recognition as a Legal and Political Act

Much doctrinal debate concerns the nature of recognition, namely its status as a source of law and, should it indeed be considered such, its location amongst the traditional sources of international law. The debate is confounded by the sheer multitude of varying practice described as 'recognition', the significance accorded to it by the observer and the comparative importance and role of 'non-recognition', which is generally defined in opposition to recognition: whereas the former is a positive act, the latter is a refusal to act in a certain way. As such, non-recognition may be more difficult to identify (because it is usually easier to pinpoint acts than their absence). As Brownlie remarked, '[t]here is no such thing as a uniform type of recognition or non-recognition' and '[i]n any case "recognition" is not a term of art'.[18]

To conceptualise the act of recognition, we must fix it on two axes: along the first, recognition may be a political or legal act; along the second, it may be an international or domestic one. Thus, there are four possibilities: recognition can be a domestic legal, or an international political act, and so on. None of these exclude the others, they are merely different manifestations of the same phenomenon.

The political–legal dichotomy is not readily apparent. Kelsen attempted to draw a line between political and legal recognition in theory:

> The political act of recognition of a state or government means that the recognizing state is willing to enter into political and other relations with the recognized state or government, relations of the kind which normally exist between members of the family of nations. Since a state according to general international law is not obliged to entertain such relations ... political recognition of a state or a government is an act which lies within the arbitrary decision of the recognizing state.[19]

Conversely, recognition is a legal act only insofar as the legal order attaches to it certain consequences; he clarifies, 'The jurist knows that the legal order attaches a certain punishment only to a theft established by the competent court following a prescribed procedure.'[20] Thus, recognition is a legal act if it is governed by the law and produces legal consequences.

[18] Ian Brownlie, *Principles of Public International Law* (OUP 1998) 89; the sentence was omitted in later editions of the *Principles* prepared by Crawford.
[19] Kelsen (n 2) 605.
[20] ibid 606.

Kelsen's view rests on two premises: first, recognition is political if it is a discretionary act of States, and second, it is legal if it is governed by law (by producing legal consequences or taking place in a legal procedure). This approach to the political–legal dichotomy is clearly too narrow. Kelsen rather seems to be discussing the effects of recognition, which can be both political and legal or only political ('apolitical recognition' is only possible *in abstracto*). In the latter sense, recognition is declaratory and does not, in principle, produce results in international law. Yet even if a State's recognition of an object were merely declaratory, it could still be regarded as a legal act, just as recognition producing legal rights and duties may be firmly political in a given context.

Any act of recognition can be analysed for its legal and political implications which coexist. The latter are the domain of the study of international relations and political science. In this work, I focus narrowly on the legal act of recognition, which is a notion separate from that of its legal effects *stricto sensu*. Recognition is therefore a legal act insofar as it amounts to a reaction to a legal fact and intends to produce legal effects.

2.2 Recognition as a Domestic and International Act

Recognition is properly dealt with as an international act, and that is the way I will examine it here. But it will synchronously produce legal consequences in many national legal systems: this presupposes that it is also a domestic legal act. Even if recognition were declaratory under international law, it could still be constitutive domestically, as is the case in many common law systems where unrecognised States will be denied certain rights such as legal standing in domestic courts if they are not recognised by the executive. As we will see, it can sometimes be very difficult to discern whether domestic courts discuss in various cases recognition as a domestic or international act, namely whether they are evaluating it from the perspective of national or international law.

I am not aware of domestic legislation expressly foreseeing the legislative nature or power of acts of recognition by the State's executive. Its effects vary from one domestic jurisdiction to another and are usually interpreted by local judges who typically understand recognition primarily as an international act. Yet if recognition could produce any legal effects in domestic law, then we must infer that it is also a domestic act, however one might categorise it in a given system. In several countries, such as the United States, the United Kingdom, or Serbia, the rights of a foreign State under domestic law will largely depend on whether it has been recognised by the national government. The validity of such an act can therefore be evaluated in terms of national law. For example, the US Supreme Court has confirmed that only States recognised by the US government may enjoy legal standing in American courts.[21] As foreign States are not entitled to legal standing in municipal law, we may infer that recognition by the US government is constitutive of their legal standing in domestic fora. French courts have taken the view that a state of war, which may be much more important to municipal law than it is to contemporary international law, could only exist between States that recognise each other.[22] Again, recognition by the French government would thus be a requirement for the exercise of war powers under national legislation.

My focus is nevertheless on recognition as an international legal act, its domestic manifestations being very diverse and largely incidental. As an international act, recognition takes place within the framework of international law and seeks to produce results within its domain.

In an ideal-type scenario, this comes to pass when a new State A is recognised by existing State B. B's recognition is a formal act of which A's ministry in charge of foreign affairs is notified in a formal *note verbale* containing a solemn greeting and closing remarks as customary in diplomatic practice. Examples of this abound whenever a new State is created and its statehood is uncontested, as was the case when Montenegro and South Sudan were proclaimed independent and swiftly admitted to UN membership. This type of recognition represents the 'default' form of the act. Although there may be disagreement as to its effects, there are no additional difficulties in its analysis, as it is clear what B wishes to achieve by recognition.

Practice, of course, is much more complex than the ideal-type situation. Let us assume that A is recognised by some States but that others have made declarations that they will not recognise it; a third group of States takes no explicit view either way. State B finds itself in this third group. It may entertain diplomatic relations with A and even open an embassy in its territory without ever having formally recognised its statehood: but what if B insisted, while opening a representation, that it did not thereby recognise the recipient's statehood, as Greece did when opening a liaison office in Priština?[23] Or if B accepted passports issued by A? What if B concluded a treaty with A? To make matters more complicated, B may not engage directly with A at all, but they may still become members of the same regional organisation, or of the United Nations. All these situations may lead to different legal consequences: what they have in common is that there is no formal act of recognition for us to analyse.

The difference between formal diplomatic recognition and implied recognition is therefore of great interest to this study. If recognition is cognisance and acceptance, these functions need not be achieved through any formal declaration: they

[21] See eg *Pfizer Inc v India* (1978) 434 US 308.

[22] See *War in Korea (Self-Mutilation Case)* (1953) 20 ILR 591 and the discussion in Andrew Clapham, *War* (OUP 2021) 7–8.

[23] At this moment, however, Greece does not maintain that it has diplomatic relations with Priština, maintaining for example that its liaison office is open in 'Kosovo-UNMIK'; see more at the website of the liaison office at <https://www.mfa.gr/missionsabroad/en/pristina-en> last ccessed 30 May 2024.

can be deduced from a mere conclusive action (*acte concluant*, *Konkludentes Halten*).[24] Whether recognition has taken place is a very separate matter from that of the effects of recognition or non-recognition: the rights associated with statehood may become opposable even in the absence of recognition. Yet in colloquial parlance and even some serious academic discussions, one may still hear that admission into the United Nations signifies 'recognition' of the acceding State by existing members.[25] In the following sections, I will also consider whether such situations may be considered a form of recognition, whether it is explicit or implicit.

3. Recognition as an Explicit Act

Legal acts are usually categorised according to how many parties they gather—recognition is no exception. Mainstream scholarship usually classifies recognition as a unilateral act.[26] This may be the most common way in which recognition is done, but there is no *a priori* reason to exclude other iterations which are in fact quite common. We may therefore examine it as a unilateral, bilateral, or multilateral act.

3.1 Recognition as a Unilateral Act

Recognition typically involves a formal act by an existing State towards a new one in which it accepts the latter's statehood. The act is expressly directed at the recipient, although it will also be of interest to third States, particularly the Parent State of a secessionist entity. This is most commonly done unilaterally, for example when State A notifies State B of its recognition—State B may or may not respond, but it will be said to have been 'recognised' by A regardless.

3.1.1 Of Unilateral Acts in General

States may undertake unilateral acts that produce legal consequences and create a new legal situation that is henceforth opposable to them. Insofar as the author

[24] It is not possible to provide a perfect translation of this term in English; the concept most closely resembles the notion of 'implied in fact', as in the case of a contract that is implied in fact by inference from the parties' statements or conduct. The term 'conclusive action' has been employed in some translations from French, German, Russian, and Serbo-Croatian legal literature and legislation and seems to be the closest correlate.

[25] This is of course imprecise as the UN is not entitled to give external recognition itself.

[26] See eg Cavaglieri (n 5) 352; Kelsen (n 2) 609; Lauterpacht (n 5) 57; Joe Verhoeven, *La reconnaissance internationale dans la pratique contemporaine* (Pedone 1975) 2; James Crawford, 'Chance, Order, Change: The Course of International Law: General Course on Public International Law' (2014) 365 RCADI 9, 148; Shaw (n 10) 90; and many others.

intended to produce a legal obligation, others may rely upon the act and invoke it against them. In international law, such an act is referred to as a 'unilateral act' or 'unilateral declaration'. Both in practice and in doctrine, there is a tendency to mix the terms as if interchangeable. While most unilateral acts assume the form of declarations, not every act is a declaration, wherefore these terms are not synonymous. Nevertheless, as noted by the International Law Commission (ILC) Special Rapporteur Víctor Rodríguez Cedeño in his first report to the UN General Assembly, '[i]t is difficult in practice to find substantive unilateral acts that are not expressed or embodied in a declaration'.[27] Accordingly, I find it acceptable—if imprecise—to equate unilateral acts and declarations for the larger part of my analysis, unless the act under scrutiny is obviously not a declaration but a conclusive action as with tacit recognition. The applicable normative regime will be identical in either case.

According to the ILC's 2006 Guiding Principles on Unilateral Declarations, '[d]eclarations publicly made and manifesting the will to be bound may have the effect of creating legal obligations'.[28] The mechanism whereby this comes to pass was described by the ICJ judgment in the *Nuclear Tests* case in 1974, although the principle that a unilateral statement may produce binding effects has been accepted at least as early as the Permanent Court of International Justice's (PCIJ) *Eastern Greenland* case.[29] Australia and New Zealand, opposed to French nuclear testing in the South Pacific because of its significant environmental impact, instituted proceedings against that State arguing that France was obliged to refrain from testing because of the fallout spreading to their territory. The Court ruled instead that France had undertaken an obligation to desist further testing in a binding unilateral declaration, and in proper Solomonic fashion found the claims groundless and dismissed them (because the question of whether France had accepted the obligation to stop nuclear testing had therefore been settled).[30] As regards unilateral acts, the Court stated:

> It is well recognized that declarations made by way of unilateral acts, concerning legal or factual situations, may have the effect of creating legal obligations. Declarations of this kind may be, and often are, very specific. When it is

[27] *First report on unilateral acts of States, by Mr Víctor Rodríguez Cedeño, Special Rapporteur* (5 March 1998) A/CN.4/486, para 73.

[28] 'Guiding Principles Applicable to Unilateral Declarations of States Capable of Creating Legal Obligations, with Commentaries Thereto' (2013) II(2) Yearbook of the International Law Commission 2006 160–66 (hereafter 'Guiding Principles on Unilateral Declarations'), Principle 1; cf Christian Eckart, *Promises of States under International Law* (Hart Publishing 2012).

[29] *Legal Status of Eastern Greenland*, Judgment of 5 April 1933, Ser A, No 53 (hereafter *Eastern Greenland* case) 71.

[30] See *Nuclear Tests Case (Australia v France)*, ICJ Reports 253, Judgment of 20 December 1974 (hereafter *Nuclear Tests* case).

> the intention of the State making the declaration that it should become bound according to its terms, that intention confers on the declaration the character of a legal undertaking, the State being thenceforth legally required to follow a course of conduct consistent with the declaration. An undertaking of this kind, if given publicly, and with an intent to be bound, even though not made within the context of international negotiations, is binding.[31]

Finding that 'the French Government conveyed to the world at large, including the Applicant, its intention effectively to terminate these tests' and that '[i]t was bound to assume that other States might take note of these statements and rely on their being effective', the Court determined that the French statement renouncing further nuclear tests resulted in an obligation, undertaken *erga omnes*, to respect that promise.[32] Accordingly, Australia and New Zealand—but also any other member of the international community—could rely on the French declaration as a source of law.

International law imposes no requirement on the form of unilateral undertakings, which may be aimed at one or more States or be made *erga omnes*. Form and context will certainly facilitate the determination of a declaration's legal content to distinguish it from political, non-binding commitments. As the Court cautioned in a later case, when declarations are made towards no single, identifiable recipient (implying the entire international community as their beneficiary), there is 'a duty to show even greater caution' when ascertaining binding legal status.[33]

The question of who makes the statement has also been examined by the Court. In *Congo v Uganda*, it was deemed that 'it is a well-established rule of international law that the Head of State, the Head of Government and the Minister for Foreign Affairs are deemed to represent the State merely by virtue of exercising their functions, including for the performance ... of unilateral acts having the force of international commitments'.[34] Others may also do so if possessing adequate authorisation to act on behalf of the State,[35] by analogy to treaty law.[36] Ministers may be presumed to possess the authority to make binding statements on behalf of a State if the matter typically falls within their department's mandate,[37] which suggests *a contrario* that sufficient proof that an individual has been acting *ultra vires*

[31] ibid 267.
[32] ibid 269.
[33] *Case Concerning the Frontier Dispute (Burkina Faso/Mali)*, ICJ Reports 554, Judgment of 22 December 1986 (hereafter *Frontier Dispute* case) para 39.
[34] *Case Concerning Armed Activities on the Territory of the Congo (New Application: 2002) (Democratic Republic of the Congo v Rwanda)*, ICJ Reports 6, Judgment of 3 February 2006 (hereafter *Armed Activities* case) para 46.
[35] ibid para 47.
[36] See Vienna Convention on the Law of Treaties, 1155 UNTS 331 (adopted 23 May 1969, entered into force 27 January 1980) (hereafter VCLT).
[37] *Armed Activities* case (n 34) para 48.

will discredit claims of obligation in a statement.[38] This point is of limited value for this study, wherefore I am content to recall that only the will to be bound is of any relevance to the binding nature of unilateral acts: who may speak for the State, and under what circumstances they may do so, is ephemeral to the intrinsic qualities of a declaration, and merely serves as an indicator of the State's consent to be bound by a new legal rule.[39]

3.1.2 Unilateral Acts as Formal Sources of International Law

The question of the place of unilateral acts or declarations in the typology of legal sources is not however obvious. The commonly accepted list of sources, reproduced in Article 38 of the ICJ Statute,[40] lists as sources to be applied by the Court only international conventions, international custom and general principles of law. Unilateral acts cannot be summarily reduced to any of these, although this is necessary unless we regard them as a separate source of law that the Court has 'read into' Article 38.[41]

For example, it is possible to regard a unilateral act as an inchoate international treaty which becomes complete when the commitment is accepted by its recipient, in an explicit or tacit fashion. Some basis for this view may be found in the *Eastern Greenland* judgment when the PCIJ found that Norway and Denmark had renounced their respective claims to Greenland and Spitzbergen in a series of ministerial statements.[42] One could easily argue that the same logic applies to unilateral statements that otherwise applies to treaties, and it is possible to think of them as informal treaties, albeit their one-sided nature ultimately makes this approach counterintuitive.[43]

It is clearly the better approach to explain the binding nature of unilateral acts by reference to general principles of law. The ILC thus recalls that 'the binding character of [unilateral] declarations is based on good faith'.[44]

There is some proof in the literature that at least unilateral declarations, such as estoppel, do indeed find their basis in the principle of good faith.[45] The ICJ

[38] The State must nevertheless control such claims, as discussed by the ICJ in *Case Concerning Delimitation of the Maritime Boundary in the Gulf of Maine Area (Canada/United States of America)*, ICJ Reports 246, Judgment of 12 October 1984, paras 128ff.

[39] See *Case Concerning Military and Paramilitary Activities In and Against Nicaragua (Nicaragua v United States of America)*, ICJ Reports 14, Judgment of 27 June 1986, paras 257–261.

[40] Statute of the International Court of Justice, 33 UNTS 993 (adopted 26 June 1945, entered into force 24 October 1945) (hereafter ICJ Statute) art 38(1).

[41] There exists some controversy as to whether art 38 should be regarded as an exhaustive list of sources of international law: its wording does not exclude other sources, merely foresees which sources may be applied by the Court. Thus, unilateral acts could either be considered a separate type of source, or as based on the principle of good faith as a general principle of law under art 38.

[42] *Eastern Greenland* case (n 29) 70–71.

[43] This theory was also rejected by the ICJ in the *Nuclear Tests* case (n 30) para 43.

[44] 'Guiding Principles on Unilateral Declarations' (n 28) 160–66, Principle 1.

[45] Crawford, *Brownlie's Principles* (n 1) 406–07; cf *Case Concerning the Temple of Preah Vihear (Cambodia v Thailand)*, ICJ Reports 6, Judgment of 15 June 1962, 39–66 (Separate Opinions of Judges Alfaro and Fitzmaurice).

found in the *Gulf of Maine* judgment that 'in any case the concepts of acquiescence and estoppel, irrespective of the status accorded to them by international law, both follow from the fundamental principles of good faith and equity'.[46] Special Rapporteur Rodríguez Cedeño, who regards Article 38 of the ICJ Statute as incomplete, nevertheless agrees that 'good faith has a role to play as a basis of [a unilateral act's] obligatoriness', finding evidence for this in the ICJ's *Nuclear Tests* judgment.[47] If therefore we accept that good faith is a principle coming within the purview of Article 38(1)(c) (and I see no reason why it should not), then it seems safe to describe that provision as a more-or-less precise restatement of the formal sources of international law, and unilateral acts as firmly grounded within them.

3.1.3 The Content and Form of Unilateral Acts

An analysis of ICJ case law and the ILC's Guiding Principles demonstrates that international law merely proscribes a necessary content, but not a required form, for binding unilateral acts: it is the content, and not the form of the act, that serves to distinguish it from a political commitment and bring it within the scope of positive law. The act's legal effect—the creation of a situation that is opposable to its author—depends solely on this content, which is nothing else than the issuing State's will to make a legal commitment.

The form of an act has probative value in establishing its content. It does not appear that the ILC's Guiding Principles distinguish between unilateral acts and declarations in this sense[48]—the framework is always the same—although the Commission focuses on declarations, which 'may be formulated orally or in writing'.[49] In a broader sense, 'acts' could also arise from an omission: '[B]ehaviours capable of legally binding States may take the form of formal declarations or mere informal conduct including, in certain situations, silence, on which other States may reasonably rely.'[50] This possibility is only mentioned in passing in the Principles' preamble and is not specifically referred to in their substantive part. There can be no doubt however that any conduct of States may be scrutinised for legally binding content, by analogy with the importance of State behaviour when recognising or objecting to the formation of rules of customary law.[51] The

[46] *Case Concerning Delimitation of the Maritime Boundary in the Gulf of Maine Area (Canada/United States of America)*, ICJ Reports 246, Judgment of 12 October 1984, para 130.

[47] *First report on unilateral acts of States, by Mr Víctor Rodríguez Cedeño, Special Rapporteur* (5 March 1998) A/CN.4/486, paras 43 and 156–159; Rodríguez Cedeño also identifies a rule of customary law requiring that promises be kept.

[48] This is stated in the Preamble, where the ILC states that 'the following Guiding Principles ... relate only to unilateral acts *stricto sensu*, ie those taking the form of formal declarations formulated by a State with the intent to produce obligations under international laws'; 'Guiding Principles on Unilateral Declarations' (n 28) 160–66 preambular para 6.

[49] ibid Principle 5.

[50] ibid preambular para 3.

[51] See Crawford (n 1) 25–28; Emmanuel Decaux and Olivier de Frouville, *Droit international public* (Dalloz 2018) 56–60 ('Même l'inaction peut apparaître comme une pratique, mais encore faut-il qu'elle traduise une intention "délibérée"'); and more generally, Olufemi Elias, 'Persistent Objector' in

United States of America welcomes the birth of a new nation.'[62] Recognition may otherwise be extended in an official letter or *note verbale*; such was the case when France,[63] Germany,[64] and others[65] recognised the unilaterally declared independence of Kosovo in 2008.

If diplomatic recognition may be considered a unilateral act as a formal source of law, then it must be subjected to the same or similar principles with respect to its content, form, and effects.

In terms of contents, we must first ask ourselves whether the recognising State is expressing legally relevant will to be bound by a certain commitment. In my view, this question must be answered in the affirmative. Consider the language used in the statement by President Obama in relation to South Sudan, reproduced above, which is representative of general practice. As President Sarkozy wrote to Mr Sejdiu:

> J'ai l'honneur de vous informer que la France … tirant les conséquences de la résolution adoptée par l'Assemblée du Kosovo le 17 février 2008, reconnaît dès à présent le Kosovo comme un État souverain et indépendant.[66]

Also the British Foreign Secretary's statement in Parliament on the same matter:

> Bringing all these elements together … the Government considers that UK recognition of Kosovo is fully justified. My right hon[ourable] Friend the Prime Minister wrote to President Sejdiu on 18 February indicating to the Kosovo government that the United Kingdom recognises Kosovo's independence. I have also written to Prime Minister Thaçi proposing the establishment of diplomatic relations.[67]

[62] The White House, 'Statement of President Barack Obama Recognition of the Republic of South Sudan' (9 July 2011) available at: <https://obamawhitehouse.archives.gov/the-press-office/2011/07/09/statement-president-barack-obama-recognition-republic-south-sudan> last accessed 30 May 2024.

[63] Présidence de la République, 'Lettre de M Nicolas Sarkozy, Président de la République, adressée à M Fatmir Sejdiu, Président du Kosovo, reconnaissant le Kosovo comme un Etat souverain et indépendant' (17 February 2008) available at: <https://www.elysee.fr/nicolas-sarkozy/2008/02/18/lettre-de-m-nicolas-sarkozy-president-de-la-republique-adressee-a-m-fatmir-sejdiu-president-du-kosovo-reconnaissant-le-kosovo-comme-un-etat-souverain-et-independant-le-17-fevrier-2008> last accessed 30 May 2024.

[64] Formal recognition was communicated in a letter from the German President Horst Köhler to Fatmir Sejdiu, the President of Kosovo, in a letter dated 20 February 2008.

[65] See in this regard Colin Warbrick, 'Kosovo: The Declaration of Independence' (2008) 57(3) The International and Comparative Law Quarterly 675.

[66] Présidence de la République, 'Lettre de M Nicolas Sarkozy, Président de la République, adressée à M Fatmir Sejdiu, Président du Kosovo, reconnaissant le Kosovo comme un État souverain et indépendant' (17 February 2008) available at: <https://www.elysee.fr/nicolas-sarkozy/2008/02/18/lettre-de-m-nicolas-sarkozy-president-de-la-republique-adressee-a-m-fatmir-sejdiu-president-du-kosovo-reconnaissant-le-kosovo-comme-un-etat-souverain-et-independant-le-17-fevrier-2008> last accessed 30 May 2024.

[67] HC Deb 19 February 2008, vol 472, cols 21–22WS.

The wording of various acts of recognition may differ slightly, but invariably it revolves around the terms 'State' (or 'statehood'), 'sovereignty', and 'independence': these of course mean the same thing, namely that the object of recognition is a State and that the granter acquiesces to treat it as such. From this we must infer, irrespective of whether diplomatic recognition is constitutive or declaratory of statehood, that the act necessarily implies an opposability to the State extending recognition. As the French submission to the ICJ ahead of its advisory opinion on Kosovo's unilateral declaration of independence recalls, recognition amounts to an 'irrevocable decision' (*une décision irrévocable*) taking cognisance of the quality of an independent and sovereign State and establishing inter-state relations with it.[68]

As with other unilateral acts, international law places few formal requirements that need to be met for recognition to produce legal consequences. If form is not essential, the act must at least fulfil the standard of 'notoriety', which requires, 'beyond mere publicity of the act, that is, knowledge of the act and its content on the part of the addressee, is another constituent element of the act of recognition. Indeed, the act must be known to the addressee in order to produce its legal effects'.[69] This serves a very obvious practical purpose, but nowadays also reflects a general unease with secret and obscure law-making, by analogy with secret treaties.[70] Notoriety is a formal requirement for the entire plethora of unilateral acts currently known in State practice. Recognition is however subjected to additional substantive criteria that we will discuss in the following chapters.

3.2 Recognition as a Bilateral Act

As we have seen, recognition is usually treated in doctrine as a unilateral act. This conclusion draws from the usual manner of recognising new States by means of a diplomatic act. However, not all acts of direct recognition take place in the same fashion: recognition may also be a bilateral or a multilateral act, assuming a varying form.

Doctrine considers bilateral recognition according to two approaches. The first takes it at as a bilateral act *per definitionem*, meaning that all acts of diplomatic recognition should be treated as bilateral acts. The other treats it as a unilateral act by default but does not exclude that it may take place bilaterally as well, in either a written or oral agreement. Although practice invariably supports the latter view,

[68] *Accordance with International Law of the Unilateral Declaration of Independence in Respect of Kosovo*, Written Submission by the French Republic, 18 April 2009, para 9.

[69] *Sixth report on unilateral acts of States, by Mr Victor Rodríguez Cedeño, Special Rapporteur* (30 May 2003) A/CN.4/534, 63; cf *Case Concerning Delimitation of the Maritime Boundary in the Gulf of Maine Area (Canada/United States of America)*, ICJ Reports 246, Judgment of 12 October 1984, para 131ff.

[70] See on this Richard Caddell, 'Treaties, Secret' in Anne Peters and Rüdiger Wolfrum (eds), *Max Planck Encyclopedias of International Law* (OUP 2006) <https://opil.ouplaw.com/display/10.1093/law:epil/9780199231690/law-9780199231690-e1489?prd=EPIL> last accessed 13 June 2024.

the former deserves to be considered for highlighting some of the challenges raised by recognition in legal theory.

3.2.1 Anzilotti's Theory of Mutual Constitutive Recognition

The idea of recognition as an 'agreement' (*Vereinbarung*) was formulated at least as early as Heinrich Triepel[71] and later entertained by Alfred Verdross.[72] However, the theory of what Lauterpacht calls 'mutual constitutive recognition'[73] finds its true paragon in Dionisio Anzilotti. A strict positivist, Anzilotti finds the basis of all international law in agreements between States and the principle of *pacta sunt servanda*. Just as international law determines its own subjects, so too does it regulate how they come into being, wherefore recognition is a phenomenon regulated by law.[74] Accordingly, a subject of law comes into being only by concluding its first agreement: for relations between legal persons are nothing other than contractual relations. Thus, recognition (which he considers a misnomer) must also be considered a treaty:

> La reconnaissance donc n'est autre chose qu'un pacte conclu sur la base de la règle *pacta sunt servanda*: la personnalité internationale, rendue possible par cette norme, devient effective et concrète par la reconnaissance. La reconnaissance, selon nous, est purement et simplement l'accord initial auquel se rattache la naissance de normes juridiques pour des sujets donnés et par suite leur personnalité l'un à l'égard de l'autre; de par sa conception même elle est réciproque et constitutive.[75]

Anzilotti believes that State consent is a necessary component to create a norm of international law, but that only the norm, and not consent itself, must be seen as a source of law. He raises this argument to overcome the problem of how an unrecognised State could express legally relevant will, which he finds pointless as the relevant norms (presumably the rule *pacta sunt servanda*) proscribing the effects of recognition have an independent and separate existence in international law. In other words, recognition takes places within a legal framework that exists independently of its actual or potential subjects and their individual will: even if a State

[71] 'Namentlich die sogenannte Anerkennung von Neustaaten ist hier von grösster Bedeutung. Sie ist regelmässig nicht bloss eine formelle Deklaration des Wunsches oder der Bereitwilligkeit, mit dem Neuling in Verkehr zu treten, sondern soweit sie als Erwiderung oder Provokation entsprechender Erklärung der Gegenseite zu Tage tritt, zugleich Bestandtheil einer Vereinbarung, die eine ganze Reihe, wenn auch natürlich nicht alle innerhalb der "Völkerrechtsgemeinschaft" in Kraft stehenden Normen auf den jungen Staat ausdehnt.' Heinrich Triepel, *Völkerrecht und Landesrecht* (Verlag von C L Hirschfeld 1899) 102.

[72] Verdross, 'Règles générales du droit international de la paix' (n 11) 329.

[73] Lauterpacht (n 5) 39.

[74] Dionisio Anzilotti, *Cours de droit international, Premier volume; Introduction—Théories générales* (Librairie du Recueil Sirey 1929) 160–61.

[75] ibid 161.

is not recognised, and therefore legally 'invisible' to existing States, its acceptance is governed by a rule already created by the latter. Anzilotti resorts to this unwieldy line of thought to deny the unilateral character of recognition, for accepting the latter would be tantamount to saying that existing States can extend the application of the international legal order outside its very boundaries.[76] This is not so, claims Anzilotti, if we regard recognition as a treaty.

Considerable and convincing criticism has been levelled at this theory of Anzilotti's. Although Kelsen in his essay on recognition does not explicitly mention Anzilotti when discussing the theory of mutual constitutive recognition, there can be little doubt that it was Anzilotti's interpretation he had in mind when briefly remarking that '[r]ecognition of a community as a state is not a treaty. A treaty is only possible between two subjects already existing in relation to each other, not between an existing subject and a subject to be created by the former's act of recognition.'[77] This criticism is echoed by Cavaglieri.[78] Lauterpacht finds a more practical issue with Anzilotti's theory, namely that 'in actual experience there is no mutuality at all in the process of recognition since the recognizing State appears to grant a benefit without a compensating *quid pro quo*.'[79] Lastly, Verdross, while not reacting directly to Anzilotti, criticises the notion that the act of recognition is solely governed by the principle of *pacta sunt servanda* and concludes that a new State, whose only obligations would then stem from what it agrees to specifically, would not even be bound by customary law. An unrecognised State would be altogether incapable of violating international law.[80]

I agree with these arguments against mutual constitutive recognition. Anzilotti's theory, which is designed to solve the conundrum of how a legal community's normative could be extended to incorporate outsiders, ultimately falls into this same 'trap': even the 'initial agreement' must be governed by some law to produce legal effects. More cogently, it is not very useful to overly rationalise law-making for doctrinal coherence if it means sacrificing our ability to explain an observable phenomenon. In this sense, Anzilotti's inspired but unsuccessful theoretical exercise causes more problems than it resolves.

Even if we disagree with his conclusion, Anzilotti's starting point and identification of a potential logical gap in explaining how a State is treated by a normative system to which it is not initially subjected are still of great value. This means that the act of recognition must be re-evaluated in light of its apparent effects. In this respect, I must raise two points. First, it is simply a matter of practice that

[76] ibid 162.

[77] Kelsen (n 2) 609.

[78] 'Si la capacité juridique dérive uniquement du droit, comment peut-on admettre que des États, dont la volonté et l'activité sont encore en dehors du droit international, aient une capacité préjuridique d'échanger entre eux des manifestations de volonté qui aient une valeur et des effets juridiques?' Cavaglieri (n 5) 352.

[79] Lauterpacht (n 5) 39–40.

[80] Verdross (n 11) 327ff; Verdross otherwise accepts the idea that recognition is a bilateral act.

recognition is typically not a bilateral act: when State A recognises State B, no treaty thereby materialises between them—to conclude otherwise is to insist on a legal fiction. Second, it is not really so difficult to explain how unrecognised States become bound by international law. By raising a claim of statehood or independence, the new State is really accepting to comply with an existing legal system and submit itself to its existing concepts, norms, and institutions. Its statehood may not be opposable to States withholding recognition, but this does not excuse it from respecting general international law. There are thus less complicated and more realistic ways of achieving Anzilotti's purpose than to subscribe to his mutual recognition theory.

3.2.2 Recognition by Means of a Treaty

Although typically a unilateral act, recognition is sometimes contained in a treaty. This is not a theoretical 'initial agreement' governed by *pacta sunt servanda*, but an empirically demonstrable source of international law.

Throughout history, States have often granted recognition not by way of a unilateral act but through a treaty—very often, a peace treaty. This is because peaceful settlements in many cases required the Parent State to accept the independence of an erstwhile colony, dominion, or other dependent territory at the end of a war of secession. A typical example is the 1783 Treaty of Paris, whereby King George III was forced to recognise the independence of the United States after the American Revolution:

> His Brittanic Majesty acknowledges the said United States, viz., New Hampshire, Massachusetts Bay, Rhode Island and Providence Plantations, Connecticut, New York, New Jersey, Pennsylvania, Maryland, Virginia, North Carolina, South Carolina and Georgia, to be free sovereign and independent states, that he treats with them as such, and for himself, his heirs, and successors, relinquishes all claims to the government, propriety, and territorial rights of the same and every part thereof.[81]

Such practice was not confined to early modern times and continued well into the twentieth century—there exist numerous treaties granting independence to colonial countries after the Second World War. Emblematic of these treaties are elaborate provisions whereby the Parent State vows to treat the new State as sovereign: exemplary are the Treaty of Manila,[82] between the

[81] The Paris Peace Treaty of 30 September 1783, art 1. Similar wording was employed in the 1825 Treaty of Rio de Janeiro, whereby the Kingdom of Portugal recognised the independence of the Empire of Brazil.

[82] 'The United States of America agrees to withdraw and surrender, and does hereby withdraw and surrender, all right of possession, supervision, jurisdiction, control or sovereignty existing and exercised by the United States of America in and over the territory and the people of the Philippine

United States and the Philippines, and the Evian Accords between France and Algeria.[83]

Bilateral recognition in a treaty is not granted only by the Parent State but also by third States whose involvement in the situation may be at best indirect, although this is comparatively rare: third States usually recognise separation or secession in a unilateral act, as demonstrated by US practice towards former Spanish colonies in the Americas in the nineteenth century.[84] A treaty may however be preferable when the recognising State and the recipient of recognition wish to settle some matters of their relations from the outset, such as diplomatic representation. Thus, the Holy See concluded a treaty with the State of Palestine in 2015 whereby, '[i]n recognition of the right of the Palestinian people to self-determination, including the right to their independent and sovereign state, the Holy See recognizes the State of Palestine and welcomes its admission to the United Nations as a Non-Member Observer State'.[85] Following the agreement, Palestine established an embassy in Rome.

3.2.2.1 *The separability of recognition from treaties*

The fact that recognition may be contained in a treaty raises interesting questions about the implications of a withdrawal, suspension, or termination of that treaty in relation to recognition. The Belavezha Accords and subsequent Alma-Ata Declaration formalised the dissolution of the Soviet Union: like a line of previous agreements,[86] the Declaration[87] foresaw the 'mutual recognition' of the Union's former units and the consequent applicability of international law to their relations, in addition to establishing the Commonwealth of Independent States (CIS) and its governing principles. Therefore, when Georgia withdrew from the

Islands ... The United States of America further agrees to recognize, and does hereby recognize, the independence of the Republic of the Philippines as a separate self-governing nation ....' Treaty of General Relations and Protocol, 7 UNTS 3 (adopted 4 July 1946, entered into force 22 October 1946) art I.

[83] '*The Algerian State* will exercise its full and complete sovereignty both internally and externally. This sovereignty will be exercised in all spheres, in particular in defense and foreign affairs.' France-Algeria Independence Agreements, 1:2 ILM 214 (adopted 18 March 1962) 216, Chapter II, A(I).

[84] See in this regard M Romero, 'The United States and the Liberation of the Spanish-American Colonies' (1897) 165(488) The North American Review 70; William Spence Robertson, 'The First Legations of the United States in Latin America' (1915) 2(2) The Mississippi Valley Historical Review 183–212; William Spence Robertson, 'The Recognition of the Hispanic American Nations by the United States' (1918) 1(3) The Hispanic American Historical Review 239; and William Spence Robertson, 'The United States and Spain in 1822' (1915) 20(4) The American Historical Review 781.

[85] Comprehensive Agreement between the Holy See and the State of Palestine, 108 *Acta Apostolicae Sedis* 168 (adopted 26 June 2015) art 1; cf Leonard Hammer, 'The 2015 Comprehensive Agreement Between the Holy See and the Palestinian Authority: Discerning the Holy See's Approach to International Relations in the Holy Land' (2017) 6(1) Oxford Journal of Law and Religion 162.

[86] See Armenia-Azerbaijan-Belarus-Kazakhstan-Kyrgyzstan-Moldova-Russian Federation-Tajikistan-Turkmenistan-Uzbekistan-Ukraine: Agreements Establishing the Commonwealth of Independent States 31:1 ILM 138 (adopted 8 and 21 December 1992).

[87] ibid 148, preambular para [3].

CIS and these accords, did it also withdraw from a normative system on which its recognition by the other members had been predicated? Did this move entail 'de-recognition'? The best view, argued convincingly by Robert Kolb, is to accept the separability of recognition from the treaty containing it.[88] There are several ways this could be explained.

(1) We could say that the treaty itself, regardless of its object, presupposes statehood as a necessary condition, and that this act of recognition (as a separate unilateral act) serves the function of initially rendering the new State opposable to the existing one, whereas the treaty itself is a mere manifestation of an already existing legal relationship between the two legal persons. This view was defended by Hersch Lauterpacht:

> In these and similar treaties recognition, although expressed in the treaty, does not form part of the contractual arrangement. The treaty is merely a convenient and suitable opportunity for registering the fact of recognition. If the treaty were to lapse, for instance, as the result of a subsequent declaration of war, the recognition expressed therein would nevertheless remain in full vigor. Recognition is independent of the content of the treaty.[89]

Robert Kolb also expresses a preference for this view and refines it by introducing separability. This approach has the advantage of avoiding the 'fragmentation' of legal sources (namely, by maintaining the unilateral character of recognition regardless of the existence of the treaty) and explaining how a State recognised in a treaty does not become 'de-recognised' if the treaty itself were to lose force by allowing the separability of recognition. As far as recognition is concerned, this approach deprives the treaty of any legal effect,[90] as recognition was already achieved through the posited prior unilateral act of which the treaty is merely probative.

(2) We could also say that a unilateral act of recognition and recognition by means of a treaty are distinct phenomena according to their nature and their place in the sources of international law, but that they are nevertheless the same in terms of their object and effects (in line with Brownlie's view that recognition is not a 'term of art'). In this case, treaty-based recognition should be regarded in exactly the same way as the unilateral act of recognition: if the latter cannot in principle be withdrawn, neither can recognition contained in a treaty, meaning that the matter is separable from any other issues discussed in said instrument.

(3) In the *Territorial Dispute* case, the ICJ ruled that the border fixed in a treaty between Libya and France remained valid for Libya and Chad regardless of the

[88] The credit for this concept goes to Robert Kolb, who raised it several times in his feedback and communication with the author of this book.

[89] Lauterpacht (n 5) 57.

[90] Only in relation to recognition: in practice, treaties of this kind regulate many different points that are not related to statehood or recognition.

further life of that treaty.[91] There is no reason why this should not also be the case for recognition of statehood, regardless of how one arrives at the conclusion. This suggests that there exists an exception—to be found either in customary law or in the general principles of law—to the regime of Article 44(1) of the Vienna Convention on the Law of Treaties (VCLT) regarding recognition and the inviolability of borders.[92]

Whichever approach one takes to explain it, it seems that the separability of recognition from treaties may be presumed in the current state of international law.

3.3 Recognition as a Multilateral Act

Multilateral recognition may come about in two ways: first, it may be based on the provisions of a multilateral treaty to which a number of States are party; and second, it may result from the act of an international organisation ('collective recognition'). The latter, if it results from the act of a single common organ, can only be regarded as 'multilateral' with caution, for this term is reserved for the joint action of several separate States with a view to achieving a common purpose.

3.3.1 Recognition in a Multilateral Treaty

Recognition of new States at international congresses and conferences is an old practice; the new States may or may not be invited to ratify the resulting accords and may not even have any representatives involved in the negotiations. In 1878, the independence of Serbia, Montenegro, and Romania from the Ottoman Empire was agreed at the Congress of Berlin and foreseen in the resulting treaty between the Great Powers.[93] The former vassal principalities, which had already enjoyed *de facto* independence from the Porte, were not asked to join the treaty themselves. Bulgaria was also not invited to join, and the country remained an autonomous part of the Ottoman Empire even though its representatives had been acting externally since 1876. At other times, the new State is also invited to join: after the First World War, Czechoslovakia and Poland became parties to the Treaties of Versailles, Trianon, and Saint-Germain-en-Laye granting them independence from the German and Austro-Hungarian empires.[94]

[91] *Case Concerning the Territorial Dispute (Libyan Arab Jamahiriya/Chad)*, ICJ Reports 6, Judgment of 3 February 1994, para 72.

[92] Foreseeing that '[a] right of a party, provided for in a treaty or arising under article 56, to denounce, withdraw from or suspend the operation of the treaty may be exercised only with respect to the whole treaty unless the treaty otherwise provides or the parties otherwise agree'. VCLT (n 36) art 44(1).

[93] Treaty between Austria-Hungary, Germany, Great Britain and Ireland, Italy, Russia, and the Ottoman Empire for the Settlement of Affairs in the East (adopted and entered into force 13 July 1878).

[94] See Treaty of Peace between the Allied and Associated Powers and Germany, 225 CTS 188 (signed 28 June 1919, entered into force 10 January 1920); Treaty of Peace between the Allied and Associated Powers and Hungary, 113 BSP 486 (signed 4 June 1920, entered into force 26 July 1921); and Treaty of

Recognition provided in a multilateral treaty does not greatly differ from recognition in a bilateral treaty and can also be regarded as severable from other treaty provisions. Issues of recognition and statehood could arise if one or more States were to leave the treaty regime, such as when Ukraine and Georgia left the CIS. As neither State's independence was brought into question at the time, continued recognition by other CIS members may be presumed. In my view, the separability of recognition continues to play a role, although this may be different in cases of contested statehood, namely when the Parent State does not join the relevant multilateral treaty.

3.3.1.1 Recognition and treaty reservations

Unlike bilateral treaties, multilateral treaties with a significant number of parties are commonly subjected to reservations. Of course, a State refusing to recognise another will not join a treaty whose primary purpose is to confirm the latter's statehood, but it may still disagree with certain provisions and try to modify their effects towards itself. Admittedly, there are few examples of such reservations in practice, and in the best-known case the State considering reservations ultimately did not join the treaty regime.

Namely, at the end of the First World War, the US Senate was unable to ratify the Treaty of Versailles or the other multilateral peace treaties ending the war as this would have entailed US membership in the League of Nations. A number of complex reasons figured in the senators' discussions and prevented a sufficient majority to form in support of membership in the League. The Republican Senator Lodge prepared a set of reservations in this regard, but even this watered-down proposal was defeated and the Senate ultimately never ratified the peace agreements.[95] The United States concluded separate peace treaties with the Central Powers[96] and recognised Poland and Czechoslovakia unilaterally.[97] But what if the United States

Peace between the Allied and Associated Powers and Austria, 226 CTS 8 (signed 10 September 1919, entered into force 16 July 1920).

[95] On this, see Leo Gross, 'The Charter of the United Nations and the Lodge Reservations' (1947) 41(3) The American Journal of International Law 531; James E Hewes Jr, 'Henry Cabot Lodge and the League of Nations' (1970) 114(4) Proceedings of the American Philosophical Society 245; and David Mervin, 'Henry Cabot Lodge and the League of Nations' (1971) 4(2) Journal of American Studies 201.

[96] Treaty of Peace Between Austria and the United States of America, 7 LNTS 156 (adopted 24 August 1921, entered into force 8 November 1921); Treaty Concerning the Re-Establishment of Peace Between Germany and the United States, 12 LNTS 192 (adopted 25 August 1921, entered into force 11 November 1921); Treaty of Peace Between Hungary and the United States of America, 48 LNTS 191 (adopted 29 August 1921, entered into force 17 December 1921). See more on this topic in Bernadotte E Schmitt, 'The Peace Treaties of 1919–1920' (1960) 104(1) Proceedings of the American Philosophical Society 101 and George W Egerton, 'Britain and the "Great Betrayal": Anglo-American Relations and the Struggle for United States Ratification of the Treaty of Versailles, 1919–1920' (1978) 21(4) The Historical Journal 885.

[97] The United States recognised the Polish Provisional Government in 1919. The situation was more complicated with Czechoslovakia, whose National Council had been recognised by as a belligerent in 1918, but US diplomatic recognition was offset by unsettled Czechoslovak war debt. Nevertheless, the United States eventually deployed a minister in Prague and concluded its first treaty with the

had ratified the Treaty of Versailles with reservations? Would these have affected the US recognition of any of the States resulting from Versailles or Saint-Germain-en-Laye? What if the reservations had been invalid, which could imply that the reserving State cannot be considered a party to the treaty in the first place?[98]

Once again, this matter concerns the question of the effects of recognition, which must here be distinguished from the effects of an invalid reservation to a treaty. This situation is largely hypothetical but still warrants some reflection. Recognition still appears to be separable from the rest of the treaty, as is the case with bilateral instruments. Assuming that the treaty itself conforms to international law and is not rendered null and void by a violation of peremptory norms, then clearly any reservations have to be considered in light of the usual requirements of treaty law: they must be valid and accepted expressly or tacitly by other parties for the underlying provisions to produce bilateral legal effects. If the reservation was deemed invalid for violating the treaty's object and purpose—and if this determination was made by a competent judicial authority rather than inferred from the reactions of other contracting States, whose views would produce effects *inter partes*—then the reserving State should not be considered a party to the treaty unless it signals otherwise (other views are certainly possible and have been argued in doctrine). This means, of course, that the effects of any reservation—whether valid or invalid or simply objected to by other parties—can only be ascertained on a case-by-case basis, although I see no reason why, exceptionally, the question of recognition could not be regarded as severable from other treaty provisions in case of an invalid reservation: thus, the reserving State would not join the treaty regime, but its recognition could nevertheless be inferred, perhaps as a presumed previous unilateral act, as argued by Lauterpacht and Kolb. However, it is impossible to resolve this matter with any certainty in the absence of more elaborate practice.

3.4 Collective Recognition

Before the Second World War, some scholars—notably those subscribing to a constitutive view of recognition, such as Lauterpacht[99]—deplored the lack of a

new republic a few years later. See on this topic Josef Kalvoda, 'Masaryk in America in 1918' (1979) 27(1) Jahrbuch für Geschichte Osteuropas 85; see also Matthew Vink, 'The Competition for Self-Determination in Czechoslovakia, 1918–1919' (2012) 46 New Zealand Slavonic Journal 41.

[98] As per one interpretation of the Vienna Convention on the Law of Treaties, 1155 UNTS 331 (adopted 23 May 1969, entered into force 27 January 1980) arts 19–21 (of course, this treaty is not as such applicable to the peace treaties ending the First World War, which long precede its adoption and entry into force); cf *Reservations to the Convention on the Prevention and Punishment of the Crime of Genocide*, ICJ Reports 15, Advisory Opinion of 28 May 1951, 24; but an opposing view is possible by analogy with art 44(3) of the VCLT and the doctrine of separability.

[99] Lauterpacht (n 5) 61ff.

centralised mechanism for the recognition of new States, such that recognition would no longer be given or withheld by individual States and subjected to the vagaries of their particular interests, but left to the 'international community', decided according to rules of international law and producing effects *erga omnes*. The reconstitution of the global order within and around the United Nations gave some reason to hope that such a role could be played by the Organisation itself, and while it cannot be maintained, in my view, that the United Nations is entitled to recognise States in the true sense of the word, at least full membership in the United Nations today arguably entails irrefutable proof of statehood.

Already at the San Francisco conference in 1945, it was suggested by the Norwegian delegation that the future United Nations be vested with explicit powers in relation to the recognition of new States or governments. This would have been done through the General Assembly, which would, according to the amendment, have had 'the right to present recommendations to member states with regard to the recognition of new Governments or new States'.[100] The proposal was not accepted,[101] and several years later Secretary-General Trygve Lie—who had led the Norwegian delegation in Dumbarton Oaks—recalled, in relation to Chinese representation at the United Nations, that 'States have refused to accept any such rule and the United Nations does not possess any authority to recognize a new State or a new government of an existing State'.[102] Such authority, he added, would require either amending the Charter or adopting a treaty to which all UN members would adhere.[103] To date, this has not been done, and formally, the Organisation does not possess the capacity to issue an act of recognition in the same way its Member States can.

Nevertheless, whether the UN could act as a forum for collective recognition has piqued the interest of lawyers since the Organisation's earliest days. The matter was addressed by scholars as diverse as Jessup[104] and Lauterpacht,[105] both of whom accepted that the UN could help 'certify' an entity's statehood before it is recognised but could not itself extend recognition in the absence of a specific procedure; Wright,[106] who argued that the United Nations could provide 'general' but

[100] *Documents of the United Nations Conference on International Organization, San Francisco, 1945: Volume III, Dumbarton Oaks Proposals, Comments and Proposed Amendments* (United Nations 1945) 366.

[101] See John Dugard, 'The Secession of States and Their Recognition in the Wake of Kosovo' (2013) 357 RCADI 9, 58.

[102] Letter dated 8 March 1950 from the Secretary-General to the President of the Security Council Transmitting a Memorandum on the Legal Aspects of the Problem of Representation in the United Nations (8 March 1950) S/1466, 3.

[103] ibid.

[104] Phillip C Jessup, *A Modern Law of Nations: An Introduction* (Macmillan 1948) 47.

[105] Lauterpacht (n 5) 403.

[106] Quincy Wright, 'Some Thoughts About Recognition' (1950) 44(3) The American Journal of International Law 548, 550ff.

not 'particular recognition'; and Kelsen,[107] who concluded that common membership in the Organisation at least carried implied recognition. More recently, the idea of collective recognition through UN membership has been defended by John Dugard.[108]

In Dugard's view, admission to UN membership is tantamount to recognition, and not only in the eyes of the Organisation: it also requires individual Member States to recognise the new member's statehood.[109] The roots of this idea stretch back to the League of Nations, when the question of recognition—either as a precondition of membership or as flowing from it—was raised in relation to the admission of new members by several delegations and in discussions in the Fifth Committee of the League Assembly and in the Assembly itself.[110] Focusing on UN practice during decolonisation—when membership was extended to former colonies with little regard for the famous criteria of the Montevideo Convention—he infers that 'admission [to the UN] is today regarded as the definitive acknowledgment of [the former colonies'] independence and statehood by the international community ... It is likewise impossible to avoid the conclusion that the international community has delegated the authority to recognize decolonized entities as States to the United Nations.'[111] Later, new States created in the wake of the dissolution of the USSR, Yugoslavia, and Czechoslovakia also sought speedy admission into the United Nations as an imprimatur of their statehood: 'Once they are members of the international community of nations, States may disapprove of them politically and decline to enter into diplomatic relations, but their existence as international legal persons is secure. Admission to the United Nations is of paramount importance to seceding States as it puts the success of the secession beyond all doubt.'[112]

Although 'recognition' (in reality, admission into membership) is done by the United Nations itself through the General Assembly and Security Council, all Member States—even those refusing to extend bilateral recognition and voting against such membership—are henceforth required to accept the new member's statehood under the Charter and general international law. Admission into the United Nations does not merely signify implicit recognition by its members, but essentially replaces it: just as members cannot amongst themselves deny the applicability of the provisions of the Charter, so too they cannot deny each other's statehood.[113] It is the United Nations' near-universality, and the universal outlook

[107] Hans Kelsen, *The Law of the United Nations: A Critical Analysis of Fundamental Problems* (Steven & Sons 1950) 79.

[108] See more generally Dugard, *Recognition and the United Nations* (n 13) and 'The Secession of States and Their Recognition' (n 101) 57ff.

[109] Dugard, *Recognition and the United Nations* (n 13) 78ff.

[110] ibid 14ff; this was notably the case in relation to Albania and Lithuania.

[111] ibid 73, 78–80.

[112] Dugard, 'The Secession of States and Their Recognition' (n 101) 58.

[113] 'Admission to the United Nations constitutes "legal" or "general" recognition that will be respected by all Member States of the United Nations.' ibid 72.

inherent in its constitutional framework, that allows the Organisation to act as the avatar of the international community. Framed in such terms, Dugard's concept of collective recognition fulfils both Lauterpacht's desire for a centralised mechanism of recognition[114] and Chen's prediction that, once membership in the United Nations had become universal, it would obviate the need for bilateral recognition altogether.[115] This theory, sometimes referred to as 'constitutive-collective recognition'—has proven influential and drawn both praise and criticism from the legal community.[116]

In my view, it is necessary to distinguish the act of recognition from its effects. As I discuss in Chapters 9 and 10, the essential effect of recognition is to render its object opposable to the author. The content of opposability is dictated by the object and the author's intention when extending recognition. By its nature, diplomatic recognition involves cognisance that certain legal facts have occurred and an acceptance of those facts in the eyes of the author: namely, that the object is a State (according to certain criteria) and that it shall henceforth be treated as such.

The United Nations is clearly not authorised to issue an act of recognition like its individual members. The Organisation's legal personality and authority are determined functionally according to its constitutional framework, which empowers the United Nations to accept peace-loving States into its ranks but not to formally recognise them. A power of recognition cannot therefore be implied from the Charter, as confirmed by the Organisation's representatives on several occasions. In this regard, neither can the United Nations through its various bodies formally recognise a State, nor can the legal fact of membership amount to an act of recognition. UN members have not delegated power over recognition to the Organisation and admission into membership does not replace individual recognition by its members. Arab States that do not recognise Israel cannot be said to have recognised it simply because they are all UN members.

Nevertheless, the establishment of relations under the UN Charter may itself render the statehood of its parties opposable to each other regardless of bilateral recognition. As I discuss in Chapter 9 of this work, common UN membership (and perhaps common membership in some other international organisations) does indeed render individual members' recognition declaratory. This means that

[114] Lauterpacht tried to remedy the absence of such a mechanism by arguing for a duty of recognition; see Lauterpacht (n 5) 61ff.

[115] Ti-Chiang Chen, *The International Law of Recognition* (Stevens & Sons Limited 1951) 222.

[116] See eg Gerhard Erasmus, 'Criteria for Determining Statehood: John Dugard's *Recognition and the United Nations*' (1988) 4(2) South African Journal on Human Rights 207; Lynn Berat, 'John Dugard's *Recognition and the United Nations*' (1989) 24 Texas International Law Journal 501; and François Finck, 'The State Between Fact and Law: The Role of Recognition and the Conditions Under Which it is Granted in the Creation of New States' (2016) XXXVI Polish Yearbook of International Law 51, 73ff, for generally positive views of collective recognition; and David Raič, *Statehood and the Law of Self-Determination* (Kluwer Law International 2002) 41ff and Glen Anderson, 'Secession in International Law and Relations: What Are We Talking About?' (2013) 35 Loyola of Los Angeles International & Comparative Law Review 343, 365ff for a more critical view of the theory.

common UN membership has the effect of bilateral recognition (it is constitutive) but does not replace it: as the United Nations is not authorised to issue an act of recognition, this may only be said to have taken place once the members have explicitly or implicitly accepted each other's statehood.[117] For example, recognition may still be required for the application of relevant provisions of domestic law. It also cannot be said that Member States are under an obligation to formally recognise each other, as such an obligation would need to be provided explicitly in a binding legal source. I do however agree with Professor Dugard's understanding of admission into UN membership as a form of collective recognition, albeit in a broader sense of the word, because of the effects it produces under international law.[118]

In this regard, 'collective recognition' through the United Nations may not be limited to admission into membership but also flow from certain acts of its organs such as the General Assembly and the Security Council. Neither of these are vested with the authority to recognise *stricto sensu*, but this has not prevented them from coming conspicuously close to recognising both States and governments on a number of occasions.

Cohen recalls that the General Assembly 'recognised' Korea in Resolution 195 (III).[119] During the decolonisation era, the General Assembly similarly supported the right to independence and ultimately admitted into membership many former colonies regardless of whether they met the traditional criteria of material statehood and in the absence of universal recognition by the Organisation's members.[120] Dugard also argues that the General Assembly has a role to play in the recognition of States that do not want to, or for political reasons cannot, become members of the Organisation, such as the Holy See and Palestine.[121]

[117] A similar interpretation of the League of Nations Covenant was made by Graham; see Malbone W Graham, *The League of Nations and the Recognition of States* (University of California Press 1933) 39.

[118] Naturally, whether they would have effects under domestic law would have to be ascertained according to that body of law; this is another reason why collective recognition through the UN presently does not replace recognition by States.

[119] Rosalyn Cohen, 'The Concept of Statehood in United Nations Practice' (1961) 109(8) University of Pennsylvania Law Review 1127–71, 1155. The Resolution declares, *inter alia*, that 'there has been established a lawful government ... having effective control and jurisdiction over that part of Korea ... in which the great majority of the people of all Korea reside; that this Government is based on elections which were a valid expression of the free will of the electorate of that part of Korea and which were observed by the Temporary Commission; and that this is the only such Government in Korea.' UNGA Resolution 195 (III) (1948) para 2.

[120] See eg Resolutions 1573 (XV) (1960) and 1724 (XVI) on Algeria; 1742 (XVI) (1960) on Angola; 1811 (XVII) (1962) on Zanzibar; 1812 (XVII) (1962) on Kenya; and many others. These resolutions confirmed the colonial countries' right to independence and were followed by their swift admission into the UN.

[121] John Dugard, 'What Is a State in International Law? How Is This to Be Determined?' in Niels M Blokker, Daniëlla Dam-de Jong, and Vid Prislan (eds), *Furthering the Frontiers of International Law: Sovereignty, Human Rights, Sustainable Development: Liber Amicorum Nico Schrijver* (Brill/Nijhoff 2021) 110.

The Security Council has also called for respect of a State's territorial integrity and independence even before its admission into the United Nations, recognition by all members, and without fulfilling one or more Montevideo Convention criteria.[122] In theory, this practice raises a number of questions as to the effects of such resolutions: for example, did violations of the territorial integrity of Bosnia and Herzegovina after the Security Council had confirmed it in a resolution violate a right of that State, or more narrowly an obligation towards the United Nations? If the Council orders States to refrain from using force against a non-member whose statehood is dubious, does it make statehood itself legally opposable, or is this only the case with certain elements of statehood listed in the resolutions, such as territorial integrity and the obligation of non-intervention? In practice this issue does not carry much weight as all non-members benefiting from such resolutions were eventually accepted into UN membership. It appears to me that at least some effects normally reserved for recognition can also be achieved through the acts of UN bodies and may therefore come within the scope of collective recognition as contemplated by Dugard. After all, as these bodies already play a crucial role in collective non-recognition, I do not see why they should not be able to play a role in collective recognition as well, at least to some extent.

There can be no doubt that admission into UN membership entails a final and general determination of legal statehood, and not merely for the purposes of the Charter as argued by some scholars.[123] Certain acts by principal UN bodies, chiefly the Security Council, may produce a similar effect. In this sense, I agree that the Organisation can engage in some form of collective recognition by producing the effects of recognition under international law, but this does not actually replace recognition given by individual States.

4. Implicit (Implied) Recognition

In terms of whether it is contained in a formal act or must be inferred in its absence, recognition is usually described as either 'express' or 'implicit'.[124] The two merely differ in form, as the latter is also 'founded upon the will and intent of the state that is extending the recognition'.[125] Recognition is implicit if it may be deduced from conclusive facts[126] (*faits concluants*) that precondition the acceptance of a legal

[122] See eg Resolutions 242 (1967) on the Middle East; 384 (1975) on East Timor; 787 (1992) on Bosnia and Herzegovina; and others.

[123] See Colin Warbrick, 'States and Recognition in International Law' in Malcolm Evans (ed), *International Law* (OUP 2006) 251–52.

[124] See eg Verdross (n 11) 331; Anzilotti, Cours de droit international, Premier vol (n 74) 170; Cavaglieri (n 5) 344; and Crawford (n 1) 139.

[125] Shaw (n 10) 343.

[126] Thus, Anzilotti writes: 'Aussi distingue-t-on une reconnaissance expresse, résultant d'une déclaration explicite par traités, notes diplomatiques, etc., et une reconnaissance tacite, résultant de faits concluants, tels que la stipulation d'un traité, l'envoi ou la réception d'agents diplomatiques, etc.'

situation. This is most visible with recognition of statehood: even though States may, and do, engage with certain entities without recognising them as States,[127] certain acts, conduct, and statements imply that statehood has indeed been accepted even in the absence of an explicit statement.

Bearing in mind the inconsistent use of the term in the past, implied recognition is a potentially confusing doctrine; Lauterpacht rightly decries its 'vagaries and ... artificialities'.[128] In pre-Second World War doctrine, the general understanding was that, for reasons of diplomatic tradition or expediency, States could simply forego the act of recognition altogether and engage with a new State as peers. Issuing a formal act of recognition could come at a significant political price even if the recognising government had no qualms about the recipient's statehood. As Shaw puts it, 'State practice has restricted the possible scope of operation of this concept of implied recognition to a few instances only and all the relevant surrounding circumstances will have to be carefully evaluated before one can deduce from conduct the intention to extend recognition. States like to retain their control of such an important political instrument as recognition and are usually not keen to allow this to be inferred from the way they behave.'[129]

Even within legal circles, the notion of implied recognition is sometimes misconstrued as a way of proving that a certain fact has become opposable to a State in spite of its insistence to the contrary. Although most States having implicitly recognised the statehood of another will not be too reluctant to admit it, situations may indeed arise when the previously established opposability of a fact must be 'proven' against the claims of a now reticent State. The matter then comes within the doctrine of estoppel, according to which 'a representing State or organization is barred—estopped or precluded—from successfully adopting different, subsequent statements on the same issue, without regard to their truth and accuracy, provided that such statements or conduct cause harm and prejudice to another party and thus frustrate legitimate expectations as to the conduct of said State or organization'.[130] There exist extensive notions of estoppel in international law,[131] but even

Anzilotti (n 74) 170; cf Cavaglieri (n 5) 344: 'Mais la reconnaissance peut être également tacite, si elle peut se déduire de faits concluants qui la supposent logiquement (conclusion de traités avec l'État nouveau, envoi ou réception de ses agents diplomatiques, consulaires, etc.).'

[127] Lauterpacht (n 5) 8; cf Shaw (n 10) 343–44.

[128] Hersch Lauterpacht, 'Recognition of States in International Law' (1944) 53(3) The Yale Law Journal 385, 392; subsequent editions of *Recognition in International Law* only retain the reference to 'vagaries'. See Lauterpacht (n 5) 8.

[129] Shaw (n 10) 344.

[130] Thomas Cottier and Jörg Paul Müller, 'Estoppel' in Anne Peters and Rüdiger Wolfrum (eds), *Max Planck Encyclopedias of International Law* (OUP 2021) para 1 <https://opil.ouplaw.com/display/10.1093/law:epil/9780199231690/law-9780199231690-e1401?prd=EPIL> last accessed 30 May 2024.

[131] cf *Case Concerning the Factory at Chorzów (Claim for Indemnity) (Merits)*, Judgment of 13 September 1928, Ser A, no 17, 31 and *Eastern Greenland* case (n 29) 69–71.

a restrictive notion should be adequate to dismiss such inconsistent claims. This should nevertheless be an exceedingly rare occurrence and implied recognition remains above all a form of recognition and not a means of contesting a State's claims of non-recognition.

The concept of estoppel may be relevant for both explicit and implied recognition, as ultimately both forms of the act lead to the same result. The 'narrow' notion, which may be more widespread in doctrine,[132] is summarised by Judge Spender in the *Temple* case as 'prevent[ing] a State contesting before the Court a situation contrary to a clear and unequivocal representation previously made by it to another State, either expressly or impliedly, on which representation the other State was ... entitled to rely and in fact did rely, and as a result that other State has been prejudiced or the State making it has secured some benefit or advantage for itself'.[133] The 'broader' notion does not insist on actual prejudice having occurred to another party and recalls the Latin maxim *venire contra factum proprium non valet*. Cottier and Müller argue against such a wide approach, writing that '[m]ere recognition of certain facts or legal positions, however, does not automatically have an effect of estoppel, as broad concepts suggest'.[134]

An unqualified application of the concept of estoppel could lead to awkward results. If we posit that recognition—explicit or implied—merely signifies acceptance of the fact of statehood but does not produce any other palpable results on which the recipient may rely and thus be harmed by their possible repudiation, then recognition either has no effects at all, or it does not come within the scope of estoppel; this is, in my view, an untenable position. Recognition of statehood is not recognition of a simple fact such as possession over an object or the enjoyment of a specific right. It rather signifies the acceptance of an entire spectrum of rights to be enjoyed vis-à-vis the issuing State. Therefore, it is rather difficult to imagine how any denial of statehood recognition, once given, could not come within the narrower notion of estoppel requiring detrimental reliance.

Implied recognition should also not be confused with declaratory non-recognition. North and South Korea do not recognise each other, and it would be counterintuitive to say that they do so implicitly because of common UN membership. Whether explicit or implicit, recognition is always a willing act by a State, not a situation in which it finds itself.

[132] See Cottier and Müller, 'Estoppel' (n 130) paras 2–3, who list Bowett, Dominicé, Martin, Müller, and Kolb as favouring the narrow notion of estoppel, and Cheng, MacGibbon, Schwarzenberger, Koskenniemi, and McNair, amongst others, as favouring a broader notion.

[133] *Case Concerning the Temple of Preah Vihear (Cambodia v Thailand)*, ICJ Reports 6, Judgment of 15 June 1962, 143–44 (Dissenting Opinion of Sir Percy Spender).

[134] Cottier and Müller (n 130) para 3.

4.1 Implied Recognition in the Narrow Sense

Implied or implicit recognition is deduced from a State's behaviour necessitating the previous acceptance of a certain legal situation: such behaviour is called a conclusive action or fact. It is impossible to come up with a final list of specific acts that would imply recognition, although interaction without explicit recognition should nevertheless be interpreted restrictively, in such a way as to presume consistent non-recognition. An omission to act may not necessarily lead to implied recognition. Drawing from Lauterpacht, Brownlie and Crawford conclude that recognition may safely be deduced from 'the conclusion of a bilateral treaty which regulates comprehensively the relations between the two states, the formal initiation of diplomatic relations, and, probably the issue of consular exequaturs, justify the implication'.[135] In such cases, no other explanation is possible for a State's behaviour other than that it has accepted the statehood of the entity in question. According to Charpentier, 'La reconnaissance est implicite lorsque la conduite d'un État laisse présumer son intention de reconnaître'.[136]

4.1.1 Entering a Bilateral Treaty

States may negotiate and enter treaties with non-state actors and States they do not recognise without any intention of accepting their statehood. Although the degree of formality accorded to such treaties is normally not the same as when a treaty is concluded with a recognised State, there is usually no doubt that they instil a binding legal relationship governed by treaty law. Sometimes, however, the very purpose of the treaty is to elevate the two countries' relations to the realm of inter-state relations. When this is done explicitly, there is of course no problem to conclude that the treaty constitutes recognition; but sometimes, political and even domestic law constraints render the word 'recognition' unacceptable.

An excellent example of such an agreement is the German Basic Treaty of 1972, which was signed and ratified by the Federal Republic of Germany (FRG) and the German Democratic Republic (GDR) after Willy Brandt's chancellorship had abandoned the Hallstein Doctrine in favour of *Ostpolitik* and gradual rapprochement between the two German States. Prior to the basic treaty, the two Germanies—which never expressly recognised each other—had divergent views of their statehood and provenance: whereas the FRG consistently expressed the view that it shared the identity of the occupied German Reich, the GDR eventually abandoned this idea and accepted the existence of 'two States in Germany'.[137]

[135] Crawford (n 1) 139.

[136] Jean Charpentier, *La reconnaissance internationale et l'évolution du droit des gens* (Pedone 1956) 250.

[137] Bruno Simma, 'Legal Aspects of East-West German Relations' (1985) 9(1) Maryland Journal of International Law 97, 98; see also more generally Walther Hubatsch, *Die deutsche Frage* (A G Pleotz 1964) and Karl E Birnbaum, *East and West Germany: A Modus Vivendi* (Lexington Books 1973).

The parties stipulated a number of general principles that would henceforth govern their relations, promising to 'develop normal, good-neighbourly relations with each other on the basis of equal rights'[138] and that '[t]he Federal Republic of Germany and the German Democratic Republic proceed on the assumption that neither of the two States can represent the other in the international sphere or act on its behalf'.[139]

The ratification of the treaty in West Germany was challenged as unconstitutional, leading to a controversial Constitutional Court decision that found that the Basic Treaty did not violate the Basic Law of the FRG. The Constitutional Court determined that there were, as a matter of fact, two States 'belonging' to Germany that could not consider themselves 'foreign'.[140] As regards the treaty itself, it occupied a peculiar status under both international and domestic law:

> What is special in this Treaty is that it is a bilateral treaty between two states to which the rules of international law apply and which has the force and validity like any other treaty under international law, but between two states that are parts of a comprehensive state of all Germany which still exists, even though it is incapable of acting because it is not yet reorganized, with a unitary population, within borders which it is not necessary here to define more precisely. From this there results the special legal closeness of the two states to each other (...).[141]

The Court added that the Basic Treaty did not merely regulate the two States' relations *inter se* but also, in the absence of a proper domestic constitutional system, acted as a sort of constitutional arrangement for Germany as a whole, by analogy with federal States.[142] This is a strange argument, suggesting that the FRG and GDR were, at the same time, independent States and parts of the same Parent State of Germany whose constitutional system was directly based on international law. This bizarre idea was never fully accepted by lawyers in the FRG and the GDR was rather perceived as having successfully 'seceded' from the German Reich.[143] Whatever the case, the Constitutional Court correctly identified both the FRG and the GDR as States, in spite of formal non-recognition, as this flowed from the treaty itself. Specific solutions for relations between the FRG and GDR, such as the idea

[138] Treaty Concerning the Basis of Relations between the Federal Republic of Germany and the German Democratic Republic (adopted 21 December 1972, entered into force 21 June 1973) art 1.

[139] ibid art 4; cf art 6: 'The Federal Republic of Germany and the German Democratic Republic proceed on the principle that the sovereign jurisdiction of each of the two States is confined to its own territory. They respect each other's independence and autonomy in their internal and external affairs.'

[140] Kurt Wilk, 'Federal Republic of Germany Case Note' (1976) 70(1) The American Journal of International Law 147, 150.

[141] ibid 151.

[142] ibid 152.

[143] Bruno Simma, 'Legal Aspects of East-West German Relations' (n 137) 108ff.

to establish 'permanent missions' rather than embassies in each other's territory,[144] do not diminish the fact that their statehood was no longer contested under international law.

In principle, entering a bilateral treaty on any issue in due and proper form will be enough to establish recognition: a good example may be found in the Treaty of Amity and Commerce negotiated between France and the revolutionary United States in 1778.[145] However, even formal treaty relations will not lead to implicit recognition if a party's non-recognition has been made clear in the negotiation or text of the treaty.[146] Thus, in a 2020 judgment, the General Court of the European Union determined that the EU's maintenance of treaty relations with Kosovo did not amount to diplomatic recognition, recalling that 'on no occasion has the European Union adopted a position on the status of Kosovo as a State in the light of international law, as evidenced by the provisions ... which make clear that that the [Stabilisation and Association Agreement with Kosovo] does not constitute recognition of Kosovo by the European Union as an independent State or affect the individual positions of the Member States on its status'.[147] It was argued that EU law in this regard spoke of 'third countries', which could encompass entities other than sovereign States. On appeal, the Grand Chamber disagreed with the General Court's interpretation of the notion of 'third country', finding that there was no room to conclude that the relevant provisions of European law referred to anything other than a State; nevertheless, these grounds of appeal were rejected based on the fact that the agreements with Kosovo—which, in the Chamber's reasoning, treat it as another State, and not just an entity of uncertain status—expressly negated recognition by either the Union or individual Member States.[148] Therefore, recognition cannot be deduced from a treaty, however formal, that explicitly negates it. It should also be noted that purely political agreements which do not amount to treaties in the sense of international law cannot in any case give rise to recognition, regardless of their content, as they are not legal acts and do not produce legal consequences.

[144] Treaty Concerning the Basis of Relations between the Federal Republic of Germany and the German Democratic Republic (adopted 21 December 1972, entered into force 21 June 1973) art 8.

[145] Treaty of Amity and Commerce between the United States of America and the Kingdom of France (signed 6 February 1778, entered into force 17 July 1778).

[146] Charpentier, *La reconnaissance internationale* (n 136) 255; see also Olivier Corten and Pierre Klein, 'Are Agreements between States and Non-State Entities Rooted in the International Legal Order?' in Enzo Canizzaro, *The Law of Treaties Beyond the Vienna Convention* (OUP 2011) 3.

[147] T-370/19 *Spain v Commission* [2020] ECLI:EU:T:2020:440, paras 32–33. The Court also recalled that the EU had entered into international agreements with other non-state entities such as the Palestine Liberation Organisation; the Separate Customs Territory of Taiwan, Penghu, Kinmen and Matsu; the Government of the Hong Kong Special Administrative Region of the People's Republic of China; and the Macao Special Administrative Region of the People's Republic of China.

[148] C-632/20 P *Spain v Commission* [2023] ECLI:EU:C:2023:28, paras 37–65.

4.1.2 Establishing Diplomatic Relations

Diplomatic practice and relations have been regulated by law at least since the time of the Greek city-states and the Roman Republic, and today of course they are governed by international law. Traditionally, the label 'diplomatic' was used exclusively to refer to relations between States participating in the European legal community: other forms of foreign representation, such as the practice of sending emissaries of European powers to indigenous tribes in the New World or to Far Eastern empires such as China, was not regarded as enjoying the same status as late as the nineteenth century when guarantees of diplomatic privileges became more widespread with non-European States.[149] The state-centrism of nineteenth-century doctrine is exemplified in Pradier-Fodéré's definition of diplomacy: '[L]a *diplomatie* est l'art de représenter le gouvernement et les intérêts de son pays auprès des gouvernements et dans les pays étrangers . . . .'[150]

This view was still dominant when the Vienna Convention on Diplomatic Relations was adopted in 1961,[151] although Langhorne notes with irony that the Convention 'marked both the culmination and the beginning of the end of classical diplomacy'.[152] Indeed, it was not long thereafter that non-traditional, non-state diplomacy began to proliferate at great speed. Nevertheless, diplomatic relations continue to carry an aura of statism. This is why, in the limited context of recognition, we must examine whether the establishment of diplomatic relations in the absence of express recognition of statehood may be seen as a form of implicit recognition.

According to Denza, 'the right to conduct diplomatic relations is now generally regarded as flowing from recognition as a sovereign State'.[153] In the League of Nations era, States regarded diplomatic relations as reserved for States and therefore as implying recognition.[154] The Vienna Convention does not exclude diplomatic relations between States and international organisations or between international organisations from the category of 'diplomatic' relations, but neither does it regulate them. Realising that the purpose of diplomatic privileges 'is not to benefit individuals but to ensure the efficient performance of the functions of

[149] Richard Langhorne, 'The Regulation of Diplomatic Practice: The Beginnings to the Vienna Convention on Diplomatic Relations, 1961' (1992) 18(1) Review of International Studies 3, 4–6.

[150] Paul Pradier-Fodéré, *Cours de Droit Diplomatique: A l'Usage des Agents Politiques du Ministère des Affaires Etrangères des États Européens et Américains* (Paris 1899) 2.

[151] Vienna Convention on Diplomatic Relations, 500 UNTS 95 (adopted 18 April 1961, entered into force 24 April 1964) (hereafter VCDR).

[152] Richard Langhorne, 'The Diplomacy of Non-State Actors' (2005) 16 Diplomacy and Statecraft 331, 331.

[153] Eileen Denza, *Diplomatic Law: Commentary on the Vienna Convention on Diplomatic Relations* (OUP 2016) 19.

[154] Thus, the Yugoslav Foreign Minister regarded the establishment of diplomatic relations with Estonia in 1926 as 'quite naturally [implying] the judicial recognition of the Republic of Estonia by the Government of the Kingdom of Serbs, Croats and Slovenes'. Dugard, *Recognition and the United Nations* (n 13) 21.

diplomatic missions as representing States',[155] this treaty deals exclusively with relations between sovereign States.[156] Although the fact that the Vienna Convention does not apply to relations between non-state entities does not exclude the application of broader customary law, no such rules seem to exist at the sub-state level. Denza therefore concludes that the existence of diplomatic relations *necessarily* entails the recognition of statehood.[157] A typical example of recognition granted this way may be found in the UK's establishment of diplomatic relations with Namibia in the 1990s.[158]

It would therefore appear that at least the formal and unqualified establishment of diplomatic relations implies recognition of statehood and may be taken as proof of an intention to recognise the new State.[159] The 'formal' and 'unqualified' criteria are distinct and would, in my view, both need to be met for recognition to occur. Informal relations, whatever their practical purpose, do not suffice for the recognition of a State or government: they are informal precisely because the State engaging in them wishes to avoid recognition. Whereas only a few UN members maintain full diplomatic relations with Taiwan, many others that formally recognise the Beijing government still have informal relations with Taipei.[160] Taiwanese unofficial missions dispense with duties typically associated with an embassy, but do not enjoy diplomatic privileges and immunities (although the receiving State may 'turn a blind eye' and afford some special treatment *ex gratia*).[161] Such relations demonstrate the receiving States' desire to engage in commercial and other exchanges with the Republic of China (ROC) without accepting its statehood or capacity to speak for the whole of China, which also means that simply informal relations—however well developed—do not amount to implied recognition.

The notion of 'formal diplomatic relations' should in this context be taken narrowly: permanent diplomatic missions should be established, and diplomatic

155 VCDR (n 151) preambular para 5.

156 See eg ibid arts 1–3, and most of its other provisions.

157 Eileen Denza, *Diplomatic Law* (n 153) 24; see also Crawford (n 1) 139 for a similar view. In the well-known *Clerget* case, a French tribunal thus inferred recognition of North Vietnam from the French government's decision to extend diplomatic immunity to a North Vietnamese commercial delegation, see summary in Matthias Herdegen, 'Clerget v Banque commerciale pour l'Europe du Nord Case' in Anne Peters and Rüdiger Wolfrum (eds), *Max Planck Encyclopedias of International Law* (OUP 2007) <https://opil.ouplaw.com/display/10.1093/law:epil/9780199231690/law-9780199231690-e1077> last accessed 30 May 2024.

158 Crawford (n 1) 94.

159 See also Charpentier (n 136) 253; in Charpentier's view, however, the establishment of consular relations does not imply recognition.

160 On this topic, see Thomas J Bellows, 'Taiwan's Foreign Policy in the 1970s: A Case Study of Adaptation and Viability' (1976) 16(7) Asian Survey 593; Gary D Rawnsley, *Taiwan's Informal Diplomacy and Propaganda* (Palgrave Macmillan 2000); Timothy Ka-ying Wong, 'Changing Taiwan's Foreign Policy: From One China to Two States' (2000) 24(1) Asian Perspective 5; and, for a perspective on the relations between the European Union and Taiwan, Paul Lim and Sigrid Winkler, 'The European Union's Relations with the Republic of China (Taiwan)' in Jens Damm and Paul Lim (eds), *European Perspectives on Taiwan* (Springer 2012) 170.

161 See more in Erik Pajtinka, 'Between Diplomacy and Paradiplomacy: Taiwan´s Foreign Relations in Current Practice' (2017) 11(1) Journal of Nationalism, Memory & Language Politics 39.

agents vested with diplomatic privileges and immunities accredited with the host government. Liaison or commercial offices do not qualify, nor do meetings between heads of State or government or foreign ministers. The five EU members that do not recognise Kosovo occasionally meet its representatives while confidently maintaining that this does not amount to diplomatic recognition.

In addition, consular relations alone may not amount to recognition as the sending State will sometimes choose to preserve its consular activity for the benefit of its own nationals and private parties abroad. The USSR maintained a consulate in Manchukuo even though it refused to recognise it as a State.[162] Faced with a similar situation today, one might be tempted to think of the ICJ's dictum in *Namibia* that States had an obligation 'to abstain from sending consular agents to Namibia' in light of South Africa's unlawful presence in that territory.[163] However, to refrain from sending consular agents or withdraw those already deployed today comes within the broader scope of non-recognition obligations when facing violations of peremptory norms: it does not mean that the mere maintenance of consular relations amounts to recognition.

The requirement that diplomatic relations be 'unqualified' will be fulfilled if the States in question do not dispute that recognition has thereby taken place. States typically do not establish formal diplomatic relations with States they do not recognise, but it has been suggested that such relations can exist without amounting to recognition. South Africa maintained diplomatic relations with Rhodesia between 1965 and 1980 while insisting that it did not thereby recognise its statehood; Dugard is of the view that South Africa's 'express denial' of recognition was 'decisive' to conclude that implied recognition had not occurred.[164] Along these lines, the idea was recently put forward that Israel could establish diplomatic relations with Kosovo without recognising its statehood.[165] Although States do not typically maintain diplomatic relations with States they do not recognise, I do not believe that anything prevents them from doing so: certainly, there is a presumption that diplomatic relations entail recognition of statehood, but if a State were to explicitly

[162] David Turns, 'The Stimson Doctrine of Non-Recognition: Its Historical Genesis and Influence on Contemporary International Law' (2003) 2(1) Chinese Journal of International Law 105–43, 123, fn 74; the USSR insisted that this did not amount to recognition; for the consular activities of other States, see ibid 112–13.

[163] *Legal Consequences for States of the Continued Presence of South Africa in Namibia (South West Africa) Notwithstanding Security Council Resolution 276 (1970)*, ICJ Reports 16, Advisory Opinion of 21 June 1971 (hereafter *Namibia* case) para 123.

[164] John Dugard, *International Law: A South African Perspective* (Juta 2011) 92.

[165] See Rami Ayyub, 'Israel and Kosovo establish diplomatic relations in virtual ceremony' (*Reuters*, 1 February 2021) <https://www.reuters.com/article/us-israel-kosovo-relations/israel-and-kosovo-establish-diplomatic-relations-in-virtual-ceremony-idUSKBN2A12S0> last accessed 30 May 2025 and Raphael Ahren, 'Serbia won't open Jerusalem embassy if Israel recognizes Kosovo—Serbian source' (*Times of Israel*, 9 September 2020) <https://www.timesofisrael.com/serbia-wont-open-jerusalem-embassy-if-israel-recognizes-kosovo-serbian-source/#gs.g6t8w7> last accessed 30 May 2024. Israel did in fact formally recognise Kosovo before establishing diplomatic relations.

waive acceptance of the other's sovereign status, then its position should be given overriding weight when determining if implied recognition has occurred.

4.1.3 Voting for Membership in an International Organisation

Although it is more traditional to recognise a State before supporting its membership in international organisations, this is not always the case: the vote for membership itself could be intended to signify recognition. New States created in the former Yugoslavia and USSR whose statehood was uncontested were quickly admitted into the United Nations, giving individual members very little time to recognise them before voting in the General Assembly. Thus, the United Kingdom 'regarded its vote in favour of UN membership for the former Yugoslav republic of Macedonia as amounting to recognition of that entity as a state'.[166] If an organisation is open exclusively to States, then voting for membership can typically be taken as constituting recognition of the applicant. However, the matter is not always so straightforward.

First, not all international organisations have the same membership criteria, nor is membership always limited to States. There exist many different organisations today, many of which are open to non-sovereign entities. If an organisation is open exclusively to States, such as the United Nations, then a vote for membership can typically (but not always) be taken to constitute recognition. If it is open to both States and non-state entities, then their admission may be subjected to different procedures, and of course it will depend on the procedure used for a given applicant how voting may be understood. Membership in UNESCO (the United Nations Educational, Scientific and Cultural Organization) is possible through a two-track process based on whether an applicant is to become a member or associate member, the latter being reserved for territories that are not responsible for the conduct of their international relations.[167] When the Åland Islands became an associate member in 2021 at the request of Finland, its unanimous admission at the General Conference clearly cannot be taken to constitute recognition by any participating State.[168]

Membership in the United Nations occupies a special place in discussions of statehood and voting for the admission of a new member is properly taken as a form of recognition. As the Organisation is open to 'peace-loving states which accept the obligations contained in the [UN] Charter',[169] admission into the United Nations is considered a strong indicator of statehood.[170] The ICJ itself interpreted

[166] Shaw (n 10) 344.

[167] Constitution of the UNESCO, 4 UNTS 275 (adopted 16 November 1945, came into force 4 November 1946) art II.

[168] See *First plenary meeting of the 41st session of the General Conference: Unedited transcript* (9 November 2021) 41 C/VR.1 Unedited, 6ff.

[169] Charter of the United Nations, 1 UNTS XVI (adopted 26 June 1945, entered into force 24 October 1945) (hereafter UN Charter) art 4.

[170] See eg Wright, 'Some Thoughts About Recognition' (n 106) 550 and Cohen, 'The Concept of Statehood' (n 119) 1127.

the criteria for UN membership in an advisory opinion and determined that the candidate must be a State.[171] The Charter foresees that '[t]he admission of any such state to membership in the United Nations will be effected by a decision of the General Assembly upon the recommendation of the Security Council'.[172] Daillier, Forteau, and Pellet argue that it will be difficult to contest the statehood of an entity whose membership in such an organisation was supported by the voting State.[173] This is a reasonable conclusion, but it should also be borne in mind that, exceptionally, Belarus, India, and Ukraine were all admitted into the Organisation before their independence.[174] As founding members, these countries were not subjected to the Article 4 procedure, but it is not difficult to imagine that similar arrangements might again be made in the future. Should this be the case, a vote need not be interpreted as recognition.

Voting in favour of observer status at the United Nations does not imply recognition. In 2012, Palestine was accorded non-member observer State status by the General Assembly; the resolution even '[*e*]*xpresses the hope* that the Security Council will consider favourably the application submitted ... by the State of Palestine for admission to full membership in the United Nations'.[175] One could infer that members supporting the resolution also consider Palestine to be a State. However, the favourable votes included several members, such as Belgium, France, or Switzerland, that did not recognise Palestinian statehood at the time. The Swiss representative explained that the decision to support the resolution 'was motivated by our desire to resolve the current stalemate in Israeli-Palestinian negotiations and to relaunch the peace process' but also that this 'does not involve a bilateral recognition of a Palestinian State, which will depend on future peace negotiations'.[176] The Belgian delegate highlighted that 'the resolution adopted today by the General Assembly does not yet constitute a recognition of a State in the full sense. The establishment of a fully legal State must result from negotiations between Israelis and Palestinians.'[177] Both States thus agreed that the vote itself did not amount to recognition.

Voting for full membership in specialised agencies may probably be considered the same as voting for membership in the United Nations itself, although this is not always clear. When Kosovo unsuccessfully applied for membership in 2015, a few States insisted that a favourable vote would have nothing to do with recognition

[171] *Conditions of Admission of a State to Membership in the United Nations (Article 4 of the Charter)*, ICJ Reports 57, Advisory Opinion of 28 May 1948, 62.

[172] UN Charter (n 169) art 4.

[173] Patrick Daillier, Mathias Forteau, and Alain Pellet, *Droit international public* (LGDJ—Léxtenso éditions 2009) 630.

[174] The relevant provision for founding members art 3 of the Charter, which nevertheless refers to 'States'.

[175] UNGA Resolution 67/19 of 4 December 2012, para 3.

[176] *Official Records of the 44th Plenary Meeting* (29 November 2012) A/67/PV.44, 15–16.

[177] ibid 16.

of Kosovo as a State.[178] Nevertheless, the resolution was not supported by a single State that did not recognise Kosovo.[179]

It is not possible to conclude *a priori* whether voting for membership in international organisations amounts to implied recognition. This will always have to be determined on the basis of the organisation's constitutional framework and any statements made by members during voting. As a rule of thumb, we could assume the following: when membership in an organisation is open exclusively to States or is submitted to a procedure foreseen for States, a favourable vote may be presumed to imply recognition unless stated otherwise; when membership is more loosely defined and open to entities other than States, no such presumption should exist.

4.1.4 Recognising State and Personal Immunities

The recognition of State and personal immunities in respect of an authority not formally recognised as a State or government will usually amount to implied recognition. In the *Clerget* case, a French tribunal inferred recognition of North Vietnam from the government's grant of immunity to Vietnamese representatives.[180] Many domestic tribunals predicate immunities on recognition,[181] so it is not difficult to understand why they might understand the executive's extension of immunity to a foreign delegation as implying recognition.

Like the establishment of full diplomatic relations, recognition of State and personal immunities may be considered implicit recognition, although, as with diplomatic relations, it is not currently possible to determine with any certainty whether a 'qualified' grant of immunity could represent an exception to this rule. It will be crucial to determine whether immunities are granted out of a sense of legal obligation or for policy reasons. In the latter case, one should exercise caution before concluding that recognition has occurred.

4.2 By Common Membership in an International Organisation

As discussed earlier, States which do not recognise each other sometimes become members of the same international organisations. Scholars such as Dugard have argued that membership in organisations such as the United Nations replaces recognition by individual members and even acts as a form of collective recognition.[182]

[178] According to the US representative, 'This is not a question of recognition or non-recognition. Countries that do not recognize Kosovo have supported its membership in specialized United Nations agencies including the World Bank, and the International Monetary Fund (IMF).' *Tenth plenary meeting of the 38th session of the General Conference: Unedited Transcript* (9 November 2016) 38 C/VR.10 Unedited, 8.

[179] For the voting results, see ibid 14–15.

[180] Herdegen (n 157).

[181] See eg *Mighell v Sultan of Johore* (1894) 1 QB 149; *The Arantzazu Mendi* (1939) AC 256; and *United States v Lumumba* (1984) 741 F2d 12.

[182] See Dugard, *Recognition and the United Nations* (n 13).

Others, notably Kelsen, have rejected this interpretation, but suggested that the constitutional workings of certain organisations might lead to mutual implied recognition in case of common membership.[183] Because such common membership might produce the international law effects of recognition, these authors list it as a form of implicit recognition. Ker-Lindsay gives it the catchy title of 'indirect collective recognition'.[184]

Because explicit and implicit recognition only differ in form, the concept of indirect collective recognition is essentially the same as that of collective recognition. Common membership in an organisation such as the United Nations renders the statehood of its members mutually opposable but does not displace the need for individual recognition for political reasons and the purposes of domestic law. In my view, individual recognition by all members cannot be implied from joint membership of an international organisation.

4.3 By Being a Party to the Same Multilateral Treaty

As with bilateral treaty relations, becoming a party to the same treaty as an unrecognised State does not imply recognition: there must first be a demonstrated intention to recognise.[185] This position has also been taken by the ILC.[186] As a State could become a party to a multilateral treaty subsequently to one or more States that do not recognise it, not even a lack of protest or reaction by non-recognising States should lead to a presumption that they have changed their position. Nevertheless, such States will typically protest or state explicitly that they do not consider themselves to have treaty relations with the newcomer, let alone recognise it, simply because the depositary has accepted its instrument of accession or ratification.

When the Dutch government, as the depositary of the Hague Apostille Convention,[187] accepted Kosovo's instrument of accession in 2015, numerous non-recognising States Parties made declarations that the treaty would not enter into force between them and Kosovo.[188] At its 2016 meeting, the Council on

[183] Hans Kelsen, *The Law of the United Nations: A Critical Analysis of Fundamental Problems* (Steven & Sons 1951) 79.

[184] James Ker-Lindsay, 'Engagement Without Recognition: The Limits of Diplomatic Interaction with Contested States' (2015) 91(2) International Affairs 1, 7.

[185] '[L]a capacité de traiter du nouvel Etat ne suffit pas à impliquer sa reconnaissance de la part de son cocontractant: son intention de reconnaître doit être démontrée ....' Charpentier (n 136) 255. See also Manley O'Hudson, 'Recognition and Multipartite Treaties' (1929) 23(1) The American Journal of International Law 126 for a convincing argument and practice overview against presuming recognition through common multilateral treaty membership.

[186] *Report of the International Law Commission* (2011) A/66/10/Add.1, 95.

[187] Hague Convention Abolishing the Requirement of Legalisation for Foreign Public Documents, 527 UNTS 189 (adopted 5 October 1961, entered into force 24 January 1965).

[188] A list of these States is available on the website of the Hague Conference on Private International Law at <https://www.hcch.net/en/instruments/conventions/status-table/notifications/?csid=1319&disp=type> last accessed 30 May 2024.

General Affairs and Policy of the Conference recalled that 'different views [were] expressed' on the role of the depositary regarding new ratifications or accessions to the treaty and that '[w]hen, following the deposit of an instrument of ratification, approval, or accession, the Depositary subsequently receives an objection from a Contracting State, including based on the issue of statehood, the Depositary brings the matter to the attention of all Contracting States to the Convention concerned'.[189] The majority view was that States were free to object to the accession to a treaty of a State they did not recognise and that this would prevent the treaty from entering into force between them. States that do not recognise Palestine have similarly protested its accession to treaties such as the Geneva Conventions or the Nuclear Non-Proliferation Treaty.[190]

However, in 2019, the UN Committee on the Elimination of Racial Discrimination (CERD) took a different view regarding an inter-state communication between Palestine and Israel.[191] The latter insisted that it did not have any relations under the CERD with Palestine and underscored its non-recognition of a 'Palestinian entity'.[192] The Committee noted 'treaty relations do not need to exist among all the parties to a multilateral treaty, as it is recognized that treaty relations may be excluded in cases in which a State party expresses an objection to entering into treaty relations with an entity which it does not recognize' and that, 'according to a well-established practice, a State's participation in a treaty to which an entity that it does not recognize as a State is a party, does not amount to recognition'.[193] Nevertheless, the Committee boldly concluded that these principles were inapplicable to the Convention on the Elimination of All Forms of Racial Discrimination, which has a 'special character' and protects a norm with *erga omnes* effect. Therefore, 'given the nature of racial discrimination and, consequently, of the obligations contained in the Convention which are subject to a collective guarantee and enforcement, a State party cannot bar another State party, through a unilateral action, from triggering an enforcement mechanism created by the Convention'.[194] The Committee thus ignored the position of the UN Office of Legal Affairs and found the communication admissible, eliciting a strong reaction from a minority of its members.[195] This is a regrettable decision which may be easily criticised under positive international law. All the same, it reaffirms the validity of the same principle from which it seeks to carve an exception, namely that

[189] HCCH Council on General Affairs and Policy, Conclusions & Recommendations Adopted by the Council, 15–17 March 2016, para 4.

[190] See in this regard Shadi Sakran and Mika Hayashi, 'Palestine's Accession to Multilateral Treaties: Effective Circumvention of the Statehood Question and its Consequences' (2017) 25(1) Journal of International Cooperation Studies 81–99.

[191] *Inter-State Communication Submitted by the State of Palestine against Israel* (12 December 2019) CERD/C/100/5.

[192] ibid para 3.3.

[193] ibid paras 3.10 and 3.12.

[194] ibid para 3.37.

[195] ibid 13ff.

being a party to the same multilateral treaty does not automatically lead to treaty relations between non-recognising States and that it certainly does not imply recognition.

5. Conclusion

Regardless of its actual effects, recognition is always a legal act based on the principle of good faith. It will doubtless have political implications and commonly be governed by political considerations; but it cannot be relegated to a merely political role. Moreover, recognition is an international legal act: this does not exclude that it may (and will) produce effects in the domestic legal system of the recognising State.

Every act of recognition has a cognitive and normative aspect. The cognitive aspect manifests itself in the issuing State's awareness that certain legal criteria have been met that authorise it to recognise the object in question. Its normative aspect reflects the State's acceptance of a new legal situation that is henceforth opposable to it. Opposability is the necessary product of a lawful act of recognition, although other norms of international law may also render statehood opposable when certain conditions have been met.

Recognition may be explicit or implicit. In the former case, it assumes the form of a unilateral act or declaration and may sometimes be contained in a bilateral or multilateral treaty. Recognition may be implied by a State's actions, such as the establishment of diplomatic relations or the adoption of a treaty with the recipient in due form. Whether explicit or implicit, recognition must be intended: there is no such thing as accidental recognition.

Some form of collective recognition by the international community has been discussed since at least the League of Nations era and is perhaps even more relevant today when UN membership is nigh universal. Common membership in the United Nations produces effects that are otherwise reserved for bilateral recognition. This does not however replace recognition by individual members of the Organisation as the grant of recognition has not been outsourced to the United Nations.

Non-recognition is the flipside of recognition, but it is a stance rather than a legal act. It means that the non-recognising State either refuses to accept the normative implications of the situation at hand or that it finds the situation to amount to, or flow from, a violation of international law. States may refuse to recognise the situation because they consider themselves legally obliged to refrain from such actions, but sometimes also because they feel at liberty not to accept the normative modification even if it conforms to international law.

3
Types of Recognition

1. Type and Effects

In the previous chapter I discussed the nature of recognition as a legal act and the distinction between explicit and implicit or implied recognition. As implicit and explicit recognition merely differ in the way they are given, they may be considered 'forms' of recognition. As we have seen, international law sets no formal requirements for unilateral acts, including recognition, to produce effects. Nevertheless, the legal vocabulary has evolved to include other specific 'types' of recognition whereby the author wishes to imbue the act with different consequences.

Recognition is typically granted without qualification: it is full and unconditional. Sometimes, State A's recognition of State B is said to be *de facto*, or it may recognise B on condition that the latter comply with certain requirements or demands. Legal literature also speaks of external and internal recognition. All of these may be considered different types of recognition that differ based on the act's intended effects, who it comes from, and its temporal scope or revocability. I now turn to each of these categories individually.

2. *De Facto* and *De Jure* Recognition

The concept of *de facto* recognition frequently arises in practice and literature, although it is sometimes confounded with implied recognition: because A has established diplomatic relations with B, it is said to have *de facto* recognised it.[1] This is a misconception. In fact, whether recognition is given *de jure* or *de facto* rather pertains to its scope and, perhaps, the political message its author thereby wishes to convey.

It is also easy to confuse *de facto* and *de jure* recognition with *de facto* and *de jure* States or governments. There is a tremendous difference between saying that 'A is a *de facto* State' and 'A is recognised by B *de facto*'. The first statement denotes a quality of A: it possesses 'real' or material statehood, but not necessarily the legal status of a State under international law. Somaliland may today be described as a *de facto* State that enjoys neither *de jure* nor *de facto* recognition from any other

[1] See Joe Verhoeven, *La reconnaissance internationale dans la pratique contemporaine* (Pedone 1975) 633–34.

Recognition of States in International Law. Pavle Kilibarda, Oxford University Press. © Pavle Kilibarda 2024.
DOI: 10.1093/oso/9780198905653.003.0003

uncontested State. The second statement rather describes the nature of B's recognition, which naturally entails A's legal (*de jure*) existence towards B, but not in the same way as full, unqualified, or *de jure* recognition. At the end of the First World War, the United Kingdom recognised Estonia *de facto*, which meant that it accepted to treat it legally as a State although it was not sure that Estonia's material statehood would fully come about in light of the chaotic events prevailing in Eastern Europe at the time. *De facto* and *de jure* recognition therefore refer to the manner in which a State or government is recognised but also the content of recognition.[2] For this reason, several authors consider the dichotomy a misnomer.[3]

There are at least four ways in which *de jure* and *de facto* recognition have been interpreted in legal doctrine. The most common view is that the chief difference between recognition *de facto* and recognition *de jure* is that the former is provisional and the latter is permanent.[4] A State issuing *de facto* recognition is making it known that its recognition may be withdrawn should certain circumstances arise (or fail to arise) whereas *de jure* recognition is final and irrevocable. Cavaglieri records an interpretation according to which the distinction is based on whether or not diplomatic relations are actually established,[5] but this seems to be a minority view: a State may recognise another *de jure* without establishing such relations for practical or political reasons. A third view, discussed by the British Court of Appeal, suggests that the two types of recognition differ in their scope *ratione temporis*: recognition *de jure* produces retroactive effects whereas recognition *de facto* only has effects *ex nunc*.[6] It has also been raised in jurisprudence that *de jure* recognition merely has a political effect by highlighting the recipient's legitimacy (meaning that *de facto* recognition could be seen as a less than friendly act).[7]

The origins of *de facto* recognition are to be found at the end of the First World War: earlier doctrine does not discuss it.[8] The collapse of European multinational

2 Alfred Verdross, 'Règles générales du droit international de la paix' (1929) 30 RCADI 271, 331.

3 See eg Dionisio Anzilotti, *Cours de droit international, Premier volume; Introduction—Théories générales* (Librairie du Recueil Sirey 1929) 170–71; James-Leslie Brierly, 'Règles générales du droit de la paix' (1936) 58 RCADI 1, 60; and Hans Kelsen, 'Recognition in International Law: Theoretical Observations' (1941) 35 (4) The American Journal of International Law 605, 613

4 Arrigo Cavaglieri, 'Regles générales du droit de la paix' (1929) 26 RCADI 311, 350–51; Verdross, 'Règles générales du droit international de la paix' (n 2) 330; Brierly, 'Règles générales du droit de la paix' (n 3) 60; Kelsen, 'Recognition in International Law' (n 3) 612; Gerald Fitzmaurice, 'The General Principles of International Law Considered from the Standpoint of the Rule of Law' (1957) 92 RCADI 1, 26–29; Andrew Clapham, *Brierly's Law of Nations* (OUP 2012) 157; Malcolm N Shaw, *International Law* (CUP 2017) 341; on this issue, see also more generally Amos S Hershey, 'Notes on the Recognition of De Facto Governments by European States' (1920) 14 (4) The American Journal of International Law 499–518; Thomas Baty, 'So-Called "De Facto" Recognition' (1922) 31 (5) The Yale Law Journal 469; and Charles L Cochran, 'De Facto and De Jure Recognition: Is There a Difference?' (1968) 62 (2) The American Journal of International Law 457.

5 Cavaglieri, 'Regles générales du droit de la paix' (n 4) 351.

6 *Luther v Sagor* (1921) 3 KB 532, 543–44.

7 ibid 551.

8 Cavaglieri (n 4) 351; Hershey, 'Notes on the Recognition of De Facto Governments' (n 4) 499; Verdross (n 2) 330.

empires led to conditions of revolution and disarray that eventually gave birth to several new States in Central and Eastern Europe. Under the circumstances, determining whether the independence of Finland and the Baltic States had achieved a sufficient degree of permanence to merit recognition was no easy task.[9] Several Allied governments decided to proceed with *de facto* recognition, which really meant that their recognition was provisional and could be withdrawn if the fragile Eastern European polities did not survive.

This interpretation of *de facto* recognition is supported by British jurisprudence of the time. Seized in relation to the capture as a prize of a Russian vessel by the Estonians, the Court of Appeal had to determine whether Estonia was entitled to State immunity from the jurisdiction of British courts. The Court accepted that *de facto* recognition was sufficient in this regard:

> I read the letters of the Foreign Office as being statements which do recognise, and recognise to the full, the sovereignty of Esthonia, but with the limitation that in the exceptional conditions due to the setting up of the Peace Conference no undertaking could be given to continue the recognition if conditions altered ... The Attorney-General says that 'Our own Government—and looking at the affidavits in this case I see the statement is no less true whether of the Government of France or the Government of Italy—has for the time being provisionally, and with all necessary reservations as to the future, recognised the Esthonian National Council as a *de facto* independent body, and accordingly has received a certain gentleman as the informal diplomatic representative of the Provisional Government. The state of affairs is of necessity provisional and transitory'....[10]

In a well-known example, the Truman administration recognised Israel within a few hours of its declaration of independence:

> This Government has been informed that a Jewish state has been proclaimed in Palestine, and recognition has been requested by the (provisional) government thereof.
>
> The United States recognizes the provisional government as the de facto authority of the new State of Israel.[11]

The US only recognised Israel *de jure* in early 1949 after a new government had been elected.[12] It should be borne in mind that, in spite of the references to a new

[9] James Crawford, *The Creation of States in International Law* (OUP 2007) 51.
[10] *The Gagara* (1919) Probate 95, 103–04.
[11] President Harry S Truman, Letter Dated 14 May 1948 Recognising the Provisional Government of Israel, available at <https://www.archives.gov/education/lessons/us-israel> accessed 6 May 2024.
[12] Press Release (31 January 1949) Truman Papers, Official File OF 204-D: Jewish State, 1948–1949.

government, the US government is recognising the State of Israel.[13] Recognising a '*de facto* authority' was a common course of action in historic cases of secession or the proclamation of new States, but one cannot, in principle, recognise the government of a new State without recognising the State itself.[14]

Bearing in mind the above, it is clear that the only distinction between recognition *de jure* and *de facto* is the latter's provisional character. The term '*de jure* recognition' actually refers to the most common form of recognition granted by States and would be a pleonasm but for the possibility of opposing it to *de facto* recognition.[15] Any distinction in the treatment accorded to an authority recognised *de facto* is merely incidental and does not amount to 'partial' recognition.[16] It simply means that the issuing State feels that the factual circumstances are not yet fully clear, but it is presumed that the recognised entity will prove its stability and permanence and that *de facto* recognition will eventually become *de jure*. This should not be confused with recognition as a *de jure* object, in which case the author is also passing a legitimacy or constitutionality judgment on the recipient, most often the government of a recognised State.

3. External and Internal Recognition

Some authors distinguish between internal and external recognition of statehood based on the organ undertaking it. 'External' recognition is granted by a State's executive authority; 'internal' recognition is undertaken by its courts and may only be called recognition in the widest sense. Some authors maintain that only a State's highest executive authority, its government, can grant recognition (which, in this dichotomy, corresponds to 'external' recognition).[17] There does not seem to be any consensus on this matter in either theory or practice.[18] As municipal courts

[13] Thus, Warren R Austin, the US representative on the Security Council, stated: 'I should regard it as highly improper for me to admit that any country on earth can question the sovereignty of the United States of America in the exercise of that high political act of recognition of the *de facto* status of a state.' See 'Memorandum on the Legal Aspects of the Problem of Representation in the United Nations, Transmitted to the President of the Security Council by the Secretary-General (Lie), March 8, 1950' (1950) 4 (2) International Organization 356, 357.

[14] 'There can be and are however, *de facto governments*, administrations and authorities of various kinds, and it may also be proper to speak of the government *de facto* of an unrecognized entity, or even of an, as yet, unrecognized or not fully recognized State.' Fitzmaurice, 'The General Principles of International Law' (n 4) 26.

[15] cf Verdross (n 2) 330.

[16] An argument to the contrary has been made by Fitzmaurice, who feels that it would be 'unusual' to grant full jurisdictional immunities to agents of such an authority; see Fitzmaurice (n 4) 27–29.

[17] See eg Robert Piédelièvre, *Précis du droit international public ou droit des gens: Des États et de leurs relations en temps de paix* (Pichon 1894) 99–100.

[18] In most States, domestic courts would rely on the government to determine whether an entity is a State by means of an executive certificate; see John Dugard, 'What Is a State in International Law? How Is This to Be Determined?' in Niels M Blokker, Daniëlla Dam-de Jong, and Vid Prislan (eds), *Furthering the Frontiers of International Law: Sovereignty, Human Rights, Sustainable Development: Liber Amicorum Nico Schrijver* (Brill/Nijhoff 2021) 109.

typically do not possess authority to issue acts within the domain of foreign relations, and certainly not extend recognition, their judgments and decisions will remain within the purview of domestic law.

Since the nineteenth century, American courts have, under certain conditions, accepted to scrutinise legislative acts of States otherwise not recognised by the US government. In 1869, the Supreme Court issued its ruling in *Texas v White*[19] concerning US bonds sold by Texas during the Civil War. It was determined that all acts of the secessionist State were null and void under the Constitution, however the Court raised that certain legal acts of the Confederate States could be recognised when in the interest of 'peace and good order among citizens'.[20] A similar principle was accepted in recent years by British judges, who, in *Emin v Yeldag*,[21] accepted a divorce act issued by the 'Turkish Republic of Northern Cyprus', while maintaining that this did not have any implications for the recognition of this entity as a State. The International Court of Justice (ICJ) itself confirmed this approach in *Namibia*, when it was established that UN Member States had an 'obligation to refrain from lending any support or any form of assistance to South Africa with reference to its occupation of Namibia'[22] but also that 'the non-recognition of South Africa's administration of the Territory should not result in depriving the people of Namibia of any advantages derived from international co-operation'.[23] Clearly, such internal 'recognition' of a foreign State's legislation, typically done by local judges on questions of private law, does not amount to recognition of statehood. In this regard, it would also appear that there exists no rule of general international law obliging States to accept any act issued by a State they do not recognise, even in strictly private matters such as marriage, death, and birth certificates.

4. 'Conditional' Recognition

The concept of 'conditional recognition' has been regarded with much suspicion by legal doctrine since its first appearance in the early nineteenth century. Lauterpacht relates Foreign Secretary Canning's 1822 dispatch to the British minister in Madrid regarding the recognition of former Spanish colonies in Latin America, expressing the view that 'the Recognition [of the new States of Latin America] or any other Power [than Spain] may undoubtedly be given or withholden at its own

[19] *Texas v White* (1868) 74 US 700.

[20] ibid para 16.

[21] *Emin v Yeldag* (2001) 1 FLR 956; see more on this case in Yaël Ronen, 'Recognition of Divorce without Recognition of Statehood' (2004) 63 (2) The Cambridge Journal of International Law 268.

[22] *Legal Consequences for States of the Continued Presence of South Africa in Namibia (South West Africa) Notwithstanding Security Council Resolution 276 (1970)*, ICJ Reports 16, Advisory Opinion of 21 June 1971, para 119.

[23] ibid 125.

good Pleasure and may be made contingent or conditional'.[24] Since then, recognition has occasionally been conditioned upon the recipient's compliance with certain norms of international law such as the prohibition of slavery or respecting minority rights, but also guaranteeing certain privileges of the recognising State. The notorious practice of openly trading recognition for various benefits became less prominent after the First World War, although more patronising language draped in references to universal principles remains common to this day: just as Great Britain recognised Czechoslovakia on the condition that the new State enact a democratic constitution,[25] so too was recognition promised by the European Community to Croatia if it integrated the protection of human and minority rights in its constitution.[26]

Conditional recognition should not be confused with the (pre-)conditions for recognition. According to Verhoeven, 'Au sens large, les conditions de la reconnaissance s'entendent de l'ensemble des éléments qui en déterminent la légalité en droit des gens, alors que la reconnaissance conditionnelle s'entend de la reconnaissance affectée de charges particulières qui relèvent de ses modalités éventuelles ... Ces charges constituent des conditions de la reconnaissance, de manière générale, mais elles déterminent l'efficacité de la reconnaissance plutôt que sa légalité'.[27] While the law of nations spells out criteria for lawful recognition—be it full, provisional or conditional—a conditional recognition means that a specific act of recognition, performed by one or more existing States towards a new State, is predicated upon the existence of factors that are external to that act and which may or may not depend on the behaviour of the recipient.[28]

There are two ways of understanding conditional recognition in contemporary practice. First, it may be said to be a simple commitment to recognise but not an act of recognition as such: only if the conditions are met will the recipient be recognised. Second, conditional recognition may be equated with provisional recognition and therefore withdrawn if the required conditions cease to exist or fail to materialise. This question is important as a simple political commitment does not produce legal effects whereas an act of provisional recognition does. State practice could be read as supporting either approach: while the approach of European

[24] Hersch Lauterpacht, *Recognition in International Law* (CUP 2013) 13; see also in this regard Hersch Lauterpacht, '*De Facto* Recognition, Withdrawal of Recognition, and Conditional Recognition' (1945) 22 British Year Book of International Law 164, 186; the author gives the examples of the conditional recognition by the United States or the United Kingdom of Albania, Mexico, Brazil, Liberia, Bolivia, and the former Belgian Congo.

[25] See Lauterpacht, '*De Facto* Recognition' (n 24) 186.

[26] 'Conference on Yugoslavia Arbitration Commission: Opinions on Questions Arising from the Dissolution of Yugoslavia, 11 January and 4 July 1992' (1992) 31 ILM 1488, 1504–05; cf Colin Warbrick, 'Recognition of States' (1992) 41 (2) The International and Comparative Law Quarterly 473, 479.

[27] Verhoeven (n 1) 537.

[28] In Verhoeven's terms, 'A proprement parler celle-ci est une reconnaissance assortie d'une condition au sens technique du terme qui peut être définie de manière générale comme l'événement futur et incertain dont dépend la naissance ou l'extinction, normalement rétroactives, d'un droit'. ibid 649.

States towards Croatia initially amounted to a promise of recognition, and thus a political commitment, British recognition of Estonia at the end of the First World War was a legal act whose ultimate validity was predicated on the outcome of the peace conference.[29] In this sense, conditional recognition may be a form of provisional or *de facto* recognition.

Kelsen testifies to a strain of thought inferring from conditional recognition an agreement between the granting and receiving States: the former will extend recognition insofar as the latter acts in a certain way. Recalling the 1878 Congress of Berlin, when recognition was promised to Serbia, Romania, and Montenegro if they committed to respect religious freedom, he refutes the existence of a 'recognition agreement' by raising that the Balkan States were excluded from acceding to the final act, which only foresaw an obligation for Great Powers to recognise them if the criteria were met.[30] However, Kelsen also proposes a 'two agreements approach' wherein recognition is given at the same time as an additional agreement specifying its condition is accepted between the State extending recognition and the one receiving it: this precludes the conclusion that the recognised State should no longer be regarded as a State if it were to fail to dispense with the 'conditions' of its recognition.[31] This resembles the doctrine of separability discussed earlier in this work and could be an adequate explanation of certain situations.

5. Conclusion

The vocabulary of international law and international relations knows several different forms of recognition beyond full and unqualified diplomatic recognition. In each case, the issuing State resorts to a given form of recognition in the intention of modifying or qualifying the effects of its act.

De facto and *de jure* recognition are typically considered a dichotomy. As both are ascribed several different meanings, it is important not to take instances of either at face value and to consider them in a broader context in which the issuing State is acting. The most widespread view is that *de facto* recognition is provisional, whereas *de jure* recognition is permanent (corresponding to 'full' recognition). *De facto* recognition will become *de jure* recognition only once the recognising State becomes fully convinced of the recipient's stable nature and durability as a State, but may be withdrawn should this not come to pass. The distinction may also be perceived in political terms, *de facto* recognition meaning that a State or government is legally accepted out of necessity but not regarded as legitimate by

29 See eg *The Gagara* (1919) Probate 95, 103–04.

30 See Hans Kelsen, 'Théorie générale du droit international public: Problèmes choisis' (1932) 42 RCADI 117, 283–84.

31 ibid 284.

the author, whereas *de jure* recognition involves a statement on the legitimacy of its object regardless of whether it exists in fact (most commonly, this relates to a constitutional government that has been toppled through violent, revolutionary means). *De facto* and *de jure* recognition should not be confused with *de facto* and *de jure* States or governments: whereas the latter terms describe a quality of the object of recognition itself, the former are modalities under which the act of recognition is extended.

Some scholars also distinguish between external and internal recognition: external recognition is done by a State's government, while internal recognition is made by its judiciary. Only external recognition can be considered recognition in the true sense of the word. However, domestic judicial findings on a foreign State or government could have important implications under domestic law and influence the government's behaviour towards an entity it did not previously recognise.

Recognition is sometimes made conditional upon the recipient conforming to certain demands made by the issuing State. Doctrine has not been favourable to the theory of conditional recognition which nevertheless persists in practice. If recognition has indeed occurred, then it may be best to regard recognition as a separate act from its condition. It is also possible to regard conditional recognition as provisional and thus revocable in case the condition is not met, but this approach could lead to absurd conclusions.

4
Non-Recognition

1. Non-Recognition as a Stance

The act of recognition cannot be properly understood without reflecting on its antinomy, which is, of course, non-recognition. There are different stances that States can take towards a new legal situation: they may recognise it, ignore it, or explicitly refuse to recognise it. States adopting the last position may in fact be very vocal in their views, as were many States opposing the establishment of an 'independent' Manchukuo by Japan in northern China in 1932.[1] The initiative to condemn Japan's actions was led by Henry Stimson, the US Secretary of State who would also lend his name to the eponymous doctrine of non-recognition.

The Stimson Doctrine in relation to Manchuria was laid out thus: as Japan had renounced international warfare by ratifying the Kellogg–Briand Pact of 1928, its invasion of China violated international law. Consequently, the creation of an independent Manchukuo,[2] originating in unlawful use of force, could not be seen as producing legal results without violating the principle of *ex injuria jus non oritur*.[3] Identical notes were transmitted by Stimson's ministry to the Chinese and Japanese governments, stating that the United States government could not 'admit the legality of any situation *de facto* ... which may impair the treaty rights of the United States or its citizens in China, including those which relate to the sovereignty, the independence, or the territorial and administrative integrity of the Republic of China ... and that it does not intend to recognize any situation, treaty, or agreement which may be brought about by means contrary to the covenants and obligations of the Pact of Paris of August 27, 1928 ....'[4] The League of Nations followed suit and a few months later adopted a resolution declaring that 'it is incumbent

[1] See David Turns, 'The Stimson Doctrine of Non-Recognition: Its Historical Genesis and Influence on Contemporary International Law' (2003) 2(1) Chinese Journal of International Law 105–43.

[2] The official Japanese position on Manchukuo was unclear and contradictory, and the Japanese representative's statement to the Council of the League of Nations rather suggests that Japan regarded Manchuria a province of China subject to the exclusive and permanent occupation of Japan; see ibid 122–23.

[3] ibid 114ff; as this principle does not have clear independent effects in international law, the violation of Japan's treaty commitments under the Pact of Paris are probably the real reason for non-recognition of its acquisitions in China. For more on this principle in international law, see Robert Kolb, 'La maxime "*Nemo ex propria turpitudine commodum capere potest*" (nul ne peut profiter de son propre tort) en droit international public' (2000) 1/2000 Revue belge de droit international 84–136, in particular 116ff on the tension between the principles *ex injuria jus non oritur* and *ex facto oritur jus*.

[4] Turns, 'The Stimson Doctrine of Non-Recognition' (n 1) 105.

Recognition of States in International Law. Pavle Kilibarda, Oxford University Press. © Pavle Kilibarda 2024.
DOI: 10.1093/oso/9780198905653.003.0004

upon the Members of the League of Nations not to recognize any situation, treaty or agreement, which may be brought about by means contrary to the Covenant of the League of Nations or the Pact of Paris'.[5] Dugard finds the impact of the Stimson Doctrine also in the approach of American States to two conflicts that immediately followed the Manchukuo crisis, namely, the 1932 Chaco War between Bolivia and Paraguay, and the 1933 Leticia Conflict between Peru and Colombia.[6]

There have been other 'doctrines' of non-recognition adopted by one or more States at different points during the twentieth century. In Latin America, a 'Tobar Doctrine' (after a foreign minister of Ecuador) emerged at the beginning of the century, requiring States not to recognise revolutionary and unconstitutional *de facto* governments in the region.[7] This was seen as a necessary reaction to pervasive instability and forceful regime change in Latin America at the time. In 1955, an unwritten 'Hallstein Doctrine' was developed in West Germany as a reaction to the recognition of East Germany by third States. West Germany insisted that it was the sole representative of Germany and the German people and regarded recognition of an independent East Germany as an unfriendly act.[8] West Germany would go so far as to break off diplomatic relations with third States who recognised the independence of East Germany, although such extreme measures were not consistently applied.

Not all these doctrines of non-recognition have stood the test of time. Although the Stimson Doctrine was eventually integrated into general international law and in some form confirmed by the International Court of Justice (ICJ) in the *Namibia* case,[9] the Tobar Doctrine was soon abandoned, and West Germany eventually discarded the Hallstein Doctrine in favour of its new *Ostpolitik* and rapprochement with East Germany. Nevertheless, all these policies of non-recognition possessed a common element in that they were conceived as a reaction to situations regarded as either unlawful or unfriendly.

Non-recognition is thus a mirror image of recognition: if the latter requires cognisance and acceptance, then the former signifies their absence. Non-recognising States assume a stance towards a new legal situation because they either regard it as unlawful or because they do not wish it to become opposable to them even if it were lawful. However, non-recognition cannot be regarded as a legal act, as it does not seek to create new normative circumstances, but rather to prevent changes to the existing legal order.

[5] ibid 123.

[6] John Dugard, *Recognition and the United Nations* (Grotius Publications Limited 1987) 35.

[7] See Charles L Stansifer, 'Application of the Tobar Doctrine to Central America' (1967) 23(2) The Americas 251–72.

[8] See Sandrine Tesson, 'La doctrine Hallstein, entre rigueur et pragmatisme (1955–1969)' (2002) 110 Relations Internationales 219–34, 219ff.

[9] See *Legal Consequences for States of the Continued Presence of South Africa in Namibia (South West Africa) Notwithstanding Security Council Resolution 276 (1970)*, ICJ Reports 16, Advisory Opinion of 21 June 1971 (hereafter *Namibia* case) para 119.

Frowein writes that '[n]on-recognition may be a sanction … for unlawfulness, it may be an indication that some element necessary for arriving at a legal result is lacking, or it may show that a State claims a certain discretion for political reasons not to accept another State or government fully and/or on an equal footing'.[10] Thus, States may assume a different 'posture' depending on the purpose of their non-recognition.

(1) Non-recognition is typically accompanied by some form of protest: not only does the State refuse to accept the new situation but it considers it to be unlawful. This was, of course, the case with Manchukuo in the 1930s, but States have reacted the same way to the proclamation of Rhodesia, Northern Cyprus, Russian-annexed Crimea, and the separatist republics in Eastern Ukraine. Some States regard secession as inherently unlawful and the recognition of secessionist entities always to amount to a violation of the Parent State's territorial integrity. Many States that refused to recognise Kosovo did so while reiterating their commitment to the territorial integrity of Serbia, its Parent State, which in turn protested any recognition of Kosovo as a violation of international law.[11] The Tobar Doctrine also belongs to this category of reactions, although it considers domestic, rather than international, illegality. Thus, the non-recognising State's goal is not only to prevent the situation from becoming opposable to itself, but also to preclude other States from accepting it. When such a position is taken by an overwhelming number of States—as was the case with Rhodesia, Northern Cyprus, and the Donbas region—then, certainly, this will be proof that the situation genuinely does not conform to international law.
(2) Sometimes, States may refuse to recognise a situation without insisting that it is unlawful. This means that the non-recognising State does not itself accept the creation of a new State, but it also does not believe that others would be prevented from granting recognition themselves; non-recognition is therefore not based on considerations of the common interest but of the State's own interest. Such cases are relatively rare: a good example is the present Greek stance towards Kosovo. Thus, the Greek foreign ministry reiterates that Greece is 'one of the five EU member-states that do not recognize Kosovo's unilateral declaration of independence' but also that Greece is following 'a constructive political approach' towards Kosovo.[12] Similar

[10] Jochen A Frowein, 'Non-Recognition' in Anne Peters and Rüdiger Wolfrum (eds), *Max Planck Encyclopedias of International Law* (OUP 2011) para 2 <https://opil.ouplaw.com/display/10.1093/law:epil/9780199231690/law-9780199231690-e1073> last accessed 30 May 2024.

[11] See in particular States' submissions to the ICJ in relation to the *Kosovo* advisory opinion available at the Court's website at <https://www.icj-cij.org/en/case/141> last accessed 3 June 2024.

[12] As stated on the Kosovo page of the website of the Greek foreign ministry, available at <https://www.mfa.gr/en/blog/greece-bilateral-relations/pristina/> last accessed 3 June 2024.

is the stance of the United States towards Somaliland: 'The United States currently engages the Somaliland administration ... Our policy on recognition is to allow the African Union to first deliberate on the question. We do not want to get ahead of the continental organization on an issue of such importance'.[13] The United States is thereby saying that the independence of Somaliland does not violate international law, wherefore recognition may be possible, but that it does not wish to undertake such a step independently of the African Union.[14]

(3) States may also ignore a newly declared State and make no statements about it. Presented with a request for recognition, their officials may avoid the issue as 'sensitive' and perhaps maintain that the matter is still 'under consideration'. Several States reacted this way to Kosovo's declaration of independence. The Zambian government has been 'considering' recognition of Kosovo since the declaration of independence in 2008, although no official decision to either extend or refuse recognition seems to have been taken so far.[15] Although States may not have a clear position on the recognition or non-recognition of a new State, they must be presumed not to recognise it unless their actions demonstrate otherwise.

2. Non-Recognition as a Legal Duty

As opposed to the duty of recognition, which may only exists *de lege ferenda*, the obligation to refrain from recognising a new State may arise under certain conditions in positive international law. This is only the case in situations when the creation of a new State involves a violation of certain norms of *jus cogens*, such as the prohibition of aggression and the principle and right of self-determination. In other situations where States refrain from recognition, they may not do so out of a sense of legal obligation but from a desire for their legal position not to change. This also means that the interests protected by, or leading to, non-recognition are not the same in all cases. Hence, States that refuse to recognise a new State out of a sense of legal duty do so to safeguard the common interest; conversely, failing to

[13] US Bureau for African Affairs, 'United States Policy on Somaliland' (5 December 2007) <https://2001-2009.state.gov/p/af/rls/fs/2007/96359.htm> last accessed 3 June 2024.

[14] More recently, US President Donald Trump reacted favourably to the strengthening of ties between Somaliland and Taiwan, with the latter apparently recognising the independence of Somaliland even in the absence of formal diplomatic relations. See Ben Blanchard, 'Outflanked by China in Africa, Taiwan eyes unrecognised Somaliland' (*Reuters*, 1 July 2020) <https://www.reuters.com/article/us-taiwan-somaliland-idUSKBN2424UI> last accessed 3 June 2024 and Abdur Rahman Alfa Shaban, 'US "backs" Taiwan—Somaliland cooperation' (*Africa News*, 7 October 2020) <https://www.africanews.com/2020/07/10/us-backs-taiwan-somaliland-cooperation//> last accessed 3 June 2024.

[15] One of several reports by the Kosovar side is available at <https://web.archive.org/web/20131103223543/http://www.1deputyprimeminister-ks.net/?page=2,6,1173> last accessed 3 June 2024.

recognise a State whose creation is otherwise not prohibited by international law rather protects the non-recognising State's particular interests.

The link between the duty of non-recognition and the common or public interest of all States is most evident in relation to *jus cogens* provisions that are owed to the 'international community as a whole'. Indeed, it does not appear that the fact of statehood is ever separable from any violations of *jus cogens* involved in its creation. Both in practice and in doctrine, the approach so far has been to negate in full the statehood of the entity thus created, although non-recognising States may still maintain some level of interaction with the *de facto* regime for practical reasons. This approach is consonant with the one taken by the International Law Commission (ILC) in its 2019 report to the United Nations General Assembly regarding the role of *jus cogens* in treaty law, when the separability of treaty provisions violating peremptory norms was rejected.[16]

Thus, violations of *jus cogens* cannot produce legal consequences, other than the ones foresees by secondary norms governing non-recognition. The same is true of new States created, for example, through aggression; these must be regarded as a legal nullity, even though it may be impossible to ignore them in practice.

Early practice and policies such as the Stimson Doctrine were eventually carried over to the United Nations, and the Organisation's members have so far committed to collective non-recognition of States created through unlawful use of force (most recently, in relation to the breakaway republics in Eastern Ukraine)[17] or in violation of the principle and right of self-determination.[18] Calls for the non-recognition of certain *de facto* States have been made by both the Security Council and the General Assembly.[19]

The legal regime governing non-recognition of unlawful territorial acquisitions (which, in my view, fully applies to new States created in this manner) was elaborated by the ICJ in the *Namibia* advisory opinion. The Court determined that the continued presence of South Africa in Namibia was unlawful and thus required all United Nations members not to recognise it. This entails an obligation 'to refrain from lending any support or any form of assistance to South Africa with reference to its occupation of Namibia', 'to abstain from entering into treaty relations with

[16] 'A treaty which, at the time of its conclusion, conflicts with a peremptory norm of general international law (*jus cogens*) is void in whole, and no separation of the provisions of the treaty is permitted.' *Report of the International Law Commission* (20 August 2019) A/74/10, 144.

[17] See eg UNGA Resolution ES-11/1 of 2 March 2022.

[18] See more in Frowein, 'Non-Recognition' (n 10); a list of situations where the United Nations invoked a duty of recognition is given in Kolb, 'La maxime "*Nemo ex propria turpitudine commodum capere potest*"' (n 3) 120ff; cf John Dugard, 'The Secession of States and Their Recognition in the Wake of Kosovo' (2013) 357 RCADI 9, 69ff. For an overview of the situation in Transkei following independence from South Africa, see John Dugard, 'South Africa's "Independent" Homelands: An Exercise in Denationalization' (1980) 10 Denver Journal of International Law and Policy 11, 15ff.

[19] For the practice of the Security Council, see eg Resolutions 216 (1965), 402 (1976), 541 (1983); for the General Assembly, see eg Resolutions 341 1 D (XXX) (1975) and more broadly 68/262 (2014) on Crimea and ES-10/L.22 (2017) on the Holy City of Jerusalem.

South Africa in all cases in which the Government of South Africa purports to act on behalf of or concerning Namibia', and to 'to abstain from sending diplomatic or special missions to South Africa including in their jurisdiction the Territory of Namibia, to abstain from sending consular agents to Namibia, and to withdraw any such agents already there'.[20] The sole exception to these duties, described as 'implicit' in non-recognition, were actions of a humanitarian nature intended to relieve the population of Namibia.[21] These principles were reiterated in the 2004 *Wall* advisory opinion in relation to Israel's construction of a fence in the Occupied Palestinian Territory.[22]

So far, non-recognition of statehood and territorial acquisitions has only extended to those stemming from aggression or violating self-determination. It is unclear whether other *jus cogens* norms could come into play in the future. According to the approach taken by the ILC, States shall not recognise any situation created by a breach of *jus cogens*.[23] However, the scope of the relevant norms extends much further than territorial claims. This raises the question of whether any *jus cogens* norm may, from a practical perspective, annul the creation of a State; for example, it is difficult to imagine how the *jus cogens* prohibition of torture could come into play. Some other peremptory norms, such as the prohibition of genocide, come across as more relevant, but there is currently no substantial practice in this regard. Nevertheless, I do not believe that the regime of non-recognition should be *a priori* limited to aggression and self-determination.

Jus cogens violations can only negate statehood at its inception and if there is a causal connection between the violation and statehood—the statehood of an existing State does not flow from any subsequent unlawful conduct and therefore cannot be invalidated by it.[24] It is also important to highlight that the duty of non-recognition discussed above only seems pertinent regarding territorial acquisitions made by States. It is not at all evident in international practice, let alone

[20] *Namibia* case (n 9) paras 119 and 122–123.

[21] ibid paras 125ff.

[22] *Legal Consequences of the Construction of a Wall in the Occupied Palestinian Territory*, ICJ Reports 136, Advisory Opinion of 9 July 2004, para 159.

[23] *Responsibility of States for Internationally Wrongful Acts* (28 January 2002) A/RES/56/83 [Annex] art 41.

[24] The case of Kosovo is interesting in this regard: assuming that NATO's intervention against Yugoslavia in 1999—which ultimately led Yugoslav forces to withdraw from the province and thus paved the way for Kosovo's 2008 declaration of independence—had been illegal, this would have implications for Kosovar statehood as well. For States which do not recognise Kosovo, no problem arises, but those that do must accept one of the following premises: that the 1999 intervention was lawful (i) by accepting the 'humanitarian intervention' exception to the prohibition on the use of force in some cases or (ii) by interpreting Security Council Resolution 1244 as retroactively legalising NATO's use of force; or otherwise (iii) maintain that the proclamation of an independent State was unrelated to the 1999 intervention (namely, that the causal link between a serious breach of international law and the creation of statehood was somehow interrupted). The fact that States are currently almost equally divided on the matter of Kosovo's independence means that they have different views on all of these points, and it is impossible to take a position on this issue with any certainty. However, in my view, Resolution 1244 prevents a unilateral declaration of independence in relation to the territory of Kosovo.

the jurisprudence of the ICJ, that non-recognition should extend to governments. Governments that engage in aggression, genocide, or other violations of *jus cogens* do not thereby cease to be their State's government. Unlike States, governments are not subjects of international law, and the establishment of a new government does not itself lead to a change in the international legal order requiring other States to modify their behaviour. Had this been the case, States would have been obliged to see as null and void all actions taken by South Africa's apartheid governments, which was certainly not the case. Of course, States may consider such governments illegitimate, as they often do with revolutionary governments, and refuse to recognise them *de jure*, but, as Frowein correctly remarks, the impact of such non-recognition is more akin to the 'refusal to establish diplomatic relations'[25] (the government's capacity to legally represent the State will otherwise be unaffected). Any further interventionist actions that bring into question an effective government's capacity to represent its State will most likely amount to unlawful interference in that State's internal affairs, regardless of the high-minded motives that may underscore them.

One aspect of *jus cogens* in this context must be scrutinised with great care. Because a violation of a peremptory norm of international law serves to nullify all acts stemming from it, it could have a serious impact on peace agreements. This matter has come to the forefront of legal and political discussions following Russia's full-scale invasion of Ukraine in 2022. As they stem from aggression, Russian annexations of Ukrainian territory are certainly illegal and may not be recognised; nevertheless, the argument may sometimes be heard that Ukraine should be prepared to make territorial concessions to secure peace.[26] The question is whether, at the end of a war of aggression, territorial concessions made by the victim could be accepted as actually leading to a change in territorial title.

Michael Schmitt recently tackled this issue, and, in an excellent analysis, concluded that no such changes could materialise under the circumstances, based on rules governing coercion in treaty law and the violations of *jus cogens* more generally.[27] I fully agree with his reasoning, which is the only possible interpretation of the secondary rules on *jus cogens* violations and non-recognition. However, I cannot help but wonder to what extent such a rigid approach would be practical or even desirable. Although land-for-peace deals must be discouraged to disincentivise aggression, they may sometimes be understandable on humanitarian grounds; and

[25] Frowein, 'Non-Recognition' (n 10) para 4.

[26] See eg Brad Dress, 'NATO official says remarks about Ukraine giving up territory to gain membership were "mistake"' (*The Hill*, 16 August 2023) <https://thehill.com/policy/international/4154918-nato-official-says-remarks-about-ukraine-giving-up-territory-to-gain-membership-were-mistake/#:~:text=NATO%20chief%20of%20staff%20Stian,the%20statement%20a%20%E2%80%9Cmistake.%E2%80%9D> last accessed 3 June 2024.

[27] Michael N Schmitt, 'Ukraine Symposium—Territorial Acquisition and Armed Conflict' (Articles of War, 29 August 2023) <https://lieber.westpoint.edu/territorial-acquisition-armed-conflict/> last accessed 13 June 2024.

if such an arrangement were accepted by most States or approved by the Security Council, the conclusion may well be different.

Otherwise, the *Namibia* regime only applies to certain *jus cogens* violations; the effect of such violations is *erga omnes*. We must consider in this respect the role of Security Council resolutions. As discussed earlier in relation to the *Kosovo* advisory opinion, the views of the Security Council describing a violation of *jus cogens* (notably aggression) will typically be regarded as an authoritative determination.[28] However, it is not always clear whether the Council—whose mandate, under the UN Charter, does not really include pinpointing violations of international law but rather the maintenance of international peace and security—is establishing the existence of a violation or simply enacting a decision in pursuit of its broader mandate. Although resolutions on Namibia, Rhodesia, Transkei, and Northern Cyprus have all condemned specific violations of *jus cogens* and called upon States to refrain from recognising them, this is not the case with resolutions on Bosnia and Herzegovina, Georgia, or Azerbaijan, which simply recall the obligation to respect these States' territorial integrity.[29] Two questions stand out in this regard: first, what is the value of Security Council resolutions that do not obviously pertain to aggression or self-determination; and, second, what is to be made of actions that contradict them?

In relation to the first question, it should be borne in mind that it is a violation of *jus cogens*, and not a Security Council resolution, that triggers the *Namibia* regime of non-recognition. Such violations are normally identified by the Security Council when its members are not exclusively guided by their own selfish interests; the role of these resolutions is then to prove the existence of a violation. However, it is not quite apparent that the refusal by third States to recognise a Bosnian Serb or Bosnian Croat territorial entity during the war in Bosnia was a reaction to foreign aggression (no formal determination of aggression in Bosnia has ever been made by an international tribunal or the Security Council). This suggests that non-recognition may have stemmed from the relevant Security Council resolutions themselves and not from considerations of *jus cogens*. If this is the case, then an obligation to refrain from recognition could also draw strength from the UN Charter, and not simply *jus cogens*.

At first glance, this distinction does not seem to carry great practical value. However, Article 25 of the Charter is not a peremptory norm, which raises the question of the implications of non-compliant practice. Let us imagine that, upon its proclamation in 1992, one or more States recognised Republika Srpska in spite of the Council's position. Would this have been regarded in the same manner as the

[28] See more on this matter in Marko Divac Öberg, 'The Legal Effects of Resolutions of the UN Security Council and General Assembly in the Jurisprudence of the ICJ' (2006) 16(5) The European Journal of International Law 879–906

[29] See eg UNSC Resolutions 787 (1992), 853 (1993), and 1808 (2008).

recognition of a situation created in violation of *jus cogens*, and therefore null and void, or would it have been a violation of the Charter that nevertheless produced legal consequences on a bilateral level? The former possibility would require, as Divac Öberg remarks correctly, that Security Council resolutions be vested with overriding binding force: 'Recognizing such overriding binding force would give a secondary source of UN law (decisions) a greater normative value than many primary sources of international law (treaties)—thereby giving the SC a potentially very disruptive power—and would ultimately place great faith in the SC truly acting on behalf of all Member States.'[30] This author recalls that the ICJ made a preliminary finding supporting this notion when ordering provisional measures in *Lockerbie*: the Court invoked Article 103 of the Charter to find that the obligations of Libya and the United Kingdom under Security Council resolutions prevailed over their obligations under the Montreal Convention.[31] Assuming that the regime of Article 103 (which only refers to treaties) could be expanded to the unilateral act of recognition, the Council's decisions may be regarded as possessing a force comparable to *jus cogens*.[32]

While normative Security Council resolutions have considerable legal strength, it is less likely that they may be presumed to trigger the same non-recognition regime discussed by the ICJ in *Namibia*—unless, of course, the Council were to expressly foresee this. For example, it is unclear whether engagement short of recognition with a breakaway entity in the territory of a State whose territorial integrity has been reaffirmed by the Security Council would violate those resolutions in the same way that such engagement might violate customary law in case of *jus cogens* violations. I speak here of engagement with entities whose material statehood may not be in doubt: a case in point could be Somaliland in light of resolutions reaffirming the territorial integrity of Somalia.[33] As noted earlier, Somaliland does have some interaction with other States in spite of its lack of recognition.[34] Although the ICJ has sometimes taken a fairly restrictive approach to interpreting Security Council resolutions—again, the *Kosovo* opinion comes to mind[35]—such interaction with the authorities of Somaliland by UN members does not come across as consonant with either the relevant Security Council resolutions or the

[30] Divac Öberg, 'The Legal Effects of Resolutions of the UN Security Council and General Assembly' (n 28) 884.

[31] *Case Concerning Questions of Interpretation and Application of the 1971 Montreal Convention Arising from the Aerial Incident at Lockerbie (Libyan Arab Jamahiriya v United Kingdom)*, ICJ Reports 3, Order of 14 April 1992, para 39.

[32] Of course, unlike *jus cogens*, this effect would only extend to members of the United Nations.

[33] See eg UNSC Resolutions 897 (1994) and 2592 (2021).

[34] See more in Dugard, 'Secession' (n 18) 53 and 138ff and Scott Pegg, 'Somaliland' in Gëzim Visoka, John Doyle, and Edward Newman (eds), *Routledge Handbook of State Recognition* (Routledge 2020) 417–29.

[35] *Accordance with International Law of the Unilateral Declaration of Independence in Respect of Kosovo*, ICJ Reports 403, Advisory Opinion of 22 July 2010, paras 113ff.

territorial integrity of Somalia that they seek to protect. Thus, I believe that the *Namibia* doctrine should also extend to cases such as this one.

Finally, an obligation of non-recognition does not apply to a case of secession that neither violates *jus cogens*, nor is it prevented by a Security Council resolution. Clearly, the premature recognition of an entity seeking statehood would violate the Parent State's right of territorial integrity. However, the concept of non-recognition more properly applies to States existing *de facto*, which excludes the object of premature recognition. If the breakaway State fulfils the criteria set by international law, its recognition is authorised, but not required. The same is true, *mutatis mutandis*, of non-recognition.

3. Conclusion

International law imposes an obligation of non-recognition regarding modifications of territorial status stemming from violations of certain rules of *jus cogens*, particularly the prohibition of aggression and the principle and right of self-determination. States will be required not to recognise entities thus created either explicitly or implicitly, not to engage in treaty relations with them, nor to deploy diplomatic or consular agents. A similar obligation is likely to exist in relation to entities whose creation does not violate *jus cogens* but contradicts a Security Council resolution. Conversely, there is no obligation of non-recognition regarding States that meet the criteria of effectivity and legality and whose recognition is therefore not prohibited by international law. These criteria are further discussed in Chapter 10.

5
States in International Law

1. Statehood, Law, and Recognition

The vast majority of human beings live and die within the territory of a State. We model our livelihoods in accordance with rules dictated by the State, conduct our affairs in its economic confines, and sometimes seek to perform public office in its political system. In the broadest sense, a State is an institution, 'a system whereby individuals establish relations among themselves in order to secure certain objects, the most fundamental being a system of order within which they can carry on their activities'.[1] The sheer variety of States and political systems makes any attempts at defining them a difficult endeavour: a scientific explanation of statehood will largely depend on one's scientific background. This means that a sociological or political science view may be different from a legal understanding of the same phenomenon.

It is questionable, perhaps even doubtful, whether law is well equipped to define a State. Statehood involves so many structural, social, normative, and symbolic dynamics that a legal explanation must seem a fruitless endeavour, if it is even possible. However, the legal act of recognition is, by definition, a reaction to the birth of a new State as an observable phenomenon. Statehood is a legal fact if it authorises or triggers the application of legal rules: the law must therefore have some conception of it.

There are two ways in which a legal concept of statehood may be elaborated. One is to tie the legal definition to external, non-legal elements. This approach became dominant during the nineteenth and early twentieth centuries, as exemplified by Jellinek, and is still the preferred textbook approach.[2] This understanding highlights the State's material existence—its existence as an effectivity—from which doctrine draws legal implications.

The other position emphasises the State's legal personality: legal conclusions are drawn from legal premises. A State is not a bundle of material elements but a collection of legal rights and duties that constitute a common denominator of all other members of the same group of subjects. Although such conceptualisations

[1] Andrew Clapham, *Brierly's Law of Nations* (OUP 2012) 139.

[2] ibid 139ff; James Crawford, *Brownlie's Principles of Public International Law* (OUP 2019) 117ff; Vojin Dimitrijević and others, *Osnovi međunarodnog javnog prava* (Belgrade Centre for Human Rights 2007) 71ff; Malcolm N Shaw, *International Law* (CUP 2017) 156ff; Emmanuel Decaux and Olivier de Frouville, *Droit international public* (Dalloz 2018) 185ff; and others.

Recognition of States in International Law. Pavle Kilibarda, Oxford University Press. © Pavle Kilibarda 2024.
DOI: 10.1093/oso/9780198905653.003.0005

are emblematic of legal positivism, they build upon older treatises on sovereignty. Doctrine usually distinguishes statehood from sovereignty, but the differences are not quite clear. As the legal description of statehood focuses on a State's intrinsic normative components, all of which could be lassoed under the concept of sovereignty, then the terms become synonymous.

When speaking of the State as an object of recognition, it is not always easy to conceptually divorce these two approaches. Do States recognise others because of their effective existence or do they take cognisance of them as persons of law? Do a State's rights and duties form the object of recognition or part of its effects? How to distinguish between material statehood and the preconditions of recognition, and between legal statehood and the effects of recognition?

There is no clear answer to any of these questions. The material and legal paradigm may each dominate in a given context: a State may recognise another because of its effective existence but also because it wishes to treat it as a legal subject regardless of effectivity. In my view, both the material and legal aspects of statehood come within the ambit of 'object of recognition'; material statehood overlaps (but is not identical) with the preconditions of recognition,[3] whereas the possible effect of recognition is the opposability of the rights and duties forming legal statehood.

I now turn to material conceptions of statehood before discussing the State as a person of law.

2. States in Legal Doctrine

There is no settled definition of 'statehood' in international law.[4] Some lawyers even advance that any attempt to provide a comprehensive definition is doomed to failure. During the preparatory work on the International Law Commission's (ILC) Draft Declaration on the Rights and Duties of States, Brierly pointed out that the word 'State' was 'commonly used in documents and speech, and its meaning had been understood without definition', wherefore there was no reason to conceive a definition while preparing the document.[5] To date, the ILC has not dealt with either statehood or recognition, and it is unlikely that this body will approach the matter in the foreseeable future.[6]

[3] The relationship between the Montevideo criteria and the conditions of recognition has also been noticed by John Dugard; see John Dugard, 'The Secession of States and Their Recognition in the Wake of Kosovo' (2013) 357 RCADI 9, 30.

[4] '[T]here is no generally accepted definition of statehood in international law, despite longstanding efforts by international lawyers (end episodic efforts by States) to develop one'; Hennie Strydom (ed), *International Law* (OUP 2016) 37.

[5] *Yearbook of the International Law Commission 1949: Summary Records and Documents of the First Session including the report of the Commission to the General Assembly* (United Nations 1956) 64–65.

[6] According to John Dugard, 'any suggestion that the question of statehood or recognition be examined by the ILC was dismissed out of hand by colleagues' during his time on the Commission; John Dugard, 'What Is a State in International Law? How Is This to Be Determined?' in Niels M Blokker,

However, some elements commonly arise in jurisprudence and doctrine. It is usually said that States are both the original and 'dominant' subjects of international law,[7] that they are law-makers and a 'total' subject of law, while all others are merely particular. Today, this notion has been challenged by the rise of international organisations and the pervading influence of multinational companies, some of which are wealthier and more influential than many States. Yet international law remains fundamentally state-centric, and old dogmas are difficult to weed out. To quote Decaux and de Frouville, 'Pendant des siècles le droit international a été un droit interétatique, fait par les États pour les États, dans une société relationnelle, cernée de frontières.'[8]

Positivist scholars tend to give broad outlines of what constitutes a State as a material fact from which legal consequences flow according to the will of the States that may accept to engage with it.[9] The State's effectivity or *de facto* existence is thus incidental and not intrinsic to its legal existence. During the nineteenth century, at the height of the 'States only' paradigm, the statehood of an entity was up to other States to determine in whichever way they found appropriate.[10] Statehood is thus a legal term, to be examined, conceptualised, and re-conceptualised according to legal tools and vocabulary.

The alternative view highlights the fact that statehood 'pre-dates' law and cannot exclusively be explained by State practice.[11] Law requires the existence of a State, making statehood a non-legal notion, at least insofar as law does not create a State. This view shares a common genealogy with rationalist views of the seventeenth and eighteenth centuries and exists today in very refined forms.[12] Effectivity may not be the sole criterion considered, but it is certainly the most important one.

Daniëlla Dam-de Jong, and Vid Prislan (eds), *Furthering the Frontiers of International Law: Sovereignty, Human Rights, Sustainable Development: Liber Amicorum Nico Schrijver* (Brill/Nijhoff 2021) 97.

[7] 'States are the central subjects of international law and, through the related notion of sovereignty, continue to play a dominant role in structuring the international legal order ... In fact, states are central not just to international law, but to the modern legal, political and social imagination generally.' Strydom, *International Law* (n 4) 36.

[8] Decaux and de Frouville, *Droit international public* (n 2) 181.

[9] This manner of reasoning is particularly visible in the doctrines of Anzilotti, Cavaglieri, and Kelsen; see eg Dionisio Anzilotti, *Cours de droit international: Premier volume: Introduction: Théories générales* (Librairie du Recueil Sirey 1929) 159ff; Arrigo Cavaglieri, 'Regles générales du droit de la paix' (1929) 26 RCADI 311, 322ff; and Hans Kelsen, 'Théorie du droit international public' (1953) 84 RCADI 1, 129–32; see more in Hans J Morgenthau, 'Positivism, Functionalism, and International Law' (1940) 34(2) American Journal of International Law 260; and Roberto Ago, 'Positive Law and International Law' (1957) 51(4) American Journal of International Law 691.

[10] 'According to predominant nineteenth-century doctrine there were no rules determining what were "States" for the purposes of international law; the matter was within the discretion of existing recognized States.' James Crawford, *The Creation of States in International Law* (OUP 2007) 5.

[11] This is the understanding of eg Johann Caspar Bluntschli, *Allgemeines Staatsrecht* (München 1857) 36 (in a later work, Bluntschli would emphasise legal personality); Gerald Fitzmaurice, 'The General Principles of International Law Considered from the Standpoint of the Rule of Law' (1957) 92 RCADI 1, 23ff; and, largely, Crawford, *The Creation of States* (n 10) 4ff.

[12] See in this regard Robert Kolb, *Theory of International Law* (Hart Publishing 2016).

In principle, it might be possible to demonstrate which entities States treat as peers and under what circumstances. This would allow us to induce their common characteristics and form a comprehensive theory. Unfortunately, practice is diverse and inconsistent and does not allow us to discern with any degree of certainty the necessary and sufficient conditions for a State to arise. This is one of the main reasons for which lawyers such as Cavaglieri[13] and Dimitrijević[14] conclude that international law simply does not regulate the creation of States.

2.1 The Conceptual Evolution of Statehood in Law

Most scholars are nevertheless of the view that the genesis of States *is* a matter governed at least in part by international law. They find support for this view in State and judicial practice. Scholarship often discusses conditions or elements of statehood to describe a State as an entity consisting of or possessing them. Crawford traces this understanding to Francisco de Vitoria, who wrote in the seventeenth century that '[a] perfect State or community ... is one which is complete in itself... [and] has its own laws and its own council and its own magistrates'.[15] Vattel makes the same observation: 'Any nation that governs itself', he writes, 'under what form soever, without dependence on any foreign power, is a sovereign state. Its rights are naturally the same as any other state ....'[16]

Manuals of international law published in the nineteenth and early twentieth centuries also focus on a notion of statehood in general, and not only for the purposes of international law. This means that law deals with the same phenomenon as sociology, history, and other social sciences. Examples of such reflections we find with Wheaton,[17] Bluntschli,[18] and Pradier-Fodéré.[19] The most influential definition by far was however provided by Jellinek, who describes the State as a 'body of a settled people, endowed with original authority' (*mit ursprünglicher Herrschermacht ausgerüstete Körperschaft eines seßhaften Volkes*).[20] Jellinek's

[13] Cavaglieri, 'Regles générales du droit de la paix' (n 9) 340.

[14] Dimitrijević and others, *Osnovi međunarodnog javnog prava* (n 2) 73.

[15] *De Indis ac de Iure Belli Relectiones* (ed Simon 1696); *De Iure Belli*, para 7, ss 425–426, quoted from Crawford (n 10) 7.

[16] Emer de Vattel, *The Law of Nations* (Liberty Fund Inc 2008) 83.

[17] Coleman Phillipson, *Wheaton's Elements of International Law* (Steven and Sons Ltd 1916) 32.

[18] Bluntschli (n 11) 36; he would later define a State, from an international law perspective, as quite simply a person of international law and the highest legal subject; see Johann Caspar Bluntschli, *Das moderne Völkerrecht der civilisirten Staten als Rechtsbuch dargestellt* (Druck und Verlag der C H Beck'schen Buchhandlung 1872) 66.

[19] Paul Pradier-Fodéré, *Traité de droit international public européen & americain, Volume I* (G Pedone-Lauriel 1885) 144–45.

[20] Georg Jellinek, *Allgemeine Staatslehre* (Verlag von O Häring 1914) 180; cf Alphonse Rivier, *Principes du droit des gens: Tome premier* (Arthur Rousseau 1896) 45 ('Envisagé en sa qualité de personne du droit des gens, l'État peut être défini: une communauté indépendante, organisée d'une manière permanente sur un territoire.').

'scientific' approach to statehood synthesised earlier thinking and resulted in a concept that was not specific to law—something that resounded with the academic fashion of the time.

After the First World War, it became more common for lawyers to deal with a concept of statehood specific to law. Thus, Kelsen advanced that statehood in international law must be understood in its own terms and inferred from State practice as part of customary international law.[21] This 'legal concept' of statehood includes the elements of a 'coercive, relatively centralized legal order' that is effective for a certain territory and the individuals living there and is independent from that of another community of the same type; '[a] community meeting these three conditions is a state', concludes Kelsen.[22]

Hersch Lauterpacht espouses a similar view. He submits that a State must first possess an independent government: 'there must exist a government actually independent of that of any other State, including the parent State'.[23] That government must exercise effective authority within its territory, guaranteeing 'a sufficient degree of internal stability as expressed through the functioning of a government enjoying the habitual obedience of the bulk of the population'.[24] Third, the State must have a reasonably well-defined territory.[25] This list of criteria is 'exhaustive' according to Lauterpacht, who rejects additional outdated elements (such as religion, legitimacy of origin, political system, or 'degree of civilisation') which had been present in earlier legal thought.[26] Lauterpacht identifies the criteria of statehood as identical to the preconditions of recognition.[27]

Lauterpacht and Kelsen espouse similar views of statehood despite having different notions of international law. Still today, the 'core elements' of statehood seem to be a matter of consensus among lawyers with very different sets of beliefs and coming from different schools of thought. For example, Ti-Chiang Chen (a critic of positivism) draws on Oppenheim (a positivist) to define a State as an entity consisting of its people, country, government (internal aspect), and sovereign government (external aspect of statehood).[28] Ian Brownlie and James Crawford define a State as 'a stable political community supporting a legal order to the exclusion of others in a given area'.[29] Decaux and de Frouville highlight the elements of territory, government, and population, but notice that these conditions are not specific to the definition of statehood as they may also be possessed by intra- or supra-state

[21] Hans Kelsen, 'Recognition in International Law: Theoretical Observations' (1941) 35(4) American Journal of International Law 605, 607.
[22] ibid 607–08.
[23] Hersch Lauterpacht, *Recognition in International Law* (CUP 2013) 26.
[24] ibid 28.
[25] ibid 30.
[26] ibid 31–32.
[27] ibid 26.
[28] Ti-Chiang Chen, *The International Law of Recognition* (Stevens & Sons Limited 1951) 54–62.
[29] Crawford (n 2) 119.

entities.[30] The Badinter Commission of the Conference on Yugoslavia famously recalled 'that the state is commonly defined as a community which consists of a territory and a population subject to an organized political authority' and 'that such a state is characterized by sovereignty';[31] it is added that all of these criteria need to be met with a certain degree of permanence.[32] In their submissions to a Pre-Trial Chamber of the International Criminal Court (ICC) on the matter of Palestinian statehood, several prominent lawyers recalled these elements as crucial to the notion of statehood under international law.[33] Therefore, defining States through their material elements—population, territory, government, and, typically, independence—seems to be the dominant trend in legal scholarship.

2.2 Material and Legal Statehood

There exists another strain of thought in law which does not put these material elements into the foreground. For example, Jean Charpentier defines a State through its personality, by means of which it becomes opposable to other States, forcing them to adapt their behaviour towards it: '[s]i l'on définit la *personnalité de l'État* comme l'aptitude d'une nation organisée à l'intérieur d'un territoire à être titulaire des compétences étatiques, celles-ci étant les compétences exercées par un organe gouvernemental dans l'intérêt de l'État, le critère de l'opposabilité des compétences étatiques n'est autre que le critère de la personnalité de l'État'.[34] This definition focuses on the possession of the competencies of a State. Although it is possible to distinguish between statehood and its legal personality, from a legal perspective, it is also legitimate to equate them. Verhoeven explains:

[30] 'Selon la conception classique de l'État, trois éléments constitutifs sont nécessaires pour qu'un État puisse exister: un territoire, une population et un gouvernement. En fait ces éléments constitutifs ne sont pas spécifiques à la définition de l'État puisqu'ils caractérisent aussi bien les collectivités infra-étatatiques, qui sont des "démembrements de l'État", ou les regroupements supra-nationaux, dans le cadre du fédéralisme … ou, de manière *sui generis*, avec la construction originale de l'Union européenne.' Decaux and de Frouville (n 2) 185.

[31] 'Conference on Yugoslavia Arbitration Commission: Opinions on Questions Arising from the Dissolution of Yugoslavia, 11 January and 4 July 1992' (1992) 31 International Legal Materials 1488 (hereafter Badinter Commission) 1495.

[32] 'A new state comes into existence when a community acquires not momentarily, but with a reasonable probability of permanence, the essential characteristics of a state, namely an organized government, a defined territory, and such a degree of independence from control by any other state as to be capable of conducting its own international relations.' Clapham, *Brierly's Law of Nations* (n 1) 149.

[33] See in particular the submissions under Rule 103 of the ICC Rules of Procedure and Evidence by Eyal Benvenisti of 16 March 2020, Robert Badinter and others of 16 March 2020, and Malcolm Shaw of 4 February 2021 in *Situation in the State of Palestine* ICC-01/18; cf Dugard, 'What Is a State in International Law?' (n 6) for an in-depth analysis and critical reflection of some of these views.

[34] Jean Charpentier, *La reconnaissance internationale et l'évolution du droit des gens* (Pedone 1956) 160.

> Entendu comme personne souveraine, l'État est fondamentalement une effectivité 'menée à terme', pour reprendre l'expression du président Charles De Visscher. Cette effectivité est avant tout constituée de relations 'comme État' qui se construisent au départ d'un donné matériel traditionnellement défini par référence à trois notions: une population, un territoire, une autorité organisée. Cette effectivité est l'*objet* de la reconnaissance d'État, alors que son apparition en forme l'*occasion*.[35]

For Verhoeven the State is an effectivity which flows from its material elements (population, territory, government), but which expresses itself in inter-state relations, namely in the exercise of the competencies of a State.[36] This seems to be the more refined view as it is appropriate to distinguish the State's outward legal personality from the material conditions which may give rise to it.

The definitional approaches examined above focus either on the criteria of statehood or its intrinsic qualities. These are intensional definitions which seek to describe the necessary (and often sufficient) conditions for an entity to be termed a State. As with other social sciences, the study of international law cannot define statehood in absolute terms. The differences between these two strains of thought are not intrinsic: they simply emphasise different elements of the same phenomenon.

In my view, the State as the object of recognition must therefore be understood to mean a legal subject possessing certain material elements and attributes which are not shared by other subjects of international law. From an external perspective, statehood is thus both a material and a legal phenomenon; for the recognising State, these two facets conform to the cognitive and normative functions of recognition—these are intertwined and cannot exist without each other. In order to conceptualise the State as an object of recognition, it is thus necessary to establish a common core of elements required for material statehood.

3. Material Statehood in Positive Law

Faced with the question of how to approach the possible statehood of former Yugoslav federal units which had just proclaimed independence, the Badinter Commission described a State as 'a community which consists of a territory and a population subject to an organized political authority',[37] and which is

[35] Joe Verhoeven, *La reconnaissance internationale dans la pratique contemporaine* (Pedone 1975) 8.

[36] This recalls the work of Jean Bodin, who wrote: '[La] République est un droit Gouvernement de plusieurs familles, et de ce qui leur est commun, avec puissance souveraine'. Jean Bodin, *Six livres de la république* (Librairie générale française 1993), Book I, Chapter VIII, 111–12. Bodin combines the material aspects of statehood (a 'multitude of families and their possessions') with its legal manifestation (sovereign power).

[37] Badinter Commission (n 31) 1495.

therefore vested with sovereignty. These elements had earlier been adopted for the Montevideo Convention[38] and thus introduced into positive law.

Although some lawyers, such as Hersch Lauterpacht, believe otherwise, the elements of statehood are not identical with the preconditions of recognition. As we will see, an entity corresponding to the concept of material statehood may nevertheless not be recognised for reasons of legality; conversely, recognition may sometimes be possible even if the recipient does not meet the material elements of statehood. The Badinter Commission is wrong to automatically infer statehood from effectivity, but effectivity is nevertheless a fitting start for an analysis of statehood.

3.1 The Elements of Material Statehood in Legal Sources

Even before any attempt was made to codify the criteria of statehood in a treaty, legal doctrine had tried to discern the necessary conditions for an entity to be described as a State. It was first necessary to identify elements common to existing States and, at a later stage, how they could be differentiated from other similar entities such as federal units and non-self-governing territories.

This is obvious already in Jellinek's classical definition of a State as a community established by a sedentary people (*sesshaftes Volk*),[39] excluding nomadic communities,[40] and explicitly laying the groundwork for what would eventually be accepted as the permanent population criterion. Indirectly, Jellinek's definition also implies the other two usual criteria, namely possessing a common government (for a community must possess some sort of common political institutions) and a more-or-less defined territory (inhabited by the sedentary people). Independence, too, is implicit in Jellinek's approach. These elements are also identified by Kelsen,[41] Lauterpacht,[42] and other lawyers.[43]

There also exists some jurisprudence to support these elements. Although the International Court of Justice (ICJ) stated in the *Western Sahara* advisory opinion that '[n]o rule of international law ... requires the structure of a State to follow any particular pattern, as is evident from the diversity of the forms of State found in the world today',[44] it practically excluded, in the same case, nomadic tribes from the

[38] Montevideo Convention on the Rights and Duties of States, 165 LNTS 19 (adopted 26 December 1933, entered into force 26 December 1934) art 1.

[39] Jellinek, *Allgemeine Staatslehre* (n 18) 180.

[40] That nomadic communities cannot form a State is a view shared by Bluntschli, who nevertheless thought that such peoples could be treated as States if they had adequate representation at the international level; see Bluntschli, *Das moderne Völkerrecht der civilisirten Staten* (n 18) 67.

[41] Kelsen, 'Recognition in International Law' (n 21) 607–08.

[42] Lauterpacht, *Recognition in International Law* (n 23) 26ff.

[43] See eg Slobodan Jovanović, *Država: Knjiga prva* (Belgrade 1936) 30.

[44] *Western Sahara*, ICJ Reports 12, Advisory Opinion of 16 October 1975, 43–44; the ICJ took into account the fact that the political organisation of Western Sahara during Spanish colonisation had been based on religion rather than territory.

notion of effective control over territory.[45] Other bodies have been more willing to confirm the government–territory–population triptych, both at the international and domestic levels.[46] In so doing, these courts invariably refer to the 1933 Montevideo Convention.

3.1.1 The 1933 Montevideo Conference

The Montevideo Convention on the Rights and Duties of States is often taken as the starting point when analysing the criteria of statehood. The treaty is a regional instrument, adopted at the Seventh International Conference of American States in 1933. It has a limited number of States Parties[47] and its customary status regarding the criteria for statehood should not be presumed. There are at least four reasons for which the Convention enjoys a place of honour in scholarship: first, the criteria listed in Article 1 correspond to the ones usually identified in doctrine; second, the Convention is a source of positive law; third, its provisions have been invoked by other authorities such as the Badinter Commission;[48] and fourth, there exists no other treaty with the same subject matter as the Montevideo Convention. According to Dugard, '[c]ontemporary State practice shows that States do by and large follow the requirements of the Montevideo Convention in their recognition policy and practice'.[49] Some provisions of the Montevideo Convention were reproduced using similar language in later instruments such as the Friendly Relations Declaration[50] and the Helsinki Final Act,[51] but this is not the case with the definition of statehood itself.

Neither statehood nor recognition were much discussed by the States participating in the Seventh Organization of American States (OAS) Conference in Montevideo. The draft treaty had been prepared by the Second Sub-Committee appointed by the Committee on International Law taking into account 'the fact

[45] ibid 48–49; for an opposing view, see the separate opinion of Judge Forster, ibid 95 ('It is Africa of former times which is in question, as to which it cannot arbitrarily be required that its institutions should be a carbon copy of European institutions, for on that basis almost the entire African continent would have to be declared *terra nullius* … It is from this viewpoint that the "legal ties" recognized in the Opinion should be confronted with the classic notions conveyed by the expression "State" and "sovereignty".')

[46] See *Prosecutor v Slobodan Milošević* IT-02-54-T (16 June 2004) [Decision] paras 83ff; for domestic jurisprudence, see *Kadic v Karadzic* (1995) 70 F 3d 232, 245 and *République de Chine (Taïwan) c Organisation internationale de Normalisation* (2010) as reproduced in Lucius Caflisch (ed), *La pratique suisse en matière de droit international public 2011* (Bern 2013) 27.

[47] The OAS website lists only sixteen States Parties at the time of writing of this book; see <http://www.oas.org/juridico/english/sigs/a-40.html> last accessed 4 June 2024.

[48] Badinter Commission (n 31) 1495. The Opinions do not specifically invoke the Montevideo Convention but they have been interpreted as an 'endorsement' of Montevideo; see John P Grant, *International Law Essentials* (Edinburgh University Press 2010) 41.

[49] Dugard, 'The Secession of States and Their Recognition' (n 3) 56.

[50] See *Declaration on Principles of International Law Concerning Friendly Relations and Cooperation Among States in Accordance with the Charter of the United Nations* (24 October 1970) A/RES/2625(XXV).

[51] See Final Act of the Conference on Security and Cooperation in Europe, 14 ILM 1292 (signed 1 August 1975).

that in America there exist certain principles of International Law which are definitely accepted';[52] the research and draft were listed under 'methods for the progressive codification of international law'.[53] In spite of the importance given to the Convention by contemporary lawyers, these matters were not of great interest to the delegates in Montevideo: controversy rather surrounded draft Article 11 on the use of force and territorial acquisitions. This provision had been the subject of a minority report by the Peruvian delegation, who felt that its formulation was unnecessarily precise and could cause problems in relation to Article 2 of the earlier Anti-War Pact of Rio de Janeiro regarding non-recognition of forceful territorial claims.[54] The sessions were also marked by tensions between the United States and Cuba regarding the United States refusal to recognise the Cuban revolutionary government and its involvement in that country's internal affairs.[55] The Roosevelt administration therefore submitted a lengthy general reservation, with Brazil and Peru making reservations to Article 11.[56]

The fact that the *travaux préparatoires* do not cast more light on this topic is important to understand the approach of the Montevideo delegates. First, OAS members clearly did not find Articles 1 and 3 of the draft controversial. This might indicate the existence of consensus on a point of international law by the participating States.[57] Nevertheless, the statements and behaviour of some States Parties demonstrate a reluctance to be bound by at least some of the treaty's provisions, which could reflect these States' understanding of customary law at the time. This point is also backed by the delegates' awareness that the treaty amounted to 'progressive codification' of international law. Scholarly debates in the years following the Conference did not generally single out Articles 1 and 3 for analysis, if they invoked the Convention at all.[58]

3.1.2 The Montevideo Criteria

The elements of statehood are listed in Article 1 of the Convention:

[52] See *Seventh International Conference of American States: First, Second and Eighth Committees: Organization of Peace, Problems of International Law, International Conferences of American States: Minutes and Antecedents* (OAS 1933) Report of the Second Subcommittee.

[53] ibid Program of the Seventh International Conference of American States Approved by the Governing Board of the Pan American Union in the Session of 31 May 1933.

[54] ibid 166.

[55] ibid 103ff.

[56] See 'Convention on the Rights and Duties of States' (1934) 28(2) American Journal of International Law 75, 78; for an evolution of legal thinking on intervention in the Americas, see J M Yefes, 'Les problèmes fondamentaux du droit des gens en Amérique' (1934) 28 RCADI 1, 77ff.

[57] However, it is possible that the reason for the lack of debates on these matters lies in the participants' preoccupation with other political issues at the Conference. Care should therefore be taken when making assumptions regarding the existence of consensus on such legal matters or at least what relevance to attribute to States' silence in this regard.

[58] See eg Herbert Wright, 'The Montevideo Conference and Organization for Peace' (1934) 97(2) World Affairs 100.

> The state as a person of international law should possess the following qualifications:
> (a) a permanent population;
> (b) a defined territory;
> (c) government; and
> (d) capacity to enter into relations with the other states.[59]

Paragraphs (a) to (c) correspond to the material criteria developed by legal doctrine as demonstrated earlier. Paragraph (d) may be interpreted as both material and legal.

3.1.2.1 Permanent population

In nineteenth-century conceptions of international law, the State was a product of its people or 'nation'.[60] A people may share an ethnicity, culture, religion, and language across a State's territory—or it may be very heterogenous. There is no minimum population that a territory under a common government should possess to call itself a State.[61]

How is a permanent population identified in practice? The link between States and groups/individuals is primarily expressed through nationality.[62] Nationality is of fundamental importance in international law. It may authorise, or even oblige States to act in a certain way, for example by exercising diplomatic protection in favour of their nationals abroad.

Every State must have nationals. Does a permanent population then refer to nationals? Crawford disputes this, finding that '[n]ationality is dependent upon statehood, not vice versa'.[63] Nevertheless, matters of nationality feature prominently in cases of secession, as a new State necessarily 'inherits' some nationals of its parent. It is therefore necessary for a State to at least claim a group as its own nationals for there to exist a permanent population as an element of statehood: nationality must exist, even though it need not be pervasive among the population. The Badinter Commission proposed that members of the Serbian community in Croatia and Bosnia be offered the possibility of choosing their nationality between that of these countries or another Yugoslav republic.[64] Crawford therefore suggests that, '[i]n

59 Montevideo Convention (n 38) art 1.

60 Nations have sometimes themselves been the object of recognition separately from States; see Jean J A Salmon, *La reconnaissance d'état* (Librairie Armand Colin 1971) 12–13.

61 N A Maryan Green, *International Law* (Pitman Publishing 1987) 42.

62 The concepts of a State's 'nationals' and its 'permanent population' are not however identical.

63 Crawford (n 10) 52.

64 Badinter Commission (n 31) 1498–99; this was seen as a manifestation of self-determination. Conversely, compulsory changes of nationality could also violate self-determination and even prevent the establishment of an independent State, as exemplified by South Africa's 'independent' homelands; see John Dugard, 'South Africa's "Independent" Homelands: An Exercise in Denationalization' (1980) 10 Denver Journal of International Law and Policy 11, 21ff.

the absence of agreement to the contrary, persons habitually resident in the territory of the new State automatically acquire the nationality of that State, for all international purposes, and lose their former nationality, but this is subject to a right in the new State to delimit more particularly who it will regard as its nationals'.[65]

Doctrine still insists on the fact that this population 'must be settled, not nomadic'.[66] This is seen as inherent in the 'permanency' requirement. Brownlie writes that '[t]his criterion is intended to be used in association with that of territory, and connotes a stable community. Evidentially this is important, since in the absence of the physical basis for an organized community, it will be difficult to establish the existence of a state.'[67]

Discussions of what constitutes a 'people' also feature in jurisprudence. Of particular interest is the distinction between a people or population as an element of an existing State and as a precondition for the establishment of a new one. In 1897, the US Supreme Court delivered a judgment on the seizure of an armed vessel, the *Three Friends*, intended to aid Cuban rebels in their insurrection against Spain. This raised the question of whether the US Neutrality Act had been triggered by the insurrection.[68] The US Government had not recognised the rebels as belligerents. Nevertheless, the wording of the Act prohibited the United States from furnishing assistance to 'any colony, district or people' engaged in hostilities against a foreign prince or State with whom the United States was at peace. The Supreme Court therefore found that the words 'colony, district or people' implied no necessity of political recognition[69] and analysed these terms *a contrario* to the notion of statehood.[70] It found that the word 'people' could mean 'the entire body of the inhabitants of a state, or the state or nation collectively in its political capacity, or the ruling power of the country... [T]aken in connection with the words "colony" and "district", [its meaning] covers, in our judgment, any insurgent or insurrectionary "body of people acting together, undertaking and conducting hostilities", although its belligerency has not been recognized.'[71] Consequently, there was no obstacle to the application of the Nationality Act.

This case is illustrative of the challenges involved in the determination of the criterion of a people or population, for in a possible determination of Cuban statehood (a matter not addressed by the Court) one must first establish the existence of a Cuban population as distinct from that of Spain. International law provides

65 Crawford (n 10) 53.

66 Green, *International Law* (n 61) 42.

67 Crawford (n 2) 118.

68 *The Three Friends* (1897) 166 US 1.

69 ibid 56.

70 The Supreme Court found in an *obiter dictum* that a State under the Act is 'a political community whose independence has been recognized'. ibid.

71 ibid 62–63; cf Final Report and Recommendations of an International Meeting of Experts on the Further Study of the Concept of the Right of People for UNESCO, SNS-89/CONF.602/7 (22 February 1990) for more recent views.

no clear way of making such a determination. Zimmerman therefore writes of the 'manifold problems' of nationality arising in State succession: 'The most important issue is the criteria that the successor State may use to determine its initial set of nationals ... [I]t is also important to determine those groups of people that the predecessor State may continue to consider as its own nationals without violating pertinent rules of customary international law.'[72] In practice, the determination of whether there exists a permanent population (and who belongs to it) may need to be settled on a case-specific basis. Recognition by third States may also play an important role indicatively.[73]

While exceptions can be made, international law proscribes that, in principle, a new State that amicably separates from its parent inherits that State's sovereignty not only over the territory in its possession but also over its population ('personal sovereignty'). In recognising the separation, the parent relinquishes its claims of territorial and personal sovereignty to the recipient, and its own nationals from that moment on become nationals of the new State. This principle was recalled by the Supreme Court of Japan in *Kanda v The State*, when the Korean plaintiff's claim to Japanese nationality—which she held by birth—was rejected on account of Japan having relinquished its sovereignty over Korea in the Treaty of San Francisco. The Court observed:

> A State is composed of people, territory and a Government as its essential requisites for existence, and if it lacks any one of these it cannot exist as a State. Recognition of the independence of Korea is recognition of Korea as an independent State; it is none other than the recognition that Korea possesses the people, territory and Government appertaining to it. Accordingly, by the Peace Treaty Japan has renounced sovereignty over the people belonging to Korea. This means that the people belonging to Korea have been divested of Japanese nationality.[74]

The Court also remarked that '"People belonging to Korea" are properly construed to mean persons who had legal status as Koreans under Japanese domestic law after the union of Japan and Korea.'[75] This is an important and realistic observation,

[72] Andreas Zimmermann, 'State Succession and the Nationality of Natural Persons' in P M Eisenmann and M Koskenniemi (eds), *State Succession: Codification Tested against the Facts* (Brill/Nijhoff 2000) 614.

[73] '[T]here are many cases where laws have been made against the will of the sovereign by persons engaged in rebellion or revolution; then until such persons or the government which they set up have been granted *de facto* recognition by the Government of this country, their laws cannot be recognised by the courts of this country, but after *de facto* recognition such laws will be recognized.' *Carl Zeiss Stiftung v Rayner & Keeler Ltd* (1967) 1 AC 853, as reproduced in L C Green and Georg Schwarzenberger (eds), *International Law through the Cases* (Steven & Sons Limited 1970) 149, 149.

[74] *Kanda v The State* (1966) 32 ILR 170–85, 173–74.

[75] ibid 174.

meaning that domestic law arrangements in force prior to independence will have a bearing on personal status in its aftermath.

3.1.2.2 Defined territory

All States exist and are created within a certain territory, and almost the entire habitable surface of the Earth belongs today to a sovereign State. On the other hand, few States are not involved in some sort of territorial dispute with one or more of their neighbours, whether the dispute concerns the delineation of a land border or the limits of the territorial sea. In some cases, there exist conflicting claims to regions of considerable size. As an element and criterion of statehood, a 'defined territory' is therefore particularly difficult to pinpoint.

An entity calling itself a State must exist within a reasonably identifiable part of the Earth's surface distinguishable from the territory of other States and allowing the territorial State to exercise its jurisdiction.[76] The term employed by Hersch Lauterpacht, namely a 'sufficiently determined territory' (*un territoire suffisamment déterminé*)[77] seems more appropriate than the strict wording of the Montevideo Convention. The same author recalls: 'Most of the new States which arose after the First World War were recognized *de facto* or *de jure* before their frontiers were finally laid down in treaties—although as a rule such recognition was accompanied by stipulations relating to the acceptance by the State concerned of the frontiers to be laid down by the Peace Conference.'[78] There is no requirement that the territory attain a certain minimum surface or be contiguous, yet 'statehood implies exclusive control over *some* territory'[79] so that the State may dispense with its international obligations. As the traditional criteria of statehood only fulfil their purpose in unison, this is the territory over which the corresponding government should exercise exclusive control. However, new States have been recognised even when the government only controlled a small portion of their claimed territory, such as Bosnia and Herzegovina in 1992.[80] Zemanek explains this by the 'eroding territoriality' of international law, whereby territory is no longer as important for States perform their social functions as it had been earlier.[81]

[76] The purposive nature of this element of statehood has been indirectly recognised in jurisprudence: 'Territorial sovereignty ... involves the exclusive right to display the activities of a State. This right has as corollary a duty: the obligation to protect within the territory the rights of other States, in particular their right to integrity and inviolability in peace and in war, together with the rights which each State may claim for its nationals in foreign territory. Without manifesting its territorial sovereignty in a manner corresponding to circumstances, the State cannot fulfil this duty.' *Island of Palmas Case* (1928) 2 RIAA 829, 839.

[77] Hersch Lauterpacht, 'Règles générales du droit de la paix' (1937) 62 RCADI 95, 255; cf Crawford (n 10) 48 and Shaw, *International Law* (n 2) 158.

[78] Lauterpacht (n 23) 30; cf Crawford (n 2) 118 ('In 1913 Albania was recognized by a number of states in spite of a lack of settled frontiers, and Israel was admitted to the UN in spite of disputes over its borders.').

[79] Crawford (n 10) 48.

[80] Shaw (n 2) 159–60.

[81] See Karl Zemanek, 'The Legal Foundations of the International System: General Course on Public International Law' (1997) 266 RCADI 229, 68ff.

When categorising territorial disputes based on their impact on an entity's capacity to meet the elements of statehood, one should distinguish situations where the entirety of a State's territory is claimed by another State (unilateral secession) from those where only a part of it is contested (border disputes). Crawford advocates such an approach.[82] Simple territorial disputes do not bring into doubt the very existence of one or more States, whereas contested statehood brings into question the opposability of the unrecognised State's acts in general. This is why the existence of a dispute between Italy and France regarding the ownership of the Mont Blanc summit does not render the acts of one State unopposable to the other. Opposability may however be controversial in relations between the two Koreas or North and South Vietnam prior to unification. Aware of this problem, Crawford goes so far as to deny altogether the requirement of possessing a defined territory and subordinates it to the possession of independence and an effective government.[83]

Thus, although there are no exact rules on how to delimit a new State's territory under international law, a number of different factors have been taken into account in doctrine and practice. The element initially considered crucial by scholars was the effectivity of the State's control over the territory, but delimitation has more recently been performed according to the Parent State's internal divisions and domestic law,[84] the approach of UN bodies such as the General Assembly, and even the principle and right of self-determination.[85] It is clear that, although a degree of effective control over territory is still in principle required for statehood, the proper extent of a new State's territorial possessions can only be determined on a case-by-case basis and could remain controversial long after its statehood has been accepted.

3.1.2.3 Government

Governments, as a form of institutionalised political authority over a territory and population, exist on many levels, from sub-national (local, municipal) to supranational. Only the national or federal government is relevant for the determination of statehood, because it is such authorities that speak on behalf of the State. The term 'government' is used here as a generic term; it does not apply to any individual government, cabinet, or administration but to their continuity as exercising

[82] Crawford (n 10) 48–49.

[83] 'Thus even a substantial boundary or territorial dispute with a new State is not enough, of itself, to bring statehood into question. The only requirement is that the State must consist of a certain coherent territory effectively governed—a formula that suggests that the requirement of territory is rather a constituent of government and independence than a distinct criterion of its own.' ibid 52.

[84] This was the practice in relation to former colonial countries such as Burkina Faso and Mali as well as in the former Yugoslavia.

[85] The ICC recently resorted to both UNGA practice and the principle of self-determination to delineate Palestinian territory in order to establish its jurisdiction under the Rome Statute, see *Situation in the State of Palestine* ICC-01/18 (5 February 2021) [Decision].

governmental control over a territory. 'The existence of effective government, with centralized administrative and legislative organs', writes Brownlie, 'is the best evidence of a stable political community'.[86]

From an international law perspective, the purpose of a government is to represent a State towards others: it acts as a mouthpiece, having no separate legal personality of its own.[87] Kelsen writes, 'A government, according to the norms of international law, is the individual or body of individuals which by virtue of the effective constitution of a state, represents the state in its relations with other states, *i.e.*, is competent to act on behalf of the state in its relations with the community of states.'[88] This role will usually be played by the State's traditional executive branch, namely the council of ministers or presidential cabinet. Who these individuals are or what titles are bestowed upon them is determined by domestic law as part of the State's constitutional autonomy.

Accurately identifying the central government, as opposed to the government of federal units or municipalities (which do not in principle speak for a State externally),[89] is crucial for a State's enjoyment of international law rights. For example, the incumbent head of government is vested with full powers to represent the State[90] and absolute immunity from foreign jurisdiction.[91] Although the determination of who the government is must normally be done according to domestic law, this is not always the case: thus, even an unconstitutional government may speak for a State if it is effective. This principle was famously stated in the *Tinoco Concessions* arbitration by William Taft[92] and is today widely accepted in legal doctrine.[93]

Even if well established in principle, effectiveness (or effectivity) is not always easy to identify in practice. Green breaks the principle down into three constituent

[86] Crawford (n 2) 119.

[87] See Charpentier (n 34) 15.

[88] Kelsen (n 21) 615.

[89] Consider in this respect the role of the central government to speak for the *entirety* of a State's territory: Vienna Convention on the Law of Treaties, 1155 UNTS 331 (adopted 23 May 1969, entered into force 27 January 1980) art 29. The ILC bore in mind various 'federal clauses' when drafting this provision; see Barbara Miltner, 'Territory and its Relationship to Treaties' in Michael J Bowman and Dino Kritsiotis (eds), *Conceptual and Contextual Perspectives on the Modern Law of Treaties* (CUP 2018) 468, 473ff.

[90] Vienna Convention (n 89) art 7.

[91] See *Case Concerning the Arrest Warrant of 11 April 2000 (Democratic Republic of the Congo v Belgium)*, ICJ Reports 3, Judgment of 14 February 2002, paras 53–54.

[92] 'What is true of the non-recognition of the United States in its bearing upon the existence of a *de facto* government under Tinoco for thirty months is probably in a measure true of the non-recognition by her Allies in the European War. Such non-recognition for any reason, however, cannot outweigh the evidence disclosed by this record before me as to the *de facto* character of Tinoco's government, according to the standard set by international law.' *Tinoco Claims Arbitration (Great Britain v Costa Rica)* (1923) 1 RIAA 369, 381.

[93] See eg Elihu Lauterpacht (ed), *International Law: Being the Collected Papers of Hersch Lauterpacht QC, LLD, FBA: Volume 3: The Law of Peace Parts II–VI* (CUP 1977) 115; Colin Warbrick, 'Recognition of Governments' (1993) 56 The Modern Law Review 92–97; and *Republic of Somalia v Woodhouse Drake & Carey (Suisse) SA* (1992) 1 QB 54.

elements: '(1) [the government] must represent the state, in the sense that it speaks in the name of the population; (2) it must be able to govern this population, in the sense that it can impose its will; (3) it must have some likelihood of permanence, in that, even if the actual government loses office it will be replaced by another.'[94] Schwarzenberger is also right to highlight that a different understanding must be given to the notion of effectivity depending on the nature of the territory, the terrain, climate, and whether it constitutes part of a contiguous land territory or an islet: 'In cases of islets and rocks, or jungle country, limits are set to physical appropriation … Normally, however, effective possession manifests itself by the establishment of proper state machinery for purposes of defense and administration of the occupied territory and the actual display of state jurisdiction.'[95] As we will see, recognition by third States may play an indicative role to determine whether a government is effectively in control of a State's territory.

A State does not cease to exist even if it loses its government, nor can it be extinguished by foreign occupation.[96] Nevertheless, beyond States discontinuing their existence by merging or joining others, recent practice pertaining to Yugoslavia has accepted that a State may extinguish itself through 'dissolution'.[97] As there still existed a Yugoslav federal government nominally representing the entirety of the Socialist Federal Republic of Yugoslavia at the time of the Yugoslavia Peace Conference in 1991 and 1992, it is difficult to ascertain what specific facts were taken by the Arbitral Commission to reach such a conclusion. Insofar as the desire and efforts of federal units to dismember a federation could lead the federal government to lose effective control over its country—perhaps irreversibly so—finding that the State itself thereby ceases to exist comes across as inconsistent with the traditional understanding of the extinction of statehood.[98] The only caveat in this regard could be the inception of new claims to the dissolving Parent State's territories and succession by its federal units.

3.1.2.4 *Capacity to enter into relations with other States*

This particular criterion is usually omitted from older doctrine,[99] not because it is not relevant but because it is subsumed in the criterion of an effective government (if a State's government is incapable of entertaining international relations, then either it is not a government, or it does not represent a State). A number of authors,

[94] Green (n 61) 43.

[95] Georg Schwarzenberger, 'Title to Territory: Response to a Challenge' (1957) 51(2) American Journal of International Law 308–24, 315–16.

[96] Shaw (n 2) 164ff.

[97] Badinter Commission (n 31) 1497.

[98] It might have been different had no federal unit subsequently claimed continuation of the legal personality of the federation, which in Yugoslavia was not the case; in cases where all former federal units seek new legal personality and succession, the Parent State may indeed be said to have ceased to exist.

[99] See Decaux and de Frouville (n 2) 185; cf Jovanović, *Država* (n 43) 30; Kelsen (n 21) 605, 607–08; Lauterpacht (n 23) 26–32; and many others.

such as Brownlie[100] and Green,[101] describe this criterion as referring to independence; others, such as Crawford,[102] understand it as a '*capacity* to enter into the full range of international relations' regardless of whether the entity enjoys diplomatic recognition; and a third group, including John Dugard and John Grant, specifically understand it as requiring recognition by other States.[103]

Although there is no consensus on how to interpret the criterion, it is noteworthy that doctrine generally requires entities to be independent before they can be considered States for the purposes of international law. Depending on the context, this may refer to either *de facto* or *de jure* independence. Entities such as vassal States, federal units, or provinces within a federal State or realm are not regarded as States in this sense because they do not possess an independent government enabling them to interact with other States on an equal footing: 'The proper usage of the term "independence" is to denote the status of a state which controls its own external relations without dictation from other states.'[104] Such independence is commonly equated with sovereignty.

But dependent entities have also historically been able to conduct independent foreign policy. In the nineteenth century, Serbia, Bulgaria, and the Danubian Principalities of Moldavia and Wallachia were nominally tributaries of the Ottoman Empire, but given their *de facto* independence, they engaged in active foreign policy—sometimes with open hostility towards the Porte. For example, the vassal Principality of Serbia was able to conclude an anti-Ottoman military alliance with the Kingdom of Greece in 1867. Before its sovereignty was formally acknowledged by France and Spain in 1993, Andorra exhibited similar qualities. Independence therefore cannot merely refer to a situation wherein a territorial entity is objectively responsible for its own domestic and foreign policy: a legal claim of statehood, including a refusal to recognise the superior authority of any other State, is crucial. There do not exist proper examples of such 'semi-sovereign' States today, yet at a conceptual level it is important to keep these older examples in mind: even a significant degree of independent foreign policy-making does not make an entity a sovereign State.

Insofar as independence is understood as freedom from a higher authority, it is not particularly useful to treat it as a separate prerequisite of statehood. Emphasis

[100] 'In the enumeration contained in the Montevideo Convention, the concept of independence is represented by the requirement of capacity to enter into relations with other states.' Ian Brownlie, *Principles of Public International Law* (OUP 1998) 70–72; cf Crawford (n 2) 119–20.

[101] Green (n 61) 42–45. Note that Green does not take the Montevideo Convention as a starting point in his analysis, but rather the ICJ's *Western Sahara* advisory opinion; see *Western Sahara*, ICJ Reports 12, Advisory Opinion of 16 October 1975.

[102] Crawford (n 10) 61.

[103] Grant writes: 'To satisfy the conditions of statehood, a State must be able to interact with other States, and an entity that cannot interact with other States because these other States will not interact with it is not a State.' John P Grant, *International Law Essentials* (Edinburgh University Press 2010) 42.

[104] Clapham (n 1) 143; cf Ricardo J Alfaro, 'Rights and Duties of States' (1969) 97 RCADI 91, 95 and Green (n 61) 45.

should rather be put on the existence of a claim of statehood or independence, because even entities that meet the criteria of statehood will not be considered sovereign States if they do not view themselves as such.[105]

Another view, espoused by John Dugard, sees this criterion as referring to recognition. According to this scholar, '[a] State cannot comply with the fourth requirement of statehood under the Montevideo Convention without recognition by some States, as it will not be able to demonstrate a "capacity to enter into relations with other States"'.[106] In *Caglar v Billingham (Inspector of Taxes)*, British Special Commissioners of Inland Review maintained that non-recognition of Northern Cyprus meant that that entity does not have 'functional independence as it cannot enter into relations with other States' and therefore 'does not satisfy the fourth requirement of statehood'.[107] This echoes the view of the 'Belgian school' of recognition, advocated by Charles de Visscher, Jean Salmon, and Joe Verhoeven,[108] which takes the existence of widespread recognition to be an element of statehood in its own right. However, this is not a mainstream reading of Article 1(d) of the Montevideo Convention. Although the extent of recognition will certainly be crucial for an entity claiming statehood to meet the material requirements of Montevideo, it nevertheless remains an extrinsic quality that should not be confounded with the existing intrinsic elements: even an unrecognised State may exist unto itself.

3.1.2.5 Claim of statehood

As Crawford remarks, 'Statehood is a claim of right based on a certain factual and legal situation'.[109] There is more to this point than meets the eye, because to take the three elements of statehood as described above and apply them indiscriminately to all the various entities that possess them would lead to awkward results and we would be forced to treat as States entities that claim no such status.

Yaël Ronen calls such entities 'quasi-states'. She gives as examples 'the political entity in the Palestinian territories' until 2011, Taiwan, and Puerto Rico.[110] Ronen also believes that Andorra until 1993 fell within this category, when its sovereignty was recognised by France and Spain in a treaty,[111] whereafter the principality

[105] See Yaël Ronen, 'Entities that Can Be States but Do Not Claim to Be' in Duncan French (ed), *Statehood and Self-Determination: Reconciling Tradition and Modernity in International Law* (CUP 2013) 23; it is important here to highlight that the entity should regard itself as a State under international, not domestic law.

[106] Dugard (n 3) 51.

[107] *Caglar v Billingham (Inspector of Taxes)* (1996) STC (SCD) 150, (1996) 1 LRC 526.

[108] See Charles de Visscher, *Problèmes d'interprétation judiciaire en droit international public* (Pedone 1963) 190ff; Salmon (n 60); and Verhoeven, *La reconnaissance internationale* (n 35) 666–67.

[109] Crawford (n 10) 156.

[110] Ronen, 'Entities that Can Be States but Do Not Claim to Be' (n 105) 23–59, 25ff.

[111] Treaty of Good Neighbourliness, Friendship and Cooperation Between the Kingdom of Spain, the French Republic and the Principality of Andorra, 1872 UNTS 195 (signed 1 and 3 June 1993, entered into force 1 December 1994) art 1.

joined the United Nations; Andorra arguably fulfilled the criteria of statehood long before that, and was sometimes described as a 'country' rather than a State for the purposes of international law.[112] Quasi-states are in principle excluded from the law applicable to States.[113] Ronen's quasi-states resemble Frowein's '*de facto* regimes'[114] but are distinguished from them by *not* claiming the status of a State (whereas *de facto* regimes do, but do not enjoy full or even partial recognition of their claim).

Therefore, there exist very good reasons to posit the existence of a statehood claim as one of the essential criteria of statehood. It is evident that quasi-states (as understood by Ronen) are not regarded as States under international law: unless the entity seeks statehood, it cannot be considered a State. Doctrine identified a voluntaristic aspect in statehood genesis already in the nineteenth century, when Pradier-Fodéré raised the 'will to statehood' to the same level as its material elements: '[U]n État existe de fait dès qu'il réunit les éléments nécessaires, c'est-à-dire la volonté unie à la force et aux moyens indispensables pour défendre son indépendance ....'[115] Such a claim, expressing a political will, could even be seen as a form of 'self-recognition'[116] and explains how the new State is joined to the system of international law. This is congruent with a normative framework that is still predominantly based on consent and allows us to bridge the gap between material and legal statehood by explaining how an entity possessing certain factual qualities becomes a subject of international law bound by its universal customary rules.

3.2 Exceptions to the Traditional Approach

Not all entities enjoying the legal personality of States fulfil the material criteria of statehood. In addition to the two historic exceptions I consider here, namely the Holy See and the Order of Malta, regarding whose status there exists much confusion under international law, more recent contested entities such as Palestine and

[112] Ronen (n 105) 23, 28; cf *Drozd and Janousek v France and Spain* App no 12747/87 (26 June 1992) para 88 (the Court added that Andorra could only become an 'associate member' of the Council of Europe). Consider also the debate concerning the notion of 'third country' in EU law in T-370/19 *Spain v Commission* [2020] ECLI:EU:T:2020:440 and C-632/20 P *Spain v Commission* [2023] ECLI:EU:C:2023:28. Although the notion of 'third country' was essentially equated with that of 'third State' in the latter judgment, it should be borne in mind that this interpretation is restricted to the provisions of EU law.

[113] Crawford expresses the same view separately: 'The case of Taiwan raises the possibility that an entity which does not claim to be a State, even though it might otherwise qualify for statehood in accordance with the basic criteria, will not be regarded as a State.' Crawford (n 10) 156.

[114] See Jochen A Frowein, 'De Facto Regime' in Anne Peters and Rüdiger Wolfrum (eds), *Max Planck Encyclopedias of International Law* (OUP 2013) <https://opil.ouplaw.com/display/10.1093/law:epil/9780199231690/law-9780199231690-e1395> last accessed 13 June 2024.

[115] Paul Pradier-Fodéré, *Traité de droit international public européen & americain, Tome premier* (Pedone-Lauriel 1885) 229; cf Cavaglieri (n 9) 341.

[116] See Kelsen (n 21) 609.

Western Sahara may also be listed. All of these entities are either States, wherefore one or more of the material criteria of statehood are not essential, or they are not States, in which case the legal personality of States is not limited to entities possessing material statehood.

3.2.1 The Holy See

Hersch Lauterpacht examines the Holy See under the category of 'political units not as yet endowed with full statehood [treated] as subjects of international law', referring in particular to the time before the Lateran Treaty of 1929 when its rule over the Vatican City State was restored: 'In the intervening period the Holy See, although not a State in international law, concluded treaties and sent and received diplomatic representatives – it was a subject of international law.'[117]

Even today, the Holy See remains a peculiar entity on the international stage. Whereas the Vatican City State is a territorial entity described as a State under international law,[118] the Holy See is legally distinct and refers to the central governing body of the Roman Catholic Church. Unlike the Vatican, which was created by the Lateran Treaty as a new State that did not succeed the earlier Papal States, the Holy See is perceived as originating in early Christianity. Pope Pius IX was the last Pontiff to rule over the Papal States before the capture of Rome in 1870 at the end of Italian unification. While the capacity of the Holy See to engage in diplomatic relations following the capture of Rome could be attributed to the Pope's earlier temporal rule, this is not how other States regarded it at the time.[119] For its own part, the Holy See does not consider itself a State but rather a sovereign and independent entity with full international legal subjectivity that exercises control over the Vatican City State based on the Lateran Treaty; this is evident from the Holy See's reports to UN human rights mechanisms, for example their initial report to the Committee against Torture in 2012.[120] The Holy See is listed as a 'permanent

[117] Hersch Lauterpacht, 'The Subjects of International Law' in Lauterpacht (ed), *International Law* (n 93) 136–50, 138.

[118] However, not all lawyers regard the Vatican City State as meeting the requirements of statehood: 'The [Vatican City State] has no permanent population apart from Church functionaries and exists only to support the work of the Holy See. Italy carries out a substantial number of administrative functions with regard to the City. Some writers accordingly have concluded that it cannot be regarded as a state.' Shaw (n 2) 194.

[119] The mission statement of the Permanent Observer Mission of the Holy See to the United Nations recalls that, '[s]ince the fourth century, and well before the constitution of the Papal States, the Apostolic See has sent and received diplomatic missions.' See website of the Permanent Observer Mission of the Holy See to the United Nations, available at <https://holyseemission.org/contents//mission/our-history.php> last accessed 4 June 2024.

[120] See eg the Holy See's reports to UN treaty bodies: 'The Holy See is a sovereign and unique subject of international law having an original, non-derived legal personality independent of any authority or jurisdiction, which exercises its sovereignty over the territory of [the Vatican City State] ... Since 1929, the [Vatican City State] has received international recognition of its particular international nature which is intricately related to, but separate and distinct from the international nature of the Holy See. It has never been confused with the Holy See. For example, following the loss of the traditional Papal States in 1870 until the establishment of [the Vatican City State] in 1929, the Holy See continued to act as a subject of international law by concluding concordats and international treaties with

observer State' at the United Nations, but this label is better explained by the UN's institutional architecture than the legal status of the papacy.

There have been various attempts to describe the genesis of the Holy See as a person of international law. Some earlier writers, notably Fiore,[121] found the source of its personality in the universal nature of the Catholic Church, but this understanding was quickly rejected as extra-legal.[122] Anzilotti distinguished the legal personality of the Catholic Church from that of the Holy See in that the former flows from concordats, agreements reached between the Church and individual States. Although these are seen as possessing a dual nature and flowing from both canon and domestic law, they establish the Church as a legal subject and are, in his view, governed by the principle *pacta sunt servanda* regardless of how either party legally interprets them.[123] The Catholic Church is thereby a subject of international law by virtue of concordats—but also separate from the Holy See. Anzilotti dismisses the argument whereby the Papacy 'survived' in a small stretch of Roman territory in 1870, having rather been eradicated through *debellatio*.[124] The contemporary personality of the Holy See therefore derives from the rights that were accorded to it by Italy after the fall of Rome.[125]

There seems to be little doubt that the Holy See is itself a 'state-like' person of international law. With some symbolic oddities, its rights and duties are the same as those of any other State in the world, and it is vested with sovereignty. This status flows from the personality of other States that created or recognised it, chiefly Italy, its Parent State, which conferred personality on it in the Lateran Treaty and granted it territory in the Vatican.[126] The extinction and subsequent reconstitution of the Papacy is little more than an unusual case of State separation. Arguments whereby the Vatican City State does not meet the criteria of statehood are also not convincing: the Vatican City State as possessing material statehood and the Holy See as a legal personality taken together thus form a single entity. Were one to apply the 'duck test' here ('If it walks like a duck and it talks like a duck, then probably it is a duck'), one would conclude that the Vatican–Holy See duo is, in fact, a State under international law—even though it does not assume that label explicitly. Therefore, although the two are often said to have separate legal personality, this is largely a legal fiction.

States, participating in international conferences, conducting mediation and arbitration missions, and maintaining both active and passive diplomatic relations.' *Consideration of reports submitted by States parties under article 19 of the Convention: Initial reports of States parties due in 2003: The Holy See**, 8 March 2013, CAT/C/VAT/1, paras 4–5.

[121] Pasquale Fiore, *Le droit international codifié* (Paris 1890) 87–90.

[122] See Anzilotti, *Cours de droit international* (n 9) 139–40 and Henri Wagnon, 'La personnalité du Saint-Siège en droit international: Les faits—les doctrines' (1977) 30(4) Studia Diplomatica 321, 335.

[123] Anzilotti (n 122) 140–43.

[124] ibid 146.

[125] ibid 147.

[126] See Crawford (n 2) 114–15.

3.2.2 The Order of Malta

The Holy See is not the only 'odd one out' among the state-like subjects of international law. Another example, again originating in Western Christianity, is the Sovereign Military Order of Malta.[127] Unlike the Holy See, which also functions as the government of the Vatican City State,[128] the Order of Malta in its modern form has no territorial possessions. The Order originally established itself as an organisation of knights and healers that opened a hospital in Crusader-held Jerusalem at the end of the eleventh century. Having secured a papal bull[129] from Paschal II—regarded as the basis of their independence and sovereignty—the Knights were allowed to choose their grand master without the external interference of any other authority. When, following the Siege of Acre in 1291, the last stronghold of the Crusader Kingdom of Jerusalem fell to the Mamluks, the Knights briefly retreated to the island of Cyprus, and from there to Rhodes, which they governed until their defeat at the hands of Suleiman the Magnificent in 1523. The Order then finally settled upon Malta, which they were given 'by treaty with Charles V in 1530 as a fief of the Kingdom of Sicily'.[130] The Knights would rule Malta and become a military and naval power in the Mediterranean, even briefly colonising the Carribbean islands of Saint Christopher, Saint Martin, Saint Barthélemy, and Saint Croix in the seventeenth century. Their possession of Malta ended when Napoleon's forces occupied the island in 1798. Nevertheless, the Order, which never again enjoyed territorial possessions, continued to exist as a subject of international law. Shaw remarks that '[t]he Order already had international personality at the time of its taking control of Malta and even when it had to leave the island it continued to exchange diplomatic legations with most European countries'.[131]

The claim of sovereignty by the Order of Malta is largely, if not entirely, historic. Clearly the Order does not fulfil the requirements for material statehood, which begs the question of *how* its sovereignty may be exercised. Of course, nothing prevents States from treating the Order in a similar way as other States should they so desire. Nevertheless, as the Order is not at a State, the purposefulness of recognising its sovereignty is questionable. It is therefore best regarded as a legal oddity, a non-state actor awarded by some States rights otherwise only enjoyed by States, and nothing else.

[127] The Order's full name is 'Sovereign Military Hospitaller Order of Saint John of Jerusalem, of Rhodes, and of Malta' (*Supremus Ordo Militaris Hospitalis Sancti Ioannis Hierosolymitani Rhodius et Melitensis*).

[128] See Crawford (n 10) 226ff.

[129] The bull *Pie Postulatio Voluntatis* was issued on 15 February 1113 and is today preserved in the National Library of Malta.

[130] Shaw (n 2) 193.

[131] ibid.

3.2.3 Other Examples

There have been numerous instances of territorial entities having been treated as States legally while failing to meet the criteria of material statehood. A few examples are Bosnia and Herzegovina at the outset of the Yugoslav Wars and today Palestine and Western Sahara. Whereas Bosnia's statehood was confirmed by UN membership in 1992 in spite of the very limited extent of territorial control by the government in Sarajevo, Western Sahara, and particularly Palestine have received numerous acts of recognition from third States.[132] Practice in relation to these three territories demonstrates that other States may choose to regard as States entities that fail to meet the Montevideo formula. Hence, a State may exist legally without existing as an effectivity.

The reverse situation is also possible: an entity may possess material statehood, but be denied legal statehood by most or all existing States, especially if its creation entails a violation of imperative norms of international law. Such was the case with Southern Rhodesia, and is perhaps the case today with Northern Cyprus, if the latter may be regarded as sufficiently independent from Turkey, which is certainly debatable. One might also wonder whether an entity such as Somaliland, which has existed for decades as independent and whose creation did not violate *jus cogens* norms, should be considered a State in the sense of international law in the absence of any foreign recognition. However, it is demonstrable from practice that material and legal statehood by and largely coincide, but neither depend on nor require each other.

3.3 Expanding the List of Material Elements

Some authors, such as Crawford, suggest that there exist today new criteria of statehood in addition to the above-mentioned 'traditional' ones. These include the principle of self-determination and the prohibition on the use of force in international relations.[133] To quote Dugard, 'there is big difference between asserting that the Montevideo criteria are the starting point for such an enquiry and claiming that they are the only criteria and factors to be considered and that satisfaction of these criteria constitutes a binding customary rule'.[134] Entities may be regarded as States even though they do not conform to Montevideo, and conversely may be denied status even when they do. Southern Rhodesia, mentioned earlier, could not be regarded as a State as its creation was considered to violate the right to self-determination. The same could be said of South Africa's 'bantustans', created to assuage world opinion of the country's treatment of its black population during

[132] This is most likely by reference to the principle of self-determination.
[133] Crawford (n 10) 97ff.
[134] Dugard (n 6) 101.

apartheid.[135] While legality is clearly a crucial consideration when ascertaining legal statehood, it is less obvious whether illegality negates statehood altogether or simply its recognition by others. In the same vein, we must ask ourselves whether the force of law is sufficient to equip an entity with statehood if it otherwise does not possess it in fact.

While it is impossible to recreate a full list of elements invoked by various legal scholars, what follows are criteria either most commonly invoked in addition to those contained in Article 1 of the Montevideo Convention, or with interesting implications for the application of the law.[136]

3.3.1 Independence

I have already discussed this criterion as a possible interpretation of Article 1(d) of the Convention, and several authors advance it as the most important criterion of statehood. Such is the view of Crawford, although he considers it a separate criterion, rather than an understanding of one of the classical elements contained in the Convention.[137] The main problem is that it is not always clear what 'independence' means in each context. If sovereignty and independence overlap,[138] it would represent circular reasoning to infer that States are sovereign because they are independent. If independence is taken in a more limited sense to denote the factual lack of a superior governmental authority, then of course it is quintessential for statehood.

3.3.2 Recognition

It is commonly asserted that, according to the constitutivist theory, recognition forms a necessary ingredient of statehood.[139] Strictly speaking, this is not true: constitutivists advance that recognition is a condition of legal personality, not of statehood. Early on, Bluntschli argued that statehood arose as a matter of municipal law, while a State's international personality was regulated by international law.[140] Later constitutivists refined this approach and distinguished between the State as a material and legal fact. Oppenheim wrote that '[a] State is and becomes an International Person through recognition only and exclusively'.[141] The act or

[135] For an overview of South Africa's 'homelands policy' at the time, see John Dugard, 'South Africa's "Independent" Homelands: An Exercise in Denationalization' (1980) 10 Denver Journal of International Law and Policy 11.

[136] An excellent and extensive overview of the additional criteria proposed by some scholars is provided in Thomas D Grant, *The Recognition of States: Law and Practice in Debate and Evolution* (Praeger Publishers 1999).

[137] Crawford (n 10) 62ff.

[138] See in this regard Ricardo J Alfaro, 'Rights and Duties of States' (1969) 97 RCADI 91, 95ff.

[139] Crawford (n 10) 93.

[140] 'Die Frage, ob, aus welchen Ursachen und in welcher Form ein neuer Stat enstanden sei, ist voraus statsrechtlich. Die Frage dagegen, ob und in welcher Stellung ein neu gebildeter Stat in der Genossenschaft der Staten Zutritt erhalte, ist wesentlich völkerrechtlich.' Bluntschli (n 18) 71.

[141] Lassa Oppenheim, *International Law: A Treatise, Volume I: Peace* (Longmans, Green and Co 1912) 116; cf Anzilotti (n 9) 161; Cavaglieri (n 9) 348; Kelsen (n 21) 605–06; and others.

recognition is thus merely constitutive of legal relations between the recognising and recognised States, but it does not create its recipient other than in terms of legal relations with other States. Kelsen points towards the distinction between theft as a real and legal fact: only the latter, he claims, is of relevance to the application of the law (theft becomes a legal fact once a judge has determined that theft has occurred).[142]

The views described above are representative of the traditional constitutivist understanding of recognition which, evidently, does not require recognition for statehood to arise. However, there do exist doctrinal positions to the contrary. A notable example is the 'Belgian doctrine' of recognition, initially developed by De Visscher before receiving a more refined treatment by Verhoeven. The essence of their argument is that recognition does not lead to the opposability of statehood but must be taken into consideration to determine effectivity.[143] Recognition then truly becomes an element of statehood, at least if it is sufficiently widespread. This theory may be easily criticised, but it represents a remarkable and intelligent approach to the politics of recognition that is even more worthy of note for not coming from constitutivist sources.

Barring the existence of specific circumstances that would render it declaratory, recognition is doubtless necessary for an entity to enjoy legal statehood on a bilateral level.[144] Recognition by at least some States is also realistically necessary for it to survive as a *de facto* regime. However, there is no good reason for recognition to be considered a material criterion of statehood. If effectivity is a precondition of recognition, then including recognition in the material criteria of statehood would make the act its own prerequisite. A *de facto* State therefore must be presumed to exist and functions regardless of recognition; recognition, as a legal act, may be necessary for legal existence, but this is an altogether different matter from effectivity.

3.3.3 Democratic Legitimacy

Since the end of the Cold War, the question of whether international law does or should recognise a principle of democratic legitimacy, or a right to democratic governance, has drawn much attention from legal scholarship.[145] The analysis is mostly theoretical, but some authors identify specific points in international

[142] ibid Kelsen (n 21) 606.

[143] Verhoeven (n 35) 666ff.

[144] 'The simple fact is that without substantial recognition on the part of other States or admission to the United Nations, a would-be State is not a State.' Dugard (n 6) 108.

[145] See eg Thomas M Franck, 'The Emerging Right to Democratic Governance' (1992) 86(1) American Journal of International Law 46; Sean D Murphy, 'Democratic Legitimacy and the Recognition of States and Governments' (1999) 48(3) The International and Comparative Law Quarterly 545; Gregory H Fox and Brad R Roth (eds), *Democratic Governance and International Law* (CUP 2000); Susan Marks, *The Riddle of All Constitutions: International Law, Democracy, and the Critique of Ideology* (OUP 2000); and Jean d'Aspremont, 'The Rise and Fall of Democracy Governance in International Law: A Reply to Susan Marks' (2011) 22(2) European Journal of International Law 549–70.

practice where such a principle is allegedly established or recognised. Of particular interest is Security Council Resolution 940 (1994), whereby the Council authorised Member States 'to form a multinational force under unified command and control and ... to use all necessary means to facilitate the departure from Haiti of the military leadership, consistent with the Governors Island Agreement, the prompt return of the legitimately elected President and the restoration of the legitimate authorities of the Government of Haiti'.[146] According to Olivier Corten, this was the first time in the history of the United Nations that the Security Council authorised force to restore democracy in a Member State.[147] Corten examines whether this signifies the emergence of a new principle of democratic legitimacy in international law. Although his analysis is grounded in the framework governing the use of force,[148] he notably compares the United Nations response in Haiti to its reaction to the situation in Southern Rhodesia, whose creation was described by the Organisation as a violation of self-determination and therefore a threat to international peace and security. If such a principle existed, then an authorisation of armed action by foreign powers against unconstitutional or undemocratic governments would *ipso facto* disenfranchise the effective government from speaking on behalf of the State. Corten rightly rejects this dangerous idea, finding that the Security Council took action, not because of the existence of an undemocratic government but because the change of government violated a peace agreement.[149] Other authors nevertheless see considerations of democratic legitimacy in actual State practice when recognising States or governments, particularly in relation to the former Yugoslavia.[150] The Western occupation of Afghanistan after the 9/11 attacks was also said to end after a new government had been elected in free elections[151] (the free choice of government by the people of Afghanistan presumably resulted in an indigenous authority that did not overtly depend on the whim of Occupying Powers).[152] While the possession of a democratic government may

[146] UNSC Resolution 940 (1994) para 4.

[147] Olivier Corten, 'La résolution 940 du Conseil de sécurité autorisant une intervention militaire en Haïti: L'émergence d'un principe de légitimité démocratique en droit international?' (1995) 6(1) European Journal of International Law 116, 125.

[148] Corten examines whether a violation of the principle of democratic legitimacy may amount to a threat to international peace in the sense of the UN Charter; see ibid 121ff.

[149] 'Il est en effet fondamental de relever que le non-respect du résultat des élections n'a pas été directement sanctionné en Haïti, mais ne l'a été que dans la mesure où ce résultat a été incorporé dans un accord de paix prévoyant un encadrement international, par l'envoi de Forces des Nations Unies ayant pour mission d'accompagner le processus.' ibid 130.

[150] See Sean D Murphy, 'Democratic Legitimacy and the Recognition of States and Governments' (1999) 48(3) The International and Comparative Law Quarterly 545.

[151] The International Committee of the Red Cross relied on the fact that a new Afghan government was convened in a *loya jirga* or 'grand assembly' to reclassify the situation as a non-international armed conflict, with the former Taliban government now considered a non-state actor. See *Commentary on the First Geneva Convention: Convention (I) for the Amelioration of the Condition of the Wounded and Sick in Armed Forces in the Field* (ICRC 2016) para 400.

[152] A more realistic view is that occupation ended because the Security Council accepted the new government in a resolution. See Marco Sassòli, *International Humanitarian Law: Rules, Controversies, and Solutions to Problems Arising in Warfare* (Edward Elgar 2019) 273ff.

influence a factual evaluation of whether the traditional criteria of statehood have been met, and will certainly factor in the political decision whether to extend recognition, nothing points towards the emergence of a new criterion of either statehood or government in international law.

3.3.4 Self-Determination

Self-determination shares a common purpose with democratic legitimacy in that it purports to diminish the importance of effectivity in some situations when identifying a new State. Unlike the latter, it is well-established in positive law.[153] Its precise content remains a matter of some debate: in UN practice, it was initially invoked to achieve independence for colonial nations and peoples.[154] Self-determination was thus conceived as an entitlement to statehood for certain peoples that did not already possess a State of their own. Whatever such an entitlement does for legal statehood, it cannot be seen as an element of statehood on its own. As Dugard correctly points out, '[t]he right of a people to self- determination cannot be seen as an interpretation or elucidation of the Montevideo Convention'.[155]

It is true that entities which do not possess effectivity, or do not possess it fully, often rely on self-determination to insist on being treated as States: this is famously the case with Palestine and Western Sahara, both of which have received numerous acts of recognition on these grounds. But self-determination is notoriously context-specific: it will function in one way in French Polynesia and another in East Timor. For countries such as Palestine, whose right to external self-determination has been continuously reaffirmed by the UN General Assembly and the ICJ, the right facilitates recognition and could even serve to base a claim of legal statehood. However, self-determination cannot act in lieu of material statehood.

It is interesting to note in this regard that the right to self-determination was developed as a corrective element in the international system. If the Sahrawi Republic does not meet the Montevideo criteria, this is because of occupation by Morocco; if colonial countries were not States, this was because of their subjugation by European powers. External self-determination precisely serves to 'soften' or even displace Montevideo. As such, it cannot be regarded under the same lens as the elements of territory, population, and effective government.

153 See Charter of the United Nations, 1 UNTS XVI (adopted 26 June 1945, entered into force 24 October 1945) arts 1(2) and 55–56; International Covenant on Economic, Social and Cultural Rights, 993 UNTS 3 (adopted 16 December 1966, entered into force 3 January 1976) art 1; and International Covenant on Civil and Political Rights, 999 UNTS 171 (adopted 16 December 1966, entered into force 23 March 1976) art 1.

154 See *Declaration on the Granting of Independence to Colonial Countries and Peoples* (14 December 1960) A/RES/1514(XV).

155 Dugard (n 6) 106.

3.3.5 Lawfulness and Legality

It constitutes long-standing UN practice that a State created in violation of the prohibition of the use of force or of the principle and right of self-determination shall not be treated as a State regardless of effectivity. In 1965, the Security Council condemned the 'unilateral declaration of independence made by a racist minority in Southern Rhodesia' and called upon all States not to recognise or assist the 'illegal' and 'racist' minority regime.[156] There exists similar practice in relation to Bosnia and Herzegovina, Northern Cyprus, Ukraine, and other territories that we will revisit in later chapters. In my view, contemporary practice clearly confirms that statehood may not arise when inextricably linked to a *jus cogens* violation.

On the other hand, some well-known lawyers such as Stefan Talmon[157] insist that statehood is a purely material fact that is excluded from appreciations of lawfulness. A State either exists or it does not exist; there is no such thing as an 'illegal' State. Thus, even entities such as Southern Rhodesia or Northern Cyprus must be considered States despite the violation of peremptory norms involved in their creation. Non-recognition then becomes, according to Talmon, a form of sanction against the offending State. At some level, such views are of course correct, for even an 'illegal' State can be a State materially. I do not, however, see the added value of engaging in such intellectually taxing theoretical work and casting the offending State as some sort of rude wedding crasher, only to deny it the legal rights of States anyway. Certainly such 'mental gymnastics' is performed to honour declaratist dogma, but that does not make it correct.

4. Conclusion

Statehood is a complex phenomenon that has dual meaning in international law. Traditionally, States have been described as real or material phenomena (material statehood), entities possessing certain empirical qualities regardless of their status under international law. To such entities lawyers impute legal qualities or a legal personality of a specific type (legal statehood). Material and legal statehood normally coexist, but they may also be present separately: a *de facto* State may not be legally treated as a State by one or more other States, while this may be the case with an entity that does not possess material statehood. The reasons for the existence of such exceptional cases are of a normative nature and may only be discerned in terms of the law itself, which accords legal personality to some entities while denying it to others.

[156] UNSC Resolution 216 (1965) of 12 November 1965, paras 1–2.

[157] See Stefan Talmon, 'The Constitutive Versus the Declaratory Theory of Recognition: *Tertium Non Datur*?' (2004) 75(1) British Yearbook of International Law 101.

Material statehood is therefore not determinative of legal statehood. It is a precondition of legal statehood in situations where the latter cannot be inferred from another norm of international law. Material statehood is normally understood as a syndrome of several natural facts such as the existence of a government in effective control over a defined territory with a permanent population. These criteria have long been identified in doctrine and are reproduced in the 1933 Montevideo Convention, which adds to them the capacity to enter into relations with other States, an aspect which is otherwise implicit in the criterion of effective government. Although it is doubtful that the Montevideo Convention reflects customary law in this regard, the fact remains that there exists no alternative definition of material statehood in positive law.

Despite some lawyers' attempts at refining or extending the Montevideo formula, it seems neither necessary nor justified to do so, at least in relation to material statehood. A *de facto* State exists when the criteria of effective government, defined territory, and permanent population are all met; there is no additional requirement. However, some aspects of these criteria are not obvious at first glance: the entity in question must claim statehood under international law; it must be factually independent from the authority of any other State and act as the highest legal order in the territory it claims; and it must achieve these qualities with reasonable prospects of permanence. An entity fulfilling these criteria possesses material statehood but it will not necessarily achieve legal statehood.

6
The Legal Personality of States

1. Defining States through their Legal Personality

We have seen that legal scholarship tends to approach States as empirical phenomena and considers their legal personality a consequence of their objective existence. In law, however, it is not empirical but legal existence that must come into the foreground: whether an entity is a State in the absolute is less important (and perhaps wholly irrelevant) compared to whether others are required by law to regard it as such.

The act of recognition has a crucial role to play in linking empirical and legal existence. Recognition entails an acceptance of a fact or situation relevant to the application of the law—in this case, it signifies the acceptance of another's existence as a State. Personality is thus nothing more or less than a bundle of rights and duties provided under the law to all States.[1] To describe personality is therefore to explain what it *means* to be a State in international law.

'In any legal system', writes Shaw, 'certain entities, whether they be individuals or companies, will be regarded as possessing rights and duties enforceable at law ... Legal personality is crucial. Without it institutions and groups cannot operate, for they need to be able to maintain and enforce claims'.[2]

For a long time, the sovereign State was seen as the quintessential subject of international law.[3] It alone possessed international rights and duties, the capacity

[1] This is the view of Grant, who writes that 'statehood is probably best described as a bundle of rights, obligations, and functions'. Thomas D Grant, *The Recognition of States: Law and Practice in Debate and Evolution* (Praeger Publishers 1999) 1. In Crawford's terms, 'To be a State is to have a range of powers and responsibilities at [the international] level.' James Crawford, *The Creation of States in International Law* (OUP 2007) 44. cf Alfred Verdross, 'Règles générales du droit international de la paix' (1929) 30 RCADI 271, 321ff and Karl Zemanek, 'The Legal Foundations of the International System: General Course on Public International Law' (1997) 266 RCADI 229, 29ff (both espouse an interesting perspective on statehood and membership in the international community).

[2] Malcolm N Shaw, *International Law* (CUP 2017) 155; cf Johann Caspar Bluntschli, *Das moderne Völkerrecht der civilisirten Staten als Rechtsbuch dargestellt* (Druck und Verlag der C H Beck'schen Buchhandlung 1872) 66 (explaining that a legal person is a being capable of acquiring and mainting rights and undertaking obligations: 'Person im rechtlichen Sinn des Worts heisst ein Wesen, welches fähig ist, Rechte zu erwerben und zu behaupten und Verpflichtungen auf sich zu nehmen') and Hersch Lauterpacht, 'The Subjects of International Law' in Elihu Lauterpacht (ed), *International Law: Being the Collected Papers of Hersch Lauterpacht: Volume I: The General Works* (CUP 1970) 136–50, 136.

[3] 'The classical system was based on the recognition of the modern sovereign state as the only subject of international law. This system was composed of numerous sovereign states considered as legally equal and who accepted the unlimited right to wage war to enforce claims and protect national interests. In essence it reflected the interaction among European powers and the imposition of their international

Recognition of States in International Law. Pavle Kilibarda, Oxford University Press. © Pavle Kilibarda 2024.
DOI: 10.1093/oso/9780198905653.003.0006

to bring claims under international law and to create legal norms through its consent. Attempts to provide an abstract definition of the concept of legal personality are relatively recent: at a time when the State was the only subject of international law, there was no need to define subjectivity as anything other than statehood itself.[4] Thus, Robert Kolb remarks correctly that, insofar as the law revolved around a single pre-eminent subject, it was not necessary to elaborate an abstract notion of legal personality, as the notions of subjectivity and statehood were largely synonymous.[5]

1.1 Pinpointing Legal Personality

Although today there are many ways in which legal scholarship describes subjectivity (which is synonymous with 'personality'),[6] it is most often described through an entity's capacity to possess rights and obligations under the law—here, specifically, under international law.[7] The multiplication of stakeholders in the international arena has made this question controversial, and a final list of subjects has not been settled in international law; a common approach is to avoid the central conundrum by singling out specific entities as subjects without clearly identifying what makes them such.[8] Lawyers would therefore do well to take heed of Crawford's warning and beware of providing definitions which 'only tend to obscure'.[9]

legal order upon the rest of the world in the three centuries following the Peace of Westphalia.' Peter Malanczuk, *Akehurst's Modern Introduction to International Law* (Routledge 1997) 10.

4 'L'étude du sujet dans la littérature des internationalistes est relativement récente—on peut la dater du début du XXe siècle, lorsque débuta la contestation de l'exclusivisme de la subjectivité des États.' Michel Cosnard, 'Rapport introductif' in Société française pour le droit international, *Colloque du Mans: Le sujet en droit international* (Pedone 2005) 13, 13. For specific examples of such scholarly approaches, see Paul Pradier-Fodéré, *Traité de droit international public européen & americain, Volume I* (G Pedone-Lauriel 1885) esp 117ff; Georg Jellinek, *Allgemeine Staatslehre* (Verlag von O Häring Berlin 1914); and Coleman Phillipson, *Wheaton's Elements of International Law* (Steven and Sons Ltd 1916).

5 'Tant que le droit international se coagule autour de ce seul sujet éminent, il n'est pas nécessaire de recourir à une notion abstraite de personnalité juridique internationale. Le sujet, c'est l'État. Aussi peut-on se permettre de le désigner directement sans intercaler une espèce de synonyme.' Robert Kolb, 'Le droit international comme corps de droit privé et de droit public: Cours général de droit international public' (2021) 419 RCADI 9, 232. The findings of Verhoeven are similar: 'L' "État" a longtemps constitué, s'il ne le demeure aujourd'hui, le sujet par excellence, voire même exclusif, du droit des gens.' Joe Verhoeven, *La reconnaissance internationale dans la pratique contemporaine* (Pedone 1975) 168.

6 A somewhat superficial distinction seems to appear with Pradier-Fodéré, who defines a person of international law as an immediate subject of international law; see Pradier-Fodéré, *Traité de droit international public européen & americain* (n 4) 118.

7 Such is already the definition of Bluntschli; see Bluntschli, *Das moderne Völkerrecht der civilisirten Staten* (n 2) 66.

8 '[L]e droit international ne contient pas de règles explicites définissant de manière positive, à l'instar du droit interne, quelles sont les personnes juridiques'. Cosnard, 'Rapport introductif' (n 4) 13, 14.

9 Crawford, *The Creation of States in International Law* (n 1) 28.

Indeed, it has become rare for contemporary international lawyers to produce treatises specifically focusing on the notion of international subjectivity or personality.[10] Many notable manuals and courses on public international law either treat the topic ephemerally or skip it altogether.[11] This stands in contrast to some of the older continental doctrine which gives the more abstract notions of subjectivity, sovereignty, personality, and capacity a position of prominence, although the question of non-state actors has become quite fashionable in our times.

The terms 'subject' and 'legal person' are generally synonymous in international law.[12] As Portmann explains, they are 'principally employed to distinguish between those social entities relevant to the international legal system and those excluded from it'.[13] For Shaw, the concepts refer to the capacity to possess rights and duties enforceable at law.[14] Similar is the laconic understanding of Maryan Green: 'The subjects of a legal system are those upon whom the law bestows, or in whom it recognizes, a capacity to act ... The personality of a subject of international law is the measure of its capacity to act.'[15] It is uncertain whether, in his understanding, subjectivity and personality are identical, although this seems to be the case; both terms, revolving around the 'capacity to act', correspond to the actual possession of rights and duties under the law.[16] A broader concept is advanced by Dimitrijević, for whom international legal subjectivity means that a certain unit is the bearer of rights and obligations under international law, that it acts in line with the rules of that law, and that it is directly subjected to the international legal order.[17] While many authors focus on possessing rights and obligations at law, others highlight the capacity to exercise those rights: Cosnard argues that the capacity to exercise rights is the most frequently invoked criterion to confirm or deny the legal personality of a particular entity, demonstrating the direct character of legal rights and duties.[18]

[10] A rare general treatise on personality published in recent years is Roland Portmann, *Legal Personality in International Law* (CUP 2010), which was originally developed as the author's doctoral thesis at the University of St Gallen; see also Société française pour le droit international, *Colloque du Mans: Le sujet en droit international* (Pedone 2005).

[11] See eg *Malanczuk, Akehurst's Modern Introduction to International Law* (n 3) 75ff and Shaw (n 2) 155ff, among many others; for a recent work dealing with subjectivity, see Kolb, 'Le droit international comme corps de droit privé' (n 5) 228ff.

[12] See Malanczuk (n 3) 91.

[13] Portmann, *Legal Personality in International Law* (n 10) 1.

[14] Shaw (n 2) 155.

[15] N A Maryan Green, *International Law* (Pitman Publishing 1987) 30.

[16] Even if a theoretical distinction may be made between these two definitions, it would arguably be strained and certainly deprived of any practical relevance.

[17] Vojin Dimitrijević and others, *Osnovi međunarodnog javnog prava* (Belgrade Centre for Human Rights 2007) 70; this comprises legal capacity (enjoyment of rights and fulfilment of obligations that emanate from the principles and rules of international law); business capacity (*poslovna sposobnost* in the original Serbian, which partially corresponds to the French *capacité commerciale* and here refers to the capacity to acquire and dispose of rights and obligations); procedural capacity (the capacity to initiate international proceedings in order to realize the subject's rights); and the capacity to be responsible for violations of international law (*deliktna sposobnost*, most closely corresponding, rather than to accountability, to responsibility for wrongful acts).

[18] Cosnard (n 4) 13, 43.

The necessary elements of subjectivity in international law are therefore not settled. Some scholars are happy to opt for a broad approach, accepting the simple fact of possessing (or even the mere capacity to possess) rights and duties at law as sufficient to create an entity as a subject of law.[19] Others add to this the capacity to bring international claims,[20] a quality the former may only reserve for a specific group of subjects. Some go as far as to require the capacity to create general international law in their definitional approaches.[21] This restrictive approach, which has been disproven by contemporary practice,[22] would limit the subjects of international law to sovereign States.[23] However, were we to scrutinise the matter from a top-down perspective we would see that the great controversies only arise as we sufficiently distance ourselves from our point of departure, which is of course the State itself: if doubts still linger about the nature of personality in general, it is not questionable whether States possess it.

Different concepts of subjectivity or personality all have a descriptive role: they tell us something about the phenomenon that they relate to. In some cases, they may also have a prescriptive or normative function. The latter serves to infer that if entity A is a legal person because of possessing the quality B, then it must also possess quality C.[24] This prescriptive function is not uniformly identified in legal literature: Kelsen notably relegated the personality of an entity to the sum of legal norms 'addressing and constituting it'.[25] Because personality thus understood does not imply *a priori* qualities for entity observed, these may only be ascertained through an *a posteriori* analysis of the subject's circumstances or by interpreting

[19] See Malanczuk (n 3) 155; Crawford (n 1) 28; this also seems to be the approach of Verhoeven, who writes: 'II n'y a cependant aucune difficulté d'ordre logique ou structurel à admettre l'existence dans l'ordre juridique international de sujets de droit distincts des Etats, revêtus de droits et d'obligations spécifiques mesurés aux besoins de la société internationale auxquels ils entendent donner satisfaction.' Verhoeven, *La reconnaissance internationale* (n 5) 170.

[20] See eg James Crawford, *Brownlie's Principles of Public International Law* (OUP 2019) 105–06 and Dimitrijević and others, *Osnovi međunarodnog javnog prava* (n 17) 70.

[21] This is typical of authorship at the time the 'States-only' paradigm was dominant, mainly before the First World War.

[22] In its *Reparation for Injuries* case, the International Cout of Justice (ICJ) confirmed that the United Nations was a legal person in international law as it was 'capable of possessing international rights and duties' and had 'capacity to maintain its rights by bringing international claims'. *Reparation for Injuries Suffered in the Service of the United Nations*, ICJ Reports 174, Advisory Opinion of 11 April 1949 (hereafter *Reparations* case) 179.

[23] As with so many other concepts, this criterion could also potentially be interpreted in different ways, as stringent or as watered down as the scholar desires. While it would usually be interpreted as the capacity to create norms of international law, which would exclude individuals, it could also be read as a capacity to create any law, which could include the domestic level, where individuals and private organisations are recognised as legal subjects. There is no logical reason to exclude this approach *a priori*, but it would essentially equate domestic and international legal personality, rendering discussions of the latter pointless.

[24] This is often the case with authors who try to establish the individual as a subject of international law, who may sometimes infer from the fact that an individual possesses rights under international law thereby also necessarily has the capacity to enforce them as a matter of international law, at a court of law; see eg Lauterpacht (n 2) 136–50.

[25] Portmann (n 10) 184.

the legal norms addressed to it.[26] In other words, is an entity a subject because it possesses rights and duties under international law, or does it possess them because it is a subject? This issue remains of great interest for the theory of international law, although, from a practitioner's perspective, it is of marginal importance.

1.2 The Legal Personality of States in Particular

Portmann distinguishes five conceptions of personality in legal doctrine: the States-only conception, the recognition conception, the individualistic conception, the formal conception, and the actor conception.[27] These conceptions are not always mutually exclusive, and the authors he recognises as belonging to the same vein do not arrive at their common conclusions in a uniform way. Among them, he highlights the first one (States-only) as historic, and the second one (recognition) as its modern offshoot that seemingly 'represents the dominant conception of international personality today'.[28] According to the recognition conception, States are the original and full subjects of international law, but other entities may also be legal persons provided that they are recognised as such by States. This conception does not imply any specific qualities that should be seen as emanating from recognition, unless the entity is recognised as a State, which has concrete legal meaning. According to Portmann, the original manifestation of this manner of thinking in international jurisprudence may be identified in the ICJ's *Reparation for Injuries* advisory opinion,[29] used by many textbooks as a starting point for discussions of subjectivity. The World Court, answering the question of the legal personality of the UN, did so by opposing its subjectivity to that of States:

> Whereas a State possesses the totality of international rights and duties recognized by international law, the rights and duties of an entity such as the [United Nations] Organization must depend upon its purposes and functions as specified or implied in its constituent documents and developed in practice.[30]

The State is therefore a totality of rights and duties,[31] a subject of international law 'with the full capacity to act, or in other words with full international personality',[32]

[26] See eg Hans Kelsen, 'Théorie du droit international public' (1953) 84 RCADI 1, 66ff; this also seems to be implied by the ICJ in the *Reparations* case (n 22) 178.

[27] Portmann (n 10) 29.

[28] ibid 80.

[29] *Reparations* case (n 22).

[30] ibid 180.

[31] 'Seuls les États sont appelés à l'observance de la totalité des règles générales du droit de la paix, sont qualifiés pour exercer les droits et accomplir les devoirs qui en dérivent.' Arrigo Cavaglieri, 'Règles générales du droit de la paix' (1929) 26 RCADI 311, 318.

[32] Green, *International Law* (n 15) 31.

and finds itself at the extreme end of a spectrum. Beneath States on that spectrum there lie the other subjects of international law, those who are neither full nor original but derived, and whose subjectivity is fluid and defined in opposition to that of States.

How this last situation came to be is another matter. Much has been written about the origins and evolution of international law and the reader is advised to look to treatises specific to this subject matter for a more in-depth study.[33] The classical narrative will suffice for this chapter. Like any body of legal norms, international law is created by its law-makers, the first players in the modern legal system—commonly known as Westphalian States[34]—who were in a position to set the rules; these rules then included provisions on who else may join the gaming table. Fenwick refers to 'charter members' of the international community when describing these 'older states which were in existence at the time international law began to take definite shape in the [seventeenth] century' and which are called upon to recognise the existence of new members without having been subjected to recognition themselves.[35] Because they were the ones who established the system, they were able to fashion its elements without having themselves previously been subjected to it, and the system was established in such a manner that the stakeholders' freedom, rather than obligation, had to be presupposed. This is because, since the dawn of international law, the State is sovereign.

Sovereignty, which we shall examine at greater length, is a crucial element of the State as a subject of international law. Sovereignty is not a right of States—it is a key element of their nature, and while the subjectivity of States may (perhaps) not be reduced to their sovereignty, their statehood cannot be understood without it.

Amongst the various subjects of international law, scholarship usually distinguishes between those which are 'original', or 'natural', and those which are 'derived'. According to Robert Kolb, the natural subject of international law possesses, 'as an entity, the totality of international legal positions; the derived subject is only such if it possesses at least one. Between the two situations we see a continuum'.[36] Malanczuk refers to this as 'unlimited' personality, reserved for States, whereas other subjects, including international organisations, only have certain rights and obligations as established by their founding treaty.[37]

[33] See more in Bardo Fassbender and Anne Peters (eds), *The Oxford Handbook of the History of International Law* (OUP 2012) and Ignacio de la Rasilla, *International Law and History* (CUP 2021).

[34] The system established in Europe following the Treaty of Westphalia in 1648 is seen as one of sovereign States possessing the monopoly of violence within their own territory.

[35] Charles G Fenwick, *Cases on International Law* (Callaghan and Company 1935) 51.

[36] 'En un mot: le sujet naturel n'est tel que s'il possède en l'abstrait (i.e. en tant qu'entité) la totalité des positions juridiques internationales; le sujet dérivé n'est tel que s'il en possède au moins une. Entre les deux situations il y a, on le note, un continuum.' Robert Kolb, 'Nouvelle observation sur la détermination de la personnalité juridique internationale' (2002) 57 Zeitschrift für Öffentliches Recht 229–41, 232.

[37] Malanczuk (n 3) 91–92.

States themselves insist on this in official publications. In a short official document entitled *ABC du droit international public*, the Swiss Federal Department of Foreign Affairs adds that the State, as the primary subject, is also the purpose of international law:

> L'État est l'élément juridique principal du droit international. Les États sont les sujets 'primaires' du droit international. Leur capacité juridique leur est propre par essence: ils sont à la fois les créateurs et les destinataires des normes et des obligations de droit international, ils sont libres de conclure des *traités* et peuvent contribuer à l'évolution du *droit international coutumier*.[38]

It is further added:

> Le droit international public au sens classique a été conçu par des États pour des États. Pendant longtemps, seuls les États pouvaient être sujets de droit international. Dans l'optique du droit international public, tout État est considéré comme étant souverain et mis sur un pied d'égalité avec les autres États, qu'il soit grand ou petit, riche ou pauvre.[39]

In this line of reasoning, which is still widely echoed in scholarship,[40] only the State is the principal or full subject of international law; 'secondary' or derived subjects do not possess original personality but draw it from the will of States, the wellspring of legal subjectivity.[41] Thus, the crucial aspect of State personality is their sovereignty.

2. The Concept of Sovereignty in Doctrine

In the vocabulary of international law, few terms are as fundamental, or as widely contested, as sovereignty. This concept, originally developed as an empiric term by scholars struggling to describe the phenomenon of statehood since the sixteenth century, today provokes impassioned debate amongst its proponents and

[38] *ABC du droit international public* (Swiss Federal Department of Foreign Affairs 2009) 21.

[39] ibid 4.

[40] To quote a few examples: 'Some subjects have ... the full measure of legal personality. These are the fully sovereign and independent states.' Green (n 15) 30; 'Staaten sind die Hauptvölkerrechtssubjekte, die sogennanten "geborenen" Völkerrechtsubjekte.' Anne Peters, *Völkerrecht: Allgemeiner Teil* (Schulthess 2006) 24; 'L'État reste le sujet principal du droit international, jouant sur le double registre de la souveraineté interne et de la souveraineté internationale.' Emmanuel Decaux and Olivier de Frouville, *Droit international public* (Dalloz 2018) 185.

[41] Hersch Lauterpacht recalls the earlier notion (the 'traditional view') that 'States [are the] only and exclusive subjects of international law'. Lauterpacht (n 2) 136, 136. This is certainly no longer the case.

opponents, having turned into a politicised golem that has lost much of initial scientific value.

It is difficult to categorise sovereignty in early doctrinal works as either a legal or political term. Certainly, we do not find it in the early vocabulary of international law, which it also pre-dates by a full century. And yet, it is safe to say that modern international law finds its source primarily in the concept of sovereignty as incorporated in the Treaty of Westphalia and exemplified in its historic principles, notably that of *cuius regio eius religio* (while such principles have today become outdated, the underlying notion of sovereignty has not).[42] Nevertheless, the early authors on sovereignty focus on the internal, rather than external aspects of sovereignty: the latter is merely incidental to the explanation of a relationship that first existed between a single ruler and his subjects, and only much later the 'disembodied' State and its citizens. To explain the aspects of sovereignty and its origins was the chief concern of political philosophy in Western Europe for well over two centuries and culminated in the creation of a vast body of philosophical and legal literature.

2.1 Conceptualising Sovereignty in the Works of Bodin, Hobbes, and Grotius

While discussions of sovereignty may be found as early as Plato and Aristotle,[43] the first modern and subject matter-specific treatise on sovereignty was written by the French legal academic Jean Bodin and published in 1576. In his *Six livres de la république*, Bodin tries to define sovereignty by first pinpointing what it is not; and it is not, he finds, the power of a Roman dictator, nor that of an archon of Athens, nor that of a regent governing fully on a king's behalf (*Le lieutenant général et perpétuel d'un Prince avec puissance absolue*); for, he writes, 'la souveraineté n'est limitée, ni en puissance, ni en charge, ni à certain temps'.[44] Only absolute authority (*summa potestas*), with no boundaries other than those dictated by the laws of God, nature (the 'higher legal order' from which it flows)[45] and the law of nations, may be styled sovereign. To illustrate his vision, Bodin recounts a romanticised tale of the election of a new King of Tartary upon the death of his predecessor, whereupon the people implore the king-elect to rule over them without restraint,

[42] See on this topic Derek Croxton, 'The Peace of Westphalia of 1648 and the Origins of Sovereignty' (1999) 21(3) The International History Review 569 and Andreas Osiander, 'Sovereignty, International Relations, and the Westphalian Myth' (2001) 55(2) International Organization 251.

[43] See on this topic W A Dunning, 'The Politics of Aristotle' (1900) 15(2) Political Science Quarterly 273; Glenn R Morrow, 'Plato and the Rule of Law' (1941) 50(2) The Philosophical Review 105; Zbigniew Pańpuch, 'The Foundations of Classical Thought on the Sovereignty of the State' (2014) 3 Studia Gilsoniana 347; and others.

[44] Jean Bodin, *Six livres de la république* (Librairie générale française 1993), Book I, Chapter VIII, 113; the specific examples are discussed on pages 111–18.

[45] James Crawford, 'Chance, Order, Change: The Course of International Law: General Course on Public International Law' (2014) 365 RCADI 9, 76.

and the new sovereign solemnly promises that 'the word of [his] mouth shall be [his] sword' (*La parole de ma bouche sera mon glaive*).[46]

As quaint as Bodin's vision of sovereignty may seem to the modern reader, it is dictated by the strife and troubles of his time, namely the savage wars of religion that had already plagued France for decades and culminated in the slaughter of French Huguenots in the streets of Paris a few years before his work was published.[47] Only a powerful central authority, unbound by the desires of any particular group in the territory it governs, could curb such sectarian violence and ensure lasting peace in the French kingdom.

At least two aspects of Bodin's thought on sovereignty did not stand the test of time or are difficult to reconcile with reality. First, Bodin's sovereign is an individual, the ruler of a State, rather than the State itself; second, his limitless notion of sovereignty implies the sovereign's authority to revoke his legislation as he sees fit (and also that the sovereign is not subject to his own law as *legibus solutus*),[48] which is difficult to reconcile with the rule of law.[49] The first issue was soon dealt with adequately in subsequent works by philosophers such as Hobbes and Rousseau; the second still poses a conundrum to lawyers.[50] But the essential quality Bodin identifies in a sovereign, namely the power to create and revoke the law ([*La*] *puissance de donner et casser la loi*), is the one from which all other qualities emanate,[51] and it is also a key element of statehood.[52]

The basic elements of Bodin's reflections on sovereignty exerted a substantial influence on legal and political thought in the centuries to follow and were refined by later authors. In particular, Thomas Hobbes improved Bodin's work by removing sovereignty from any specific individual to an abstract commonwealth so instituted by its people in a presumed contract:

> A commonwealth is said to be instituted when a multitude of men do agree, and covenant, every one with every one, that to whatsoever man, or assembly of men, shall be given by the major part the right to present the person of them all, that is

[46] Bodin, *Six livres de la république* (n 44) 119.

[47] Besson draws attention to Bodin's preoccupation with an authority that could put an end to the wars of religion, namely 'the Republic'; see Samantha Besson, 'Sovereignty' in Anne Peters and Rüdiger Wolfrum (eds), *Max Planck Enyclopedias of International Law* (OUP 2013) para 15 <https://opil.ouplaw.com/display/10.1093/law:epil/9780199231690/law-9780199231690-e1472?prd=EPIL> last accessed 5 June 2024; cf Andrew Clapham, *Brierly's Law of Nations* (OUP 2012) 7–8.

[48] Besson, 'Sovereignty' (n 47) para 16.

[49] According to Andrew Clapham, Bodin's approach may be reconciled with more recent notions of sovereignty if we link the limits in divine and natural law, but also fundamental laws on the functioning of the State (the *leges imperii*) that he instils upon sovereignty, with modern constitutional laws; see Clapham, *Brierly's Law of Nations* (n 47) 8–9.

[50] See in this regard Crawford, 'Chance, Order, Change' (n 45) 75–84.

[51] 'Sous cette même puissance de donner et casser la loi, sont compris tous les autres droits et marques de souveraineté: de sorte qu'à parler proprement on peut dire qu'il n'y a que cette seule marque de souveraineté, attendu que tous les autres droits sont compris en celui-là ....' Bodin (n 44) 162–63.

[52] ibid 111–12.

> to say, to be their representative; every one, as well he that voted for it as he that voted against it, shall authorize all the actions and judgements of that man, or assembly of men, in the same manner as if they were his own, to the end to live peaceably amongst themselves, and be protected against other men. From this institution of a Commonwealth are derived all the rights and faculties of him, or them, on whom the sovereign power is conferred by the consent of the people assembled.[53]

Like that of Bodin, Hobbes's sovereign, the eponymous Leviathan,[54] is an answer to a pressing social concern, here again exemplified in (religious) civil war: the Puritan-led English republican experiment anointed by the beheading of King Charles I in 1649. Charles had been a devout believer in the divine right of kings, and his execution on charges of high treason for seeking to rule unfettered caused the royalist Hobbes much distress. Yet his secular notion of sovereignty grounded in consent and divorced from the mandate of Providence did not sit well with many of his fellow royalists,[55] and Hobbes (who had fled to Paris years earlier) now had to implore the revolutionary English government for asylum from offended Anglican dissidents and French Catholics.

Hobbes's disposition and anthropological pessimism led him to emphasise the view of sovereignty as a general, and not merely legal, power; the latter is but a facet of the former, the sole means whereby humankind, intrinsically flawed but collectively conscious and desirous of higher virtues, may advance itself. 'Law neither makes the sovereign, nor limits his authority', writes Clapham; 'it is might that makes the sovereign, and the law is merely what he commands'.[56] While Clapham concludes that '[t]his ... is what today we call totalitarianism pure and simple',[57] Hobbes's understanding of sovereignty does not seem very different from what

[53] Thomas Hobbes, *Leviathan: Or, The Matter, Forme, & Power of a Common-wealth Ecclesiasticall and Civill* (McMaster University 1999), Chapter XVIII, 107.

[54] According to Mintz, Hobbes's allegorical invocation of Leviathan—here representing sovereignty—is grounded in a false etymology, commonly presumed in the seventeenth century, of the name of this Biblical beast as referring to a connected or joined serpent (dragon) in the Hebrew language, which, 'by his bignesse... seemes not a single creature' but a great connected multitude; thus, 'Both Leviathan and Hobbes's sovereign are unities compacted out of separate individuals; they are omnipotent; they cannot be destroyed or divided; they inspire fear in men; they do not make pacts with men; theirs is the dominion of power.' Samuel I Mintz, 'Leviathan as a Metaphor' (1989) II Hobbes Studies 3, 5, quoting the Westminster Assembly's *Annotations* on the Bible (1641 and 1652) as reproduced in John M Steadman, 'Leviathan and Renaissance Etymology' (1967) 28 Journal of the History of Ideas 575–76.

[55] Hobbes does not however feel that it is possible for people to change their sovereign without his permission, and considers deposing a sovereign a grave injustice, even if such measures are taken in light of a new Covenant with God, which at any rate cannot be done 'but by mediation of somebody that representeth God's person, which none doth but God's lieutenant who hath the sovereignty under God'; the pretense of such a Covenant is therefore not only an unjust act, but also one of a "vile and unmanly disposition". Hobbes, *Leviathan* (n 53) 107.

[56] Clapham (n 47) 12.

[57] ibid.

Bodin (with whose work Hobbes was likely acquainted)[58] had written decades earlier.[59] At any rate, it seems overly simplistic to reduce his work to a praise of kraterocracy, where might makes right, which is also incompatible with social contract theory. By vesting sovereignty with an earthly rather than divine provenance, Hobbes, far more so than Bodin, lay the foundations for those theorists who, already in the late eighteenth century, began to abandon natural law concepts and to understand law as the product of humankind (positivism).

As both Bodin and Hobbes are reacting to internal strife in their home countries, their analysis understandably focuses on the relationship between the sovereign (whether a monarch or the State) and his subjects: this is called internal sovereignty, authority exercised within a geographically limited area. As there exist in the world many other such sovereign entities, their relationship must be analysed externally, vis-à-vis one another.[60] Both of these writers permit the existence of such multiple sovereigns, whose authority is focused inward: Hobbes sees the sovereign as possessing 'the right of making war and peace with other nations and Commonwealths',[61] all of whom exist separately to conserve peace and justice, 'the end for which all Commonwealths are instituted'.[62] But in Hobbesian terms, the multitude of sovereigns is not a desirable circumstance, and in a better world, there would be a single, all-encompassing authoritarian commonwealth (*civitas*) guaranteeing universal peace.[63] The classical authors of political philosophy have little else to add on the subject of external sovereignty, and neither do their critics in the following decades, such as Locke[64] and Rousseau (although the latter often refers to various States and forms of government, and several times scrutinises the notion of warfare as an inter-state matter).[65]

Separately from the original studies of sovereignty, we find the earliest meditations on the law of nations—today this must appear to us an oddity, as sovereignty and international law have become intrinsically entangled and can no longer be separated from each other. Yet in Hugo Grotius's landmark *De jure belli ac pacis*, of which the first edition was published in 1625, sovereignty receives but a passing

58 According to Mintz, the libraries of Hardwick Hall and Chatsworth contained, amongst other books of commentary, the works of Bodin; as Hobbes was charged with 'ordering and cataloguing these books', he may well have been acquainted with the former's writings, 'but since the presence of a book in a library is no guarantee of its having been read', this cannot be ascertained with certainty; Mintz. 'Leviathan as a Metaphor' (n 54) 6.

59 Besson (n 47) para 19.

60 For an overview of views regarding internal and external sovereignty, see J P A François, 'Règles générales du droit de la paix' (1938) 66 RCADI 1, 63ff.

61 Hobbes (n 53) 111.

62 ibid 112.

63 See Mark W Janis, 'Sovereignty and International Law: Hobbes and Grotius' in Reginald St John Macdonald (ed), *Essays in Honour of Wang Tieya* (Martinus Nijhoff 1993) 391, 393–94.

64 Locke's 1689 *Two Treatises of Government* focus particularly on inalienable rights enjoyed by individuals vis-à-vis their government.

65 See Jean-Jacques Rousseau, *Du contrat social, Ou principes du droit politique* (Athena 2023) esp Book I, Chapter IV.

treatment—unlike Bodin and Hobbes, who were spurred by civil war to focus on the relations of power existing within a country, Grotius focuses outwards, to principles of law governing inter-state relations.[66] In an attempt to wrest these relations from traditional Catholic doctrine and find common grounds for a law that would bind in equal measure the Catholic and Protestant belligerents of the ongoing Thirty Years' War, Grotius 'secularised' law and made the attempt to base his approach in reason, dealing with a diverse range of topics relevant to international relations.[67] In so doing, the Dutch lawyer reflected on the notion of sovereignty, which he described, in the manner of his peers, as a 'supreme power':

> That is called Supreme, whose Acts are not subject to another's Power, so that they cannot be made void by any other human Will. When I say, by any other, I exclude the Sovereign himself, who may change his own Will, as also his Successor, who enjoys the same Right, and consequently, has the same Power, and no other.[68]

For Grotius, the sovereignty of the State is expressed through its ruler, and while it has a separate existence from its mortal embodiment, this author never reaches the fine distinction that would characterise the work of Hobbes a few decades later (in truth, Grotius had no need to draw such a surgical distinction in the first place). But true to his purpose, Grotius subjects the sovereign to the application of the law when he has consented accordingly, because to create laws without being bound by them would create a situation of hypocrisy and injustice alien to the fundamental rules of the law of nations.[69] Thus, Grotius abolished from the law of nations the principle of *princeps legibus solutus est*, previously imported into the domestic law of medieval Europe from Roman law (although the corollary principle of *quod*

[66] Grotius is open about being incited to write his treatise by the atrocities of the Thirty Years' War, which was still ongoing at the time of writing of *De jure belli ac pacis*: 'I observed throughout the Christian World a Licentiousness in regard to War, which even barbarous Nations ought to be ashamed of: a Running to Arms upon very frivolous or rather no Occasions; which being once taken up, there remained no longer any Reverence for Right, either Divine or Human, just as if from that Time Men were authorized and firmly resolved to commit all manner of Crimes without Restraint.' Hugo Grotius, *The Rights of War and Peace, Book I* (Liberty Fund 2005) 106.

[67] On Grotius's lasting influence in the study of international law, see more in Janis, 'Sovereignty and International Law' (n 63) 391–00; Annabel Brett, 'The Subject of Sovereignty: Law, Politics and Moral Reasoning in Hugo Grotius' (2020) 17(3) Modern Intellectual History 619–45; and Martti Koskenniemi, 'Imagining the Rule of Law: Rereading the Grotian "Tradition"' (2019) 30(1) European Journal of International Law 17–52.

[68] Grotius, *The Rights of War and Peace* (n 66) 259.

[69] 'Grotius believed that sovereigns not only made rules, but were obliged to live with the rules once made. The covenants or contracts of sovereigns were legally and morally binding and not just Machiavellian temporary arrangements of mutual convenience. As men and women could bind themselves together in religious communities and to the law of God, so could sovereigns bind themselves to the law of nations.' Janis (n 63) 391–400, 397.

principi placuit, legis habet vigorem still remains fundamental to international law, if in a less tyrannical sense, pertaining to the law's primary consensual basis).[70]

The fact that the notion of sovereignty has remained essentially unaltered in international law since the time of Grotius and Hobbes stands as a testament to the classical writers' continuing relevance beyond the textbooks of international legal history. First, in vesting the sovereign with the power to create law (both domestic and international) through its will (expressed through either domestic law-making or consent to be bound by a norm of international law), they emphasised the State as the sole source of positive law and described, at the same time, how the provisions of said law and facts pertinent to its application may be made opposable to those very States. This relates to the aspect of sovereignty where it is described as supreme power. Secondly, they established a link between sovereignty and independence, which is, as we shall see, the way most of our contemporary scholars understand it.[71]

2.2 Sovereignty in Legal Doctrine Since the Nineteenth Century

Discussions regarding the nature of sovereignty have haunted the most fundamental aspects of international law for the greater part of two centuries and are still ongoing. Legal scholarship differs on almost every element relevant to the concept of sovereignty, depending on various factors: whether sovereignty is regarded as a fact external to international law, or as an inherent legal concept; whether it is construed as authority or independence; whether it is a precondition or a consequence of statehood; whether it flows from State practice or rational principles reflected in State practice but not fully explicable by it; whether it is a descriptive or prescriptive concept (a legal fact or a legal right); whether it is an abstract concept or empirical phenomenon; whether it is practically relevant or deprived of relevance; and so on. The difficulty of grasping a common stratum in this fundamental yet elusive concept is compounded by the differing importance, value, and qualities given to it by scholars coming from different schools of thought—naturalists, positivists, those who are something in between, and those who consider themselves neither

[70] For an overview of these principles and their place in the history of European thought on sovereignty, see Brian Tierney, '"The Prince is Not Bound by the Laws." Accursius and the Origins of the Modern State' (1963) 5(4) Comparative Studies in Society and History 378–400.

[71] We recall here that Grotius, similarly to Bodin, sees only fully independent States as sovereign: 'We then exclude the Nations, who are brought under the Power of another People, as were the Roman Provinces; for those Nations are no longer a State, as we now use the Word, but the less considerable Members of a great State, as Slaves are the Members of a Family.' Grotius (n 66) 259. This seems to be a common view among more recent scholarship, whereas a minority distinguishes between sovereignty and independence, both of which are crucial for legal statehood; see eg Ricardo J Alfaro, 'Rights and Duties of States' (1969) 97 RCADI 91, 95–96; the notion of sovereignty as independence was also famously restated by Max Huber in the *Island of Palmas* award; see *Island of Palmas Case* (1928) 2 RIAA 829, 838.

have all dealt with this issue—and often we find lawyers in the same legal tradition arriving at significantly different conclusions. It is in principle impossible to reject any of these antinomies as unsound (insofar as they are logically consistent), which means that the different theories of sovereignty are epiphenomena: like trains riding on different but parallel tracks, they start from different stations and have different destinations, and pass each other by with no physical contact; and the mere fact that one train does not fit our needs as travellers does not make it untrue. We must therefore conclude that sovereignty is and will remain an *aporia*, fundamentally unknowable if it even possesses a true and not merely phenomenal existence, for we cannot be sure of which premises to choose for our analysis. The abstract notion is therefore outside of the scope of scientific inquiry.

Yet sovereignty is beyond doubt a term employed in positive law, which is open to empirical investigation, and where it is a term laden with meaning. A positive law analysis of sovereignty is perforce inductive. As we will see, jurisprudence and observations of State practice show that, although there is much inconsistency in the application of the term, it is nevertheless possible to identify a core concept of sovereignty, for clearly it is a phenomenon that influences human behaviour in meaningful ways.

As far as recognition is concerned, to recognise statehood is to recognise sovereignty, and to recognise sovereignty is to recognise statehood—always and without exception. Sovereignty forms the object of recognition and thus vests the act with legal meaning: at the same time, it is a shorthand for the bundle of rights and obligations that are accepted by the recognising State after becoming cognisant that the legal and material requisites have been met. In my view, the cognisance and acceptance functions of recognition are evident even here, corresponding to the two main schools of thought on sovereignty: one emphasising sovereignty as independence (linking to the cognitive function of recognition), and the other as authority (highlighting the act's normative role).

Accordingly, we find in the works of Jellinek, Wheaton, Lauterpacht, Jovanović, Brownlie, and Crawford an overwhelming emphasis on sovereignty as authority, whereas Bluntschli, Verdross, Cavaglieri, Kelsen, Fitzmaurice, and Hart emphasise independence.

2.2.1 Sovereignty as Authority

(1) For Georg Jellinek, sovereignty is power (*Gewalt*) above which there is no other, and which is at the same time independent and highest.[72] The latter quality corresponds to internal, and the former to external sovereignty,

[72] Jellinek (n 4) 475.

although neither can exist without the other.[73] To this Jellinek adds the requirement that such power be legally limitless: it cannot even limit itself. However, because sovereignty is a legal term, sovereign power cannot exist without the law, and a State must have some sort of constitution or legal order to exist for it does not stand so far above the legal order as to be able to renounce it ('Der Staat steht nicht derart über dem Rechte, daß er des Rechtes selbst sich entledigen könnte').[74] Earlier, similar views had been expressed by Pradier-Fodéré,[75] Bonfils,[76] and Wheaton.[77]

(2) Hersch Lauterpacht exhibits a complex relationship with the notion of sovereignty[78] that cannot be adequately reproduced in a short passage. In his doctoral thesis, Lauterpacht identifies two notions of sovereignty: first, it is the theory of positive international law because it is the law's basis; and second, the notion of sovereignty as an absolute legal and moral value (*summum genus in politicis*) for which international law is a mere tool of survival, something Lauterpacht rejects.[79] The meaning of State sovereignty, far from universal, can only be decided by reference to positive law in a given moment in human history. He would later note of (territorial) sovereignty that it meant nothing else than a 'bundle of rights and competencies' (*faisceau de droits et de compétences*) that are easily modifiable and divisible and not affecting the essence of the relations governed by international law.[80] Nevertheless, there must exist a superior normative order which does not proceed from State sovereignty and which accounts for at least the most fundamental principles of international law such as that of *pacta sunt servanda.*

(3) The views of Slobodan Jovanović are inspired by Jellinek, and he attributes to sovereignty direct consequences in specific provisions of international law. Sovereignty, a purely formal term, means highest authority within

[73] 'Das erste Merkmal zeigt sich überwiegend nach außen, im Verkehr des souveränen Staates mit anderen Mächten, das zweite nach innen, im Vergleich mit den ihm eingeordneten Persönlichkeiten. Beide Merkmale sind aber untrennbar miteinander vereinigt.' ibid.

[74] ibid 477.

[75] 'La souveraineté est le pouvoir qui appartient à toute nation de déterminer sa manière d'être, de formuler se conditions de droit, de constituer l'État et le gouvernement selon l'idée qu'elle représente ou le but humain qu'elle poursuit.' Pradier-Fodéré (n 4) 159–60.

[76] Henry Bonfils, *Manuel de droit international public* (Arthur Rousseau 1894) 131ff.

[77] 'Sovereignty is the supreme power inherent in a State, by which that State is governed.' Phillipson, *Wheaton's Elements* (n 4) 34.

[78] On this topic, see Martti Koskenniemi, 'Lauterpacht: The Victorian Tradition in International Law' (1997) 2 European Journal of International Law 215; and Roman Kwiecień, 'Sir Hersch Lauterpacht's Idea of State Sovereignty—Is It Still Alive?' (2011) 13 International Community Law Review 23.

[79] Hersch Lauterpacht, *Private Law Analogies in International Law* (The British Library of Political and Economic Science 1926) 40 and 52.

[80] Hersch Lauterpacht, 'Règles générales du droit de la paix' (1937) 62 RCADI 95, 330; Koskenniemi observes: 'In Lauterpacht's mind, this was to be replaced by a comprehensive and professionally administered system of cosmopolitan law and order in the image of the liberal state.' Koskenniemi, 'Lauterpacht' (n 78) 217.

a given territory; it implies (i) the independence of the State's authority within its frontiers from the authority of any other State, and (ii) that this authority stands above all others within its territory.[81] More fundamentally, State sovereignty is nothing else but a name for State will that creates law.

(4) Brownlie and Crawford express common views on sovereignty. For the former, '[t]he sovereignty and equality of states represent the basic constitutional doctrine of the law of nations, which governs a community consisting primarily of states having a uniform legal personality'.[82] As such, they have a number of corollaries in the law, including the possession of an exclusive jurisdiction, a duty of non-intervention, etc.[83] Crawford also does not equate sovereignty and independence, and defines sovereignty by drawing from the *Reparations* case: '[S]overeignty is the term for the "totality of international rights and duties recognized by international law" as residing in an independent territorial unit—the State. It is not itself a right, nor is it a criterion for statehood (sovereignty is an attribute of States, not a precondition).'[84] Accordingly, a State is not a State because it is sovereign, but is sovereign because it is a State, making statehood a sufficient condition of sovereignty.[85] Crawford identifies five elements flowing from sovereignty: first, States have plenary competence to act on the international plane; second, they have exclusive competence in their internal affairs; third, they are not subject to compulsory international (judicial) processes without their consent; fourth, States are formally equal; and fifth, no derogations from these principles will be presumed.[86] Crawford leaves it open whether the international community must be seen, as suggested by Lauterpacht, as the true source of sovereignty, but he does believe that 'sovereignty still requires such a community to exist'.[87] For Brownlie and Crawford, sovereignty is a consequence of statehood, whereas independence is its prerequisite, and it may be examined empirically in terms of the rights and duties it entails in the normative order. We may also add to this line of thinking Brierly and Clapham.[88]

[81] Slobodan Jovanović, *Država, Knjiga prva* (Belgrade 1936) 224–26.

[82] Ian Brownlie, *Principles of Public International Law* (OUP 1998) 289; cf Crawford, *Brownlie's Principles* (n 20) 431.

[83] Brownlie, ibid 289–90.

[84] Crawford (n 1) 31; cf Crawford (n 45) 71–72.

[85] Compare this with Crawford's later reflection: 'Strictly, the term "sovereign State" is a pleonasm—the adjective is redundant. A State is sovereign because it is a State.' Crawford (n 45) 70.

[86] ibid 72–73.

[87] ibid 81.

[88] See eg James-Leslie Brierly, 'Règles générales du droit de la paix' (1936) 58 RCADI 1, 23ff; and Clapham (n 47) 7–15.

2.2.2 Sovereignty as Independence

Even before Jellinek, other lawyers felt it was prudent to stop qualifying sovereignty as absolute power. Some of them broke away with the legacy of the Hobbesian tradition and reconceptualised sovereignty by changing the premises. Sovereignty as authority is vertical: it projects from sovereign to subjects and explains the sovereign's power to create law. As independence, sovereignty is horizontal, emphasising one sovereign's legal freedom from other subjects of international law.

(1) Bluntschli's understanding of sovereignty is essentially Grotian. Sovereignty has a dual existence: it is the independence of a State from a foreign State and the assumption of exclusive jurisdiction within its territory, but it is also a freedom to determine and implement that State's will without foreign hindrance.[89] It is expressed through freedom from other sovereigns, whose multitude thus forms a 'community' of equals. The freedom of individual States is not 'absolute independence or absolute freedom' because States are limited by law.[90] In law, States enjoy full sovereignty, which entails a number of specific rights opposable to other States, namely the right to create their own constitution; to pass their own laws; to govern and administer themselves; to freely name public officials; and to name and authorise representatives abroad.[91] Sovereignty is then essentially a relationship of mutual rights and obligations between sovereign subjects.

(2) Both Verdross and Kelsen ground their approach to sovereignty in the notion of *Völkerrechtsunmittelbarkeit*, namely that independent States are directly subject to international law. Verdross distinguishes between two concepts of sovereignty: according to one, sovereignty means that States are only subject to the rule of law insofar as they accept it ('Les États sont ... des personnes souveraines qui ne sont soumises à l'empire du droit que dans la mesure où ils veulent le reconnaître').[92] The second understanding of State sovereignty distinguishes States from lesser entities and vassal powers by subordinating it to no other domestic law than its own.[93] There is thus no tension between the State's authority and the imposition of the law because sovereignty only means that a State is subjected to no other legal order but

[89] Bluntschli explains that sovereignty manifests itself in a State's independence from any other State and its exclusive territorial jurisdiction as well as the freedom to assert its will as a State without foreign interference: 'Die Souveränetät eines States zeigt sich a) in der Unabhängigkeit desselben von einem fremden State und in der Ablehnung jeder fremden Statshandlung auf seinem Gebiet; b) in der Freiheit desselben, ohne Behinderung fremder Staten seinen eigenen Statswillen selbst zu bestimmen und nach eigenem Ermessen zu äussern und zu bethätigen.' Bluntschli (n 2) 87.

[90] ibid.

[91] ibid 88.

[92] Alfred Verdross, 'Le fondement du droit international' (1927) 16 RCADI 247, 308.

[93] 'Or, dans le domaine international, la proclamation de la souveraineté de l'État ne fait que déclarer que l'État n'est plus soumis à un supérieur dans la pyramide féodale. La souveraineté constitue donc le caractère de toute puissance non vassale.' ibid 311.

international law.[94] Kelsen also espoused the view that international law could not be efficient nor States were superior to international law, which requires some sort of guarantor—this is the 'international community', of which all States are members. Because to say that the international community guarantees international law is to make it superior to individual States, State sovereignty merely signifies freedom from the national law of any other State, but not from international law itself.[95] This does not imply any intrinsic rights or duties of States (such as a right to equality),[96] although a sort of equality—meaning nothing other than the application of the law according to the law ('L'égalité devant la loi signifie application de la loi conformément à la loi')[97]—does emerge within the system. Otherwise, Kelsen rejects the doctrine of fundamental rights of States.[98]

(3) In Cavaglieri's conception of sovereignty, much like in his views on statehood, the 'sovereign State' predates the legal order and is treated by it as a given fact, not created by it (as law exists to regulate the reciprocal relations between such entities).[99] Cavaglieri defines sovereignty by its function: 'La souveraineté place les États dans une situation d'égalité juridique et rend possible, entre eux, ce rapport de coordination, sur la base duquel peut se former un système de règles fondées exclusivement sur le concours de leur volontés.'[100] Cavaglieri rejects rigid notions of sovereignty and finds the concept relevant to the study of law insofar as it signifies the independence of States from any other superior or foreign power.[101] To that end, Cavaglieri subscribes to the general content of rights labelled fundamental

[94] 'Est donc souveraine en ce sens non pas une organisation investie d'un pouvoir absolu, mais celle qui ne reconnaît comme supérieur juridique que le droit international lui-même.' Verdross, 'Règles générales du droit international de la paix' (n 1) 322.

[95] 'Le seul critère valable est que l'État ne soit pas soumis au droit national d'un autre État. Si un État conclut un traité qui en quelque domaine que ce soit le soumet au droit national d'un autre État, il cesse d'être soumis au seul droit international et n'est plus un État au sens de ce droit.' Kelsen, 'Théorie du droit international public' (n 26) 84. For more on Kelsen's views on sovereignty, see W B Stern, 'Kelsen's Theory of International Law' (1936) 30(4) The American Political Science Review 736; Hidemi Suganami, 'Understanding Sovereignty through Kelsen/Schmitt' (2007) 33(3) Review of International Studies 511, 518ff; and Lars Vinx, 'Austin, Kelsen, and the Model of Sovereignty' (2011) 24 Canadian Journal of Law & Jurisprudence 473.

[96] Kelsen (n 26) 104.

[97] ibid 105.

[98] See ibid 107. Kelsen nevertheless holds that international law sets limits to the scope of application of domestic law and accepts the existence of those rights often called 'fundamental' while denying such a characterisation; see ibid 182ff.

[99] Cavaglieri, 'Règles générales du droit de la paix' (n 31) 321.

[100] ibid.

[101] 'Si l'on voit dans celle-ci, tout simplement, l'indépendance de l'État vis-à-vis de toute puissance supérieure ou étrangère, en faisant découler ... le principe qu'il peut librement se lier envers les autres États par le seul concours de sa volonté, par l'exercice indépendant de sa faculté d'autoobligation, on aura toutes raisons de douter de la nécessité ou même de l'opportunité de renoncer à une expression traditionnelle, dont tout le monde comprend le sens et qui est encore très employée dans la pratique des États et dans les documents diplomatiques.' ibid.

for States by natural law scholars, although he regards them in a positivist light, as emanating from the collective will of States.[102]

(4) The position of other lawyers writing in the second half of the twentieth century—especially those coming from the Anglo-Saxon tradition—has usually been to relegate sovereignty to independence, and in principle not to spend too much time deciphering the matter. For example, for Fitzmaurice, State sovereignty means 'equality with and independence of one another—but not of the law'.[103] He also rejects the notion whereby there exists a presumption favouring the legality of State acts as 'unsatisfactory because it would give too free a rein to unrestricted State action'.[104] He therefore argues in favour of understanding sovereignty as giving rise not to rights, but to liberties of States: 'A right, jurisprudentially, is something actually accorded, guaranteed or protected; but also defined and circumscribed, by the law—whereas a liberty is simply a freedom of action arising out of the fact that the matter is unregulated by any positive rule.'[105] States may then be validly accused of abusing their liberties for failing to act in good faith even though no violation may be determined from their conduct if this were examined by a judicial body.

3. State Sovereignty in Positive Law

In broadest terms, sovereignty and statehood are concepts that are more often examined in theory than in practice. However, since 1945, the multiplication of judicial bodies with a mandate over various branches of public international law has led to a Copernican shift in legal culture: what used to be fertile ground for abstract reflections and deductive reasoning is now more open to legal practitioners and inductive methods. To prove the existence of certain norms of international law—particularly customary law—there is today a preference to invoke the jurisprudence of courts and quasi-judicial bodies of recognised authority, rather than to refer to the writings of individual scholars.

The basic judicial explanation of sovereignty in international law was given by the PCIJ in the famous *Lotus* case. In early August 1926, a French vessel, the *Lotus*, collided with a Turkish ship, the *Boz-Kourt*, just off the coast of the Greek island of Mytilene. Although the French crew did their best to save the passengers and

[102] For more on Cavaglieri's approach to international law, see Giulio Bartolini, 'Italian Legal Scholarship of International Law in the Early Decades of the Twentieth Century' in Giulio Bartolini (ed), *A History of International Law in Italy* (OUP 2020) 127, 143ff.

[103] Gerald Fitzmaurice, 'The General Principles of International Law Considered from the Standpoint of the Rule of Law' (1957) 92 RCADI 1, 49.

[104] ibid 52.

[105] ibid 53.

crew of the *Boz-Kourt*, which had split in half and sunk, the accident caused the death of eight Turkish nationals. When the *Lotus* then arrived in Constantinople, one of her lieutenants, who had been officer of the watch the night of the accident, was arrested on charges of manslaughter.[106] Feeling that its own jurisdiction over a vessel flying the French flag had been infringed, France brought the case to the World Court, arguing that a rule of customary law established the flag principle as the only proper basis for jurisdiction in such cases. In addition, Turkey would need to demonstrate the existence of a rule allowing it to extend its criminal laws to a French officer.[107] The Court, which ruled in favour of Turkey, did not agree with France regarding the customary status of the flag principle, and took the opposite stance regarding the nature of State obligations under international law. Far from being required to demonstrate authorisation in international law to act in certain ways, States can do as they please insofar as their conduct is not specifically prohibited by the law:

> International law governs relations between independent States. The rules of law binding upon States therefore emanate from their own free will as expressed in conventions or by usages generally accepted as expressing principles of law and established in order to regulate the relations between these co-existing independent communities or with a view to the achievement of common aims. Restrictions upon the independence of States cannot therefore be presumed.[108]

More specifically:

> In these circumstances, all that can be required of a State is that it should not overstep the limits which international law places upon its jurisdiction; within these limits, its title to exercise jurisdiction rests in its sovereignty.[109]

The bench was equally divided, with President Huber's casting vote giving effect to the judgment as we know it. Judges Loder,[110] Weiss,[111] Findlay,[112] Nyholm,[113] Moore,[114] and Altamira[115] dissented but none of the dissenting opinions disagreed with the majority's view of State jurisdiction and sovereignty. The contentious issue was rather whether the existence of jurisdiction by one State excluded another's

[106] The facts of the case as summarised by the Court may be found in *The Case of the SS 'Lotus'*, Judgment of 7 September 1927, Ser A, No 10, 10ff.
[107] ibid 22ff.
[108] ibid 18.
[109] ibid 19.
[110] ibid 34–39.
[111] ibid 40–49.
[112] ibid 50–58.
[113] ibid 59–64.
[114] ibid 65–94.
[115] ibid 95–107.

(some judges, such as Loder and Moore, had concerns about States retroactively establishing their criminal jurisdiction over individuals who were not subjected to it at the time of the impugned act's commission).

Legal doctrine has largely taken up the above findings of the Permanent Court of International Justice (PCIJ) as textbook restatements of the basis of obligation in international law and an elucidation of State sovereignty.[116] The implications of *Lotus* are best described by Crawford, who interprets the Court's approach to sovereignty as a 'set of (rebuttable) presumptions'.[117] In the words of Shaw, '[t]he starting point for the consideration of the rights and obligations of states within the international legal system remains that international law permits freedom of action for states, unless there is a rule constraining this'.[118] This means that in the event of a legal dispute involving the existence of an alleged obligation, the onus to prove its existence rests with the party invoking it, and not the respondent State.[119] The notion has been formally reaffirmed by the ICJ. In the *Nicaragua* case, the Court rejected US attempts to justify its acts as self-defence considering alleged Nicaraguan militarisation:

> It is irrelevant and inappropriate, in the Court's opinion, to pass upon this allegation of the United States, since in international law there are no rules, other than such rules as may be accepted by the State concerned, by treaty or otherwise, whereby the level of armaments of a sovereign State can be limited, and this principle is valid for all States without exception.[120]

The second aspect of the *Lotus* judgment on sovereignty is its insistence on 'freely expressed will' as a source of State obligations. When a dispute involves a treaty or unilateral declaration, such will is clear and easy to prove. However, the *Lotus* case concerned customary rules, which flow from practice accepted as law. Verdross notices with irony that the majority in *Lotus* omits to ascertain whether France and Turkey had themselves recognised the customary rule being discussed.[121]

[116] See in particular Cavaglieri (n 31) 325ff; Verdross (n 1) 295; and Crawford (n 45) 72–73.

[117] Crawford (n 45) 73. Crawford refers to the *Lotus* judgment as 'controversial'; for Shaw, the controversial aspect refers rather to the relevance of abstention from certain types of behaviour by States in the elucidation of international legal rules; see Shaw (n 2) 60.

[118] Shaw (n 2) 167.

[119] The ICJ's examination of whether the principle of estoppel could be relied upon to establish that the Federal Republic of Germany had accepted to be bound by the rule of equidistance as espoused in the 1958 Geneva Convention on the Law of the Sea is an excellent example of the practical relevance of this notion: see *North Sea Continental Shelf Cases (Federal Republic of Germany/Denmark; Federal Republic of Germany/Netherlands)*, ICJ Reports 3, Judgment of 20 February 1969 (hereafter *North Sea Continental Shelf* cases) paras 31–33.

[120] *Case Concerning Military and Paramilitary Activities In and Against Nicaragua (Nicaragua v United States of America)*, ICJ Reports 14, Judgment of 27 June 1986 (hereafter *Nicaragua* case) para 269; the Court made a similar finding ten years later in its advisory opinion on nuclear weapons, see *Legality of the Threat or Use of Nuclear Weapons*, ICJ Reports 226, Advisory Opinion of 8 July 1996 (hereafter *Nuclear Weapons* case) para 52.

[121] Verdross (n 1) 295.

Later ICJ jurisprudence is ambiguous on this point. In the *Asylum* case, the judges insisted that '[t]he party which relies on a custom ... must prove that this custom is established in such a manner that it has become binding on the other party ... in accordance with a constant and uniform usage *practised by the States in question*' (emphasis added).[122] However, in the *North Sea Continental Shelf* cases, the Court did not highlight the necessity of establishing whether Germany had accepted a customary rule on equidistance if such a rule existed.[123] Recognition of the 'persistent objector' rule in doctrine[124] and the Court's own case law[125] implies an evolution towards less stringent standards for the application of customary law as a reversal of the 'burden of proof' for State consent.[126] These developments mitigate the *Lotus* doctrine but they do not discredit it.

3.1 Sovereignty and Statehood

It is demonstrable that a rule and concept of sovereignty exist in international law. Acts of recognition often refer to sovereignty, with the author typically recognising the recipient as a 'sovereign and independent State'. As discussed in previous chapters, the word 'sovereignty' signifies here two things: (i) the issuer has taken cognisance of the fact that the recipient is a State and that it is independent, and (ii) the issuer has accepted to establish bilateral legal relations with the recipient as a fellow sovereign, namely to respect its rights as a State and expect that its own stately rights be respected in turn. Sovereignty implies independence but cannot be reduced to it. Rather, the term refers to a bundle (*faisceau*) of rules attached to a specific category of legal persons that are now applicable in the relations between the author and recipient of recognition. This includes, beyond the enjoyment of specific rights, participation in the creation of inter-state law on an equal footing.

Sovereignty has a complex and dynamic content that evolves with other legal rules governing international relations at a given point in time. As it pertains to

[122] *Asylum Case (Colombia/Peru)*, ICJ Reports 266, Judgment of 20 November 1950, 276; see also the Court's consideration of State declarations in *Case Concerning the Frontier Dispute (Burkina Faso/Mali)*, ICJ Reports 554, Judgment of 22 December 1986, para 24.

[123] *North Sea Continental Shelf* cases (n 119) paras 61–69; compare this with the Court's findings on customary law and general principles in *The Corfu Channel Case (United Kingdom v Albania)*, ICJ Reports 4, Judgment of 4 April 1949; and the *Nicaragua* case (n 120).

[124] See eg Crawford (n 20) 26; Crawford (n 45) 57; Shaw (n 2) 68; and Decaux and de Frouville (n 40) 58.

[125] See *Fisheries Case (United Kingdom v Norway)*, ICJ Reports 116, Judgment of 18 December 1951, 131.

[126] It is important however to highlight that the *North Sea Continental Shelf* cases discuss universal custom, whereas the *Asylum* case only discusses the existence of a regional rule, where it is more appropriate to ascertain the derogatory participation of States in the region; see in this regard Niels Petersen, 'The International Court of Justice and the Judicial Politics of Identifying Customary International Law' (2017) 28(2) The European Journal of International Law 357–85.

the totality of international law norms pertaining to States as such, it is also synonymous with the legal personality of a State.

3.2 Specific Elements of Sovereignty in Contemporary Law

Because the inherent rights and duties of States constitute their legal personality and fulfil the meaning of sovereignty, they also form the crucial part of the object of recognition of statehood: the recognising State accepts these norms as governing its relations with the new State. As Klüber wrote, '*Staatsheit* oder *Souverainetät* ... ist der Inbegriff aller Rechte, welche einem unabhängigen Staat in Hinsicht auf den Staatszweck zustehen.'[127] This means, above all, that the State has the authority to participate in the creation of international law and act as the original and exclusive legislator in its own territory. There are other specific rights and duties of the State contained in general (customary) international law. The following attempt to create a list is based on the provisions of the Montevideo Convention on the Rights and Duties and States, the International Law Commission's (ILC) Draft Declaration on the Rights and Duties of States, the UN Friendly Relations Declaration, and other relevant sources.

(1) *The Right to Independence.* This is the first right of States listed by the ILC.[128] It is defined as an exercise of lawful powers without the interference of other States. As discussed, independence is linked so closely with sovereignty that some lawyers consider it an inherent attribute of statehood rather than an *a posteriori* right developed in practice.[129] This right does not explicitly appear in the UN Charter, but permeates the entire document and finds its corollary in a number of Charter-based obligations of Member States. According to the Friendly Relations Declaration—an authoritative interpretation of the Charter's principles[130]—the territorial integrity and political independence of States are inviolable.[131] This does not only protect

[127] Johann Ludwig Klüber, *Europäisches Völkerrecht, Erster Band* (J G Cotta'sche Buchhandlung 1821) 45.

[128] 'Draft Declaration on Rights and Duties of States' in *Yearbook of the International Law Commission 1949: Summary Records of the First Session Including the Report of the Commission to the General Assembly* (United Nations 1956) 287–90 (hereafter ILC Draft Declaration) 287, art 1.

[129] Alfaro, 'Rights and Duties of States' (n 71) 95ff.

[130] '[O]n peut constater que la Déclaration est le premier acte formel adopté par l'Assemblée générale ... dans lequel on a procédé à une interprétation détaillée des principes de la Charte en vue de contribuer à leur mise en oeuvre plus efficace dans la pratique actuelle des États.' Milan Šahović, 'Codification des principes du droit international des relations amicales et de la coopération entre les états' (1972) 137 RCADI 242, 252.

[131] *Declaration on Principles of International Law Concerning Friendly Relations and Cooperation Among States in Accordance with the Charter of the United Nations* (24 October 1970) A/RES/2625(XXV) (hereafter Friendly Relations Declaration).

them from armed attack, but also from other forms of unlawful interference.[132] It is uncertain whether this right may be invoked against non-state actors.[133] The Montevideo Convention bestows this right upon States before they are ever recognised.[134] Nevertheless, the practical relevance of this provision for unrecognised States is unclear.

(2) *The Right of Territorial Jurisdiction.* Territorial jurisdiction is an essential element of State sovereignty and therefore at least as old as the maxim *cuius regio eius religio*. The territorial State is free to treat individuals and things in its territory according to its own judgment, and in principle free from regulation by international law unless specific rules emerge to that end.[135] The ILC's Draft Declaration otherwise only limits this right by reference to immunities recognised by international law.[136] The provision recalls somewhat the language of Article 105 of the UN Charter, which obliges Members to respect such privileges and immunities of the Organisation and its representatives as are necessary for the exercise of their functions.[137] Accredited diplomats, foreign heads of State or government or foreign ministers, the officials of the United Nations or other international organizations, and diplomatic and consular missions are all fully or partially excluded from the enforcement jurisdiction of the territorial State.[138] This right has a corollary duty of refraining from interfering in the domestic jurisdiction of other States. What constitutes interference (or even what matters are left to a State's *domaine réservé*)[139] is a matter of some debate,[140] but specific exceptions have taken shape in practice, particularly relating to breaches of human rights.[141]

132 Šahović, 'Codification des principes du droit international (n 130) 289–90.

133 *Accordance with International Law of the Unilateral Declaration of Independence in Respect of Kosovo*, ICJ Reports 403, Advisory Opinion of 22 July 2010, para 80.

134 Montevideo Convention on the Rights and Duties of States, 165 LNTS 19 (adopted 26 December 1933, entered into force 26 December 1934) (hereafter Montevideo Convention) art 3.

135 cf ILC Draft Declaration (n 128) 287, art 6.

136 ibid art 2.

137 Charter of the United Nations, 1 UNTS XVI (adopted 26 June 1945, entered into force 24 October 1945) (hereafter UN Charter) art 105.

138 See more in Xiaodong Yang, *State Immunity in International Law* (CUP 2012); Edward Chukwuemeke Okeke, *Jurisdictional Immunities of States and International Organizations* (OUP 2018); and Tom Ruys, Nicolas Angelet, and Luca Ferro (eds), *The Cambridge Handbook of Immunities and International Law* (CUP 2019).

139 'The general position is that the "reserved domain" is the domain of state activities where the jurisdiction of the state is not bound by international law ....' Ian Brownlie, *Principles of Public International Law* (OUP 1998) 293.

140 See Alfred Verdross, 'The Plea of Domestic jurisdiction before an International Tribunal and a Political Organ of the United Nations' (1968) 28(1) Zeitschrift für Öffentliches Recht und Völkerrecht 33; Charles de Visscher, 'Cours Général de principles de droit international public' (1972) 86 RCADI 445, 494ff; and Antônio Augusto Cançado Trindade, 'The Domestic Jurisdiction of States in the Practice of the United Nations and Regional Organisations' (1976) 25(4) The International and Comparative Law Quarterly 715.

141 For example, the United Nations General Assembly started taking a position on the question of race in South Africa as early as 1946, and continued to deplore apartheid in that country in spite of

(3) *The Right of Sovereign Equality.* Alfaro and several other scholars[142] suggest that equality is inherent to the very notion of sovereignty. The ILC defines sovereign equality as 'equality in law with every other State'.[143] It is now guaranteed by customary law[144] and explicitly by the UN Charter.[145] The principle of *par in parem non habet imperium* can be linked to this right, as equals do not sit in judgment over each other.[146] State practice confirms the basic formula of the Montevideo Convention that States have equal rights, emanating from the simple fact of statehood, and independently of their power in the international arena.[147]

(4) *The Right of Self-Defence.* This right[148] is well-established in the UN Charter[149] and is sometimes incorrectly equated with the right of self-preservation.[150] Narrowly construed, defence against armed attack represents one of the two exceptions to the prohibition on the threat and use of force in international relations.[151] It was most famously formulated with regard to the *Caroline* incident of 1837, which led to a diplomatic crisis between the United States and the United Kingdom.[152] Certain aspects of self-defence have drawn much controversy, such as the question of

South Africa's invocation of art 2(7) of the Charter; see eg Resolutions 44 (I) of 8 December 1946, 395 (V) of 2 December 1950, 1302 (XIII) of 10 December 1958 and 1761 (XVII) of 6 November 1962.

[142] Alfaro (n 71) 96; cf Hans Kelsen, 'The Principle of Sovereign Equality of States as a Basis for International Organization' (1944) 53(2) The Yale Law Journal 207–20 and Crawford (n 1) 32.

[143] ILC Draft Declaration (n 128) 288, art 5.

[144] '[T]he principle of the sovereign equality of States ... is one of the fundamental principles of the international legal order ....' *Questions Relating to the Seizure and Detention of Certain Documents and Data (Timor-Leste v Australia)*, ICJ Reports 147, Order of 3 March 2014, para 27.

[145] UN Charter (n 137) art 2 (1).

[146] This is described in the older case law of the US Supreme Court as '[t]he principle that the conduct of one independent Government cannot be successfully questioned in the courts of another' and that it 'rests at last upon the highest considerations of international comity and expedience'. *Oetjen v Central Leather Company* (1918) 254 US 279, 303. The principle is also linked to independence, namely 'that every sovereign State is bound to respect the independence of every other sovereign State, and the courts of one country will not sit in judgment on the acts of the government of another done within its own territory'. *Underhill v Hernandez* (1897) 168 US 250, 253.

[147] Montevideo Convention (n 134) art 4.

[148] The UN Charter, as well as reiterations of customary law, speak of a 'right' of self-defence; however, as the right of self-defence does not have a meaningful corollary obligation of another subject, it is perhaps more appropriate to regard it as a faculty or possibility than as a right.

[149] UN Charter (n 137) art 51.

[150] Alfaro (n 71) 102ff.

[151] See Josef L Kunz, 'Individual and Collective Self-Defense in Article 51 of the Charter of the United Nations' (1947) 41(4) The American Journal of International Law 872; Shaw (n 2) 861ff; and Tom Ruys, *'Armed Attack' and Article 51 of the UN Charter* (CUP 2010); although a different view, taken by Roberto Ago, rather regards *Caroline* as an instance of necessity, not self-defence; see *Eighth report on State responsibility by Mr Roberto Ago, Special Rapporteur: The internationally wrongful act of the State, source of international responsibility* (29 February, 10 and 19 June 1980) A/CN.4/318/Add.5–7, 39–40.

[152] See Michael Wood, 'The *Caroline* Incident—1837' in Tom Ruys, Olivier Corten, and Alexandra Hofer, *The Use of Force in International Law: A Case-Based Approach* (OUP 2016) 5–16.

when it is triggered[153] and whether it applies to armed attack by non-state actors.[154]

The corollary of rights are legal obligations or duties; these, too, form part of the integral notion of statehood. They include, at least, the following:

(1) *The Duty to Refrain from Intervention in the Internal or External Affairs of Any Other State.* Depending on the context, this duty corresponds to several of the above rights, and correlates to the rights to independence, self-defence, and territorial sovereignty. Described by Brownlie as a 'master principle' of international law,[155] it is contained in both treaties[156] and customary law.[157] Establishing jurisdictional boundaries between States requires their equality as well as limits to their authority where the jurisdiction of others begins. The duty of non-intervention additionally requires States to refrain from interfering with matters deemed to be internal to another State, although '[p]recisely what constitutes the internal affairs of a state is open to dispute and is in any event a constantly changing standard'.[158] It includes not only the direct use of force against a sovereign State but also fomenting rebellion and uprisings in its territory,[159] and has recently been invoked to condemn meddling in elections abroad[160] and interference in the lawful conduct of international relations between other States,[161] among other aspects.[162]
(2) *The Duty to Comply with Human Rights Law.* This modern development in international law originates in the UN Charter[163] and was subsequently

153 See Ruys, '*Armed Attack*' (n 151) 250ff.

154 In its *Wall* advisory opinion, the ICJ determined that art 51 of the UN Charter had no relevance in relation to attack by non-state actors; see *Legal Consequences of the Construction of a Wall in the Occupied Palestinian Territory*, ICJ Reports 136, Advisory Opinion of 9 July 2004, para 138.

155 Brownlie, *Principles of Public International Law* (n 139) 293.

156 UN Charter (n 137) art 2(4) and Montevideo Convention (n 134) art 8.

157 ILC Draft Declaration (n 128) arts 3 and 4; Friendly Relations Declaration (n 131); *Nicaragua* case (n 120) para 176; and *Case Concerning Armed Activities on the Territory of the Congo (New Application: 2002) (Democratic Republic of the Congo v Uganda)*, ICJ Reports 168, Judgment of 19 December 2005 (hereafter *Congo v Uganda* case) paras 162–165.

158 Shaw (n 2) 167.

159 See eg *Congo v Uganda* case (n 157) paras 162–163.

160 See *The Oxford Statement on International Law Protections Against Foreign Electoral Interference Through Digital Means* (2020) available at <https://www.elac.ox.ac.uk/the-oxford-process/the-statements-overview/the-oxford-statement-on-international-law-protections-against-foreign-electoral-interference/> last accessed 5 June 2024.

161 For example, in 2019, the German government described US sanctions against German companies involved in the Nord Stream 2 pipeline project with Russia a form of interference in its internal affairs; see 'Nord Stream 2: Germany and Russia decry US sanctions' (*BBC*, 21 December 2019) available at <https://www.bbc.com/news/world-europe-50879435> last accessed 5 June 2024.

162 See in general on this topic in Maziar Jamnejad and Michael Wood, 'The Principle of Non-intervention' (2009) 22(2) Leiden Journal of International Law 345 and Niki Aloupi, 'The Right to Non-intervention and Non-Interference' (2015) 4(3) Cambridge Journal of International and Comparative Law 566.

163 UN Charter (n 137) arts 1(3), 55, and 56.

developed in a series of declarations. There now exist general and subject-matter-specific human rights treaties within the UN framework[164] and beyond it.[165] At least the core of human rights protection, such as the prohibition of arbitrary deprivation of life or torture, is of a *jus cogens* nature.[166] There is a growing body of doctrine concerning the human rights obligations of non-state actors[167] and it seems accepted that unrecognised States are also bound to respect International Human Rights Law.[168]

(3) *The Duty Not to Endanger International Peace and Order.* This duty, restated in the ILC's Draft Declaration,[169] is closely related to the duty of peaceful settlement of international disputes, but its full contents are not quite clear. UN members join an organisation whose purpose is to 'maintain international peace and security' and are required to participate in 'effective collective measures for the prevention and removal of threats to the peace, and for the suppression of acts of aggression or other breaches of the peace, and to bring about by peaceful means, and in conformity with the principles of justice and international law, adjustment or settlement of international disputes or situations which might lead to a breach of the peace'.[170] Before the UN Charter, the Montevideo Convention had proclaimed the conservation of peace as the primary interest of States.[171] This duty entails specific positive obligations for the State 'to ensure that conditions prevailing in its territory do not menace international peace and order'.[172] An additional positive facet of this obligation may involve the State's role in ensuring the implementation of and respect for international law and the obligation to take lawful action to curb ongoing violations.[173] It is more controversial what

[164] *Universal Declaration of Human Rights* (10 December 1948) A/RES/217(III); for a list of core UN human rights treaties and their monitoring bodies, see OHCHR website at <https://www.ohchr.org/en/professionalinterest/pages/coreinstruments.aspx> last accessed 5 June 2024.

[165] For an overview of the regional treaty systems, see Daniel Moeckli, Sangeeta Shah, and Sandesh Sivakumaran (eds), *International Human Rights Law* (OUP 2018) 411–81.

[166] See Theodor Meron, *Human Rights and Humanitarian Norms as Customary Law* (OUP 1989) and Pavle Kilibarda and Robert Kolb, 'The International Court of Justice, International Humanitarian Law and Human Rights' in Robert Kolb, Gloria Gaggioli, and Pavle Kilibarda, *Research Handbook on Human Rights and Humanitarian Law* (Edward Elgar 2022) 168–87.

[167] See Andrew Clapham, *Human Rights Obligations of Non-State Actors* (OUP 2006) and Katharine Fortin, *The Accountability of Armed Groups Under Human Rights Law* (OUP 2017).

[168] See Hans-Joachim Heintze, 'Are De Facto Regimes Bound by Human Rights?' (2010) 15 OSCE Yearbook 2009 267 and Anthony Cullen and Steven Wheatley, 'The Human Rights of Individuals in *De Facto* Regimes under the European Convention on Human Rights' (2013) 13(4) Human Rights Law Review 691.

[169] ILC Draft Declaration (n 128) 288, art 7.

[170] UN Charter (n 137) art 1 (1).

[171] Montevideo Convention (n 134) art 10; the provision recalls the obligation of peaceful settlement of disputes.

[172] ILC Draft Declaration (n 128) 288, art 7.

[173] See *Legal Consequences for States of the Continued Presence of South Africa in Namibia (South West Africa) Notwithstanding Security Council Resolution 276 (1970)*, ICJ Reports 16, Advisory Opinion of 21 June 1971, para 117.

acts, beyond the threat and use of force in violation of international law, could amount to 'endangering' international peace and security.

(4) *The Duty of Peaceful Settlement of International Disputes.* This obligation is undoubtedly of a customary nature[174] and has been reiterated by the ICJ several times in its jurisprudence.[175] Although 'there is no obligation in general international law to *settle* disputes',[176] the parties to a dispute must seek a peaceful settlement,[177] particularly if the dispute may endanger international peace and security. The UN Charter proposes several routes for peaceful dispute settlement.[178] Apart from specific clauses in treaties, international law does not dictate the mechanisms to be chosen.

(5) *The Duty to Refrain from the Threat or Use of Force in International Relations.* Limitations on the right to resort to the use of force in international relations were placed on States already by the League of Nations Covenant,[179] and many States renounced war altogether in the 1928 Pact of Paris.[180] The UN Charter prohibits threat or use of force between States with very few exceptions.[181] The customary law status of this norm is well established[182] and the prohibition of wars of aggression has been recognised as a *jus cogens* and *erga omnes* rule.[183] Many studies have been conducted into the relevant legal regime, and it is not necessary to discuss it here any further.[184]

(6) *The Duty to Carry Out International Legal Obligations in Good Faith.* Much has been written[185] on the principle of good faith, which is sometimes said to be inferable from State practice rather than present within it.[186] The principle of good faith is a cornerstone of international law and codified in the

[174] ILC Draft Declaration (n 128) 288, art 8; Friendly Relations Declaration (n 131).

[175] See eg *Nicaragua* case (n 120) para 290; *Nuclear Weapons* case (n 120) para 103 *a fortiori*; *Case Concerning the Aerial Incident of 10 August 1999 (Pakistan v India)*, ICJ Reports 12, Judgment of 21 June 2000 (hereafter *Pakistan v India* case) para 53.

[176] Brownlie (n 139) 703.

[177] 'The Court's lack of jurisdiction does not relieve States of their obligation to settle their disputes by peaceful means.' *Pakistan v India* case (n 175) para 53.

[178] UN Charter (n 137) art 33.

[179] League of Nations Covenant, 225 CTS 195 (adopted 28 June 1919, entered into force 10 January 1920) art 12.

[180] See General Treaty for Renunciation of War as an Instrument of National Policy, 94 LNTS 57 (signed 27 August 1928, entered into force 25 July 1929).

[181] UN Charter (n 137) arts 2(4), 42, and 51.

[182] See ILC Draft Declaration (n 128) 288, art 9; Friendly Relations Declaration (n 131); and *Nicaragua* case (n 120) para 290.

[183] See *Report of the International Law Commission* (2019) A/74/10, 146–47 and *Case Concerning the Barcelona Traction, Light and Power Company, Limited (New Application: 1962) (Belgium v Spain) (Second Phase)*, ICJ Reports 3, Judgment of 5 February 1970, para 34.

[184] See Robert Kolb, *International Law on the Maintenance of Peace: Jus Contra Bellum* (Edward Elgar 2018) 504ff.

[185] See Robert Kolb, *Good Faith in International Law* (Hart Publishing 2017) 265ff.

[186] Crawford (n 20) 34.

Vienna Convention on the Law of Treaties[187] both as an aspect of *pacta sunt servanda* and as a rule of treaty interpretation. It has been invoked many times by the ICJ as a general principle relevant to all international legal provisions regardless of their source.[188] As such, the prohibition of acting *mala fide* binds all States. The obligation to act in good faith is an essential feature of statehood and binds States from the moment of their creation.

All the above rights and duties form the core legal personality of States. In my view, they are all today subsumed in the word 'sovereignty': to recognise a State as sovereign is to accept that it enjoys these rights and to expect that it will fulfil the related obligations. In proclaiming statehood, an entity is implicitly committing itself to this framework. The State may not be, as the ICJ suggested, a 'totality' of rights and duties under international law[189] (for what could this even mean?); but it is certainly a particularity, a package of rules necessarily contained in the shorthand term 'statehood'.

4. Conclusion

The legal personality or subjectivity of States cannot be separated from the legal notion of statehood. Unlike material statehood, statehood in the legal sense describes the rights to which an entity considered a State under international law is entitled and the duties to which it may be held. In legal terms, this is the most relevant understanding of statehood: material statehood is of concern only insofar as it may lead to legal statehood.

The key element of legal statehood is sovereignty, an attribute possessed by States but not by other subjects of international law. There exist different concepts of sovereignty and in international law it may be used to describe different facets of statehood, such as the capacity create general international law. In the context of recognition, sovereignty should not be seen as a simple but a complex quality, a 'bundle' of rights and duties incumbent upon an entity vested with statehood. Thus, to recognise an entity as sovereign is to recognise it as a State and vice versa.

[187] Vienna Convention on the Law of Treaties, 1155 UNTS 331 (adopted 23 May 1969, entered into force 27 January 1980) arts 26 and 31 in particular.

[188] For example, 'One of the basic principles governing the creation and performance of legal obligations, whatever their source, is the principle of good faith. Trust and confidence are inherent in international co-operation, in particular in an age when this co-operation in many fields is becoming increasingly essential.' *Nuclear Tests Case (Australia v France)*, ICJ Reports 253, Judgment of 20 December 1974, para 46; cf *Lake Lanoux Arbitration (France v Spain)* (1957) 12 RIAA 281, 15–16; and other sources.

[189] 'Whereas a State possesses the totality of international rights and duties recognized by international law, the rights and duties of an entity such as the [United Nations] Organization must depend upon its purposes and functions as specified or implied in its constituent documents and developed in practice.' *Reparations* case (n 22) 180.

The bundle of rights and duties constituting sovereignty is a minimum common denominator for the legal status of all States. At present, general international law guarantees the rights to independence, territorial jurisdiction, sovereign equality, and self-defence, and imposes the duties of non-intervention, respect for human rights, preservation of international peace and order, the peaceful settlement of international disputes, non-use of force and acting in good faith, as the core elements of this bundle.

7
Recognition in Treaties, Jurisprudence, and Practice

1. The Problem of Practice

There exists abundant State practice regarding recognition. The twentieth century saw, in close succession, the dissolution of Europe's great multinational empires, several waves of decolonisation, and the disintegration of large socialist federations at the end of the Cold War. Every stage saw the creation of one or more new States, requiring other States to react by accepting or condemning them, and the increased frequency with which governments had to mull over questions of recognition and statehood naturally brought about more jurisprudence in various jurisdictions.

Yet all the practice brings us no closer to properly understanding recognition. As a rule, practice is opaque and incoherent, and views do not merely differ at the international level, but domestically as well. For example, the Swiss Federal Tribunal first described recognition of States as merely political in one case, then gave it preponderant weight in another. The same inconsistencies may be remarked in the United States, the United Kingdom, and elsewhere.

Nevertheless, even if practice is blurry and inconsistent, this too should tell us something about the phenomenon of recognition. The very different positions taken by domestic and international bodies that I will examine in this chapter point to the conclusion that international law simply does not contain a rule governing the effects of recognition in all cases. This inference is quite reasonable bearing in mind the way the legal regulation of recognition might infringe on the fundamental, jealously guarded particular interests of all States.

I turn now to the few treaties containing provisions on recognition and to the colourful practice of courts, pseudo-judicial mechanisms, and some expert bodies on recognition of States.

2. Recognition in Treaty Law

The only treaty to deal with recognition in general is the Convention on the Rights and Duties of States adopted at the Seventh International Conference of American

Recognition of States in International Law. Pavle Kilibarda, Oxford University Press. © Pavle Kilibarda 2024.
DOI: 10.1093/oso/9780198905653.003.0007

States in Montevideo in 1933.[1] The relevant provisions would be reproduced verbatim in the 1948 OAS Charter,[2] but it is the 1933 treaty that is most often referred to regarding statehood and recognition.

The 'Montevideo formula' seemingly adopts the declaratist approach.[3] Statehood is separated from recognition, whose purpose is described as follows:

> The political existence of the state is independent of recognition by the other states. Even before recognition the state has the right to defend its integrity and independence, to provide for its conservation and prosperity, and consequently to organize itself as it sees fit, to legislate upon its interests, administer its services, and to define the jurisdiction and competence of its courts. The exercise of these rights has no other limitation than the exercise of the rights of other states according to international law...
>
> The recognition of a state merely signifies that the state which recognizes it accepts the personality of the other with all the rights and duties determined by international law. Recognition is unconditional and irrevocable.[4]

For lack of a better source in treaty law, the Montevideo Convention is commonly cited as the most relevant document in respect of recognition of statehood. There are several reasons why this idea should be taken with a grain of salt.

First, the Montevideo Convention has merely sixteen States Parties, all of which are located in the Americas.[5] The adoption of and adherence to a treaty by a dozen-and-a-half States is not necessarily indicative of the opinion or practice of the broader international community. It may of course be considered as a regional approach to the matter of recognition, whereby the participating States subscribe to a more detailed normative framework than the one provided under general public international law (just as States could individually opt for a different framework, as long as this does not violate international law). There is no doubt that some provisions of the OAS treaties reflect customary law but this cannot be said of the agreements as a whole; Besson recalls that 'unlike countless international law textbooks and certain international law scholars, [international courts] have only rarely referred to the Montevideo Convention as evidence of the customary nature of the

[1] Montevideo Convention on the Rights and Duties of States, 165 LNTS 19 (adopted 26 December 1933, entered into force 26 December 1934) art 3.

[2] Charter of the Organization of American States, 119 UNTS 3 (adopted 30 April 1948, entered into force 13 December 1951) art 13.

[3] See Hersch Lauterpacht, *Recognition in International Law* (CUP 2013) 41, fn 2; *Sixth report on unilateral acts of States, by Mr Victor Rodríguez Cedeño*, Special Rapporteur (30 May 2003) A/CN.4/534, paras 84–87; and others.

[4] Montevideo Convention (n 1) arts 3 and 6.

[5] These are Brazil, Chile, Colombia, Costa Rica, Cuba, the Dominican Republic, Ecuador, El Salvador, Guatemala, Haiti, Honduras, Mexico, Nicaragua, Panama, the United States, and Venezuela. However, as the same provisions are reproduced in the OAS Charter, to which all American States are parties, it may be said that the 'Montevideo formula' has been accepted by all of them.

international law of statehood'.[6] A much more significant problem than the relevant provisions' customary status plagues the OAS documents, leading me to my second point.

Namely, the wording of Article 6 of the Montevideo Convention, and Article 14 of the OAS Charter, is very ambiguous regarding the legal effects of recognition. That recognition '*merely* signifies that the state which recognizes it accepts the personality of the other with all the rights and duties determined by international law' (emphasis added) seems to flow from a conscious effort to diminish the effects of this act, specifically by denying its power to create its own object or confer upon its legal personality—but it says nothing of said object's opposability to the author of recognition. A significant number of scholars—perhaps the majority—take these provisions to foresee the 'pure' declaratory approach, namely, that opposability does not require acceptance.[7] But Dugard correctly highlights a different perspective: while States typically follow the Montevideo criteria in their recognition policy, '[w]hether they do so because they believe that the entity in question is already a State on the ground that it meets the conditions of the Montevideo Convention or because they wish to confer international legal personality on an entity that they consider in their judgment meets these conditions is seldom clear'.[8]

Unfortunately, the treaties' *travaux préparatoires*[9] do not shed any light on the interpretation to be given to these provisions, which is reflected in the US criticism (as expressed in its reservation to the 1933 Convention) that 'it is unfortunate that during the brief period of this Conference there is apparently not time within which to prepare interpretations and definitions of these fundamental terms ... Such definitions and interpretations would enable every government to proceed in a uniform way without any difference of opinion or of interpretations'.[10]

[6] Samantha Besson, 'International Courts and the Jurisprudence of Statehood' (2019) 10(1) Transnational Legal Theory 30–64, 39. Besson refers additionally, but erroneously to the ICJ's *Asylum* case as proof that the Montevideo Convention is not customary. In the *Asylum* case, the Court is actually discussing the 1933 Montevideo Convention on Political Asylum. Other authors have also expressed doubts about the customary status of Montevideo, see eg Thomas D Grant, 'Defining Statehood: The Montevideo Convention and its Discontents' (1998–1999) 37(2) Columbia Journal of Transnational Law 403 and Jure Vidmar, 'The Importance of Legal Criteria for Statehood: A Rejoinder to Dapo Akande' (2013) *EJIL:Talk!* <https://www.ejiltalk.org/the-importance-of-legal-criteria-for-statehood-a-rejoinder-to-dapo-akande/> last accessed 13 June 2024.

[7] See eg Josef L Kunz, 'Critical Remarks on Lauterpacht's "Recognition in International Law"' (1950) 44(4) The American Journal of international Law 713–719; Rodríguez Cedeño, *Sixth report on unilateral acts of States* (n 3) paras 86–87 (discussing the provisions of the OAS Charter which are identical to the relevant articles of the Montevideo Convention) and Stefan Talmon, 'The Constitutive Versus the Declaratory Theory of Recognition: *Tertium Non Datur*?' (2004) 75(1) British Yearbook of International Law 101, 106.

[8] John Dugard, 'The Secession of States and Their Recognition in the Wake of Kosovo' (2013) 357 RCADI 9, 56.

[9] See *Seventh International Conference of American States: First, Second and Eighth Committees: Organization of Peace, Problems of International Law, International Conferences of American States: Minutes and Antecedents* (OAS 1933) Report of the Second Subcommittee.

[10] The United States' reservation was expressed at the time of its ratification of the treaty on 29 June 1934.

The crux of the matter is that the Montevideo Convention is neither truly useful as a regional instrument on statehood nor can it attest to a uniformity of State practice on recognition. Indeed, although the question of recognition was not directly discussed in the International Court of Justice's (ICJ) 2010 advisory opinion on the unilateral declaration of independence of Kosovo, several American States (parties to either the OAS Charter or both to the Charter and the 1933 Convention) expressed views that seemingly contravene the declaratory theory, should this really be the approach of the OAS documents. Argentina,[11] Bolivia,[12] Brazil,[13] and Venezuela[14] all stated that the unilateral declaration of independence on behalf of Kosovo or the recognition thereof violated international law, either by infringing upon the territorial integrity of Serbia, or, more narrowly, Security Council Resolution 1244 (1999).[15] Bearing in mind that none of these States raised the argument that Kosovo did not, at the time, meet the criteria of statehood under the Montevideo Convention, whether or not these were met does not seem to have been at all relevant to their position (it is safe to assume that, had it been otherwise, these States would have at least have tried to refute such a claim). They rather insist on the illegality of the declaration and/or recognition, meaning that either (i) the Montevideo criteria are not exhaustive, and there exists an additional or overarching criterion of legality in addition to the material criteria; or (ii) that opposability does not stem from effective statehood, at least not under all circumstances. Both options cast a long shadow on the Montevideo formula's place of honour amongst the sources listed in favour of the declaratory approach.[16]

Accordingly, I find that, as regards the effects of recognition, the OAS documents are less then helpful, and far from constituting proof of general practice accepted as law, they are too vague to even guarantee uniform practice among their States Parties.

3. Jurisprudence and Other Relevant Practice

Contemporary doctrine rarely analyses diplomatic recognition in the centuries and decades preceding the American Revolution and the US Declaration of Independence at the end of the eighteenth century. Recognition in some form

[11] See *Accordance with International Law of the Unilateral Declaration of Independence in Respect of Kosovo*, Written Comments of the Argentine Republic of 17 July 2009, in particular para 63 ('Recognition cannot cure the illegality of the [Unilateral Declaration of Independence]').

[12] Written Submission of Bolivia of 17 April 2009.

[13] Written Submission of the Federative Republic of Brazil of 17 April 2009.

[14] Position of the Bolivarian Republic of Venezuela with Respect to the Unilateral Declaration of Independence of the Serbian Province of Kosovo: Violation of International Law of 17 April 2009.

[15] This was the view of Brazil.

[16] It could be argued, as does Vidmar, that recognition is in general declaratory but constitutive in cases of secession against the wishes of the Parent State; if so, the Montevideo criteria would be of limited value indeed.

long predates the Peace of Westphalia: thus, in 1609, the Spanish King recognised the independence of the Dutch United Provinces after many decades of conflict. It is difficult to analyse the legal effects of recognition given at a time when international law itself was merely nascent. Recognition was certainly the sovereign's prerogative, placing the decision to recognise within the domain of executive authority. Courts would not actually become involved with the matter until the early nineteenth century. Since then, recognition has been as much a matter of law as of judicial policy. It is arguably the latter factor that has had the greatest influence on judges' understanding of recognition: early deference to the executive resulted in overwhelmingly constitutivist views, whereas declaratism gained popularity as domestic courts started analysing recognition with greater autonomy from their governments.

3.1 The Domestic Origins of Jurisprudence on Recognition

Predictably, the earliest case law on recognition comes from national jurisdictions. The increasing complexity of international relations and commerce arising after the Industrial Revolution, the great upheavals of the Napoleonic Wars, and the successful struggle for independence of colonies in North and South America meant that judges would inevitably be asked whether a given foreign entity could be considered a State. Later, judicial practice was reinvigorated by the attempted secession of the Confederacy during the American Civil War, allowing the US Supreme Court to pass judgments on statehood and recognition that greatly influenced subsequent practice in other parts of the world.

At first, domestic courts regarded recognition as an executive matter, deferring to the government on the status of foreign territorial entities. In the United Kingdom, this is still referred to as the 'one voice' doctrine.[17] The first cases were brought during the Napoleonic Wars and involved the status of Switzerland, which had been transformed into the Helvetic Republic following the French invasion of 1798. The move was not recognised by the British government, and in 1804 the High Court of Chancery under Lord Eldon denied legal standing to the City of Bern for claims against the Bank of England and the South Sea Company.[18]

The question of Swiss investments prior to 1798 would be revisited the following year when the Swiss cantons again demanded the dividends they were owed. This

[17] *The Maduro Board of the Central Bank of Venezuela (Appellant) v The Guaidó Board of the Central Bank of Venezuela (Respondent)* (2020) EWCA Civ 1249, paras 93–94.

[18] 'The *Lord Chancellor* would not make the Order; observing, that he was much struck with the objection; and it was extremely difficult to say, a judicial Court can take notice of a Government, never authorized by the Government of the Country, in which that Court sits; and, whether the Foreign Government is recognized, or not, is a matter of public notoriety.' *The City of Berne in Switzerland v The Bank of England* (1804) 9 Ves 347.

time, their representatives claimed to be the same State as had existed before the Republic, which the debtors disputed. Lord Eldon admitted that a new State could arise from a revolution, but if it did, he was unsure whether, 'if a new state was to arise in *Europe*, a Court of Justice is to take notice of it'.[19] The defendants were tasked with demonstrating that the Helvetic Republic was indeed a new State, recognised by Britain. The Attorney General got involved in 1806, maintaining that the cantons had ceased to exist, wherefore the dividends were now the property of the King of England that could be paid—should the King be so inclined—to a future Swiss government (this was reportedly done).[20] Again, the judiciary relied on recognition, or lack thereof, by the government to determine whether Switzerland was a State.

This trend continued throughout the nineteenth century. In *Taylor v Barclay*, the Court of Chancery dismissed a case regarding the sale of obligations issued by the Federal Republic of Central America on account that the insurgent Spanish colony could not be considered an independent and sovereign State for lack of recognition by the British government.[21] '[T]he Courts of the King', it was said, 'should act in unison with the Government of the King.'[22] In the unusual case of *Mighell v Sultan of Johore*, the Court of Appeal unanimously confirmed that the Sultan was a head of State with sovereign immunity by virtue of British recognition, and thus could not be the object of a complaint before British courts by a certain Miss Mighell, to whom he had falsely promised marriage while covertly travelling through British territory.[23] In *Foster v Globe Venture Syndicate*, regarding the question of whether the Suss tribes were independent of Morocco, Judge Farwell explicitly deferred this matter to the government, stating that it was not up to the courts to make such a determination.[24]

This judicial policy persisted until the end of the First World War. In *The Gagara*, a Court of Appeal case concerning the capture as a prize of a Russian vessel by Estonians at a time Estonia had not yet been recognised *de jure* by the United Kingdom,[25] the Court was required to determine whether the Estonian government could invoke sovereign immunity before the British courts.[26] The

[19] *Dolder v Lord Huntingfield, St Didier v Lord Huntingfield* (1805) 11 Ves Jun 283, 295. Emphasis in the original.

[20] Geoffrey Marston, 'The Personality of the Foreign State in English Law' (1997) 56(2) The Cambridge Law Journal 374, 383.

[21] *Taylor v Barclay* (1828) 2 Sim 213; cf 1; *Yrisarri v Clement* (1825) 2 Carr & Payne 223 and *The Charkieh* (1873) LR 4 Adm & Eccl 59.

[22] *Taylor v Barclay* (n 21) 221. In a case involving contracts with unrecognised Peru, Lord Eldon asked, 'What right have I, as the King's Judge, to interfere upon the subject of a contract with a country which he does not recognize?' *Jones v Garcia del Rio* (1823) Turn & Russ 297, 299.

[23] *Mighell v Sultan of Johore* (1894) 1 QB 149; cf *The Charkieh* (n 21) *a contrario*.

[24] *Foster v Globe Venture Syndicate* (1901) 1 Ch 811.

[25] Estonia had proclaimed independence in early 1918 and soon became embroiled in a war against Soviet Russia which lasted until the Tartu Peace Treaty of 1920, when Russia recognised Estonia's independence *de jure*.

[26] *The Gagara* (1919) Probate 95.

plaintiffs demanded that the ship, moored in British waters, be returned to them, because the Estonian government could not avail itself of State immunity in British courts. Clarification was sought from the Foreign Office, which clarified that the Estonian government had received *de facto* recognition.[27] The Court of Appeal inferred that the Foreign Office's statements 'recognize, and recognize to the full, the sovereignty of Esthonia'[28] and that it could not exercise jurisdiction over the acts of Estonia, a foreign sovereign. That same year, the seizure of Estonian vessels by the Provisional Government of Northern Russia was raised in *The Annette* case.[29] The Admiralty Division was satisfied that the United Kingdom had neither formally nor 'informally' recognised the Provisional Government as an independent State and the motion for sovereign immunity was dismissed. The judicial logic was therefore one of deference, putting recognition at the heart of discussions of statehood.

The US Supreme Court adopted the same reasoning. Before the Civil War, the Court had taken a simplified view of recognition, making little distinction between recognition of statehood, governments, and belligerency. Recognition by the US government was always given preponderant weight, followed by specific provisions of domestic law. The approach was formulated in *Rose v Himeley*[30] and further developed in *Gelston v Hoyt* when the Court found that '[n]o doctrine is better established than that it belongs exclusively to governments to recognize new states in the revolutions which may occur in the world, and until such recognition either by our own government or the government to which the new state belonged, courts of justice are bound to consider the ancient state of things as remaining unaltered'.[31]

In 1852, in *Kennett v Chambers*,[32] the Supreme Court was asked to decide the validity of a private contract concluded under Texan law in September 1836, several months after that State had declared independence from Mexico. At the time, the United States had not yet recognised the independence of the Republic of Texas, despite President Jackson's understanding that 'the civil authority of Mexico [had] been expelled, its invading army defeated, the chief of the republic himself captured, and all present power to control the newly organized Government of Texas annihilated within its confines'.[33] Because the US government had still regarded Texas as part of Mexico, any contract created under the laws of the Republic of Texas were to be regarded as 'illegal and absolutely void' at the time they were

[27] ibid 97.

[28] ibid 103.

[29] *The Annette; The Dora* (1919) P 105, 35 T L R 288.

[30] *Rose v Himeley* (1808) 8 US 241.

[31] *Gelston v Hoyt* (1818) 16 US 246, 324; cf *The Santissima Trinidad* (1822) 20 US 283, 337; *The Brig Amy Warwick; The Schooner Crenshaw; The Barque Hiawatha; The Schooner Brilliante* (1863) 67 US 635; and *The Three Friends* (1897) 166 US 1, 56–57.

[32] *Kennett v Chambers* (1852) 55 US 38.

[33] ibid 48.

created.[34] Not even the subsequent recognition of the independence of Texas and its admission into the Union swayed the Court's approach in this regard, although it would eventually give recognition a retroactive effect.[35]

The Supreme Court refined its approach after the Civil War. In *Williams v Bruffy*, the defendant from Virginia argued that his debt to the plaintiff, loyal to the Union, was annulled by the government of the Confederate States of America as being towards an 'enemy national'. He claimed that that the Confederate States had been an independent nation: '[The Confederate government] was a government *de facto*, complete in all its parts, exercising jurisdiction over a well-defined territory, which included that portion of Virginia where the deceased resided, and as such ... possessed, and was justified in exercising within its territorial limits, all the rights of war which belonged to an independent nation ....'[36] The Court rejected these arguments, finding that a secessionist entity could only be considered an independent nation if it had achieved permanence *and* recognition.[37] An exception was allowed in *Thorington v Smith* for private contracts and debts under Confederate law, to the benefit of US citizens, as though the Confederate States had been a foreign occupying power.[38] However, acts of the Confederate States could not themselves be considered opposable to the US in the absence of recognition.

3.2 The Fusion of Recognition of States and Governments Until the Second World War

By the time of the League of Nations, court practice on recognition had greatly increased and finally reached the international level. The First World War had led to the creation of several new States in Europe and the establishment of a Bolshevik government in Russia that other European powers unsuccessfully attempted to remove, then begrudgingly ignored. Late in the interwar period, the Spanish Civil War gave an additional spur to recognition jurisprudence, particularly in the United Kingdom. At all instances, lawyers did not properly distinguish between the recognition of States, governments, and belligerency, mixing diverse principles of law for either declaratory or constitutive effect. The constitutive view was still dominant, although some jurisprudence both domestically and internationally began to espouse declaratist views.

[34] ibid 51.

[35] See *Underhill v Hernandez* (1897) 168 US 250, 253, where recognition was said to have retroactive effect regarding the recipient's domestic acts.

[36] *Williams v Bruffy* (1877) 96 US 176, 184.

[37] ibid 186; cf *Shortridge v Macon* (1867) 22 F Cas 20.

[38] *Thorington v Smith* (1868) 75 US 1, 11ff. It was determined that, as the Confederate notes constituted the local currency at the time, their use among private citizens as a result of 'irresistible force' employed by the insurgent government could not be held against them.

Two arbitral awards from this period remain influential and are frequently referred to in doctrine. In *Tinoco*,[39] William H Taft adjudicated a contentious matter regarding the validity of the acts of Tinoco's unconstitutional government Costa Rica. The award is sometimes invoked in favour of the declaratory theory of State recognition[40]—incorrectly, in my view, as it concerns the status of effective governments. Namely, Tinoco's government had given concessions to foreign companies that would be nullified after he had been removed from power. The United Kingdom had never recognised Tinoco's government but maintained that it was nevertheless 'the only government of Costa Rica *de facto* and *de jure* for two years and nine months' and that 'during that time there [was] no other government disputing its sovereignty, that it was in peaceful administration of the whole country, with the acquiescence of its people'.[41] Taft agreed that, in ruling 'effectively and peaceably', the Tinoco government was 'an actual sovereign government' and that its non-recognition could not 'outweigh the evidence disclosed by this record ... as to the *de facto* character of Tinoco's government, according to the standard set by international law'.[42]

In 1929, a German-Polish Mixed Arbitral Tribunal issued an award in the case of *Deutsche Continental Gas-Gesellschaft v The Polish State*.[43] The Tribunal was called to determine the consistency with the Treaty of Versailles of the liquidation of the property of a German company by Polish authorities in what had until recently been the territory of the Russian Kingdom of Poland. The plaintiff argued that the rights of the Polish State to liquidate 'enemy property' were restricted to the territory which had been ceded to Poland by the German Reich and did not extend to what remained of *de jure* Russian possessions until such time as the question of the Russian-Polish border had been settled. The Tribunal found that 'the recognition of a State is not constitutive but merely declaratory. The State exists by itself (*par lui même*) and the recognition is nothing else than a declaration of this existence, recognised by the States from which it emanates'.[44] Poland was therefore entitled to exercise sovereign authority over all of its liberated territory, and the powers represented at Versailles were free to recognise it within its claimed borders.

The approach of domestic judges was guided as much by doctrinal positions as it was by national interest. States created in the aftermath of the war particularly demonstrated a preference for declaratory positions on recognition. The Polish Supreme Court ruled in 1923 that a State came into being 'as a result of having

[39] *Tinoco Claims Arbitration (Great Britain v Costa Rica)* (1923) 1 RIAA 369.

[40] See eg Rodríguez Cedeño (n 3) para 89 and James Crawford, *The Creation of States in International Law* (OUP 2007) 23.

[41] *Tinoco Claims Arbitration* (n 39) 377.

[42] ibid 380–81.

[43] *Deutsche Continental Gas-Gesellschaft v The Polish State* (1929) 5 ILR 11.

[44] ibid 13.

gained power over the territory and having suppressed the old power and organised the new power' and that 'its title is based on the fact of the creation of a new State will which is able to exclude the influence of another State will in the territory in question'.[45] Poland, which had become a State by ousting Germany from its territory and establishing itself as the new effective sovereign, was not bound by the legislation or legal obligations of the Parent State. In 1925, the Supreme Administrative Court of Czechoslovakia examined the dissolution of a Hungarian association in Slovakia for acts preceding the Treaty of Trianon and similarly determined that the dissolution had been lawful because Czechoslovakia came into existence with the popular revolution against Austro-Hungarian rule in October 1918, rather than international treaties subsequently adopted.[46]

The approach was very different in Western Europe, especially in the United Kingdom. In *Luther v Sagor*, British judges strongly reaffirmed the necessity of recognition of foreign authority by their own government, even if that authority is the effective government of its country. The case concerned a failed delivery of wood from Ukraine after the contractor company had been nationalised by the Soviet Council of Commissars. At the High Court of Justice, Judge Roche summarised the traditional Anglo-American position: 'If a foreign government is recognized by the Government of this country the Courts of this country may and must recognize the sovereignty of that foreign government and the validity of its acts ... If a foreign government, or its sovereignty, is not recognized by the Government of this country the Courts of this country either cannot, or at least need not, or ought not, to take notice of, or recognize such foreign government or its sovereignty/'[47] Roche could not conclude whether the Foreign Office had recognised the Soviet government,[48] but it was later clarified to the Court of Appeal that the British government had recognised the Soviet government *de facto*.[49] The discussion on appeal turned to whether recognition had a retroactive effect: the judges were reluctant to accept this view in general, but as the Foreign Office specifically referred to acts of the Soviet government preceding recognition, retroactive effects were allowed *in casu*.

Recognition was explicitly understood to have constitutive character. Lord Bankes wrote: 'The Government of this country having, to use the language just quoted, recognized the Soviet Government as the Government really in possession of the powers of sovereignty in Russia, the acts of that Government must

[45] 'Graffowa and Wolanowski v Polish Ministry of Agriculture and State Lands' (1933) 2 *Annual Digest of Public International Law Cases* 55–57, 56.

[46] *Establishment of Czechoslovak State Case* (1929) 3 *Annual Digest of Public International Law Cases* 13–14.

[47] *Luther v Sagor* (1921) 1 KB 456 [King's Bench Division] 474.

[48] The Foreign Office accepted that the Russian delegation in the case represented a 'State Government of Russia' and regarded them 'for a certain limited purpose ... as exempt from the process of the Courts', but also maintained that 'His Majesty's Government have never officially recognised the Soviet Government in any way'. ibid 456.

[49] *Luther v Sagor* (1921) 3 KB 532 [Court of Appeal] 536.

be treated by the Courts of this country with all the respect due to the acts of a duly recognized foreign sovereign state.'[50] Warrington quoted Oppenheim and opined that, through recognition, 'the government in question acquires the right to be treated by the recognizing state as an independent sovereign state'.[51] Scrutton added that '[State] immunity follows from recognition as a sovereign state. Should there be any government which appropriates other people's property without compensation, the remedy appears to be to refuse to recognize it as a sovereign state.'[52]

The House of Lords later expressed the same views in *Arantzazu Mendi*.[53] The British government had concurrently recognised Franco's regime as *de facto* and the Republican authorities as the *de jure* government of Spain. The House of Lords regarded *de facto* recognition as full legal recognition, and *de jure* recognition as political, giving the former precedence on the grounds of effectivity.[54] It was however recognition, and not effectivity, that led the Court to its conclusion, and the latter merely served as an interpretive principle to determine the substance of the British position.[55]

The interwar period also saw the establishment of the Permanent Court of International Justice. It is debatable to what extent the World Court's jurisprudence has anything to say about recognition. Thormodsgard and Moore find in the Court's refusal to issue an advisory opinion touching the interests of Soviet Russia without its presence in the *Eastern Carelia* case, at a time when that State, 'aside from not being a member of the League of Nations, had been recognized only by ... a group forming roughly a mere tenth of the states of the world',[56] indicates a dismissal of the relevance of recognition by the Permanent Court of International Justice (PCIJ). This is incorrect, as it is the Bolshevik government, not the existence of the Russian State, that was disputed.[57] It is also unclear how recognition could impact legal standing at an international court more generally.[58] Neither of these points

[50] ibid 543.

[51] ibid 551.

[52] ibid 556.

[53] *The Arantzazu Mendi* (1939) AC 256, as reproduced in L C Green, *International Law Through the Cases* (Steven & Sons Ltd 1970) 136–38.

[54] See also *Haile Selassie v Cable and Wireless Ltd (No 2)* (1939) Ch 182 for a similar situation stemming from the Italian annexation of Ethiopia, when for a time the Ethiopian government was recognised by the United Kingdom as the *de jure* government of that country, and the Italian government as its *de facto* government.

[55] 'In those circumstances it seems to me that the recognition of a Government as possessing all those attributes in a territory while not subordinate to any other Government in that territory is to recognise it as sovereign, and for the purposes of international law as a foreign sovereign State ... For these reasons I think that it was established by the Foreign Office letter that the Nationalist Government of Spain at the date of the writ was a foreign sovereign State and could not be impleaded.' *The Arantzazu Mendi* (n 53) 136–38.

[56] O H Thormodsgard and Roger D Moore, 'Recognition in International Law' (1927) 12(2) Washington University Law Review 108, 112.

[57] *Status of Eastern Carelia*, Advisory Opinion of 23 July 1923, Ser B, No 5, 13ff.

[58] Thus Crawford recalls the peculiarity that '[t]he Free City of Danzig was a State for the purposes of Article 71 (2) of the Rules of the Permanent Court; whether it was a State for all purposes has been doubted'. Crawford, *The Creation of States* (n 40) 31.

would have escaped a committed constitutivist such as Anzilotti, who supported the majority on the bench. The International Law Commission Special Rapporteur Rodríguez Cedeño[59] finds that the constitutive theory was 'argued unsuccessfully' in the *Eastern Greenland* case,[60] but as the matter concerned a territorial dispute between mutually recognising States, I cannot agree with his interpretation.

However, the *Case Concerning Certain German Interests in Polish Upper Silesia* may include an important statement on recognition. To determine the lawfulness of certain Polish expropriations of the property of German nationals under the German-Polish Convention, the PCIJ had to ascertain whether Poland could invoke the Armistice Convention and the Protocol of Spa foreseeing the transfer of ownership of German public property to the new sovereign power. The Court found that Poland could not have been a party to either, as its belligerency had not yet been recognised by Germany: '[I]t is, however, only on the basis of such recognition that an armistice could have been concluded between those two Powers.'[61] It was added: 'The Principal Allied Powers had, it is true, recognized the Polish armed forces as an autonomous, allied and co-belligerent (or belligerent) army ... [T]he Court observes that these facts cannot be relied on as against Germany, which had no share in the transaction.'[62] The subsequent *de jure* recognition of Poland by Germany did not retroactively make Poland a party to the agreements.

It is controversial whether this judgment only pertains to recognition of belligerency or also to recognition of statehood.[63] In its analysis, the Court references both. It seems, on the whole, that the Court gives recognition in general a constitutive meaning. This conclusion is supported by Lord Finlay's dissenting opinion, which finds that the Armistice had also been concluded by the Allies on behalf of Poland, 'whose army had been fighting on the side of the Allies as an autonomous army, should be bound by the terms of the Armistice and, when she came into existence as a recognized State, have the benefit of them'.[64] A more limited interpretation is certainly possible.[65]

3.3 Diverging National Perspectives

The domestic courts of many countries have had the opportunity to look into recognition since the Second World War. There is no uniformity to their approach,

[59] Rodríguez Cedeño (n 3) para 90.

[60] *Legal Status of Eastern Greenland*, Judgment of 5 April 1933, Ser A, No 53.

[61] *Case Concerning Certain German Interests in Polish Upper Silesia (Germany v Poland)*, Judgment of 25 May 1926, Ser A, No 7, 28.

[62] ibid.

[63] Crawford (n 40) 19, fn 75.

[64] *Polish Upper Silesia* (n 61) 84.

[65] See in particular Joe Verhoeven, *La reconnaissance internationale dans la pratique contemporaine* (Pedone 1975) 727–28.

and courts within the same country may espouse different views in different cases. In certain jurisdictions, judges have ruled in favour of the constitutive role of recognition at the highest level; in others, they have accepted the declaratist theory. The same body—usually a supreme or constitutional court—is not necessarily consistent and the legal value it accords recognition may evolve or fluctuate. Unlike earlier jurisprudence, courts today tend to make a much more clear-cut distinction between recognition of States and government.

In the United States, the Supreme Court has generally insisted on recognition for foreign States to be regarded as such in a court of law. In *Pfizer Inc v India*, the Court stated that 'only governments recognized by the United States and at peace with us are entitled to access ... to our courts' and that 'it is within the exclusive power of the Executive Branch to determine which nations are entitled to sue'.[66] Recognition has also been accepted as a necessary condition for the enjoyment of sovereign immunity. In *Banco Nacional de Cuba v Sabbatino*, the Supreme Court reaffirmed the applicability of the act-of-state doctrine to Cuba, an 'unfriendly power', but one still recognised by the United States. The act-of-state doctrine 'in its traditional formulation precludes the courts of this country from inquiring into the validity of the public acts a recognized foreign sovereign power committed within its own territory'.[67] The Court clarified that 'the privilege of suit has been denied only to governments at war with the United States ... or to those not recognized by this country',[68] whereas 'the refusal to recognize ... signifies this country's unwillingness to acknowledge that the government in question speaks as the sovereign authority for the territory it purports to control'.[69] Other courts have followed suit. In *United States v Lumumba*, the Court of Appeals refused to accept an appeal against criminal contempt on the basis of him being a high-ranking official of a 'Republic of New Afrika'. The court simply noted that sovereign immunity 'only exists when there is recognition of another state's sovereignty by the Department of State. In other words, recognition by the executive branch ... is essential to establishing diplomatic status', and added that '[t]he United States Department of State has not recognized the Republic of New Afrika or its Provisional Government'.[70]

However, a different view of recognition was espoused by the Court of Appeals in *Kadic v Karadzic* regarding a claim brought under the Alien Tort Act by Bosnian Muslim victims of atrocities committed during the War in Bosnia. The representatives of the defendant, Bosnian Serb leader Radovan Karadžić, maintained that he was not a State actor and thus could not be held responsible for violations

[66] *Pfizer Inc v India* (1978) 434 US 308, 319.
[67] *Banco Nacional de Cuba v Sabbatino* (1964) 376 US 398, 401.
[68] ibid 408–09.
[69] ibid 410.
[70] *United States v Lumumba* (1984) 741 F2d 12, 40.

of international law.[71] The Court considered the elements of statehood in international law and the role of recognition and found that, although the 'definition of statehood requires the capacity to engage in formal relations with other states, it does not require recognition by other states'.[72] The judges clarified: 'Recognized states enjoy certain privileges and immunities relevant to judicial proceedings ... [A]n unrecognized state is not a juridical nullity. Our courts have regularly given effect to the "state" action of unrecognized states.'[73] The Court then declared unrecognised Republika Srpska a State under international law: 'Srpska is alleged to control defined territory, control populations within its power, and to have entered into agreements with other governments. It has a president, a legislature, and its own currency. These circumstances readily appear to satisfy the criteria for a state in all aspects of international law.'[74] Nevertheless, it refused to apply the act-of-state doctrine, as it 'was not asserted in the District Court and is not before us on this appeal'.[75] The judgment in *Kadic v Karadzic* does not only differ from earlier judicial practice in the United States but it is also at odds with the mainstream view that Republika Srpska did not achieve statehood under international law.[76]

Regarding the 'one voice' doctrine, the Supreme Court confirmed its continued validity in *Zivotofsky v Kerry* in 2015. The petitioner was a US national born in Jerusalem whose mother had asked the American embassy to list 'Israel' as his country of birth when issuing his passport. The embassy refused to do so, recalling that the United States did not recognise Israeli sovereignty over Jerusalem. The petitioner invoked the Foreign Relations Authorisation Act allowing citizens born in Jerusalem to have their country of birth listed as 'Israel' at their request. The Supreme Court rejected the complaint, finding that Congress could not override the executive's exclusive authority to grant or withhold recognition under international law.[77]

British courts have also continued to rely on recognition by their government, with debate again focusing on the possible retroactive effects of recognition. In *Gdynia Ameryka Linie Zeglugowe Spolka Akcyjna v Boguslawski*,[78] the House of Lords examined the purported retroactive effect of the British recognition of the Lublin government on acts of the Polish government-in-exile after recognition had been announced but before it had taken effect, and while the latter had effective

[71] *Kadic v Karadzic* (1995) 70 F 3d 232, 239.
[72] ibid 244.
[73] ibid.
[74] ibid 245.
[75] ibid 250.
[76] This is notably the case because of UN Security Council resolutions guaranteeing the territorial integrity of Bosnia and Herzegovina, such as resolutions 713 (1991), 752 (1992) and 755 (1992). See also Malcolm N Shaw, *International Law* (CUP 2017) 159–60.
[77] *Zivotofsky v Kerry* (2015) 576 US 1.
[78] *Gdynia Ameryka Linie Zeglugowe Spolka Akcyjna v Boguslawski* (1952) 2 All Eng 470.

control over Poland.[79] It was determined that the London-based Polish government continued to represent Poland for as long as it remained recognised, regardless of effectivity. In *Civil Air Transport Inc v Central Air Transport Corp*, the Privy Council examined the retroactive effects of British recognition of the Communist Government of China as that country's *de jure* government and found that 'retroactivity of recognition operates to validate acts of a *de facto* government which has subsequently become the new *de jure* government, and not to invalidate acts of the previous *de jure* government'.[80] Retroactivity could not, however, extend to acts violating local legislation.

A case often discussed in legal literature is that of *Carl-Zeiss-Stiftung v Rayner & Keeler Ltd*. The case concerned the validity of a title conferred by the German Democratic Republic which was unrecognised by the United Kingdom. Advised by the Foreign Office that only the Soviet government had been recognised as exercising *de jure* sovereignty in East Germany, the Court of Appeal unanimously refused to validate in any way the acts of East Germany and dismissed the suit of an East German company insisting on sole title over the 'Zeiss' trademark.[81] This decision was overturned by the House of Lords, which concurred that East Germany was not a sovereign State but that it was an 'organisation subordinate' to the USSR and thus drawing from the latter's sovereign rights in that part of Germany.[82] The Court of Appeal later applied the same reasoning to Ciskei in the case of *Gur Corporation v Trust Bank of Africa Ltd*, when this entity was attributed to South Africa.[83] Of note are also two cases concerning Rhodesia following its unilateral declaration of independence, an act regarded illegal by the British government. In *Madzimbamuto v Lardner-Burke*, the Privy Council examined the detention of an individual held under legislation whose application had been prolonged by the self-proclaimed State and found it to be illegal as the declaration of independence had been unconstitutional.[84] In *Adams v Adams*, the English judges refused to recognise divorce certificates issued by Rhodesia for similar reasons.[85] Recognition is therefore still a requirement for an entity to be regarded as a State by British courts.

South African practice evolved from a constitutive or at least ambiguous position to a more explicitly declaratory view towards the end of apartheid. Initially, the Supreme Court was cautious: an early and partial statement on recognition of statehood was made in 1976 regarding the continued application of an extradition

79 See Ian Brownlie, *Principles of Public International Law* (OUP 1998) 101.

80 *Civil Air Transport Inc v Central Air Transport Corp* (1952) 2 All Eng L R 733, as reproduced in 'Civil Air Transport Inc v Central Air Transport Corp' (1953) 47(2) The American Journal of International Law 328, 331.

81 See 'United Kingdom: Court of Appeal decision in Zeiss case (Effect of non-recognition of East Germany)' (1965) 4(3) ILM 551.

82 See *Carl-Zeiss-Stiftung v Rayner and Keeler Ltd and Others (No 2)* (1966) 2 All ER 536.

83 *Gur Corporation v Trust Bank of Africa Ltd* (1986) 2 Lloyd's Rep 451.

84 *Madzimbamuto v Lardner-Burke* (1968) UKPC 18.

85 *Adams v Adams* (1970) 3 AER 572. Later, in *Emin v Yeldag* (2001) 1 FLR 956, an exception was made for the internal acts of unrecognised States on purely humanitarian grounds.

agreement with Southern Rhodesia after that country had proclaimed independence from the British Crown. This independence was not recognised by South Africa or any other State. The Supreme Court reasoned: 'It is generally known that South Africa (like all other countries) did not give any formal recognition to the "new" Rhodesia ... The fact that Rhodesia does not enjoy international recognition, does not mean that it is not a State ... but the "new" Rhodesia is not the Rhodesia with which the agreement was concluded.'[86] The Court contrasted this with another treaty that South Africa had with Malawi that continued to apply after that country's independence by mutual consent of the governments of both States.[87] However, after a group of insurgents were charged with high treason for actions undertaken against the Bantustan of Bophuthatswana in 1988 and challenged the legality of the charges on the basis that Bophuthatswana could not be considered a sovereign State, the Supreme Court disagreed, stating that the declaratory view of recognition was more appropriate than constitutivism. It determined that Bophuthatswana was indeed a State under international law regardless of non-recognition by other States.[88] The Court also rejected the relevance of the question of whether the creation of Bophuthatswana violated the *jus cogens* prohibition of apartheid, determining that '[p]olitically motivated non-recognition ignores the elements of statehood which this country possesses'.[89]

In France, courts typically relied on recognition by their government but later also started to accept a more declaratory approach to recognition. This evolution is most visible in relation to their approach to Vietnam. After France had established a State of Vietnam and incorporated it into the French Union in 1949, the Paris Court of Appeal took a joint declaration by France and Vietnam to amount to French recognition of Vietnamese sovereignty and extended State immunity to Vietnam.[90] The French approach differs from Anglo-American policy in that French judges have been more willing to ascertain implied recognition by France. This was demonstrated in the *Clerget* case[91] concerning an engineer previously in the employ of North Vietnam who brought a claim for seizure of North Vietnamese funds to effect payment of his due salary and damages. The Seine Tribunal had inferred from the 1954 Geneva Accords and the fact that the French government had accorded diplomatic privileges to a Vietnamese commercial delegation that France hard recognised North Vietnam as a State. However, the Paris Court of

[86] *State v Oosthuizen* (1985) 68 ILR 3–6, 4–5.

[87] ibid 5.

[88] *S v Banda* (1989) (4) SA 519 (B); see case report in John Redgment, 'Judicial Recognition of the Independence of Bophuthatswana' (1989) 22(2) The Comparative and International Law Journal of Southern Africa 233–37.

[89] Redgment, 'Judicial Recognition of the Independence of Bophuthatswana' (n 88) 236.

[90] *Gugenheim v State of Vietnam* (1958) 22 ILR 224–25.

[91] See as summarised in Matthias Herdegen, 'Clerget v Banque commerciale pour l'Europe du Nord Case' in Anne Peters and Rüdiger Wolfrum (eds), *Max Planck Encyclopedias of International Law* (OUP 2007) <https://opil.ouplaw.com/display/10.1093/law:epil/9780199231690/law-9780199231690-e1077> last accessed 13 June 2024.

Appeal then took a firmly declaratory view of recognition, and found that, 'as the Democratic Republic of (North) Vietnam was a State, recognition could only be declaratory of this fact and that immunity from jurisdiction or execution depended on the independence of a State and not on its recognition by the government of the forum'.[92] However, the French approach is not fully declaratist and judges sitting in different courts have relied on various factors beyond recognition or effectivity to determine whether a given entity could be regarded as a State.[93] For example, the Paris Court of Appeal determined in *République de Chine (Taïwan) c République populaire de Chine* that Taiwan had legal standing at French courts even in the absence of recognition as this was necessary to protect the property of its former nationals.[94]

The Swiss Federal Tribunal has adopted a strongly declaratory view of recognition. In its 2010 judgment in the case of *République de Chine (Taïwan) c Organisation internationale de Normalisation*, it dismissed a cantonal court's views that an unrecognised State could not have legal standing in the domestic judiciary. The Tribunal opined that recognition was predominantly understood as having a declaratory effect and that it was not required for a State to enjoy rights under international law.[95] It also invoked its own earlier views on the statehood *sans* recognition of the German Democratic Republic, as well as the acceptance of Taiwanese statehood by the British and American legal systems in favour of its views. Thus, because Taiwan possessed a defined territory, population and 'undeniable independence' ('*une indépendance indéniable*') even from China, its statehood could not be affected by a lack of recognition by Switzerland.[96]

However, the Swiss Federal Tribunal has not always been quite consistent in this regard. In 2021, it issued a judgment in *A c Secrétariat d'État aux migrations*, evaluating the lawfulness of a decision by the immigration service in Fribourg to list the nationality of a Sahrawi resident as 'without nationality'. The plaintiff and his family had initially been granted asylum in Switzerland as Sahrawi nationals and were later granted permanent residence on the same basis. In 2019, his nationality was changed to 'Moroccan', and later to 'without nationality' when it was

[92] ibid para 1.

[93] For an overview of French recognition practice, see Alina Miron, 'La reconnaissance du statut d'État à des entités contestées au regard des autorités juridictionnelles françaises' in Thierry Garcia (ed), *La reconnaissance du statut d'État à des entités contestées: Approches de droits international, régional et interne* (Pedone 2018).

[94] See *République de Chine (Taïwan) c République populaire de Chine* (2008) CA Paris 07/02874.

[95] 'Selon la conception dominante à laquelle s'est rallié le Tribunal fédéral ... la reconnaissance ne produit qu'un effet déclaratif (et non constitutif), en ce sens qu'elle constate uniquement que les critères de l'existence d'un État sont réunis. En d'autres termes, la reconnaissance internationale n'est pas une condition nécessaire de l'accession au rang d'État, qui existe par lui-même et jouit de tous les droits et attributs qui y sont attachés.' *République de Chine (Taïwan) c Organisation internationale de Normalisation* (2010) as reproduced in Lucius Caflisch (ed), *La pratique suisse en matière de droit international public 2011* (Bern 2013) 27.

[96] ibid.

determined that Switzerland did not recognise Western Sahara, but neither did it recognise Moroccan claims to the territory. The Federal Tribunal agreed with this decision and the authorities' reliance on the position of the Swiss government.[97]

Conversely, the Constitutional Court of Serbia has fully embraced the constitutive theory of recognition. In its decision on constitutional review of the 2013 Brussels Agreement between Belgrade and Priština, the Court rejected a motion arguing that the agreement was unconstitutional. The Court determined that the agreement was merely political and legally non-binding and added that a new State only became sovereign through recognition by other States, with recognition producing effects *inter partes*. The Court relied on Kelsen's views of recognition and found them to reflect the 'dominant' view of international legal theory.[98] As the Serbian government had never recognised the independence of Kosovo and the 2013 agreement did not entail it, there was no violation of constitutional principles.

3.4 International Practice Since the Cold War

The breakup of the Soviet Union and the dissolution of socialist Yugoslavia allowed international bodies to revisit recognition and its role in the creation of new statehood both directly, when these matters concerned the merits of a case, and indirectly, when they had to be addressed as a preliminary matter to determine another question of law. Barring limited practice regarding Vietnam, Korea, or Biafra, the United Nations and a majority of States around the world were now presented with the opportunity to react to the creation of new independent communities outside the colonial context.

The geopolitical circumstances of the collapse of the Soviet Union and Yugoslavia understandably spurred members of the European Community to formulate an initial response. Their *Declaration on the Guidelines on the Recognition of New States in Eastern Europe and in the Soviet Union* reaffirmed the commitment to the principles enunciated in the Helsinki Final Act and the Charter of Paris as well as the right to self-determination. The legal effects of recognition are not discussed, a commitment to respect the rule of law, democracy, and human rights, and to adhere to established borders are all enunciated as conditions for new States to be recognised.[99] The peaceful breakup of the Soviet Union did not however raise much controversy at the time.

Matters were different in the former Yugoslavia where the dissolution of the federal State was marked by a series of violent armed conflicts. The European

[97] ibid para 6.2. The Tribunal justified this view by recalling that the status of Western Sahara was uncertain under international law.

[98] Constitutional Court of Serbia, IУo-247/2013, Official Gazette of the Republic of Serbia No 13/2015, s VIII.

[99] See 'Declaration on the "Guidelines on the Recognition of New States in Eastern Europe and in the Soviet Union' (1993) 4 European Journal of International Law 72–73.

Community convened a peace conference vested with an arbitration commission that is today best remembered as the 'Badinter Commission', after its president, Robert Badinter.[100] The Badinter Commission's views were not binding on any of the parties represented at the conference and its members could only advise on legal matters.[101] Nevertheless, the views of the Commission have proven immensely influential on later jurisprudence and practice.

The Badinter Commission immediately posited that the existence of a State was a matter of fact and that 'the effects of recognition by other States are purely declaratory'.[102] Sovereignty supervenes on a community consisting of 'a territory and a population subject to an organized political authority'.[103] The Yugoslav context, it was then determined, did not involve secession but dissolution, as the Yugoslav State had ceased to exist, turning internal borders into international ones.[104] The Serbian population of Croatia and Bosnia could not rely on the right of self-determination to have the borders modified as this would run contrary to the principle of *uti possidetis juris*, a principle previously applied to former colonial boundaries.[105] The Commission nevertheless did not recommend recognition before the new States had committed to integrating human and minority rights in their domestic framework. The last recommendation was duly accepted by the Community, which issued a Declaration on Yugoslavia[106] inviting all Yugoslav republics to state whether they wished to be recognised as independent States pending their acceptance of relevant human rights standards. As the peace conference was still underway, the Yugoslav government protested, claiming a violation of its rights under international law.[107] However, it was unable to prevent the recognition of Slovenia and Croatia.

The Commission's embrace of declaratism did not really dictate the approach of the European Community to Yugoslavia: it has even been suggested that recognition was ultimately constitutive, although this is debatable.[108] Regardless of the Commission's views, Croatia and particularly Bosnia and Herzegovina most likely did not factually meet the criteria of statehood when they were recognised by

[100] See 'Conference on Yugoslavia Arbitration Commission: Opinions on Questions Arising from the Dissolution of Yugoslavia, 11 January and 4 July 1992' (1992) 31 ILM 1488 (hereafter Badinter Commission Opinions) 1488–89.

[101] ibid 1488–89; cf Matthew C R Craven, 'The European Community Arbitration Commission on Yugoslavia' (1996) 66(1) British Yearbook of International Law 333.

[102] Badinter Commission Opinions (n 100) 1495.

[103] ibid.

[104] ibid 1500.

[105] Compare the ICJ's views on the *uti possidetis juris* principle in *Case Concerning the Frontier Dispute (Burkina Faso/Mali)*, ICJ Reports 554, Judgment of 22 December 1986, paras 19ff.

[106] 'Declaration on Yugoslavia and on the Guidelines on the Recognition of New States' (1992) 31(6) ILM 1485.

[107] Colin Warbrick, 'Recognition of States' (1992) 41(2) The International and Comparative Law Quarterly 473, 479.

[108] 'It has, however, been suggested that the actual practice of States respecting the dissolution of Yugoslavia may have been constitutive in effect; indeed debate continues to rage between those who attribute the troubles of Yugoslavia to premature recognition and those who blame European

European States.[109] Türk argues that the practice 'disregarded one of the classical criteria for recognition namely the criterion of effectiveness of the governments of the states which were aspiring for recognition'[110] and that ultimately recognition became a key factor in establishing the statehood of entities such as Bosnia and Herzegovina.[111]

Nevertheless, the Commission's views on statehood and recognition were taken up by the International Criminal Tribunal for the Former Yugoslavia (ICTY). A criminal court set up by the Security Council, the ICTY was not competent to determine State responsibility or decide whether former republics had become States. Nevertheless, statehood was an important preliminary matter to determine which rules of international humanitarian law governed the Yugoslav conflicts. In a decision in the *Milošević* case, a trial chamber thus had to determine whether Croatia could be considered a State for the fighting against Yugoslav forces to amount to an international armed conflict.[112]

The Chamber recalled the criteria of the Montevideo Convention—whose customary status it did not feel obliged to consider—and found that they could be relied upon to determine Croatian statehood.[113] The Chamber also refused to discuss the declaratory and constitutive theories of recognition but found that 'the formation of states is a matter that is regulated by law, that is, the criteria of statehood are laid down by law' and 'reflected in the four criteria set out in the Montevideo Convention'.[114] It was then determined that, on the date its declaration of independence became effective, Croatia had a permanent population, a defined territory, an effective government, and was effectively independent from Yugoslavia.[115] Accordingly, Croatia was a State under international law and engaged in an international armed conflict with the rump Yugoslav federation.[116] For all the judges' disclaimers regarding recognition and customary law, the decision is fully consonant with the declaratory theory.[117]

In spite of the significant legacy of the practice regarding the former Yugoslavia, declaratism has been circumvented, if not outright ignored, in recent jurisprudence

governments for not intervening earlier and more decisively.... But overall the international approach to the dissolution of Yugoslavia, unhappy as it has been, does not support the constitutive theory, still less demand that we adopt it as a general matter.' Crawford (n 40) 24–25.

[109] See Shaw, *International Law* (n 76) 342 and Colin Warbrick, 'Recognition of States Part 2' (1993) 42(2) The International and Comparative Law Quarterly 433, 434–37.

[110] Danilo Türk, 'Recognition of States: A Comment' (1993) 4 European Journal of International Law 66, 68.

[111] ibid 69.

[112] *Prosecutor v Slobodan Milošević* IT-02-54-T (16 June 2004) [Decision] paras 83–115.

[113] ibid para 86.

[114] ibid para 87.

[115] See ibid paras 94–114.

[116] ibid para 15.

[117] The Chamber relies greatly on the findings of the Badinter Commission, which it finds illuminating even though the Commission was not of a judicial nature; see ibid paras 88–92.

on Palestine. In 2019, the United Nations Committee on the Elimination of Racial Discrimination (CERD) accepted jurisdiction over an interstate communication by Palestine against Israel in spite of the latter's non-recognition but also the prevailing view that Palestine cannot be regarded as a State under the declaratory theory.[118] The Committee did not engage in a discussion of Palestinian statehood and took its accession to the Convention on the Elimination of All Forms of Racial Discrimination as sufficient proof of this fact, problematising only the question of treaty relations with Israel. The majority deemed that the Convention had a 'special character' as protecting an *erga omnes* norm, and thus 'a State party cannot bar another State party, through a unilateral action, from triggering an enforcement mechanism created by the Convention'.[119] Hence, Israeli non-recognition of Palestine did not inhibit the Committee from considering the communication. This decision is of a dubious quality,[120] albeit rather from the perspective of treaty law than rules on statehood and recognition, as the overriding power of peremptory norms does not extend to procedural matters.[121]

A more intellectually stimulating decision on admissibility was produced by the International Criminal Court (ICC) in 2021.[122] Palestine had accepted the Court's jurisdiction over crimes occurring in the Occupied Palestinian Territory since June 2014 and later also acceded to the Rome Statute.[123] The case drew considerable attention from the scholarly community and several States and prominent lawyers contributed as *amici curiae*.[124]

The Prosecutor argued that Palestine was to be considered a State Party to the Statute following the successful deposition of its instrument of accession and that no further discussion of statehood was necessary. Israel and declaratist scholars such as Malcolm Shaw and Robert Badinter countered with the declaratory view, arguing that international law had but a single notion of statehood, and that an entity could not be a State 'for the purposes of the Statute' but not for others: ergo, Palestine, which does not conform to Montevideo, could not accede to the Rome Statute.

[118] *Inter-State Communication Submitted by the State of Palestine against Israel* (12 December 2019) CERD/C/100/3-5. The Palestinian representatives argued statehood on the basis of an unusual reading of the constitutive theory that was not considered by the Committee; see para 5.16.

[119] ibid para 3.37.

[120] The majority decision was strongly criticised by the minority, who recalled that 'a State that has already ratified or acceded to a multilateral treaty [is not] under the obligation to recognize a State, such as the State of Palestine, which later becomes a party to that treaty, or to enter into a treaty relation with that State'. See ibid Annex, paras 3–5.

[121] See *Case Concerning Armed Activities in the Territory of the Congo (New Application: 2002) (Democratic Republic of the Congo v Rwanda)*, ICJ Reports 6, Judgment of 3 February 2006, para 67. The ICJ refused to consider Rwanda's reservation to art IX of the Genocide Convention as invalid.

[122] *Situation in the State of Palestine* ICC-01/18 (5 February 2021) [Decision].

[123] ibid paras 1–2.

[124] In relation to the question of Palestinian statehood, see notably the submissions under Rule 103 by Eyal Benvenisti of 16 March 2020; Robert Badinter and others of 16 March 2020; Todd F Buchwald and Steven J Rapp of 16 March 2020; and Malcolm Shaw of 4 February 2021.

The Chamber easily dismissed declaratist arguments, stating that it could not question the Secretary-General's role as depositary or the accession procedure,[125] although it also recalled that Palestine, upon accession, was active in the work of the Assembly of States Parties and that several States now opposing its legal standing as *amici* had remained silent throughout the accession process.[126] The conclusion was therefore that, 'regardless of Palestine's status under general international law, its accession to the Statute followed the correct and ordinary procedure, as provided under article 125(3) of the Statute'.[127] To demarcate Palestinian territory, the Court then gave preponderant weight to the practice of the United Nations General Assembly and the Palestinian people's right to external self-determination.[128]

To be fair to the adherents of the declaratory school, it is possible to reconcile both the CERD and ICC decisions with a more flexible understanding of declaratism that allows for statehood to arise exceptionally in pursuit of self-determination. However, the intellectual leap required for such an interpretation of the jurisprudence would produce results that are, at best, superficial. The simple truth is that treaty bodies have sensibly come up with a notion of statehood that hinges upon the mechanisms of their respective procedural frameworks. As the workings of these mechanisms will typically reflect the majoritarian views of existing members—which, in turn, may not be grounded in clear notions of statehood—the resulting concept of 'procedural statehood' cannot be adequately explained in declaratist terms.

3.5 The Kosovo Advisory Opinion

The ICJ has never dealt with the nature and effects of recognition of statehood. The Court's highly anticipated advisory opinion on Kosovo's unilateral declaration of independence proved a disappointment for many scholars when the judges opted for a restrictive approach to the question[129] asked by the General Assembly and ignored matters of recognition and statehood.[130] Nevertheless, some of the Court's statements are relevant to understanding recognition, and the submissions by

[125] *Situation in the State of Palestine* (n 122) para 99.
[126] ibid paras 100–101.
[127] ibid para 102.
[128] ibid paras 114–123.
[129] The question was: 'Is the unilateral declaration of independence by the Provisional Institutions of Self-Government of Kosovo in accordance with international law?'
[130] '[T]he question [posed by the General Assembly] is narrow and specific; it asks for the Court's opinion on whether or not the declaration of independence is in accordance with international law. It does not ask about the legal consequences of that declaration. In particular, it does not ask whether or not Kosovo has achieved statehood. Nor does it ask about the validity or legal effects of the recognition of Kosovo by those States which have recognized it as an independent State.' *Accordance with International Law of the Unilateral Declaration of Independence in Respect of Kosovo*, ICJ Reports 403, Advisory Opinion of 22 July 2010 (hereafter *Kosovo* case) para 51.

various States provide rare insight into their approach to this phenomenon. It therefore deserves special mention in any analysis of jurisprudence on recognition.

Kosovo is a province of Serbia that has since 1999 been administered by the United Nations Mission in Kosovo (UNMIK). After the failure of status talks with Belgrade, the representatives of its majority Kosovar Albanian population unilaterally seceded from Serbia in 2008. Recognised by around half of UN members as an independent State, Kosovo represents a rare instance of modern non-colonial secession to enjoy more than token recognition by other States. To determine whether the declaration of independence was legal, the Court thus had to look to general international law as well as the regime established for the territory by the Security Council.

First, the Court's most relevant but unsurprising finding was that general international law does not prohibit declarations of independence.[131] This is important as the argument was raised that the principle of territorial integrity prevents unilateral secession, but the Court found it only to apply between States.[132] By implication, this means that recognising the independence of a State created through secession does not violate international law simply because the secession is unilateral, as opposed to recognition being premature or precluded by other rules of international law. Jure Vidmar also correctly infers that 'the obligation to withhold recognition is not applicable' to declarations of independence that do not result in or from a violation of *jus cogens*.[133]

Second, the peoples of non-self-governing territories and those subject to alien subjugation, domination, and exploitation enjoy the right to independence.[134] International law does not authorise declarations of independence in general: according to the majority, 'it is entirely possible for a particular act—such as a unilateral declaration of independence—not to be in violation of international law without necessarily constituting the exercise of a right conferred by it'.[135] Evidently, acting in pursuit of a right to independence must be different from acting in the absence of such a right. The Court declined to state whether the list of situations establishing a right to independence includes the 'remedial secession' of a non-colonial territory whose population had suffered repression at the hands of the Parent State.[136]

Third, a specific declaration of independence may be prohibited by virtue of *jus cogens* and resolutions of the United Nations Security Council. The latter were a relevant consideration in relation to Kosovo.[137] As Resolution 1244 (1999)

131 ibid para 79.
132 ibid para 80.
133 Jure Vidmar, 'The *Kosovo* Advisory Opinion Scrutinized' (2011) 24(2) Leiden Journal of International Law 355, 356.
134 *Kosovo* case (n 130) para 79.
135 ibid para 56.
136 ibid paras 82–83.
137 ibid paras 85ff.

established an interim administration pending a final settlement of the status of the territory, no institution established under the UN framework would have been able to proclaim independence.[138] In one of its more controversial findings, the Court determined that the declaration of independence was not promulgated by the Assembly of Kosovo acting as a UNMIK body but as a forum hosting 'representatives of the people of Kosovo'.[139] The Court also determined that Resolution 1244 did not prohibit a declaration of independence outside of the UN framework.[140]

A remarkably large number of parties contributed to the *Kosovo* proceedings, although not all contributions refer to statehood and recognition. Recognition is discussed in the submissions of Argentina,[141] Cyprus,[142] Serbia,[143] Slovenia,[144] and Poland,[145] and some views may be inferred from the submissions of France,[146] Romania,[147] the United Kingdom,[148] and the Kosovar Albanian representatives.[149] Argentina, Cyprus, Slovenia, and Poland all refer to either the Montevideo Convention or the findings of the Badinter Commission to deny the constitutive theory of recognition. The positions of France and the United Kingdom were more ambiguous, but leant towards declaratism: France maintained that recognition was a discretionary act, but that statehood was factual,[150] while the United Kingdom admitted the crucial role of large-scale recognition (or non-recognition) to confirm the status of an entity.[151] The Serbian delegation denied the constitutive role of recognition in the creation of statehood, but maintained its importance in establishing bilateral relations between the recognising and recognised entities.[152] Serbia added that recognition could not 'legalise' an illegal declaration of independence, meaning that its validity was linked to that of the declaration, according to the principle *ex injuria jus non oritur.*

138 ibid para 108.

139 ibid paras 107–109; see discussion of this issue in Hurst Hannum, 'The Advisory Opinion on Kosovo: An Opportunity Lost, or a Poisoned Chalice Refused?' (2011) 24(1) Leiden Journal of International Law 155; Vidmar, 'The *Kosovo* Advisory Opinion Scrutinized' (n 133) 358ff; and more generally Marko Milanović and Michael Wood (eds), *The Law and Politics of the Kosovo Advisory Opinion* (OUP 2015).

140 *Kosovo* case (n 130) paras 110ff.

141 See Written Statement of the Argentine Republic of 17 April 2009 (especially para 48).

142 See Written Statement Submitted by the Republic of Cyprus of 17 April 2009, 41ff.

143 See Written Statement of the Government of the Republic of Serbia of 15 April 2009, 340ff and Written Comments of the Government of the Republic of Serbia of 14 July 2009, 199ff.

144 See Written Statement by the Republic of Slovenia of 17 April 2009, 2.

145 See Written Statement of the Republic of Poland of 14 April 2009, paras 2.1–2.3.

146 See Written Submission by the French Republic of 18 April 2009.

147 See Written Statement of Romania of 18 April 2009, para 7 (this aspect may also be interpreted in line with the constitutive theory).

148 See Written Statement of the United Kingdom of 17 April 2009.

149 See Written Contribution of the Authors of the Unilateral Declaration of Independence of 17 April 2009, 140–42.

150 Written Submission by the French Republic of 18 April 2009, 15–16.

151 Written Statement of the United Kingdom of 17 April 2009, para 5.54.

152 See eg Written Statement of the Government of the Republic of Serbia of 15 April 2009, 340ff.

4. Conclusion

The overview of practice provided above demonstrates not only a lack of consensus in national approaches to recognition, but also great variation at the international level. Both international and domestic bodies are usually laconic in their treatment of recognition, if they even discuss it at all, and there is currently a tendency for the international level to tilt towards declaratory views, albeit neither uniformly nor decisively. This is not at all adequate to infer that declaratism has won the day over constitutivism. Most of the appeal of Montevideo comes from the fact that it is really the only international instrument dealing with statehood and recognition: in truth, it does not at all seem to reflect customary law. This is demonstrated by the great diversity of practice at the domestic level, with only a minority of case law relying on Montevideo or some variation thereof. The differences of opinion between various stakeholders are sufficiently deep to show that no norm of general international law regulates either the effects of recognition or links opposability to effectivity.

This does not mean that international law does not deal with recognition of States at all. Clearly, the law prevents recognition in some cases—for example, when it is premature or involves territorial acquisitions stemming from unlawful use of force. In addition, it would also appear that entities are to be considered States regardless of recognition if a determination to this effect has been made by the United Nations Security Council or, more controversially, they enjoy a right to external self-determination. I turn to these matters in the following chapters.

8
Theories of Recognition

1. The Major Schools of Thought on Recognition

Scholarship first began seriously to deal with recognition in the nineteenth century, with a view to formulating a general rule on recognition. Such scholarly attempts are still ongoing, as attested by the present work and many others regularly published on the subject of recognition. Early doctrinal attempts were thwarted by a lack of State practice that led lawyers to deduce rules on recognition from their own preconceptions of international law. Unfortunately, to this day, State and judicial practice—while increasing rapidly in recent decades—remain so profoundly inconsistent, or so frustratingly ambiguous, that the actual views of States are often unfathomable. This means that scholarly works and reflections continue to play a role of fundamental importance in deciphering the current state of international law on recognition.

Already here we may identify the first curiosity of this domain: whereas doctrine has been so preoccupied with finding a general rule on recognition, the muddled and inconsistent State practice allowed us to identify particular rules. By focusing on the big picture, scholarship has often superficially pushed very different practice and situations into the same basket rather than try to identify how contextual specificities determined State reactions in each situation.

Adherents of the two main views of recognition have also tended to misunderstand or misattribute views to their opponents, creating a straw man against which to pit their arguments even though no one had advocated the position they criticise. For example, critics of the constitutivist approach often ridicule the idea that recognition creates statehood, even though this position is maintained by only a handful of constitutivist scholars: it is doubtful whether even the more strictly positivist lawyers such as Anzilotti or Cavaglieri would make such an argument. It is also sometimes raised that the constitutive view implies that the population of an unrecognised State is completely deprived of rights under international law, even though most constitutivist scholars go to great lengths to explain why this is not the case. Finally, the differences between most declaratist and constitutivist scholars are probably less than many of them would care to admit and depend primarily on their understanding of opposability.

Opposability is therefore the basis for categorising scholars into either group in this chapter, even though some of them have traditionally been placed into the other camp. For example, Fauchille has been considered as a proponent

Recognition of States in International Law. Pavle Kilibarda, Oxford University Press. © Pavle Kilibarda 2024.
DOI: 10.1093/oso/9780198905653.003.0008

of the declaratory view of recognition, although I believe he is better seen as a constitutivist scholar based on his views on opposability.[1] Because opposability is usually regarded in binary terms—it either requires recognition or it does not—very few theories may be genuinely regarded as 'mixed'. De Visscher, Verhoeven, Frowein, Talmon, and Dugard have been able to produce rare examples of truly mixed theories by overcoming the black-and-white opposability axis altogether.

2. The Constitutive View

The basic tenets of the constitutive doctrine may be summarised as follows: 'According to [the constitutive doctrine], [recognition] has a "constitutive" effect, so a state becomes an international person and a subject of international law only through recognition.'[2] It is said that recognition as a constitutive act sees a State as coming into existence only through the act of recognition itself: there can be no talk of statehood in the absence of this act, and the recognised State has no prior legal existence.[3] Adherents of the constitutive theory do not maintain that the State is created through recognition, but they usually advance that its legal personality derives from it.[4] This requires distinguishing between material and legal facts, which declaratory scholars sometimes object to as an unnatural dichotomy. However, there exist widely differing formulations of the constitutive theory.

For example, one strain of thought defended in the works of Strisower and Verdross traces its origins to nineteenth-century practice, when many scholars and State representatives insisted on international law as a quintessentially European product, forged in relations between Western European powers no later than the seventeenth century and extended to non-Christian States such as the Ottoman

[1] For example, Lauterpacht classifies Fauchille, along with Pradier-Fodéré and Rivier, as a declaratist; see Hersch Lauterpacht, *Recognition in International Law* (CUP 2013) 42, fn 5.

[2] Andrew Clapham, *Brierly's Law of Nations* (OUP 2012) 150; cf Ti-Chiang Chen, *The International Law of Recognition* (Stevens & Sons Limited 1951) 30 ('What is claimed [for recognition] is merely the conferment upon an already existing State of an international personality, a quality to act in the international sphere productive of legal results.').

[3] '[A]ccording to the [constitutive view] the political act of recognition is a precondition of the existence of legal rights: in its extreme form this implies that the very personality of a state depends on the political decision of other states'. James Crawford, *Brownlie's Principles of Public International Law* (OUP 2019) 136; this is also Talmon's understanding, see Stefan Talmon, 'The Constitutive Versus the Declaratory Theory of Recognition: *Tertium Non Datur*?' (2004) 75(1) British Yearbook of International Law 101, 102 ('According to the constitutive theory, only recognition makes a State a State, and thus a subject of international law'); cf Thomas D Grant, *The Recognition of States: Law and Practice in Debate and Evolution* (Praeger Publishers 1999) 2ff and Malcolm N Shaw, *International Law* (CUP 2017) 164.

[4] The blame for this common misunderstanding probably lies with constitutive writers and the often-imprecise language they use to describe the phenomenon of recognition; Wyler criticises constitutivist authors' 'vague expressions such as "recognizing the existence of State X" instead of clarifying *expressis verbis* that the recognition confers *international legal personality*'. See Éric Wyler, *Théorie et pratique de la reconaissance d'état: Une approche épistemologique du droit international* (Bruylant 2013) 141.

Empire and China through gradual acceptance by existing 'club members'.[5] An example sometimes given in the literature is the 1856 Treaty of Paris, when European Powers declared the Sublime Porte admitted to European public law and the Concert of Europe and engaged to respect the independence and territorial integrity of the Ottoman Empire.[6] The same principle was espoused in relation to the formation of independent States from former Spanish and Portuguese colonies in Latin America.[7] Strisower and especially Verdross stripped this interpretation of its Eurocentric outline and tried to distinguish between the role of recognition in the creation of States (where it is irrelevant) from their admission into the international community—a community of States governed by international law—where it is essential. This is not an understanding of recognition that most constitutivist scholars could agree with.

Indeed, there are many points, some of them fundamental, on which the constitutivist camp cannot find consensus. From the mid-nineteenth century onward, we see scholars imparting to recognition the power to transform a natural fact into a legal fact, to constitute the first norm between two consenting legal persons, or as constitutive of external but not internal sovereignty, the latter flowing from domestic law. It is often submitted that recognition is necessary for a State to express its sovereign consent to be bound by any rule of (international) law, including with respect to a new legal subject. Another view, advanced by Kelsen[8] and later Eric Suy,[9] insists on the cognitive, quasi-judicial aspect of recognition as an act requiring an examination of material facts and inferring from

[5] See Gerald Fitzmaurice, 'The General Principles of International Law Considered from the Standpoint of the Rule of Law' (1957) 92 RCADI 1–227, 25; Georges Abi-Saab, 'Cours general de droit international public' (1987) 207 RCADI 9, 52ff; Thomas D Grant, 'Defining Statehood: The Montevideo Convention and its Discontents' (1998–1999) 37(2) Columbia Journal of Transnational Law 403, 422; for a declaratory twist on this approach, see Alphonse Rivier, *Principes du droit des gens: Tome premier* (Arthur Rousseau 1896) 7ff; the club membership analogy remains a popular interpretation of the constitutive theory with constitutivist authors and their critics alike, see in particular Jan Klabbers, *International Law* (CUP 2017) 78.

[6] 'Sa Majesté l'Empereur des Français, Sa Majesté l'Empereur d'Autriche, Sa Majesté la Reine du Royaume-Uni de la Grande-Bretagne et de l'Irlande, Sa Majesté le Roi de Prusse, Sa Majesté l'Empereur de toutes les Russies et Sa Majesté le Roi de Sardaigne déclarent la sublime Porte admise à participer aux avantages du droit public et du concert européen. Leurs Majestés s'engagent, chacune de son côté, à respecter l'indépendance et l'intégrité territoriale de l'Empire Ottoman, garantissent en commun la stricte observation de cet engagement, et considéreront, en conséquence, tout acte de nature à y porter atteinte comme une question d'intérêt général.' Treaty of Paris (signed 30 March 1856) art VII.

[7] Lauterpacht, *Recognition in International Law* (n 1) 13ff.

[8] 'The legal act of recognition is the establishment of a fact; it is not the expression of a will. It is cognition rather than *re*-cognition. It has the same character as the establishment of a legally relevant fact by a court.' Hans Kelsen, 'Recognition in International Law: Theoretical Observations' (1941) 35(4) The American Journal of International Law 605–17, 608.

[9] 'En ce qu'elle contient tout d'abord la constatation de l'existence de son objet, la reconnaissance n'a donc certainement pour effet de le créer et, dans ce sens, son effet est purement déclaratif. En tant qu'acte juridique, au contraire, c'est-à-dire comme manifestation de volonté à laquelle est attachée une certaine conséquence juridique, l'acte de reconnaissance doit avoir un effet constitutif. Si elle n'était que déclaratoire, la reconnaissance ne serait pas un acte juridique.' Eric Suy, *Les actes juridiques unilatéraux en droit international public* (R Pichon & R Durand-Auzias 1962) 206–07.

them legal conclusions much the same as this would be done in a court of law. Recognition is denied a creative role but it still indispensable to exercise rights and duties vis-à-vis the recognising authority. Another major point of disagreement is whether recognition, if it confers legal personality, somehow influences an intrinsic characteristic of its object or simply its relations with the author of recognition. In the former case, the object is completely outside of the scope of international law until recognised, whereas in the latter it is a legal person from its inception and simply does not enjoy specific rights towards those who do not recognise it. Finally, several constitutivist authors reject the idea that international law can define States at all, thus relegating recognition purely to a role in the creation of legal subjectivity.

Although the constitutive view is often tied to the positivist school of law (in opposition to the naturalist school, to which the declaratory view is usually attributed),[10] there is no necessary link between positivism and constitutivism. It is true that the constitutive theory's reliance on the consent of States is compatible with the voluntaristic approach to international law that is commonly maintained by positivists. Nevertheless, some constitutivist scholars are fierce opponents of positivism. At the same time, some positivists have held declaratory views of recognition.[11] Arguing in favour or against a specific doctrine of recognition based on the intellectual background of its supporters is thus of limited value in the Great Debate.

More importantly, all questions of paradigm and even of how one understands basic legal concepts such as personality fade before the key practical concern of the effects of recognition as a legal act. If recognition establishes a relationship between two subjects of international law then we must ask whether the relevant norms result only from recognition or also have another parallel source making recognition redundant or symbolic. Thus the common thread between all constitutive theories is not the idea that recognition bestows legal personality but rather that it is necessary to make the statehood of the recipient opposable to the author. This is what truly distinguishes constitutivism from declaratism.

[10] 'In contrast to the positivist theory, the natural law theory is one which purports to furnish an explanation for the ultimate obligatory character of international law, apart from the wills of individual States. In this theory, the declaratory doctrine of recognition finds a natural alliance.' Chen, *The International Law of Recognition* (n 2) 18. See also Fitzmaurice, 'The General Principles of International Law' (n 5) 18. Talmon also expresses this view: 'The constitutive theory is an expression of an outdated, positivist view of international law as a purely consensual system, where legal relations can only arise with the consent of those concerned.' Talmon, 'The Constitutive Versus the Declaratory Theory of Recognition' (n 3) 102.

[11] 'Sir Hersch is unorthodox—a convinced naturalist who also professes strong constitutivist views.' Fitzmaurice (n 5) 18, fn 1. Brownlie finds of Kelsen that 'earlier he was a declaratist'. Crawford, *Brownlie's Principles* (n 3) 136, fn 16.

2.1 Specific Formulations of the Constitutive View

Numerous legal scholars have advocated for a constitutive view of recognition. Some merely treat the matter in passing, whereas others have seen fit to develop elaborate theories on the role of recognition in international law. It is neither possible nor useful to present them all here. What follows is a glimpse of the constitutivist landscape and its most colourful scenery, presented in roughly chronological order.

The earliest conceptualisation of the constitutive theory is to be found with Jellinek,[12] whose understanding of recognition is based on the distinction between the State as a 'natural' and 'legal' fact.[13] Law cannot define or create a State but it can govern the relations between States as sovereign entities, and it can specifically describe the process whereby a natural fact becomes a legal fact. Because sovereignty is vested in individual States and because there exists no international *civitas maxima* to determine legal personality, natural facts may only 'transform' into legal facts through mutual recognition. Therefore, recognition is an act whereby a State as a natural fact becomes a legal fact, with one State accepting another as a person of law ('Die Anerkennung ist der Act, durch welchen ein Staat einen anderen als Rechtspersönlichkeit erklärt').[14] Jellinek's approach became highly influential in the following decades with both constitutivist and declaratist scholars, and a similar theory would later be defended by Bluntschli[15] and Piédelièvre.[16] Bluntschli's approach, which was based on the concept of inclusion into the international legal community, would also be echoed in Oppenheim's doctrine, which remains one of the most influential in the field of recognition. Oppenheim drew a sharp line between statehood, which exists factually, and a State's acceptance into the 'Family of Nations', which makes it a person of law. As international law developed gradually between a small number of States, it had to be extended specifically to States which did not participate in its formation. Unrecognised States are thus not covered by international law, which takes no notice of them prior to recognition.[17] There is thus no right to recognition, and although States may be pressed politically to recognise a new State, they would not be obliged to do so even if the secession were recognised by the Parent State.[18]

[12] According to Lauterpacht, Jellinek's is the 'first modern formulation of the constitutive doctrine'. Lauterpacht (n 1) 420.

[13] Georg Jellinek, *Die Lehre von den Staatenverbindungen* (Alfred Hölder 1882) 99ff.

[14] ibid 99.

[15] Johann Caspar Bluntschli, *Das moderne Völkerrecht der civilisirten Staten als Rechtsbuch dargestellt* (Druck und Verlag der C H Beck'schen Buchhandlung 1872) 71ff.

[16] Robert Piédelièvre, *Précis du droit international public ou droit des gens: Des États et de leurs relations en temps de paix* (Pichon 1894) 96ff.

[17] Lassa Oppenheim, *International Law: A Treatise, Volume I: Peace* (Longmans, Green and Co 1912) 116ff.

[18] ibid 120.

Pradier-Fodéré builds a theory revolving around external and internal sovereignty. Internal, or constitutional, sovereignty pertains to the State's supreme right to specify the form of its 'social organism', limit individual liberties, and direct the development of its community.[19] External sovereignty refers to the State's independence from other States and its capacity to deal with them on its own behalf.[20] Pradier-Fodéré argues that declaratist doctrine does not adequately consider practice, which demonstrates that recognition is 'indispensable' for external sovereignty.[21] External sovereignty requires that all members of the society of nations recognise each other as equals to respect the others' rights.[22] This approach was taken up and further developed several decades later by Fauchille, for whom a State exists as a matter of fact as soon as the requisite material elements have been met, immediately exercising internal sovereignty,[23] but depending on recognition for external sovereignty.[24] Fauchille also distinguishes between the 'enjoyment' (*jouissance*) and 'exercise' (*exercice*) of sovereignty but makes of them a proper dichotomy; whereas even an unrecognised State may exist, and therefore enjoy sovereignty, it cannot implement (exercise) it vis-à-vis others unless it has first been recognised by them.[25] The doctrine of Verdross could also be categorised within this group of theories.[26]

Anzilotti is notable in regarding recognition as a bilateral act by nature (a notion he shares with Verdross). In his view, legal subjects are entities vested by international law with rights and duties established by legal norms; as norms are created through treaties, a subject materialises from the moment it enters into its first treaty.[27] This original contract is obligatory by virtue of the principle *pacta sunt servanda* that represents the hypothetical basis of every legal order. Anzilotti dismisses the theory whereby a State's legal personality stems only from its own constitution, whereby recognition merely serves to determine whether a State exists in fact. This doctrine 'manifestly flows from natural law' (*relève manifestement du droit naturel*)[28] and any attempt to explain the declaratory theory in terms

[19] Paul Pradier-Fodéré, *Traité de droit international public européen & americain, Tome premier* (Pedone-Lauriel 1885) 232–33.
[20] ibid 234.
[21] ibid 236–37.
[22] ibid 237.
[23] Paul Fauchille, *Traité de droit international public: Tome 1er, Première partie: Paix* (Arthur Rousseau 1922) 306.
[24] ibid.
[25] ibid.
[26] Alfred Verdross, 'Règles générales du droit international de la paix' (1929) 30 RCADI 271, 324ff.
[27] 'Les normes juridiques internationales se constituent par le moyen d'accords; les sujets de l'ordre juridique international commencent donc à exister au moment où intervient un premier accord: à ce moment même les entités entre lesquelles intervient l'accord deviennent l'une à l'égard de l'autre destinataires de la norme ou des normes résultant dudit accord et, pour autant, sujets de l'ordre juridique dont ces normes font partie.' Dionisio Anzilotti, *Cours de droit international, Premier volume; Introduction—Théories générales* (Librairie du Recueil Sirey 1929) 161.
[28] ibid 162–63.

of positive law fails because it would first be necessary to identify a rule of international law requiring that States be treated as such simply because they fulfil the material requirements of statehood. The existence of such a rule has never been properly demonstrated.[29] A similar approach, albeit not founded on mutual constitutive recognition, was advocated by Cavaglieri.[30]

Kelsen pays much attention to the matter of recognition because of its importance for his broader theories of law.[31] For him, recognition is both political and legal: political recognition is merely declaratory as it presupposes the existence of a State and produces no legal consequences of its own.[32] The legal act of recognition is very different. Every legal order, including international law, 'attaches to certain facts certain consequences', yet in jurisprudence, there are no absolute facts 'but only facts established by the competent authority in a procedure prescribed by the legal order'.[33] Accordingly, '[t]he legal act of recognition is the establishment of a fact; it is not the expression of a will. It is cognition rather than *re*-cognition. It has the same character as the establishment of a legally relevant fact by a court'.[34] Such a determination has the effect 'that the recognized community becomes in its relation with the recognizing state itself a state, i.e., a subject of rights and obligations stipulated by general international law'.[35] A new State exists only towards those which recognise it as '[t]here is no such thing as absolute existence'.[36] A declaration of independence is similar to an act of recognition received from other States, with the effect that the new State 'exists only for itself, not in relation to other states'.[37] This caveat explains how even an unrecognised State is bound by international law.[38]

For Hersch Lauterpacht, recognition is an act of legal nature. Lauterpacht believed that every State was a 'judge' in a system of international law that lacked a universal and supreme judicial authority.[39] Recognition serves a dual role: it is

[29] ibid 164.
[30] Arrigo Cavaglieri, 'Règles générales du droit de la paix' (1929) 26 RCADI 311, 340ff.
[31] See in particular Hans Kelsen, 'Théorie générale du droit international public: Problèmes choisis' (1932) 42 RCADI 117, 268ff.
[32] Kelsen, 'Recognition in International Law' (n 8) 605–06.
[33] ibid 606; he illustrates: 'It is not theft as a fact in itself to which the legal order attaches a certain punishment. Only a layman formulates the rule of law in that way. The jurist knows that the legal order attaches a certain punishment only to a theft established by the competent court following a prescribed procedure.'
[34] ibid 608.
[35] ibid.
[36] ibid 609.
[37] ibid 609.
[38] However, Kelsen does not believe that the new State thus makes itself a subject of law; instead, this is so because the objective legal order itself foresees such a possibility. Elsewhere, he ridiculed the notion of a State establishing itself as a subject of international law on its own as absurd as 'Baron Munchhausen pulling himself by his own braid from the mire in which he has fallen' ('une idée qui rappelle la tentative du baron de Munchhausen de sortir à l'aide de sa propre natte du marais où il est tombé'). Kelsen, 'Théorie générale du droit international public' (n 31) 269.
[39] See Hersch Lauterpacht, 'Règles générales du droit de la paix' (1937-IV) 62 RCADI 118, 106.

declaratory of an existing fact (statehood) but constitutive of the corresponding rights and obligations.[40] There exists sufficient State practice to infer certain general rules of international law in relation to this act. One aspect of recognition that he finds to be uncontroversial is that premature recognition amounts to an unlawful interference in the affairs of the Parent State and therefore a violation of international law.[41] Conversely, '[w]hen the struggle for independence has reached a tangible measure of success accompanied by reasonable prospect of permanency, international law authorizes third States to declare by means of recognition of the nascent community that the sovereignty of the parent State is extinct. This means that international law attaches a distinct legal effect to the situation thus created'.[42] The fact that recognition presupposes the existence of the recipient State as a fact simply means that 'recognition is not a question of unfettered discretion, of contractual bargain, or of political expediency. It means, positively, that the State called upon to grant recognition must judge whether the required conditions of fact exist, and that it is entitled to exercise its discretion in arriving at that judgment. However, this is a judicial discretion aiming at ascertaining the existence of the relevant facts'.[43] Lauterpacht goes to great lengths to establish a framework for an obligation to recognise, drawing upon the work of Blunstchli.[44] However, even if a duty of recognition exists, it cannot substitute actual lack of recognition: in his theory, the fact that a State has the right to be recognised by another does not mean that it *is* recognised.[45]

2.2 Objections to the Constitutive View

Critics of the constitutive view commonly list a few main lines of argumentation against it. These counterarguments are of a logical, ethical, and practical nature.

(1) *The Cognitive Problem.* The first argument raised against the constitutivist conception of recognition is logical. Fitzmaurice summarises it in the following question: '[H]ow can one recognize something which, until one does recognize it, has no existence? More serious still, how can mere recognition bring the nonexistent into existence?'[46] There exists a slight

[40] Lauterpacht (n 1) 1–3. In his introduction to the 2013 edition, Crawford notices that in Lauterpacht's approach 'recognition was *both* constitutive *and* declaratory', at xxxvi.
[41] ibid 7ff.
[42] ibid 9.
[43] ibid 24.
[44] ibid 61ff.
[45] Lauterpacht extensively analyses the jurisprudence of foreign States vis-à-vis newly proclaimed States to disprove the declaratory theory, finding that '[i]n *foreign* courts, the unrecognized State and its acts do not legally exist prior to recognition'. ibid 44.
[46] Fitzmaurice (n 5) 24.

variation of this argument targeting the theory of mutual constitutive recognition, namely 'that it is impossible to understand how an entity which does not possess a juridical existence can conclude a treaty which presupposes its personality'.[47] This is another version of the chicken-and-egg dilemma. Although States do not seem to have a problem 'recognising' the existence of something they had previously denied, this conundrum carries significant theoretical weight: if something does not exist, it cannot be recognised; and if it is recognised, then it must have existed before recognition. This problem dissipates if one were to slightly alter the premises, as do many constitutivists: even Jellinek accepted that a State existed as a matter of fact, but that is legal existence depended on acceptance by other States.[48] Recognition does not create but transform. An alternative resolution may be found with Kelsen, from whom recognition is a truly cognitive act, 'the establishment of the fact that in a given case a "state in the sense of international law" exists'.[49] The State exists prior to recognition, but this existence must be demonstrated in a judicial process rather than presumed. This reasoning is not dissimilar from what is commonly argued in declaratist doctrine.

(2) *The Problem of Transference.* A closely related but separate logical argument concerns the question of how an existing person of international law might confer legal personality mirroring and equal to its own upon a new entity.[50] It is uncontroversial that one or more subjects of international law can create a new one, for example an international organisation, but that one State can create another, in a process resembling cell mitosis, comes across as another matter entirely. Moreover, it is raised that this is not how States themselves perceive recognition: Charpentier consecrates a significant part of his thesis to demonstrating that States and their courts simply react (without bestowing any qualities) to *de facto* States; they do not question their existence or validity in international law.[51] Essentially, no 'transfer' of qualities takes place through recognition. A less abstract but related concern is that States cannot create obligations for a third party without that party's consent, which seems to be the case with constitutive recognition.[52] It is sometimes added that this violates the principle of equality of States.[53]

[47] Lauterpacht (n 1) 351ff.

[48] Jellinek, *Die Lehre von den Staatenverbindungen* (n 13) 99ff.

[49] Kelsen (n 8) 607.

[50] '[H]ow can mere recognition confer on an entity the characteristics of international personality?' Fitzmaurice (n 5) 24.

[51] See Jean Charpentier, *La reconnaissance internationale et l'évolution du droit des gens* (Pedone 1956) esp 204ff.

[52] '[I]t is clearly established that states cannot by their independent judgment remove or abrogate any competence of other states established by international law (as distinct from agreement or concession)'. Crawford (n 3) 137.

[53] See Talmon (n 3) 102.

Of course, many constitutivists would probably brush this argument aside by saying that these principles are not applicable to States prior to their recognition anyway. Conversely, even the declaratory doctrine may not be fully reconcilable with this problem in all circumstances: entities that meet the criteria of statehood are sometimes quite simply not accepted as States by a majority of existing members of the international community.[54]

(3) *The Problem of Legality.* Crawford writes: '[I]f State recognition is definitive then it is difficult to conceive of an illegal recognition and impossible to conceive of one which is invalid or void. Yet the nullity of certain acts of recognition has been accepted in practice, and rightly so ....'[55] This view presupposes a very specific view of recognition, as may perhaps be found with Anzilotti; many other constitutivists, including Kelsen[56] and Lauterpacht,[57] disagree that recognition takes place in a vacuum and accept that there may be an invalid or even illegal recognition. Although Crawford finds that, if recognition may be invalid, 'then the test for statehood must be extrinsic to the act of recognition', which is 'a denial of the constitutive position',[58] this does not seem to be of relevance for most of the formulations of the constitutivist theory presented above.

(4) *The Problem of Relativism.* The argument based on relativism is the most common criticism of the constitutive approach; as such, there are many variations of it.[59] Talmon recounts its most widespread form: 'What one State may consider to be a State may, for another, be a non-entity under international law. States are *natural-born*, i.e. absolute, subjects of international law and are not relative subjects of international law *created* by existing States as, for example, international organizations.'[60] According to declaratist scholars, a State either exists or it does not exist: it cannot be a State for some and not a State for others. Constitutivist scholars have

[54] Fitzmaurice recalls: '[I]t is urged that a number of individuals could join together as a group, proceed to some uninhabited part of the world, set up a few institutions, and then claim to "exist" as a statal entity and therefore to be entitled to recognition as an international person; and examples are given such as the case of the eccentric Mr. Hicky who in 1894 purported to set up a State on an island in the S. Atlantic, assumed the title of King James I, and claimed admission to the Universal Postal Union.' Fitzmaurice (n 5) 22. See also Joe Verhoeven, *La reconnaissance internationale dans la pratique contemporaine* (Pedone 1975) 684 and Jure Vidmar, 'Conceptualizing Declarations of Independence in International Law' (2012) 32(1) Oxford Journal of Legal Studies 153, 158 regarding Rhodesia; more recently, the issue has been discussed in the context of the so-called Islamic State, see Christian Tomuschat, 'The Status of the "Islamic State" Under International Law' (2015) 90(3/4) Die Friedens-Warte 223.

[55] James Crawford, *The Creation of States in International Law* (OUP 2007) 21.

[56] 'A community meeting [the] three conditions [of statehood] is a state ... The recognition of a state is the establishment of the fact that a given community has satisfied these conditions.' Kelsen (n 8) 608.

[57] See Lauterpacht (n 1) 26ff.

[58] Crawford, *The Creation of States in International Law* (n 55) 21.

[59] See eg ibid 21–22; James-Leslie Brierly, 'Règles générales du droit de la paix' (1936) 58 RCADI 1, 53–54; Fitzmaurice (n 5) 24; Shaw (n 3) 330–31; and many others.

[60] Talmon (n 3) 102.

different ways of tackling this question. Some try to mitigate it, for example by identifying an obligation to recognise, as does Lauterpacht;[61] others accept it and diminish its importance.[62] Whether the relativism inherent to the constitutive theory poses a significant hurdle to its validity ultimately lies with one's understanding of the nature of statehood, legal personality, and international law itself.

(5) *The 'Legal Vacuum' Problem.* Many critics of the constitutive approach are offput by its apparent implication that an unrecognised State is not bound by international law at all. Strydom writes: 'What is the status of an entity that possesses the attributes of a state, but which remains unrecognised by other states? Is that entity bound by international law as it applies to states?'[63] Some constitutivists, such as Anzilotti or Cavaglieri, do not have a problem to answer the latter question with a 'no';[64] those who see recognition as constitutive of or indispensable to bilateral legal relations between States, such as Fauchille,[65] do not face this dilemma. Kelsen asserted that an unrecognised State exists for itself, meaning that it is a person of international law even while other States are not bound to treat it as such: thus, the unrecognised State is still bound by international law. In reality, the advent of international humanitarian law (IHL) and international human rights law (IHRL) and the evolution of other legal provisions benefiting the human person mean that the population of an unrecognised State does not live in a legal vacuum and that it is not dispossessed of fundamental rights.

(6) *The Moral Arguments.* It is sometimes asserted that the constitutive theory is somehow 'immoral' or at least morally dubious.[66] The main objection is that it is inappropriate for third States to decide arbitrarily on the existence of another State. Among the constitutivists, at least Lauterpacht shares this criticism, wherefore he attempts to develop a 'duty of recognition'. However, most constitutivists do not seem to have moral qualms in this regard, and it

[61] Lauterpacht (n 1) 61ff.

[62] 'A state exists legally only in its relations to other states. There is no such thing as absolute existence. Since we have to acknowledge the relativity of time and space—the general conditions of natural existence—relativity of legal existence is no longer paradoxical'. Kelsen (n 8) 609. cf Anzilotti, *Cours de droit international* (n 27) 167ff ('On ne voit pas ce qu'il peut y avoir d'absurde dans le fait que la variabilité indéfinie des droits relatifs à un sujet par rapport aux autres aille, dans notre domaine, jusqu'au point où une même entité serait investie de tous les droits par rapport à certains et en serait complètement dépourvue par rapport aux autres.').

[63] Hennie Strydom (ed), *International Law* (OUP 2016) 44; see also Verdross, 'Règles générales du droit international de la paix' (n 26) 326–27 and Brierly, 'Règles générales du droit de la paix' (n 59) 54.

[64] Anzilotti (n 27) 161ff; Cavaglieri, 'Règles générales du droit de la paix' (n 30) 347ff.

[65] Fauchille, *Traité de droit international public* (n 23) 306–07.

[66] See eg John Fischer Williams, 'Some Thoughts on the Doctrine of Recognition in International Law' (1934) 47(5) Harvard Law Review 776; Edwin Borchard, 'Recognition and Non-Recognition' (1942) 36(1) The American Journal of International Law 108; Pamela P Price, 'The Impact of Constitutive Recognition on the Right to Self-Determination: An Analysis of United States Recognition Practices Utilizing the Chinese Question as a Guide' (1979) 14(1) Valparaiso University Law Review 123; and others.

is doubtful more generally whether the creation of a State can or should be asserted as a moral right except in very limited circumstances.

(7) *The Problem of Practice.* The main and most dangerous argument against the constitutive theory is that it is not supported by practice (the authors sometimes rather maintain that the declaratory theory is supported by practice—I take this to have the same implications here).[67] Interestingly, some constitutivist authors hold the contrary to be true, namely, that it is precisely the constitutive theory that is supported by State and judicial practice.[68] I discussed the main contours of the practice and case law landscape in the previous chapter, and, suffice it to say at this point, some of the more prominent sources can be interpreted in more than one way. While some jurisprudence unambiguously takes a stance in favour of either theory, such case law is too few and far between to support the conclusion that practice in general proves a particular theory.

3. The Declaratory View

On account of the declaratory theory's broader appeal today but also the constitutive doctrine's association with positivism—a school oft maligned in the aftermath of the Second World War and the Holocaust[69]—the former is perceived as the more modern, progressive position compared to its older, amoral, and relativistic counterpart.[70] As the idea of a disconnection between law and morality grows less appealing, and State sovereignty has become burdened with more negative connotations than positive ones, the main contours of the declaratory theory are hailed as more amenable to contemporary sensibilities: declaratism thus supplanted constitutivism. This is a misconception. To the contrary, as a theory of law,

[67] See eg Institut de Droit International, 'La reconnaissance des nouveaux États et des nouveaux gouvernements' (1936) 39-II Annuaire de l'Institut de Droit International 300; Talmon (n 3) 106; Shaw (n 3) 331; and *Sixth report on unilateral acts of States, by Mr Victor Rodríguez Cedeño, Special Rapporteur* (30 May 2003) A/CN.4/534, para 91.

[68] See eg Cavaglieri (n 30) 345–46 and Lauterpacht (n 1) 43ff, both of whom insist that State practice and jurisprudence overwhelmingly support the constitutive view; Verdross is unable to determine which theory is supported in practice, whereas Anzilotti remarks that the declaratory theory is 'still widespread' (*encore largement répandue*) but denies its validity regardless; see Verdross (n 26) 318ff and Anzilotti (n 27) 162–63.

[69] See on this topic eg Anthony J Sebok, 'Misunderstanding Positivism' (1995) 93(7) Michigan Law Review 2054; Andrei Marmor, 'Legal Positivism: Still Descriptive and Morally Neutral' (2006) 26(4) Oxford Journal of Legal Studies 683–794; Herlinde Pauer-Studer, 'Kelsen's Legal Positivism and the Challenge of Nazi Law' in Maria Carla Galavotti, Elisabeth Nemeth, and Friedrich Stadler (eds), *European Philosophy of Science—Philosophy of Science in Europe and the Viennese Heritage* (Springer 2014) 223; and others.

[70] For example, Fitzmaurice ties the constitutive theory to the early nineteenth-century international system which was later abandoned; see Fitzmaurice (n 5) 25.

declaratism is older that constitutivism, and it is the latter which is a reaction, rather than the former.

Were one to take the works of Bentham and Austin as the roots of legal positivism, then the reasons for this should become obvious because the origins of the declaratory doctrine pre-date them by several decades. One naturalist writer, Vattel, holds a place of honour in the history of the declaratory theory, even though he did not fashion a general theory of recognition. In the *Law of Nations*, Vattel wrote: 'Every nation that governs itself, under what form soever, without dependence on any foreign power, is a sovereign state ... To give a nation a right to make an immediate figure in this grand society, it is sufficient that it be really sovereign and independent, that is, that it govern itself by its own authority and laws.'[71]

The common origins of naturalism and declaratism are frequently remarked by legal scholarship. Chen sees the notion, essential to natural law teaching, that States are bound by laws higher than their own will, as also present in the approach of declaratist scholars: 'In contrast to the positivist theory, the natural law theory is one which purports to furnish an explanation for the ultimate obligatory character of international law, apart from the wills of individual States. In this theory, the declaratory doctrine of recognition finds a natural alliance.'[72] Fitzmaurice adds, 'For [the naturalist lawyer], while consent may be necessary for the creation of particular new rules, the obligation to conform to international law as a whole is inherent, while equally, the obligation to apply it in respect of any given entity is inherent in the situation and the facts, rather than a matter of consent and recognition.'[73] Of course, this does not mean that contemporary declaratist scholars are all naturalists, just as constitutivists need not be positivists, although the moral arguments in favour of declaratism are reminiscent of the reason-based thinking so typical of the Enlightenment. On the other hand, the influence of positivism is also evident in some formulations of the declaratory theory, particularly when the authors insist on the recognising State's exercise of judicial function in international law.

The main aspects of declaratism are succinctly drawn up by Shaw:

> [The declaratory theory] maintains that recognition is merely an acceptance by states of an already existing situation. A new state will acquire capacity in international law not by virtue of the consent of others but by virtue of a particular factual situation. It will be legally constituted by its own efforts and circumstances and will not have to await the procedure of recognition by other states. This doctrine owes a lot to traditional positivist thought on the supremacy of the state and

[71] Emer de Vattel, *The Law of Nations* (Liberty Fund, Inc 2008) 83.

[72] Chen (n 2) 18.

[73] Fitzmaurice (n 5) 18; cf Klabbers' view that declaratist scholars seek 'to strip the law from political elements'. Klabbers, *International Law* (n 5) 78.

> the concomitant weakness or non-existence of any central guidance in the international community.[74]

The word 'recognition' thus achieves its true meaning under the declaratory approach, as the State granting recognition merely observes a factual situation that produces specific legal consequences independently of its own will. This must be distinguished from Kelsen's constitutivist theory of recognition, as these legal consequences are attached to the material fact itself and not to their quasi-judicial determination. The distinction between material and legal facts thus becomes non-existent, at least in the domain of statehood, because material facts are themselves legal facts.

The declaratory 'camp' is seemingly more uniform in its views than the constitutive one, if only because most of its adherents do not feel obliged to produce elaborate treatises on the matter like their more verbose constitutivist counterparts.[75] This is because the declaratist understanding does not oblige its defenders to ask themselves whether international law can define a State, or whether recognition confers legal personality. If legal personality flows directly from statehood, then the latter must be regulated by law because surely every legal system defines its own subjects; and if independent States are subjects of the law, then that law confers on them at least some rights and duties regardless of the approval of other existing subjects. With some exceptions, declaratist scholars do not distinguish between the notion of a State 'in general' and a legal concept of statehood, or between statehood and a State's legal personality (because the latter is simply a facet of the former). This is why declaratist scholars are so vexed by constitutivist relativism, because if an entity is a State then it must be one at all times and for all purposes.[76] This simplicity stands out as an advantage of declaratism, but this alone does not rule in its favour, and the whole doctrine is typically too rigid to explain contrary practice. If the constitutivist approach, with its insistence on bilateral legal relations between subjects, is microscopic and relativist, then declaratism is macroscopic and absolutist, insisting that likes be treated alike, at least on a conceptual level. However, to describe the whole of the declaratist school as monolithic does not do it justice, and there exist some important points where its representatives diverge, such as regarding the question of whether statehood is opposable under both international and domestic law.[77] These distinctions are interesting but they

[74] Shaw (n 3) 330–31.

[75] There are, of course, lengthy and intricate reproductions of the declaratory theory, such as those of Charpentier and Verhoeven, if the latter is taken as a declaratist scholar.

[76] See as illustrative of this point Crawford's position in Crawford (n 55) 19–28 and James Crawford, 'Chance, Order, Change: The Course of International Law: General Course on Public International Law' (2014) 365 RCADI 9, 147ff.

[77] See eg Tatjana Papić, 'Derecognition of States: The Case of Kosovo' (2022) 53 Cornell International Law Journal 683–729, who espouses a declaratory view internationally but admits that recognition and derecognition are important from a domestic law perspective.

are only marginally relevant to this analysis. I therefore suggest that the school's insistence on the opposability of statehood based on effectivity, and not recognition, be taken as the principal element of declaratism.

3.1 Specific Formulations of the Declaratory View

The declaratory view dominates much of early nineteenth century literature, when it was common to equate sovereignty with independence from a foreign power. As sovereignty thus construed refers to a factual situation, it cannot depend on diplomatic recognition. For example, Klüber—who does not give much attention to the matter of recognition—finds that a State obtains sovereignty either originally, upon its historic creation, or when it frees itself from a state of submission to another (foreign) Power.[78] Neither recognition nor guarantees need be provided by foreign Powers to validate the new State's sovereignty,[79] although this State would nonetheless be wise to seek such courtesy from their part.

An early attempt to formulate a more comprehensive approach was made by Heffter. In his 1844 treatise on public international law, this author recalled that the rise of individual States, regardless of their form of government, is ruled by historical processes.[80] The creation of a State is complete when the requisite elements of statehood have been met, namely the will and power of the entity to impose itself as a State. Once this has been achieved, other States are obliged to treat the newcomer as a State and to allow it to exist peacefully. Political recognition is not required of existing States, just as a new State is not expected to recognise those already in existence. In Heffter's view, recognition is nothing else than a confirmation of international legal existence and the admission of a new member into the existing international legal system.[81]

Heffter's theory was given a more refined treatment by Rivier, who was acquainted with the former's work.[82] Unlike Jellinek and Bluntschli, whose conception of a State he otherwise agrees with,[83] Rivier argued that the definition of a State may be found in international law itself.[84] According to Rivier, a sovereign State

[78] Johann Ludwig Klüber, *Europäisches Völkerrecht, Erster Band* (J G Cotta'sche Buchhandlung 1821) 49.

[79] 'Zu ihrer rechtlichen Gültigkeit bedarf es, bei untadelhaftem Besitz, weder einer *Anerkennung* noch einer *Garantie* von Seite anderer Mächte.' ibid.

[80] 'Die Entstehung der Einzelstaaten in ihren mancherlei Nüancen ist im Allgemeinen eine Thatsache des historischen Processes.' August Wilhelm Heffter, *Das europäische Völkerrecht der Gegenwart* (E H Schroeder 1844) 38.

[81] 'Die Anerkennung ist eben nichts als die Bekräftigung der völkerrechtlichen Existenz und die Zulassung eines neuen Gliedes in das schon bestehende völkerrechtliche System.' ibid 39.

[82] In his *Principes du droit des gens* Rivier frequently invokes Heffter's *Das europäische Völkerrecht der Gegenwart*, but not expressly in relation to diplomatic recognition.

[83] Rivier, *Principes du droit des gens* (n 5) 45ff.

[84] ibid 47.

exists as soon as a community fulfils the essential criteria of statehood, however this may have come to pass.[85] Even though the definition of a State is legal, its existence is factual, which is why it cannot be described as either lawful or unlawful.[86] Recognition merely takes cognisance of the fact of statehood and represents an approval that the legal conditions of statehood have been met. The recognising State formally engages to respect the rights of the new State, although these rights exist independently of recognition and flow from the simple fact of statehood that makes the relevant community a member of the 'society of nations', Rivier's euphemism for the international legal order[87] (which he saw as a European phenomenon, limited to the 'superior races' of humanity, but one that could be extended to non-European States through the will of existing 'club members').[88]

For Brierly, the notion of a 'State' is a primordial element of international law, meaning that the international legal meaning of statehood is different from the notion as may exist in other disciplines.[89] But the State is also an institution, a community of human beings gathered for a common purpose and a means whereby they regulate their community's legal life. If the international legal order is nothing else than a collection of independent domestic legal systems, then a State could only ever exist as an effectivity: it is upon international law to provide the tools with which to determine if this is the case.[90]

A unique declaratory view of recognition is maintained by Charpentier and deserves to be recounted here in greater detail. In his influential doctoral thesis on the matter, Charpentier switches the focus of his study of recognition from the act of recognition to its underlying and preceding situation. What States recognise, he writes, is an opposability, which is not an act but a legal fact: opposability signifies the necessary reaction to a modification of the international legal order in the behaviour of a third State[91] (by 'third State' he means one which has not participated in the modification of the legal order and is thus external to it).[92] Every modification of the international legal order, regardless of whether it is a new situation or a new rule, raises the question of its opposability to third States. Although recognition is usually considered in respect of States, governments, and belligerents, States commonly 'recognise' all manner of modifications of the legal order, such

[85] ibid 54.
[86] ibid 55.
[87] ibid 57.
[88] See on this ibid 7ff. Rivier infamously believed that 'inferior races' do not possess a 'legal conscience' and cannot therefore participate in the same international legal community as 'superior' ones ('Entre nous et les peuples de races inférieures s'ouvre un abîme, analogue à celui qui séparait les Grecs des barbares, tandis qu'un gouffre moins profond, ou même un simple fossé que l'on peut franchir et que l'on franchit, nous sépare des nations de races moyennes, des États à demi-civilisés ou dont la civilisation diffère de la nôtre en quelques traits essentiels.').
[89] Brierly (n 59) 48–49.
[90] ibid 50.
[91] Charpentier, *La reconnaissance internationale* (n 51) 9.
[92] ibid 5.

as borders, claims, protectorates, even norms of customary law, in other words, 'toutes les situations juridiques subjectives résultant soit de l'établissement de compétences nouvelles ... soit de la modification des compétences'.[93] The creation of a new State produces legal effects regardless of its recognition by third States. Opposable are those modifications requiring third States to change their behaviour regardless of recognition; unopposable are those which depend on their consent (which is synonymous with recognition). Charpentier insists that just as there is nothing to prove that the extension of the effects of a modification to a third State requires its recognition, so too nothing demonstrates that recognition could achieve such an effect.[94] Thus, Charpentier denies, unlike most authors, that recognition of governments is any different from recognition of States, and argues that they are both equally opposable as an exercise of new governmental competencies.[95] Domestic jurisprudence almost equally showcases situations where judges follow the position of their executive vis-à-vis the new State or government and those where they diverge from its position. This, he argues, proves that reality and facts, and not simply the will of States, influence judges' application of foreign law, leading him to conclude that recognition, or lack thereof, by one's own State is not crucial in this regard.

For Fitzmaurice, international law relies on the principle of automaticity, meaning that it applies *ipso facto* to both existing and new States regardless of their consent to be bound by its rules.[96] However, whereas the general applicability of international law to States cannot hinge upon their consent (because this would negate the principle of the rule of law), it is less clear whether existing States are bound automatically by the existence of new States in a similar fashion. Fitzmaurice argues that the effects of recognition have evolved over time: whereas the strict constitutive view was certainly correct when international law governed the relations of relatively few States—'consisting of the States of Europe, one or two States on the European periphery, and certain States overseas possessing a European origin and cultural heritage'[97]—it was possible to regard the international community 'a sort of club, admission to which must be sought and specifically accorded'.[98] Today, this community 'is no longer like a club which is joined, but like a clan or family into which persons are born'.[99] Fitzmaurice argues that this fact has even been recognised in more recent constitutive doctrine, with more constitutivist scholars accepting the existence of an obligation to recognise when the requisite

[93] ibid 4 (emphasis in the source).
[94] 'Or, non seulement rien ne prouve que l'extension à un État tiers des effets de la modification nécessite sa reconnaissance ... mais rien ne prouve non plus que la reconnaissance ait pour effet d'étendre à l'État qui l'accorde les effets de la modification.' ibid.
[95] ibid 15ff.
[96] Fitzmaurice (n 5) 16.
[97] ibid 25.
[98] ibid.
[99] ibid.

elements have come together and given rise to a State. Such a 'moderate' constitutive view is easily reconcilable with the declaratory view, 'for such a duty can only exist if and because there is something there to be recognized: recognition in those circumstances is recognition of an already accomplished and completed situation'.[100]

Much of the more recent doctrine expresses itself in favour of the declaratory doctrine, with lawyers coming from the Anglo-American tradition particularly favourable to this approach.[101] These authors do not insist on an elaborate or comprehensive theory of recognition and are content to conclude quite simply that practice, reason and/or modern sensibilities speak in favour of the declaratory approach, however imperfect. Quite prominently, the International Law Commission's Special Rapporteur Rodríguez Cedeño embraced the declaratory theory, finding that 'the declarative theory has been confirmed by the practice of States'[102] but also that 'non-recognition also has important legal ramifications' in specific situations.[103] Nevertheless, there is still today no doctrinal consensus on this matter, and scholarship adopting the constitutive view is still widespread.[104]

3.2 Objections to the Declaratory View

Because of its comparative simplicity, the declaratory view has attracted fewer lines of criticism than the constitutive approach. This does not detract from the cogency of some of the counter-arguments.

(1) *Logical Objections.* Critics of the declaratory approach occasionally highlight aspects which are seemingly in conflict with each other. Lauterpacht identifies as a 'logical difficulty' the fact that most declaratist scholars deny the existence of an obligation to recognise, but ascribe as inherent to new States rights and duties typically attributed to recognition: 'This means, upon analysis, that the newcomer is entitled as a matter of legal right to claim what are usually regarded as the normal legal consequences

[100] ibid 26.

[101] See eg Ian Brownlie, *Principles of Public International Law* (OUP 1998) 87–88; Crawford (n 55) 19–28; Shaw (n 3) 329–36; Clapham, *Brierly's Law of Nations* (n 2) 150–52; but also Vojin Dimitrijević and others, *Osnovi međunarodnog javnog prava* (Belgrade Centre for Human Rights 2007) 80–81; and others.

[102] 'Acts of recognition in general could represent a specific category of... acts whereby States assume unilateral obligations.' Cedeño, *Sixth report on unilateral acts of States* (n 67) para 91.

[103] ibid para 92.

[104] See eg Suy (n 9) 206–07; NA Maryan Green, *International Law* (Pitman Publishing 1987) 35–36; Karl Zemanek, 'The Legal Foundations of the International System: General Course on Public International Law' (1997) 266 RCADI 9, 82–83; Jure Vidmar, 'Remarks' (2013) 107 ASIL Proceedings 215; Emmanuel Decaux and Olivier de Frouville, *Droit international public* (Dalloz 2018) 188–93; and others.

of recognition, but that it is not entitled to claim recognition as such.'[105] The solution whereby recognition is 'a political declaration of willingness into normal diplomatic relations' is, for him, 'questionable', as it is 'contrary to the practice of governments and of courts'.[106] Another argument raised by Wyler is that, if statehood is a nothing but a 'fact' for international law, then the concept of statehood must be external to the law and precede it, which ultimately denies the possibility of a legal definition of States.[107] Evidently, the weight of logical arguments against declaratism largely depends on one's own perspective, and they do not necessarily disprove it on their own.

(2) *Recognition as a Formality.* There is a widespread opinion in the constitutivist 'camp' that, if States actually engage in recognition, then surely it must serve a purpose of some sort—preferably, a legal one.[108] Dugard considers the notion that a State can exist without any recognition at all as 'errant non-sense'.[109] Although many declaratist scholars conceive of recognition as a political rather than legal act, many of them will at least concede it some limited role, for example in the evaluation of facts endowed with legal consequences, as solidifying statehood, or even give it limited constitutive effect (eg if the recipient does not otherwise meet the criteria of statehood).[110] The main objection, however, is that States themselves do not consider their recognition or non-recognition as merely political.

(3) *The Problem of Exceptions.* In reality, there is no necessary link between the effectivity and opposability of statehood. Classical declaratory doctrine cannot explain this phenomenon. Just as there exist *de facto* States to whom this quality is legally denied by a majority of the international community, so too may we find entities lacking the requisite elements of statehood that are nevertheless treated as States by others. The declaratist scholar Talmon concedes: 'in the case of collectively non-recognized States, declaratory theorists are at pains to prove the non-existence of a State. If such a State were

[105] Lauterpacht (n 1) 2.

[106] ibid 3.

[107] 'Soulignons que, sur le plan logique, l'approche "déclarativiste" stricte, dans la mesure où elle considère que la formation de l'État relève du "Fait" exclusivement, implique l'existence d'une définition de l'État hors du droit international, comme si une notion objective d'État était antérieure à l'univers juridique; c'est vraisemblablement ce présupposé qui sous-tend l'affirmation, fréquemment avancée, selon laquelle l'État serait un "fait primaire" pour le droit international.' Wyler, *Théorie et pratique de la reconaissance d'état* (n 4) 143.

[108] Cavaglieri asks: 'Quelle serait … la valeur de cette reconnaissance si elle n'entraîne pas avec elle la validité, l'acceptation de certaines règles?' Cavaglieri (n 30) 326.

[109] John Dugard, 'The Secession of States and Their Recognition in the Wake of Kosovo' (2013) 357 RCADI 9, 51.

[110] See eg Crawford (n 55) 93; Vaughan Lowe, *International Law* (OUP 2007) 163; and Shaw (n 3) 331.

actually to exist, they would face the dilemma of not being able to justify its non-recognition, and in particular the withholding of the rights which are inherent in statehood'.[111] Some declaratist authors have attempted to resolve this problem by introducing additional criteria of statehood, including 'legality' in some sense,[112] but even when this practice does not look like cherry-picking, it actually compounds the problem rather than resolve it. Others, such as Talmon, insist more consistently that entities meeting the criteria of statehood must be considered States even if they are not recognised by a single other State and if they are universally described as 'illegal'. He rejects the notion that a State's existence may be made void by reference to the principle of *ex injuria jus non oritur* and *jus cogens*, and opines that at best such States may be denied some of the rights inherent in statehood as a form of sanction.[113]

(4) *The Problem of Legal Basis.* At least some iterations of the declaratory theory presuppose the existence of a rule of positive law linking effectivity with opposability. If the fact of statehood is identical to legal statehood, then identifying the source for this apparent rule is certainly warranted. Many declaratists will doubtless argue that effectivity is inherent in international law as an *a priori* characteristic, in which case it is not necessary to identify a specific rule of positive law—that effectivity leads to opposability is then an axiom of the legal system. However, the oft-repeated argument that State practice supports the declaratory theory drapes this approach in positive law terms, for which reason their critics are right to ask that the existence of a specific norm to this effect be empirically demonstrated. If such a norm exists, then it must be possible to identify it within the commonly accepted sources of international law, presumably customary law. Several constitutivist scholars deny the existence of such a norm.[114] If a norm does not exist, then only a principle-based approach is possible, and this seems to favour the constitutive view, which does not require a similar norm insofar as recognition is a legal act capable of producing legal results: the act itself, and not a rule of general international law, leads to opposability.

(5) *The Problem of Practice.* This objection is the same as the one declaratist scholarship raises against the constitutive theory, only this time it is the opponent view making the accusation that practice does not support the declaratory doctrine.

[111] Talmon (n 3) 107.
[112] See eg Crawford (n 55) 63ff.
[113] Talmon (n 3) 143ff.
[114] See notably Anzilotti (n 27) 164 and Cavaglieri (n 30) 345.

4. The 'Mixed' Theories

A third theoretical approach is sometimes raised, usually referred to as 'mixed', that combines elements of both the declaratory and constitutive doctrines. These do not belong to a common doctrinal tradition and it is not possible to identify a common thread, particularly in light of this work's focus on opposability as the relevant yardstick for classifying any theory of recognition (the verdict on this matter is usually categorical, namely either recognition is required for opposability or it is not). Authors tend to have an extreme view of mixed approaches: if they do not dismiss them as *a priori* baseless or inconceivable,[115] they see them as the mainstream approach in contemporary practice.[116] In my view, most of the latter group of scholars may be described as either constitutivists or declaratists rather than as espousing a 'mixed' position. For example, Wyler argues for a 'mixed' view that involves joining elements of both the constitutivist and declaratist understanding: for the recipient of recognition, it is mere confirmation of statehood, and thus declaratory; but for the State granting recognition, it is an irrevocable source of obligations towards the object of recognition. In my view, if the new State is opposable to the recognising State as a result of recognition, then the act must surely be constitutive.[117] Shaw also finds that '[a]ctual practice leads to a middle position between [the constitutive and declaratory] perceptions', namely that '[t]he act of recognition by one state of another indicates that the former regards the latter as having conformed with the basic requirements of international law as to the creation of a state'.[118] Such an understanding is declaratory in this typology. Proposals advanced by authors such as Verdross, Pradier-Fodéré, and Fauchille could all be described as mixed, but it does not appear to me that drawing a line between effective statehood and admission into the international community, or between the enjoyment and exercise of sovereignty, is essentially different from the basic tenets of the constitutive theory.

It follows that a truly mixed approach is difficult to come by, for it would necessarily entail a significant modification of the basic premises regarding the role of effectivity and opposability so that recognition would either become an ingredient of effectivity itself, or opposability would have to be compartmentalised and synchronously flow both from effectivity and recognition. The most intriguing theories to that effect have been proposed by Verhoeven, Frowein, Talmon, Zemanek, and Dugard.

[115] 'One can sympathize with these views, but at a fundamental level a choice has to be made.' Crawford (n 55) 27.

[116] See eg Wyler (n 4).

[117] 'Du point de vue de l'entité étatique nouvelle, la Reconaissance ne serait qu'une attestation de naissance (effet déclaratif), alors que, du point de vue de son auteur, elle déploierait, de par son irrévocabilité, un effet constitutif... Pour d'autres, l'effet constitutif consisterait plutôt dans l'attribution d'une personnalité juridique internationale désormais opposable à l'auteur de la Reconaissance.' ibid 10.

[118] Shaw (n 3) 331.

Verhoeven made a serious attempt to conceive of recognition as a part of effectivity itself, namely a necessary element of statehood. The basis for the approach had been set by De Visscher[119] and later also accepted by Salmon[120] but it was ultimately Verhoeven who presented it in the most elaborate manner. According to this 'Belgian doctrine' (its main advocates were all Belgian lawyers), it is pertinent to distinguish between recognition as a legal act and a legal fact. Recognition is only a legal act insofar as it produces legal consequences by expressing a State's will.[121] Because an act expresses will, its effects must be identical to its content. Legal facts refer to the effects or consequences of the application of a norm of international law; thus, the facet of recognition in which it is a legal fact involves a determination of specific effects attached to it by law.[122]

In comparing recognition as a legal act and a legal fact, Verhoeven inferred from doctrine and jurisprudence that a State's existence is factual and that its acts are opposable to others regardless of recognition. The act of recognition does not produce legal consequences of its own for either its object or author—except, perhaps, regarding the rules prohibiting aggression, which may be limited to 'recognised' States, although Verhoeven himself was not favourable to this conclusion.[123]

Recognition cannot therefore be considered a legal act. On the other hand, as a material fact, recognition has probative value for determining the existence of a new State by attesting that the criteria of statehood have been met.[124] At this point, Verhoeven diverges from classical declaratist scholars by arguing that the material fact of recognition, beyond its probative value, may itself be an effectivity. The State is an 'effectivity of relations' (*effectivité de relations*) that it enjoys with other States; recognition is crucial to demonstrate the existence of a State in this regard.[125] This explains why a State with no or limited recognition, even if it 'exists' by fulfilling the three traditional criteria, cannot be said to exist at all from an international law perspective. It does not matter, he writes, whether Rhodesia met the conditions of statehood: what matters is that the United Nations did not *want* to treat it as such, obviating the need for any factual analysis of its statehood.[126] In this sense, recognition plays a constitutive role in the formation of statehood, forming part of its effectivity, but it is not an immediate source of opposability.

Frowein identifies as inherent in the 'imperfect nature' of international law that there exists no possibility 'of clarifying whether entities have the quality of States

[119] See Charles de Visscher, *Problèmes d'interprétation judiciaire en droit international public* (Pedone 1963) 190ff.

[120] Jean JA Salmon, *La reconnaissance d'état* (Librairie Armand Colin 1971).

[121] Joe Verhoeven, *La reconnaissance internationale dans la pratique contemporaine* (Pedone 1975) 666–67.

[122] ibid 667.

[123] ibid 718–19.

[124] ibid 668ff.

[125] ibid 673–74.

[126] ibid 684.

although they are not recognized as such’.[127] Although Frowein’s views of recognition are essentially constitutive,[128] he nevertheless concludes that ‘State practice shows that entities which in fact govern a specific territory for a prolonged period will be treated as partial subjects of international law’.[129] For such entities, he develops the concept of ‘*de facto* regime’, which he distinguishes from an unrecognised government effectively in control of the territory of a State. Thus, *de facto* regimes are entities ‘claiming to be States or governments, which [control] more or less clearly defined territories without being recognized—at least by many States—as States or governments ... irrespective of whether [this entity] claims to be a new secessionist State ... or whether it aims to take over the government in a recognized State but is not yet in effective control of the whole territory’[130] (*de facto* regimes differ from Ronen’s quasi-states in that they claim statehood whereas the latter do not). He believes that, even though *de facto* regimes do not enjoy the full rights accorded to recognised States, practice shows that a number of rules nevertheless apply to their relations with other States; these include the prohibition of the use of force, the *de facto* regime’s capacity to incur responsibility for violations of international law, and its ability to maintain relations with States and to conclude treaties with them (although these cannot in principle amount to full diplomatic relations).[131] Whether a *de facto* regime’s acts may be recognised in a State’s municipal law will depend on that State’s own practice, although the tendency is that effectiveness be treated as the relevant criterion at least regarding conflict of laws.[132] Therefore, in Frowein’s view, opposability largely hangs on recognition, but at least some of the rights of statehood also flow from effectivity.[133]

Talmon’s own view is exemplary of a theory compartmentalising opposability. His starting point is strictly declaratist, but this author acknowledges that declaratist scholarship has had difficulties in explaining universal non-recognition of certain entities that doubtless meet the criteria of statehood.[134] His resolution to this problem is first, to divorce statehood from considerations of legality and to accept that opposability flows from effectivity; but also second, to relativise that opposability by identifying a fairly limited number of rights inherent in

[127] Jochen A Frowein, ‘De Facto Regime’ in Anne Peters and Rüdiger Wolfrum (eds), *Max Planck Encyclopedias of International Law* (OUP 2013) para 2 <https://opil.ouplaw.com/display/10.1093/law:epil/9780199231690/law-9780199231690-e1395> last accessed 13 June 2024.

[128] Frowein does not state this position explicitly, but it is implied from ‘his intention to overcome [the] “basic weakness”’ of the constitutive theory. Talmon (n 3) 103, fn 14.

[129] Frowein (n 127) para 3.

[130] ibid paras 1 and 3.

[131] ibid paras 4ff.

[132] ibid para 10.

[133] For a criticism of Frowein’s approach, see Talmon (n 3) 103–04; cf Georg Nolte, ‘Faktizität und Subjektivität im Völkerrecht: Anmerkungen zu Jochen Froweins “Das de facto-Regime im Völkerrecht” im Licht aktueller Entwicklungen’ (2015) 75 Zeitschrift für ausländisches öffentliches Recht und Völkerrecht 715.

[134] Talmon (n 3) 120ff.

statehood.[135] Existing States are always free to withhold typical diplomatic and other courtesies (as 'optional relations') from the newcomer as they please; they are bound to respect only these minimum rights; but if the State is created unlawfully, binding third States to non-recognition, then they may invoke such unlawful creation as a circumstance precluding wrongfulness when denying even those minimal, inherent rights.[136] These rights are still opposable to other States: non-recognising States are simply justified in disrespecting them. The circumstances allowing for such a response are very limited and would involve either a Security Council resolution ordering non-recognition or the existence of a breach of a peremptory norm of international law. Non-recognition thus becomes a countermeasure, and even a sanction: 'The collective non-recognition of a new State is intended to induce the State to dissolve itself and to return to the *status quo ante*.'[137]

A concise but thought-provoking mixed theory is also provided by Zemanek, who argued that the debate between the constitutive and declaratory views is today obsolete because their proponents confused two separate aspects of recognition. On the one hand, the existence of a State is a legal fact of which recognition may only be declaratory. However, an unrecognised State is only conferred by international law such rights as stem from *jus cogens* or general international law (eg the right not to be targeted by aggression), whereas recognition is necessary for other rights and obligations to materialise in bilateral legal relations with other States.[138]

Finally, a mixed approach to recognition of States is advocated by John Dugard. Dugard criticises both the declaratory approach and extreme forms of constitutivism,[139] although he found that '[w]ithout recognition the State does not exist as far as non-recognizing States are concerned' and that '[i]n this sense recognition is constitutive'.[140] Neither do States enjoy absolute authority in determining the existence of a new State, nor can the Montevideo formula always serve as an exact, objective, and certain determinant of such existence. In practice, States typically rely on the Montevideo criteria in addition to considerations of self-determination, human rights, and democracy.[141] Recognition is particularly important in cases of secession, as secessionist entities that are not at least partially recognised as independent cannot hope to achieve statehood regardless of effectivity. However, although Dugard finds that recognition is constitutive on a bilateral level, he rejects the concept of relative existence (the idea that a State can exist for some but not for others), and posits instead that international law has to resolve the problem of recognition *erga omnes*. The crucial mechanism for proving such

[135] ibid 148ff.
[136] ibid 153ff.
[137] ibid 181.
[138] See Zemanek (n 104) 82–84.
[139] Dugard, 'The Secession of States and Their Recognition' (n 109) 54ff.
[140] ibid 56.
[141] ibid.

existence today is membership in the United Nations. Dugard writes: 'Once an entity is admitted to the United Nations with a two-thirds majority in the General Assembly on the recommendation of the Security Council its general statehood is placed beyond doubt. But when a State is not admitted to the United Nations either because it falls short of the required majority in the General Assembly—as with Kosovo—or because of a threatened veto in the Security Council—as with Palestine—no answer can be given to the question at which point an entity becomes a State *erga omnes*.'[142] On the opposability axis, Dugard's interpretation of positive law puts him closer to the constitutive camp, although his insistence on the role of collective recognition in contemporary practice (which is not merely *de lege ferenda*) also allows him to be seen as an author proposing a mixed theory.

As thought-provoking as they may be, some of the mixed theories described above do not conform to the reality of State practice. Compartmentalising opposability may be possible, but there exist at least two fundamental problems in this regard. First, it is difficult to infer from domestic jurisprudence that States accord only some rights to unrecognised States while denying them others. Rather, it seems that judges in domestic systems, being satisfied of an entity's statehood (whether based on recognition or effectivity), infer that it is entitled to the same treatment as any other State. The executive power's approach to a State it does not recognise may be more ambiguous, however such practice is markedly inconsistent and difficult to analyse as governments may refrain from undertaking certain actions based on political or strategic, instead of legal, considerations. Second, on a conceptual level, the fact that a *de facto* regime or unrecognised State enjoys some but not all or even most rights as a recognised State could mean quite simply that its statehood is not opposable: for if an entity is accepted as being a State in any way, the legal implications should be very clear—one does not cherry-pick the rights to be thus made opposable. Conversely, a 'mixed' theory that relies on the interplay of relevant norms applicable to different situations may be more realistic (this is the case with Dugard's approach to collective recognition, although bilateral recognition may still not be fully declaratory—for example, from a domestic law perspective—in case of a new State's UN membership). Thus, in some situations, there may exist rules of international law establishing the opposability of a State regardless of recognition; in others, recognition may be indispensable.

5. Conclusion

Because State practice is at best elusive, doctrinal views retain great importance in the study of recognition. Their role in this regard is manifold: first, there are

[142] ibid 57. For Dugard's approach to collective recognition, which is a key component of his theory, see in particular John Dugard, *Recognition and the United Nations* (Grotius Publications Limited 1987).

aspects on which doctrine largely agrees, regardless of the scholar's provenance and theoretical belonging; second, there are certain aspects of international law which doctrine has correctly identified in State practice, as unclear as it is; and, third, the fact that legal scholarship cannot agree on certain points also says something about the state of international law in this regard—for example, that it does not at all regulate certain aspects of diplomatic recognition.

If we take the opposability of statehood as the basis for categorising doctrinal approaches, then these may be divided into constitutivist and declaratist ones. For the constitutive view, recognition is required for an entity's statehood to become opposable to another State even if that entity possesses material statehood. For the declaratory view, opposability flows automatically from effectivity, although some versions of the theory add requirements other than effectivity to the equation. Both views have advantages and disadvantages that have been discussed extensively in legal literature and both are reflected to a certain extent in State practice, although not in a way that allows either school of thought to claim victory.

A third view, described as 'mixed', is not a uniform school of thought but an array of diverse theories that cannot be classified as either constitutive or declaratory. If opposability is the axis of classification, then only approaches compartmentalising opposability in light of recognition or somehow overcoming it altogether may properly be described as 'mixed' rather than constitutivist or declaratist. As interesting as they may be, the diverse views advocated under the mixed chapeau do not explain the creation of statehood in a fully satisfying manner.

In my view, a theory grounded in positive law must assume a normative approach. A normative theory of recognition will focus on its effects, which is to say, opposability. If opposability can flow from recognition, but could flow from another source as well (such as a rule of general international law), then opposability will sometimes depend on recognition, and at other times, it will not. I distinguish between the different normative situations in the following chapters.

9
When Recognition is Declaratory

1. A Normative Theory of Recognition

As discussed in earlier chapters, recognition in its basic and most common form is a unilateral act whereby its author expresses cognisance that the prerequisites for the application of certain legal norms have been met and accepts the new situation as opposable. A is opposable to B if B is legally required to modify its behaviour towards A.

The declaratory approach hinges on the existence of a rule of general international law linking effectivity to opposability. Such a rule would make A opposable to B if it effectively exists as a State, regardless of the latter's recognition. However, no such rule can be credibly demonstrated to exist, *ergo*, the statehood of B cannot become opposable simply because it is effective. On the other hand, as a unilateral act whose binding power flows from the principle of good faith, recognition can achieve such a result.

Nevertheless, contrary to classical constitutivist doctrine, recognition is not the only possible source of opposability in international law. Normative developments since the end of the Second World War have led to situations where the application of certain other legal rules can achieve the same result as recognition. There also exist rules preventing opposability from arising even if B recognised A.

In this respect, we may distinguish between two types of relationship between recognition and opposability: first, there is independent opposability, which means that opposability arises even in the absence of recognition, making the latter declaratory; and, second, there is dependent opposability, when opposability cannot be established in any other way than through recognition (see Figure 9.1).

Independent opposability exists when a rule of international law—such as the right of self-determination or the provisions of the UN Charter—applies to a situation in such a way to make statehood opposable, which typically occurs with *erga omnes* or *erga omnes partes* effect. If such a rule cannot be identified, then opposability could only be inferred from recognition, which, if it is given, produces effects on a bilateral level. Distinguishing between situations when opposability is independent of recognition and those where it may only be inferred from it is the essential feature of my normative theory of recognition.

Logically, an analysis of whether an entity's statehood is opposable to another should first consider whether there is an applicable rule of international law requiring such a result. Only if this is not the case will it be necessary to consider

Recognition of States in International Law. Pavle Kilibarda, Oxford University Press. © Pavle Kilibarda 2024.
DOI: 10.1093/oso/9780198905653.003.0009

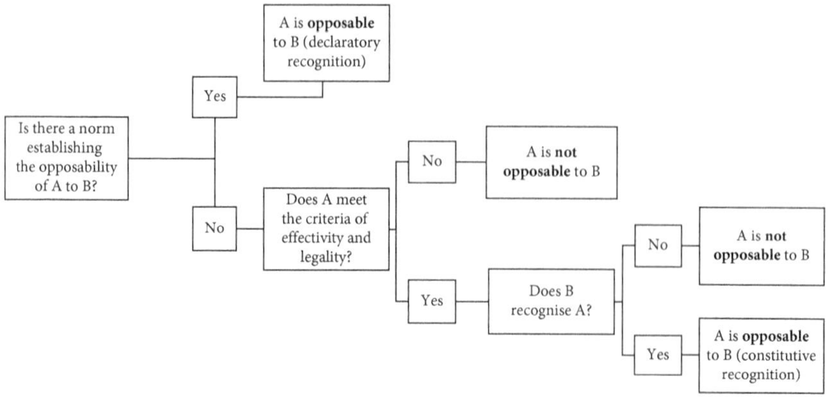

Figure 9.1 The flowchart demonstrates the relationship between recognition and opposability according to whether opposability depends on recognition. If a norm can be found establishing the opposability of State B to State A, then opposability is independent of recognition and recognition is declaratory. If not, opposability depends on recognition and the act will be constitutive. If B does not meet the criteria of effectivity and legality, not even recognition will lead to opposability. This is not the case with declaratory recognition, as situations where opposability is established by a rule of international law cannot at the same time be excluded by it.[1]

the value of bilateral recognition or non-recognition. Therefore I first turn to situations where opposability may be described as rule-based, rather than based on recognition or its bedrock, the principle of good faith. Unlike the latter, general framework of recognition, we may regard these as special regimes of recognition, as its constitutive effect is replaced by specific rules applicable to a situation.

2. Rule-Based Opposability

There is no doubt that the application of international legal norms may result in the creation of opposable statehood regardless of recognition by individual States. Earlier I argued that there is no 'law of recognition' in international law, which I understand as the existence of specific rules governing statehood before, after, or in the absence of recognition (perhaps 'law governing the creation of statehood' would be the more precise term but it is bulky and no more existent than the former). Other than to treat premature recognition as a violation of the Parent State's territorial integrity, international law does not contain particular rules on the effects of recognition, as some constitutivists would have it; neither

[1] Figure created by author.

does it establish a link between effectivity and opposability, as per the prevailing dogma of the declaratory school. However, international law contains rules of general scope—norms on membership in international organisations, on self-determination, and on the validity and effects of unilateral acts—that, when the requisite circumstances arise, result in the creation of statehood in the legal sense, and typically with *erga omnes* effects.

The main reason why recognition is becoming less legally relevant is not a decrease in the number of newly created States—almost forty States have joined the United Nations since 1990, most of them only recently independent—but rather an increase in the number of situations where the opposability of these States was not established through traditional recognition. Lauterpacht deplored the lack of a central authority charged with determining statehood and argued that leaving the matter to individual States led to a 'grotesque spectacle' whereby States could be recognised by some but not by others.[2] However, Lauterpacht wrote before the adoption of the Charter of the United Nations, before the International Court of Justice's (ICJ) advisory opinion on Membership in the United Nations and well before doctrine had become convinced that United Nations membership amounted to an imprimatur of legal statehood. Perhaps not all States are UN members, but all UN members are certainly States, and while the Organisation was never established to determine statehood, it unexpectedly became a functional surrogate for Lauterpacht's hypothetical supreme justice on recognition.

Membership in the United Nations is perhaps the most important situation where recognition by individual Member States becomes declaratory due to the independent application of specific rules of international law, in this case, the provisions of the Charter, but it is not the only one. Similar effects may arise from membership in some regional organisations, and very likely by virtue of the right of self-determination. In addition, there is nothing precluding individual or groups of States from choosing to renege on their 'right of recognition' and take up the obligation to treat new States as such from the moment they meet the criterion of effectivity. This is a point almost entirely neglected by extant doctrine, and it is possible that there exist 'self-contained regimes' on recognition.[3] Finally, the position of a new State separating with the consent of its Parent State is not identical to that of one seceding unilaterally, which may have a bearing on its opposability.

The situations described above may lead to statehood that is opposable regardless of bilateral recognition, rendering such an act merely declaratory. However, it is important to note that none of these may be explained by the classical declaratist

[2] Hersch Lauterpacht, *Recognition in International Law* (CUP 2013) 78.

[3] I employ this term here in a broad sense: recognition cannot be so 'self-contained' as to be independent of the rest of international law; for a discussion of the concept, see Eckart Klein, 'Self-Contained Regime' in Anne Peters and Rüdiger Wolfrum (eds), *Max Planck Encyclopedias of International Law* (OUP 2006) <https://opil.ouplaw.com/display/10.1093/law:epil/9780199231690/law-9780199231690-e1467?prd=EPIL> last accessed 13 June 2024.

approach, which is grounded on effectivity. In none of these cases does an entity become legally entitled to treatment as a State simply by fulfilling the vaunted criteria of statehood under general international law.

3. Membership in the United Nations and Other International Organisations

Discussing the representation of China at the United Nations, then-Secretary-General Trygve Lie, in a letter to the President of the Security Council, examined whether the Organisation could recognise a State or government. The Secretary-General took note of Lauterpacht's idea of having a body capable of providing collective recognition, and determined that the United Nations was not vested with such power: 'The fact remains … that the States have refused to accept any such rule and the United Nations does not possess any authority to recognize either a new State or a new government of an existing State.'[4] To do so, he added, would require amending the Charter, or negotiating a new treaty on the matter. The United Nations cannot formally engage in 'collective recognition', however it can determine, by collective acts, its own membership and representation in the Organisation. Neither of these depend on individual recognition by Member States.[5]

According to Article 4 of the Charter, membership in the Organisation is open to 'all other peace-loving *states* which accept the obligations contained in the present Charter and … are able and willing to carry out these obligations'.[6] That any candidate admitted into the United Nations must first be a State was confirmed by the ICJ in the *Membership in the United Nations* case,[7] although the Court did not elaborate on the meaning of statehood for the purposes of the Charter.

Membership is granted 'by a decision of the General Assembly upon the recommendation of the Security Council'.[8] This means that, according to the Charter, political bodies are bestowed with the duty and power of deciding on whether candidates fulfil legal criteria. According to Cohen, '[t]he political organs of the United Nations have the authority to admit applicants membership in that organization, subject, *inter alia*, to the condition that the applicant be a state … At the same time,

[4] Letter Dated 8 March 1950 from the Secretary-General to the President of the Security Council Transmitting a Memorandum on the Legal Aspects of the Problem of Representation in the United Nations (8 March 1950) S/1466, 3.

[5] ibid 3ff.

[6] Charter of the United Nations, 1 UNTS XVI (adopted 26 June 1945, entered into force 24 October 1945) (hereafter UN Charter) art 4; the provision relevant to original UN members, also necessarily States, is art 3. Emphasis added.

[7] *Conditions of Admission of a State to Membership in the United Nations (Article 4 of the Charter)*, ICJ Reports 57, Advisory Opinion of 28 May 1948, 62.

[8] UN Charter (n 6) art 4.

these organs must consider certain policy problems specifically relevant to the United Nations which cannot be resolved by reference to the other prerequisites of admission: those of "peace-loving" and "able and willing" to fulfill the obligations of the Charter.'[9]

The legal relationship established between UN members by virtue of Article 4 has been said to amount to 'collective recognition', even though this term is employed in an informal sense. Such recognition is achieved through the Organisation's decisions on membership and representation, respectively, for States and governments. Wright explains:

> In this sense, the United Nations, by admitting an entity to its membership, can be properly said to 'recognize' that entity as a state, and if it admits an individual appointed by a government as a representative of a state, it can properly be said to 'recognize' the appointing government as the government of that state. Admittance to the United Nations implies, of course, much more than recognition of statehood, because it adds to the rights and duties of a state under general international law, the rights and duties of a Member under the Charter, but Articles 2 (1) and 4 make it clear that every Member is regarded by the United Nations as a sovereign state with a position under general international law equal to that of other sovereign states. The question is not whether the United Nations can recognize, but whether its recognition is binding on anyone else.[10]

To answer that question, Wright distinguishes between 'particular' and 'general recognition'. 'General recognition' is what international bodies, such as an international tribunal, will take into consideration to determine whether a particular entity is 'recognised' as a State by the 'community of nations' rather than by other States individually. Wright is not able precisely to establish the elements amounting to general recognition, but certainly membership in the United Nations would result in it.[11] Individual States would still be free to grant or refuse their 'particular' recognition, although 'it would ... be difficult for a state to long maintain such an attitude, particularly if it were a member of the United Nations and consequently had to deal with the entity recognized by the United Nations as a state or a government within the organs of the United Nations'.[12] Wright does not delve into the question of the effects of particular recognition, or lack thereof, of a State or government enjoying general recognition, but he admits that the non-recognising State's courts would have to follow the political views of their own executive. Nevertheless, it

[9] Rosalyn Cohen, 'The Concept of Statehood in United Nations Practice' (1961) 109(8) University of Pennsylvania Law Review 1127–71, 1128.

[10] Quincy Wright, 'Some Thoughts About Recognition' (1950) 44(3) The American Journal of International Law 548, 550.

[11] ibid 550ff.

[12] ibid 552.

follows from his analysis that general recognition is sufficient for opposability in the sense discussed here, whereas particular non-recognition would possibly have legal effects in municipal law, but only retain political value internationally.

Although I do not believe that the distinction between general and particular recognition is very useful, I do agree with Wright's conclusion regarding the effects of general, or collective, recognition. This view is commonly expressed in doctrine.[13] The notion of collective recognition through membership in the United Nations has notably been defended by Dugard, who considers the Organisation to act on behalf of the 'international community' when accepting new members.[14] Nevertheless, for the sake of precision, I do not believe that admission into the United Nations replaces the need for bilateral recognition by individual members. Although membership in the Organisation is today almost universal, the Charter is, after all, a treaty, and thus only produces effects among its parties, not towards third States. As far as opposability is concerned, membership in the United Nations can only produce effects *inter partes*, not *erga omnes*. Therefore, it should not be assumed that the statehood of any UN member is opposable to non-members, regardless of the near-universality of its membership.

3.1 Statehood as a Prerequisite of Membership in the United Nations

A more complicated matter is whether statehood is a precondition or product of UN membership. On the face of it, the matter is clear, and statehood is clearly a prerequisite, but practice shows otherwise. The divergence stems both from the notorious obscurity of the concept of statehood as well as the fact that the admission of new members is left to political bodies in proceedings that do not have the slightest resemblance to judicial evaluation. Cohen remarked that '[i]t is a fashionable view among both lawyers and political scientists that the political organs of the United Nations have completely ignored juridical criteria when they have been called upon to assess statehood, and that they have granted or withheld recognition of statehood solely on political grounds which have borne little relation to community interests'.[15] Although she found this view to be 'dubious' and noticed a more law-oriented approach at the Security Council and General Assembly,[16] the fact

[13] See eg Georges Scelle, 'Règles générales du droit de la paix' (1933) 46 RCADI 327, 389 (speaking of admission to the League of Nations); James Crawford, *The Creation of States in International Law* (OUP 2007) 179ff; Malcolm N Shaw, *International Law* (CUP 2017) 336; and others.

[14] See John Dugard, *Recognition and the United Nations* (Grotius Publications Limited 1987) and 'The Secession of States and Their Recognition in the Wake of Kosovo' (2013) 357 RCADI 9, 57ff.

[15] Cohen, 'The Concept of Statehood' (n 9) 1128.

[16] ibid 1128ff.

remains that—in very recent practice—States have been admitted into the United Nations without meeting the criterion of effectiveness. Dugard remarked that this was particularly visible during decolonisation, when the Montevideo criteria were typically disregarded in the interest of ensuring the right to self-determination of colonial peoples and countries.[17] This would suggest that the UN bodies either have an alternative view of statehood to the Montevideo notion or that they simply ignore the criteria for statehood.

The process whereby new members are admitted is certainly not arbitrary, and, according to Chen, it is largely based on a Montevideo concept of statehood, albeit practice shows 'great variances' regarding the extent to which admitted candidates are required to fulfil it.[18] 'Other criteria' have also at times been applied to new members, and even with regard to founding members at the San Francisco Conference, when non-state entities were treated as States by the founders.[19] Belarus and Ukraine were admitted into membership even though they were, at the time, federal units of the Soviet Union.[20] India and the Philippines also became original members even though they had not yet achieved independence from the United Kingdom and the United States, respectively.[21] The Security Council recommended to the General Assembly that Bosnia and Herzegovina be admitted into the Organisation at a time when its government did not control the majority of its claimed territory, emphasising instead Sarajevo's commitment to the 'Principles and Purposes of the UN Charter'.[22] The recommendation was accepted by the General Assembly without much discussion.[23] Membership may therefore correspond to traditional notions of statehood, but it is not determined by them.

The inconsistency with which new UN members have been admitted is most likely attributable to persistent definitional problems regarding statehood and the overall failure to come up with a realistic and useful concept in international law. To clarify: that statehood is a requirement for membership in the Organisation is not problematic; the challenge is to develop the concept with organisational and operational clarity and ensure a degree of uniformity and consistency in its application. This does not have much bearing on our discussion or recognition and opposability as this aspect, at least, is separate from the criteria for UN membership: once a new member has been admitted, its statehood will become opposable to all other members as regardless of their 'particular' recognition.

[17] Dugard, 'The Secession of States' (n 14) 64ff.

[18] Frederick Tse-shyang Chen, 'The Meaning of "States" in the Membership Provisions of the United Nations Charter' (2001) 12(1) Indiana International & Comparative Law Review 25, 26.

[19] ibid.

[20] See Wright, 'Some Thoughts About Recognition' (n 10) 550, fn 1; cf Cohen (n 9) 1131–32.

[21] Cohen (n 9) 1132.

[22] UNSC Resolution 757 (1992).

[23] UNGA Resolution 46/237 of 20 July 1992.

3.2 Membership in the United Nations and Opposability

I have already discussed the language of Article 4 of the Charter, which sets up the criteria for membership in the United Nations. It may be less apparent from the provision that statehood (is not merely a prerequisite, but also a consequence of membership, vis-à-vis other members. In this respect, statehood does not refer to *de facto*, material statehood in the sense of sociology or political science; it refers to legal statehood, which means nothing else than the opposability of international law rights vested in States. The mechanism whereby this comes to pass is not particularly important: what matters is that this conclusion is almost universally supported by doctrine and practice. A Trial Chamber of the International Criminal Tribunal for the Former Yugoslavia thus determined in the *Tadić* case that '[t]he Republic of Bosnia and Herzegovina was admitted as a State member of the United Nations ... It was the *de jure* State against which the Bosnian Serb forces were in revolt.'[24] The implication is that although Bosnia and Herzegovina may have been a State earlier, its membership in the United Nations brushed off any remaining doubts in this regard.

Some rights associated with statehood in general are reproduced in the UN Charter and may be invoked between parties as a matter of treaty law. The history of the United Nations is replete with situations where various Member States refused to recognise each other but they could no longer credibly deny that their mutual relations were governed by international law simply due to a lack of recognition. This was the case, for example, with the two Germanies after both had been admitted to the Organisation following the 1972 Basic Treaty, North and South Korea following their simultaneous admission in 1991, and Israel and several States in the Middle East and North Africa since Israeli membership in 1949.

Bearing in mind the inconsistency with which the criteria of statehood have sometimes been applied when admitting States into membership, this conclusion may lead to bizarre results. One such implication was that the statehood of Belarus and Ukraine was opposable to the Soviet Union at a time when the former were not independent States. Wright observed that '[i]t follows from this that in the contemplation of the United Nations the Ukraine and Byelorussia are sovereign states, and the Union of Soviet Socialist Republics does not include those two republics'.[25] While counterintuitive, this interpretation is legally sound. In reality, because the two republics were governed by Moscow, a conflict raising the question of the value of their UN membership never materialised, and wondering what the implications might have been had it been otherwise is now mere pointless speculation.

It is clear, however, that only full membership in the United Nations could render individual recognition by other members declaratory. Lesser forms of

[24] *Prosecutor v Duško Tadić* IT-94-1-T (7 May 1997) [Trial Chamber Judgment] para 563.

[25] Wright (n 10) 550, fn 1.

involvement, such as observer status or membership in a specialised agency, do not produce such a result.[26] It is controversial whether voting for a State to be admitted as an observer amounts to recognition, although the presumption should be that it is not, and States have voted in favour of admission into observer status or membership in agencies such as UNESCO of candidates whose statehood they do not recognise; this was, notably, the case with the State of Palestine. Observers are not members and cannot base their claim of opposability on Article 4 of the Charter. Neither do they become States Parties by admission to agencies such as UNESCO (the United Nations Educational, Scientific and Cultural Organization), the International Monetary Fund (IMF), or the World Bank.[27]

3.3 Membership in Other International Organisations and Opposability

At least two regional organisations contain, in their respective frameworks, a mechanism similar to the one established under Article 4 of the UN Charter. These are the Organization of American States (OAS) and the Organization of African Unity (OAU, today replaced by the African Union).

The 1948 OAS Charter opens membership to 'independent American State[s]'[28] and in Chapter IV restates the fundamental rights and duties of States, for example that 'States are juridically equal, enjoy equal rights and equal capacity to exercise these rights, and have equal duties' and that '[e]very American State has the duty to respect the rights enjoyed by every other State in accordance with international law'.[29] I have already discussed its provisions on recognition, which will be revisited from a different perspective momentarily.

[26] For an opposing view, see John Dugard, 'What Is a State in International Law? How Is This to Be Determined?' in Niels M Blokker, Daniëlla Dam-de Jong, and Vid Prislan (eds), *Furthering the Frontiers of International Law: Sovereignty, Human Rights, Sustainable Development: Liber Amicorum Nico Schrijver* (Brill/Nijhoff 2021) 110ff. In my view, membership in a specialised agency or another international organisation with universal membership that does not possess a similar mechanism to the one existing under the UN Charter does not lead to opposability, but it will likely provide strong political impetus to a member's claim of statehood.

[27] The IMF is open to 'countries', and it still lists the Republic of China as 'Taiwan Province of China' in official country information. An invitation to join the IMF is offered by the Executive Board, as was the case with Kosovo in 2009. IMF membership is a condition of membership in the World Bank Group, where the admission of new members is otherwise conducted by the Board of Governors. Possibly due to the lack of direct participation of Member States in the admission process, State practice does not treat membership in either the IMF or the World Bank as conclusive of statehood. UNESCO is open to both States and 'territories' (although the admission procedure for either type of membership is separate). Although it opens the door for some engagement with the United Nations—such as accession to certain multilateral treaties deposited with the Secretary-General—the reaction to Palestinian membership raises doubt as to whether UNESCO membership could be regarded just as valuable as membership within the United Nations itself.

[28] Charter of the Organization of American States, 119 UNTS 3 (adopted 30 April 1948, entered into force 13 December 1951) arts 4 and 6.

[29] ibid arts 10 and 11.

Article IV of the 1963 OAU Charter allows membership to '[e]ach independent sovereign African State'.[30] In addition, Article III lists explicitly all the 'fundamental rights' of States as governing the relations of its members.[31] Similar provisions were adopted for the Constitutive Act of the African Union in 2000.[32] Like the articles of the OAS Charter, these provisions are sufficient to ensure the mutual opposability of the statehood of Member States.

The OAS and OAU are two prominent examples, and there may be others, such as the European Union, whose membership is also limited to States.[33] Ultimately, the mechanism whereby common membership of some international organisations confers opposability does not flow from the simple fact of simultaneous membership but is rather produced through treaty law. In a manner of speaking, there is little difference between the opposability bestowed by organisational membership or by a bilateral or multilateral treaty. It is incorrect, however, to regard this as implicit recognition by individual members. Implicit recognition requires that the recognising State behave in a certain way with the intention that recognition may be inferred from its behaviour. This may be lacking when deciding the membership of a candidate whose statehood is contested, and non-recognising States may actively oppose it, as demonstrated by voting in the Committee of Ministers regarding Kosovo's application for membership in the Council of Europe.[34] Although the question is really one of form and not of substance, we feel it is important to highlight this distinction.

Although, in my view, opposability resulting from membership in international organisations must be understood in terms of treaty law, a narrow interpretation of treaty provisions cannot explain this phenomenon: in vain might one look to provisions of an instrument such as the UN Charter for an explicit reference to recognition. The legal implications must rather be gleaned from practice. This explains why similar provisions on membership in different instruments do not necessarily imply that the statehood of a newly admitted candidate has become opposable to all existing members. In addition, it is important to consider the long-standing and well-established practice of existing States Parties to a multilateral agreement to object to its entry into force with a State they do not recognise at the moment of the latter's accession. As international organisations are ultimately founded on such

[30] Constitutive Charter of the Organisation of African Unity, 479 UNTS 39 (adopted 25 May, entered into force 13 September 1963) art IV.

[31] ibid art III.

[32] Constitutive Act of the African Union, 2158 UNTS 3 (adopted 11 July 2000, entered into force 26 May 2001) art 4.

[33] See Marise Cremona (ed), *The Enlargement of the European Union* (OUP 2003).

[34] 'Ministerial Committee of the Council of Europe accepts Kosovo's application for membership' (*European Western Balkans*, 25 April 2023) <https://europeanwesternbalkans.com/2023/04/25/ministerial-committee-of-the-council-of-europe-accepts-kosovos-application-for-membership/> last accessed 11 June 2024.

treaties, common membership must be precluded from producing bilateral legal effects when a declaration to that effect is made.

4. External Self-Determination

Few rights have suffered such politicisation, or been so polemicised, as the right of all peoples to self-determination. This right has been invoked by such a plethora of different stakeholders—from militant secessionist movements to anti-globalist groups—and in the most geographically diverse locations that any two situations where it has been discussed may not have even superficial resemblance. The term is commonly misused or misunderstood by the public and politicians, and it has even been summoned in developed countries to ward off perceived undue influence from abroad, as illustrated by a recent Swiss initiative against 'foreign judges'.[35] Because self-determination prominently figures in claims of statehood, its influence, if any, on recognition and opposability must be closely examined.

Although the term 'self-determination' did not enter the political and legal vocabulary until the twentieth century, the drive for nationhood and the establishment Nation States was central in European romantic nationalism in the post-Napoleonic era. The struggles for the unification of Germany and Italy are emblematic of the new conceptual paradigm pitting nationalism against feudalism,[36] and the ideals of romantic nationalism swept further across Europe, figuring prominently in the modern revival of the Balkan States that had for centuries been subjugated by the Ottoman Empire and the Habsburg Monarchy. The contemporary notion is thus usually traced to ideas advanced by Woodrow Wilson for a post-First World War Europe.[37] In his 'Fourteen Points' presented to Congress in early 1918, the American president advocated that revolutionary Russia be allowed to pursue its own political development and national policy independently, and that the borders of various European States be readjusted along lines of nationality, with the possibility of autonomous development for the peoples living in Austria-Hungary. For Wilson, national liberation thus envisaged was the key towards lasting peace in Europe.

Today, the right of self-determination is said to have an internal and an external aspect, depending on whether it is to be exercised within or outside an existing

[35] The 2018 Popular Initiative 'Swiss law, not foreign judges', which was rejected by a majority of voters in Switzerland, was also known as the Self-Determination Initiative.

[36] 'In this respect, the cases of unification of Germany and Italy are remembered as most conspicuous, having been based on the ambition that all ethnic Germans and all ethnic Italians find themselves in one respective country instead of living in a multitude of feudal statelets.' Vojin Dimitrijević, *Contemporary Right of Self-Determination of Peoples* (Belgrade Centre for Human Rights 2011) 9.

[37] See Robert McCorquodale, 'Group Rights' in Daniel Moeckli, Sangeeta Shah, and Sandesh Sivakumaran (eds), *International Human Rights Law* (OUP 2018) 344–66, 346 and Dimitrijević, *Contemporary Right of Self-Determination of Peoples* (n 36) 9.

State, namely whether it involves secession. Evidently, it is the latter possibility that is of interest to us in this chapter.

4.1 The Nature of the Principle and Right of Self-Determination

The 'principle of self-determination' was enshrined in the UN Charter and most likely had become a rule of customary law no later than 1960, when the General Assembly passed its Declaration on the Granting of Independence to Colonial Countries and Peoples.[38] It was included in both the two human rights Covenants of 1966; self-determination is therefore undeniably both a rule of general international law and a human right. It is thus natural to look to human rights practice to illuminate the content of self-determination, although the most dynamic and successful drive for self-determination took place during decolonisation under the scrutiny of the United Nations General Assembly and pre-dated the principle's appropriation by human rights law by more than a decade. Among the Assembly's numerous resolutions on the topic, the aforementioned Declaration on the Granting of Independence to Colonial Countries and Peoples must be singled out as 'the starting point for the rise of self-determination as a principle generating true legal rights'.[39] It is in this context that self-determination specifically gave rise to an entitlement to independence.

The UN Charter lists '[the development of] friendly relations among nations based on respect for the principle of equal rights and self-determination of peoples' as one of the purposes of the Organisation.[40] It further mandates the United Nations to promote, 'with a view to the creation of conditions of stability and well-being which are necessary for peaceful and friendly relations among nations based on respect for the principle of equal rights and self-determination of peoples', 'higher standards of living, full employment, and conditions of economic and social progress and development; solutions of international economic, social, health, and related problems; and international cultural and educational cooperation; and universal respect for, and observance of, human rights and fundamental freedoms for all without distinction as to race, sex, language, or religion'.[41] All Members are required to take joint and separate action in order to achieve these purposes. The Charter's provisions do not shed any more light on the content of the principle of self-determination.

[38] *Declaration on the Granting of Independence to Colonial Countries and Peoples* (14 December 1960) A/RES/1514(XV).

[39] Christian Tomuschat, 'Secession and Self-Determination' in Marcelo G Kohen (ed), *Secession: International Law Perspectives* (CUP 2006) 23–45, 23.

[40] Charter of the United Nations, 1 UNTS XVI (adopted 26 June 1945, entered into force 24 October 1945) art 1(2).

[41] ibid art 55.

The 1966 Covenants provide more detail but their wording remains just as broad and elusive. Both treaties contain an identical first article that declares the right of all peoples of self-determination.[42] The language employed is eclectic and ambiguous; the Covenants link it to economic, social, and cultural development, disposition over natural resources, and choice of political status; thus, self-determination is difficult to classify in any single 'family' of rights. According to McBeth, 'self-determination, more than any other, is a right that defies categorisation: it is a right that has simultaneously civil, political, economic, social and cultural aspects'.[43] To determine the impact of such a right, one must first determine its personal and material scopes of application.

It is not easy to distinguish between the principle of self-determination, which originates in general international law, and the human right of self-determination. The bearers of human rights are human beings, whether as groups or individuals, but the principle of self-determination acts as an obligation of States to be exercised towards both individuals and territorial entities such as colonies whether or not they have yet declared independence (certain aspects of the rule, such as the obligation to organise a status referendum, logically precede independence). Thus, an all-encompassing notion of 'self-determination' must consider both branches of law, while accounting for the specificities of each.

4.2 The Rights-Bearer(s) of Self-Determination

The bearers of the right of self-determination may not be the same as the beneficiaries of the principle of self-determination.

The Covenants, as well as the Charter before them, speak of the self-determination of 'peoples'. Unlike most other human rights, whose bearers are individual humans coming within the jurisdiction of a Contracting Power, it can be difficult to determine who is entitled to self-determination in a given case and what jurisdictional link, if any, would be necessary to claim it successfully. 'Traditional' human rights are not limited to individuals and may be enjoyed or exercised by groups or even by legal persons. However, unlike those rights where the holder may be clearly identified (even if it is a company or non-governmental organisation), 'peoples' do not have a list of members, and they only exist at a level of abstraction higher even than that of legal persons. For example, it is not difficult to determine who speaks for a company or media outlet, but it can be quite challenging to ascertain who speaks for a people. This question does not exhaust the

[42] International Covenant on Civil and Political Rights, 999 UNTS 171 (adopted 16 December 1966, entered into force 23 March 1976) art 1; and International Covenant on Economic, Social and Cultural Rights, 993 UNTS 3 (adopted 16 December 1966, entered into force 3 January 1976) art 1.

[43] Adam McBeth, Justine Nolan, and Simon Rice, *The International Law of Human Rights* (OUP 2017) 74.

problem of self-determination, which has also been described as an *erga omnes* norm, vesting any State with the legal standing to bring claims against those States violating it.

The Human Rights Committee examined the personal scope of self-determination under the International Civil and Political Rights Covenant in relation to a communication lodged by an indigenous authority against Canada. The Lubicon Lake band, represented by its chief, argued that expropriation of their ancestral lands for the benefit of corporations amounted to a violation of their right to self-determination. The Committee recalled that 'the Covenant recognizes and protects in most resolute terms a people's right of self-determination and its right to dispose of its natural resources' but also observed that 'the author, as an individual, could not claim under the Optional Protocol to be a victim of a violation of the right of self-determination enshrined in article I of the Covenant, which deals with rights conferred upon peoples, as such'.[44] This means that, for the time being, the right of self-determination is 'effectively non-justiciable' by the Committee.[45]

The notion of a people—or its relevance for external self-determination—is not easy to gauge. According to McBeth, 'the term is generally understood to mean a group that is bound together by a common identity, such as a distinct ethnicity, language, religion or culture, and that lives in a distinct area'.[46] The most reliable strategy would be to take a combination of objective and subjective factors. Such an approach was taken by a group of UNESCO experts who developed a complex definition to identify peoples, including for the purposes of self-determination. In summary, the experts found that a people is 'a group of individual human beings' who enjoy a common history, culture, language, or other common feature; that must be of a certain number that 'need not be large ... but must be more than a mere association of individuals within a State'; that must be willing to be identified as a people; and possibly possess institutions or 'other means of expressing its common characteristics and will for identity'.[47] This definition is applicable to internal self-determination; for the purposes of external self-determination, the definition may be more restrictive and limited to colonial and occupied peoples.[48]

[44] *Lubicon Lake Band v Canada* (26 March 1990) Communication No 167/1984, para 13.3, referring to the Optional Protocol to the International Covenant on Civil and Political Rights, 999 UNTS 302 (adopted 19 December 1966, entered into force 23 March 1976).

[45] McBeth, Nolan, and Rice, *The International Law of Human Rights* (n 43) 75. It has been suggested that the Committee on Economic, Social and Cultural Rights might be able to hear such a communication. The idea is based on a reading of art 2 of the 2008 Optional Protocol to the ICESCR: 'Communications may be submitted by or on behalf of individuals or groups of individuals, under the jurisdiction of a State Party, claiming to be victims of a violation of any of the economic, social and cultural rights set forth in the Covenant by that State Party ....' Optional Protocol to the International Covenant on Economic, Social and Cultural Rights, 2922 UNTS 29 (adopted 10 December 2008, entered into force 5 May 2013) art 2.

[46] McBeth, Nolan, and Rice (n 43) 75.

[47] Final Report and Recommendations of an International Meeting of Experts on the Further Study of the Concept of the Right of People for UNESCO, SNS-89/CONF.602/7 (22 February 1990).

[48] The distinction between external and internal self-determination could lead to a slight logical conundrum, namely, does it lie within the scope *ratione personae* of the right—whereby the definition of a

It may still be difficult to draw a clear line between peoples. This problem was evident in the written submissions of States to the ICJ during the proceedings in the *Kosovo* advisory opinion. The Government of Serbia submitted that Kosovo 'remains an integral part of Serbia and as such the population of that territory were, and remain, part of the "people" of Serbia'[49] and that 'there is no evidence to support the proposition that Kosovo ever constituted a self-determination unit as a recognized non-self-governing territory or that the Kosovo Albanians, being a part (albeit the majority) of the population of Kosovo, constituted a people entitled to exercise the right of self-determination in the sense of a totally free choice as to its political status up to and including secession'.[50] This view was echoed by Russia,[51] Romania,[52] Slovakia,[53] Cyprus,[54] and Argentina[55] in their written submissions and was later also highlighted in the written comments of Spain.[56] Unfortunately, the Court decided that it was not necessary to examine the possible applicability of the right of self-determination.

'people' is more restrictive for the purposes of external self-determination—or within the scope *ratione materiae*, whereby the notion of 'peoples' is the same, but the right to independence arises separately in certain circumstances? From a practical perspective, both possibilities come across as acceptable and will likely lead to the same result, but I believe that it is important to address this conceptual dilemma for the pleasure of more fastidious readers.

[49] *Accordance with International Law of the Unilateral Declaration of Independence in Respect of Kosovo*, Written Statement of the Government of the Republic of Serbia, 15 April 2009, para 571.

[50] ibid para 588.

[51] According to the Government of the Russian Federation, '[i]t is widely accepted that a population of a trust or mandated territory, of a non-self-governing territory, or of an existing State, taken as a whole, undisputedly qualifies as a people entitled to self-determination. Whether, and under which conditions, an ethnic or other group within an existing State may qualify as a people, is subject to extensive debates.' *Accordance with International Law of the Unilateral Declaration of Independence in Respect of Kosovo*, Written Statement by the Russian Federation, 16 April 2009, para 81.

[52] 'Romania's firm conviction is that, in fact, the population of Kosovo is *not* a people, but is made up of various ethnicities, which—in view of Serbia's total population—represent national minorities (*e.g.* Albanians, Turks, Bosnians), ethnic minorities (*e.g.* Goranis, Roma, Ashkalis, Egyptians) or are part of the Serb majority.' *Accordance with International Law of the Unilateral Declaration of Independence in Respect of Kosovo*, Written Statement of Romania, 14 April 2009, para 141.

[53] 'The emphasis in all relevant instruments and in the state practice on the importance of territorial integrity, means that "peoples" is to be understood in the sense of *all* peoples of given territory. All members of distinct minority groups are part of the peoples of the territory. However, minorities *as such* do not have a right of self-determination. That means that they have no right to secession, to independence, or to join with comparable groups in other states.' *Accordance with International Law of the Unilateral Declaration of Independence in Respect of Kosovo*, Written Statement of the Slovak Republic, 16 April 2009, para 15.

[54] '[N]either the population of Kosovo (which is not limited to ethnic Albanians) nor the Albanian population in Serbia as a whole, are a "people" for the purpose of the right of external self-determination.' *Accordance with International Law of the Unilateral Declaration of Independence in Respect of Kosovo*, Written Statement of the Republic of Cyprus, 17 April 2009, para 136.

[55] '[N]either within the UN nor within a regional context, is there a recognition of the applicability of the right of self-determination to a so-called "Kosovar people".' *Accordance with International Law of the Unilateral Declaration of Independence in Respect of Kosovo*, Written Statement of the Argentine Republic, 17 April 2009, para 95.

[56] *Accordance with International Law of the Unilateral Declaration of Independence in Respect of Kosovo*, Written Comments of the Kingdom of Spain, July 2009, para 7.

However, as this book is primarily interested in the external aspect of self-determination, it is important to note that such a right has traditionally been restricted to a small number of situations, and is not bestowed upon all peoples and at all times. That self-determination is 'external' relates to the material scope of the right, but there are also specific requirements in terms of the rights-holders. Self-determination was initially espoused with relation to peoples suffering under colonial dominance. The remedy envisaged by the General Assembly in its Declaration on Giving Independence to Colonial Countries and Peoples of 1960 was to allow these peoples to decide for themselves whether they wanted to establish a State of their own.[57] The General Assembly defined a colony (or a non-self-governing territory) in a subsequent resolution as (i) geographically separate, (ii) ethnically and/or culturally distinct territory from the administering State, and (iii) 'arbitrarily' in a position or status of subordination towards it.[58] This is sometimes referred to as the 'salt water theory', meaning that only a territory separated from the coloniser by a body of water may be considered a colony. Within this framework, the process of decolonisation proceeded swiftly and efficiently.[59]

Many States seem content to leave self-determination at that, as a sort of 'accomplished' or historic right; attempts to broaden the right beyond the colonial context cause much controversy, at least insofar as external self-determination is concerned.[60] Many post-colonial States are themselves strongly against the applicability of the principle or right to their own secessionist movements: Sri Lanka denied it to the Tamils and Nigeria denied it to Biafra.[61] It was nevertheless accepted that self-determination came into play in the context of foreign occupation, racist regimes, and with respect to UN trust territories and former League of Nations mandates (the latter two correspond closely but not entirely to the notion of colonial countries). The ICJ confirmed, in its *Namibia* advisory opinion,[62] that where the 'sacred trust of civilisation' existing between the holder of a mandate (or trustee) and the population of a beneficiary territory had been violated, the mandate could be terminated *ipso facto*. The first Additional Protocol to the Geneva Conventions of 1977 also explicitly recognises that the struggle of peoples against colonial domination, racist regimes, and alien occupation may all come within

57 *Declaration on the Granting of Independence to Colonial Countries and Peoples* (14 December 1960) A/RES/1514(XV).

58 *Principles Which Should Guide Members in Determining Whether or Not an Obligation Exists to Transmit the Information Called for Under Article 73e of the Charter* (15 December 1960) A/RES/1541(XV), Principles IV and V.

59 'The decolonisation process under the leadership of the United Nations was conducted and accomplished strictly within the limits defined by the blue water theory.' Dimitrijević (n 36) 26.

60 See Hurst Hannum, 'Rethinking Self-Determination' (1993) 34(1) Virginia Journal of International Law 1–69, 31–33.

61 Dimitrijević (n 36) 33.

62 *Legal Consequences for States of the Continued Presence of South Africa in Namibia (South West Africa) Notwithstanding Security Council Resolution 276 (1970)*, ICJ Reports 16, Advisory Opinion of 21 June 1971.

the purview of self-determination and may, under certain circumstances, come to constitute an international armed conflict even in the absence of statehood.[63] State practice in relation to the Occupied Palestinian Territories reaffirms the applicability of the right of self-determination in cases of belligerent occupation.[64] The more limited scope of external self-determination seems today to be the mainstream view in doctrine.

If the bearers of the human right of self-determination are peoples, this is not necessarily so with the principle of self-determination, which seems to be applicable both to peoples and territorial entities, including States as well as pre-State entities such as colonial countries.

Although this is seldom discussed, it seems that some violations of a State's territorial integrity and political independence may also amount to violations of the principle of self-determination. For example, if there is an entitlement to self-determination from belligerent occupation, this implies that at least unlawful belligerent occupation may amount to a violation of self-determination. Whether this violation would target the occupied State or its population is conceptually difficult to establish. At least in part, however, it seems to be related to the State itself.

4.3 The Duty-Holders of Self-Determination

If the rights-holders are difficult to pinpoint, then this is doubly so with the duty-holders. The simple answer may be that they are States. If a colonised nation lived in territory subjected to the effective control of a Colonial Power, or the inhabitants of an occupied territory in the control of the Occupying Power, then it may be presumed that the principle and right of self-determination is opposable to that Colonial or Occupying Power; but what of other States? If the Palestinian or Sahrawi people (or, conversely, the States they have created) enjoy self-determination from Israel and Morocco, respectively, may they also claim it towards other States—including those that do not recognise this entitlement?

Resolutions passed by the General Assembly in the decolonisation period tend to directly address Colonial or Occupying Powers.[65] But the opposability of the right may be broader. In relation to Palestine, the Assembly urged 'all States and the specialized agencies and organizations of the United Nations system to continue to support and assist the Palestinian people in the early realization of their right to

[63] Under the Protocol, international armed conflicts include 'situations … in which peoples are fighting against colonial domination and alien occupation and against racist régimes in the exercise of their right of self-determination'. Protocol Additional to the Geneva Conventions of 12 August 1949 and relating to the Protection of Victims of International Armed Conflicts, 1125 UNTS 3 (adopted 8 June 1977, entered into force 7 December 1978) art 1 (4).

[64] UNGA Resolution 72/160 of 23 January 2018, paras 1–2.

[65] See eg UNGA Resolutions 34/36, 34/37, and 34/38 of 21 November 1979.

self-determination'.[66] Third States may therefore have obligations under the principle and right to self-determination towards a given people even though they are not directly implicated in the situation.

4.4 The Content of the Principle and Right of Self-Determination

As noted above, the material scope of application of the principle and right of self-determination may be divided into external and external self-determination. External self-determination, bestowed upon peoples under colonial domination or foreign occupation, entails, quite simply, the right of that people to create its own independent State or to join (or remain within) an existing one. The right of internal self-determination is incumbent upon all peoples at all times, although it is less clear what it involves in practical terms. For Dimitrijević, 'the right of self-determination of peoples within a state, the so-called internal aspect of self-determination, is materialised though the inclusion into democratic processes of the society'.[67] This makes the right of self-determination a syndrome of a whole list of civil and political as well as social, economic, and cultural rights, bestowed both upon groups and individuals, including, but not limited to, the right of participation in public affairs, the rights of minorities, the right of non-discrimination, and so on. It may be guaranteed by vastly differing means of implementation ranging from personal or territorial autonomy[68] to freely choosing one's own citizenship,[69] to name but a few solutions.

Clearly, any implications for statehood and recognition will come from external self-determination. Practice at the United Nations has been primarily to invoke this right in support of independence for colonial peoples, and, in the *Western Sahara* case, the ICJ confirmed that 'the application of the right of self-determination requires a free and genuine expression of the will of the peoples concerned'.[70]

However, self-determination—in its classical form—does not confer statehood; it may only confer a *right* to statehood. More precisely, external self-determination bestows a people with the free expression of its political will and requires others to abide by its decision. Nevertheless, self-determination has featured prominently in declarations of independence, and it has been invoked in acts of recognition,

[66] UNGA Resolution 72/160 of 23 January 2018, paras 1–2.

[67] Dimitrijević (n 36) 47.

[68] ibid.

[69] This was foreseen by the Badinter Commission as one of the solutions to be offered to Serbs in Bosnia and Herzegovina Croatia as a means of fulfilling their minority rights, and possibly their right of self-determination; see 'Conference on Yugoslavia Arbitration Commission: Opinions on Questions Arising from the Dissolution of Yugoslavia 11 January and 4 July 1992' (1992) 31 ILM 1488, 1498.

[70] *Western Sahara*, ICJ Reports 12, Advisory Opinion of 16 October 1975, 32.

which suggests that it could have a more direct bearing on the creation of statehood. I now turn to the question of its link with opposability.

4.5 Self-Determination and Opposability

The link between external self-determination and the opposability of statehood based on the exercise of such a right is not clear in jurisprudence, although growing evidence for a judicial move towards the recognition of such a link may be found scattered among the decisions of several tribunals.

Most notably, in the *Chagos Archipelago* case, the ICJ recalled that '[b]oth State practice and *opinio juris* at the relevant time confirm the customary law character of the right to territorial integrity of a non-self-governing territory as a corollary of the right to self-determination'.[71] It is interesting that the Court is taking a right primarily associated with statehood, namely that of territorial integrity, and applying it to a non-self-governing territory, which is not a State under international law. In any event, in the eyes of the Court, Mauritian territorial integrity proceeded from its people's right to self-determination.

The necessity of elucidating at least some of these principles in the context of decolonisation is evident: for example, the United Kingdom had removed the Chagos Archipelago from Mauritius before granting independence to the latter; the Chagossian population was then expelled to accommodate a US military outpost.[72] The Court highlighted that 'the obligations arising under international law and reflected in the resolutions adopted by the General Assembly during the process of decolonization of Mauritius require the United Kingdom, as the administering Power, to respect the territorial integrity of that country, including the Chagos Archipelago' and that 'as a result of the Chagos Archipelago's unlawful detachment and its incorporation into a new colony ... the process of decolonization of Mauritius was not lawfully completed when Mauritius acceded to independence in 1968'.[73] The only possible interpretation is that, as a result of self-determination, Mauritius was vested with the right to territorial integrity before independence and therefore before it was a State. However, possessing the right to territorial integrity does not mean that a non-self-governing territory is entitled to all the rights owed to States.

It is also unclear whether territorial integrity is universally contained in the right to self-determination. Regarding the Israeli occupation of Palestine, the General Assembly has reaffirmed the 'inalienable rights' of the Palestinian people many

[71] *Legal Consequences of the Separation of the Chagos Archipelago from Mauritius in 1965*, ICJ Reports 95, Advisory Opinion of 25 February 2019, para 160.

[72] ibid paras 36ff.

[73] ibid paras 173–174.

times, which include '[t]he right to self-determination without external interference' and '[t]he right to national independence and sovereignty'.[74] However, territorial integrity is rarely mentioned, with the occupation instead derided as a direct violation of self-determination:[75] where it does figure, it is draped in unusual wording and often in the preambles of resolutions.[76] This is likely to distinguish such a case of occupation from decolonisation.

The Prosecutor of the International Criminal Court (ICC) also argued that the right to self-determination of the Palestinian people counterbalanced any lack of effective authority over its own territory and allowed the Court to conclude that Palestine was a State for the purposes of the Rome Statute.[77] The Chamber itself was more elusive in its reasoning, although the argument was essentially accepted to establish jurisdiction over the whole territory of Palestine, and it was decided that 'the above conclusion—namely that the Court's territorial jurisdiction in the Situation in Palestine extends to the territories occupied by Israel since 1967 on the basis of the relevant indications arising from Palestine's accession to the Statute—is consistent with the right to self-determination'.[78] In my view, the words 'consistent with' in this sentence could safely be replaced with 'derived from'.

There can be no doubt that the principle and right of self-determination form part of positive law. The right's *erga omnes* character has been confirmed several times by the ICJ,[79] and the International Law Commission has included self-determination in its short list of verifiable *jus cogens* norms.[80] Of course, we may debate whether this is the case only with external self-determination in the more limited colonial context. Whichever the case, there is clearly growing recognition of the possibility of justifying the possession and exercise of State rights on the basis of self-determination. Were this not so then we might legitimately ask whether self-determination serves any practical purpose.

4.5.1 External Self-Determination Before Independence

Colonialism did not function in a uniform fashion around the world, and various colonial peoples may have been subjected to different treatment and administrative

[74] UNGA Resolution 3236 (XXIX) of 22 November 1974; cf UNGA Resolution 75/172 of 16 December 2020. In Resolution ES-10/23 of 10 May 2024, the General Assembly went so far as to determine that Palestine meets the conditions of membership in the UN in accordance with Article 4 of the Charter and, in an unprecedented move, accorded it additional rights and privileges as an observer State.

[75] See eg UNGA Resolution 58/292 of 17 May 2004.

[76] '[The General Assembly,] [s]*tressing also* the need for respect for and preservation of the territorial unity, contiguity and integrity of all of the Occupied Palestinian Territory, including East Jerusalem ….' UNGA Resolution 75/172 of 16 December 2020, preambular para [10].

[77] *Situation in the State of Palestine* ICC-01/18 (5 February 2021) [Decision] para 24.

[78] ibid para 123.

[79] See eg *Case Concerning East Timor (Portugal v Australia)*, ICJ Reports 90, Judgment of 30 June 1995, para 29.

[80] *Report of the International Law Commission* (2019) A/74/10, 146–47.

divisions by Colonial Powers. However, the territory of a colony is usually well defined by the colonial administration, which inadvertently facilitated decolonisation by allowing the self-determination unit to be more readily identifiable. The principle of *uti possidetis juris* is thus indispensable, not for creating new States but for ensuring the implementation of the right of self-determination of a given people. A non-self-governing people is entitled to freely express its will and, should it so desire, it must have the right to form an independent State; a corollary of this right, the possession of a more-or-less defined territory that it inhabits, will be protected from the aspirations of other States even before independence. These claims are opposable to all States, and not only to the Colonial or Occupying Power. However, they cannot make statehood, which is non-existent and not yet claimed by an authority representing the people, opposable.

4.5.2 External Self-Determination After a Declaration of Independence

Once a people entitled to external self-determination makes it clear that it desires independence, it will have the right to form a State—the way this process is implemented may vary from one context to the other. At some point, the authority accepted as representing the people will promulgate a solemn declaration of independence, or obtain such an instrument from the Parent State. This could lead to two situations.

(1) Independence may be proclaimed in a situation where the erstwhile colony does not yet meet the criteria of statehood. This is the case in Western Sahara and in Palestine, which is seldom regarded through the colonial lens but whose legal situation is far more complex than that of a territory under belligerent occupation. Western Sahara is also today an occupied rather than colonised territory, but the link with decolonisation features prominently in its claim to self-determination and the recognition thereof by the United Nations General Assembly. One possibility is that, under the circumstances, the right to form a State would be opposable *erga omnes*, but statehood in a narrow sense may only be opposable to those States which accept the declaration of independence and recognise it. The right to self-determination therefore authorises recognition even though the material criteria of statehood have not yet been met.[81] The divided reaction of States to claims of statehood by the Sahrawi and Palestinian peoples indicates that non-recognising States typically do not regard recognition by others as contrary to international law, although they refuse to undertake such an act themselves. The other possibility is that, even in the absence of

[81] The lack of a competing legitimate claim to the territory would also factor into this equation, as a Colonial Power loses title to the territory undergoing decolonisation, and it can neither claim it for itself nor pass it to another State. As the doctrine of premature recognition exists to protect legitimate territorial claims, it has no role to play in such disputes, for there is no other lawful interest to protect.

effectivity, the colonial country's legal statehood is partially or fully opposable to others. This is reflected in the ICC decision discussed earlier, when the judges accepted the right to self-determination as a relevant justification for extending the Palestinian authority to seize the Court with regard to crimes committed in the entirety of its claimed territory.[82] In my view, this is the better understanding of self-determination in such cases.

(2) Another situation is triggered when independence is declared while the criteria of statehood have also been met. Today, it appears that all of the fundamental rights of the new State then become opposable to all other States, although is difficult to extrapolate this conclusion from practice: as most colonial countries proclaimed independence with the blessing of the Colonial Power and following its retreat from their territories, especially in Africa, and consequently enjoyed universal recognition and admission into the United Nations, one cannot be certain whether their statehood would have been considered opposable in the absence of such individual and collective recognition.[83] An interesting case in this regard is Indonesia, which proclaimed independence in 1945 but was only recognised by the Netherlands in 1949. Sukarno read the declaration while the Japanese, who had ousted the Dutch in 1942, were still withdrawing from the islands. When an initial agreement on the demarcation of jurisdiction in the islands between the Netherlands and the Indonesian Republic was concluded in Linggadjati in 1946, a number of States extended *de facto* recognition to Indonesia, while others that had previously given *de facto* recognition now declared their act to be *de jure*.[84] Both the Security Council[85] and the General Assembly[86] began to refer to the 'Republic of Indonesia' in their documents, but without prejudicing the outcome of the conflict, and universal recognition did not come before Dutch acquiescence in December 1949. It does not seem that an independent Indonesia was automatically opposable to other States, although it should be borne in mind that the example in question predates the principal developments on decolonisation at the United Nations by several years.

[82] *Situation in the State of Palestine* (n 77) paras 114–123.

[83] See Colin Warbrick, 'Recognition of States' (1992) 41(2) The International and Comparative Law Quarterly 473, 473.

[84] 'The Republic received *de facto* recognition from Australia, Burma, India, the Philippine Islands, the United Kingdom and the United States of America, while Afghanistan, Egypt, Iran, Lebanon, Saudi Arabia and Syria, who had extended *de facto* recognition after the Linggadjati Agreement had been initialled, now granted *de jure* recognition.' Ali Sastroamidjojo and Robert Delson, 'The Status of the Republic of Indonesia in International Law' (1949) 49(3) Columbia Law Review 344, 345.

[85] See UNSC Resolution 27 (1947).

[86] See UNGA Resolution 274 (III) of 11 May 1949.

In my view, a State created by a people vested with the right to external self-determination that meets the criteria of effectivity is *ipso facto* opposable to all others. It is more difficult to say whether it is the 'full package' of State rights that becomes opposable or simply the provisions on territorial integrity, non-interference, and the like. Although positive law is not entirely clear in this regard, it seems that the opposability flowing from self-determination is full, not partial. The recent General Assembly Resolution ES-10/23 of 10 May 2024 describing Palestine as a State fulfilling the conditions for membership in the UN (even though it arguably does not meet the Montevideo criteria) supports this finding. Therefore, any violations of State rights—integrity, immunities, exercise of jurisdiction, and others—would constitute violations of the right to external self-determination. In my opinion, effectivity plays little or no role in establishing the legal statehood once a claim has been made by an authority representing a people whose right to external self-determination has been recognised by the United Nations General Assembly. I admit, however, that opposing views are possible and, indeed, widespread in the legal community.

4.6 Remedial Secession

Remedial secession has sparked many heated debates among international lawyers, and there seems to be no consensus on the matter; the problem is exacerbated by the liberal mixing of moral and legal arguments that some authors feel compelled to engage in. Remedial secession is typically advocated under the aegis of self-determination, but it may also be regarded separately as an autonomous principle of international law. The concept is summarised by Del Mar as follows: '[A] minority (or a "people" who have the right to "internal self-determination"), which is located on an identifiable part of a State's territory, is transformed into a "people" who have a right to exercise ("external") self-determination and secede that territory from the State in question as a last resort to address gross violations of human rights perpetrated against them by the government.'[87] The author hastens to add that '[r]emedial secession is a legal myth: secession is not a remedy recognized in international law for violations committed by a State'.[88]

Nevertheless, the arguments in favour of remedial secession do not stem from a legal nothingness, and its proponents cite a number of sources to strengthen their claims. In 1970, the General Assembly adopted the Friendly Relations Declaration,[89] recalling principles governing relations between all States; mention

[87] Katherine del Mar, 'The Myth of Remedial Secession' in Duncan French (ed), *Statehood and Self-Determination* (CUP 2013) 79, 79.
[88] ibid.
[89] *Declaration on Principles of International Law Concerning Friendly Relations and Cooperation Among States in Accordance with the Charter of the United Nations* (24 October 1970) A/RES/2625(XXV) (hereafter Friendly Relations Declaration).

is made of both self-determination and territorial integrity. The Declaration recalls that 'all peoples have the right freely to determine, without external interference, their political status and to pursue their economic, social and cultural development' and that the 'establishment of a sovereign and independent State, the free association or integration with an independent State or the emergence into any other political status freely determined by the people constitute modes of implementing the right of self-determination by that people'.[90] The Declaration adds that the 'subjection of peoples to alien subjugation, domination and exploitation constitutes a violation of the principle [of self-determination], as well as a denial of fundamental human rights', and that it is contrary to the UN Charter.[91] The same principle was reiterated in the Vienna Declaration and Programme of Action of 1993.[92]

One of the more prominent arguments in favour of remedial secession comes from a controversial reading of a paragraph that may be found in both documents and which reiterates that their provisions may not be construed as authorising 'any action which would dismember or impair, totally or in part, the territorial integrity or political unity of sovereign and independent States *conducting themselves in compliance with the principle of equal rights and self-determination of peoples and thus possessed of a Government representing the whole people belonging to the territory without distinction of any kind*'.[93] The last phrase has been raised by some authors as an *a contrario* argument that the territorial integrity of States failing to respect human rights shall not be protected. Dimitrijević recalls: '[M]any authors believe that the right of secession, albeit exceptional, emerges and can be recognised if the discriminated minority is exposed to actions of the organs of the state which represent unquestionable and brutal violations of fundamental rights ....'[94]

It is almost impossible to distil the discussions of remedial secession to determine the existence of a mainstream or majority view. States either have no position on the matter or have argued in favour of views best aligned with their political interests.[95] Judicial and expert views have been divided. In a well-known *obiter dictum*, the Supreme Court of Canada accepted secession as an *ultima ratio* in cases of gross and systematic human rights violations.[96] The African Commission on Human and People's Rights has accepted remedial secession as an aspect of self-determination in its jurisprudence but has so far refused to apply it in practice.[97] Conversely, the Independent International Fact-Finding Commission

[90] ibid.

[91] ibid.

[92] *Vienna Declaration and Programme of Action* (12 July 1993) A/CONF.157/23, para 2.

[93] Friendly Relations Declaration (n 89); and *Vienna Declaration and Programme of Action*, ibid para 2. Emphasis added.

[94] Dimitrijević (n 36) 35.

[95] See in this respect the various written submissions and oral statements of States to the ICJ during the proceedings regarding the Kosovo advisory opinion.

[96] See *Reference re Secession of Quebec* (1998) 2 SCR 217.

[97] See *Katangese Peoples' Congress v Zaire* (1995) Comm No 75/92 and *Kevin Mgwanga Gunme et al v Cameroon* (2009) Comm No 266/03; see more in Dugard, 'Secession of States' (n 14) 173. It should

on the Conflict in Georgia expressed doubt about the status of 'remedial self-determination' as positive law.[98] The ICJ has refused to take a stance so far, although some judges, such as the late Cançado Trindade, have been favourable to the idea.[99]

It is neither possible nor necessary to address in depth the topic of remedial secession, of which much has been written elsewhere,[100] in this work. In my view, no such right has emerged in positive general international law. However, if such a right existed—and it may well emerge in the future—it would simply be an additional situation where the right to external self-determination could lead to legal statehood that is opposable *erga omnes*.

5. The Existence of a Regional or Self-Imposed Rule

An analysis of doctrine and practice concerning recognition of States suggests that there exist no rules of international law directly applicable to this act, wherefore constitutive recognition could only be guided by certain general principles. This situation is practically, if not theoretically, much more aligned with the constitutive view of recognition. However, this also means that nothing precludes States from committing individually to a more rule-based regime, insofar as this does not create obligations for third States without their consent. In fact, several States have adopted a public policy on recognition of States or governments, which may or may not be legally binding for them, but which is often considered by scholars as proof of State practice, *opinio juris*, or both. This may well be the case. Yet there is another possibility almost entirely neglected by doctrine, namely that the positions of States on recognition could in and of themselves constitute a particular legal regime whereby a new State could be opposable to them even in the absence of formal recognition.

be noted that in these cases, the African Commission is applying the African Charter on Human and Peoples' Rights and not general international law.

[98] Independent International Fact-Finding Mission on the Conflict in Georgia, *Report, Volume I* (September 2009) 17.

[99] See *Accordance with International Law of the Unilateral Declaration of Independence in Respect of Kosovo*, ICJ Reports 403, Advisory Opinion of 22 July 2010, 523ff [Separate Opinion of Judge Cançado Trindade].

[100] See eg Colin Warbrick, 'Kosovo: The Declaration of Independence' (2008) 57(3) The International and Comparative Law Quarterly 675; Jure Vidmar, 'Remedial Secession in International Law: Theory and (Lack of) Practice' (2010) 6(1) St Antony's International Review 37; Robert Kolb, 'Autodétermination et "sécession remède" en droit international public' in M Cherif Bassiouni and others (eds), *Yearbook of International Law and Jurisprudence: Global Trends: Law, Policy & Justice* (Oceana 2013) 57; Del Mar, 'The Myth of Remedial Secession' (n 87) 79–108; Dugard, 'Secession of States' (n 14) 112ff; and McCorquodale, 'Group Rights' (n 37) 351–54.

New Zealand is a prominent example of a State which has renounced formal recognition,[101] although it is unclear when this practice actually began: Talmon relates that New Zealand has maintained this approach 'since the 1970s'.[102] This author finds that New Zealand's policy on recognition was 'unsettled':

> The New Zealand Government did not perform any formal acts of recognition with regard to Namibia, the Czech Republic and Slovakia or Eritrea. It also did not issue any formal recognition statements in relation to most States resulting from the break-up of the former USSR ... [T]he same was not true with regard to the three Baltic States Latvia, Lithuania and Estonia which New Zealand formally recognized on 28 August 1991 [and] three out of five successor States of the Socialist Federal Republic of Yugoslavia ....[103]

Of course, this practice concerns primarily explicit versus implicit recognition, but it would be difficult to maintain that it does not also rest on a declaratory view of recognition. Talmon concludes:

> It is suggested that although formal acts or declarations of recognition of States are no longer made, the criteria previously applied for the express recognition of States remain the basis upon which the New Zealand Government makes any decision on implied recognition ... [T]he New Zealand Government, as a rule, will not take any action implying recognition of statehood if a new entity does not fulfil [the conditions of statehood].[104]

It is easy to see how such domestic policy, regardless of whether or not it is backed by the binding force of domestic or international law, could create expectations of a State's government and be legitimately invoked by entities claiming statehood.

What States can do individually, they can also do together. The Montevideo Convention is unique in regulating recognition, even if this is done in an inconclusive and ambiguous manner. Although most lawyers' initial reflex is to induce from the provisions of the Convention a rule of general international law (which, in my view, is incorrect), the Convention is above all an international agreement that binds its own States Parties. If indeed the Convention espouses a declaratory view of recognition, then it is these States that have committed to such a view.

[101] See Stefan Talmon, 'New Zealand's Policy of Implied Recognition of States: One Step Ahead or Falling Behind?' (2009) 7 New Zealand Yearbook of International Law 3.
[102] ibid 4.
[103] ibid 5.
[104] ibid 12–13.

6. Consensual Separation

When a part of the territory of a State secedes with the consent of the Parent State, or when a federal State is peacefully dismembered into its constituents, as was the case with Czechoslovakia, other States typically respect that decision and proceed to recognise the new State or States without delay. This was the case almost universally in the context of decolonisation, but also beyond it, in situations where self-determination did not play a significant part in the creation of new States. There have been several examples of such practice in recent years. Montenegro declared independence and dissolved its union with Serbia in June 2006 after a referendum organised in agreement with Belgrade and the European Union. The new Republic of Montenegro received almost a hundred acts of formal recognition by the end of the year and was admitted to the United Nations within a month of declaring independence. Similarly, South Sudan proclaimed independence with the consent of Sudan, its Parent State, in July 2011 and became a UN member in a matter of days. Neither State had received formal notice of recognition from all UN members by the time of admission, but this was clearly due to a lack of diplomatic and economic exchange with some other nations and for reasons of expediency, rather than because their statehood was in doubt: it has been argued that the speed with which South Sudan was admitted into the Organisation disincentivised States from offering formal recognition, and their favourable vote for membership was seen as sufficient to achieve this result.[105]

But there are more problematic cases. When the Socialist Republic of Macedonia proclaimed independence from Yugoslavia in 1991 as the Republic of Macedonia, most UN members refrained from recognising it due to Greek fears that the name implied territorial aspirations towards the eponymous region in Greece. It was not until 1993 that the 'Former Yugoslav Republic of Macedonia' was accepted as a UN member and achieved more widespread recognition. Of course, it is unlikely that any of the States initially withholding recognition would have denied that Macedonia was a State, or that they were required to treat it as such under international law.

These situations are challenging for the classical constitutive view of recognition. Applying the doctrine could lead to absurd results: a non-recognising State could hypothetically regard the territory in question as *terra nullius* and seek to establish its own claim to it. This problem is not merely theoretical, and an analogy may be found in the treatment of Western Sahara by Mauritania and Morocco after Spanish withdrawal, and in Israeli claims to Palestinian territory.

The question therefore is whether a State created with the consent of its parent requires recognition to become opposable to others. Older constitutivist authors

[105] Dugard, 'Secession of States' (n 14) 57.

such as Oppenheim would answer this question in the positive,[106] because the creation of a new State would have to be regarded simply as an act of the Parent State that cannot generate obligations for third parties without their consent. The declaratory theory would resolve this problem, but only if the new State meets the criteria of statehood to a sufficient degree.

To resolve this problem, it is necessary to introduce the concept of contestation. Every claim of statehood is by definition a territorial claim, and the fact that a given territory is claimed by only one or more States will have an impact on the position of third States regarding the dispute: this is why Bluntschli gave special importance to recognition of a new State by its parent.[107] In cases of secession, a territory to which the Parent State holds lawful title becomes subjected to a new, competing claim by the secessionist State. Recognition by the parent *ipso facto* entails a renunciation of its title over the whole or part of the territory claimed by the new State.[108] Thus, a territory is contested if there exists more than one claim to it, and statehood is contested if the ownership over the entirety of a new State's territory is claimed by another. Clearly, the claims need to be based on established legal principles. For example, the Parent State will claim a continuity of lawful title to it, while the secessionists could base their claims on effectivity, self-determination, or some other grounds. If neither claim can be clearly rejected under international law, then third States may 'choose a side' in the dispute and recognise one competing claim over another. However, in situations of consensual separation, no such dispute arises, and there is no way for third States to establish their own competing claim if the original sovereign has lawfully passed its title to the new State.

Some contemporary lawyers such as Jure Vidmar agree with the importance of consent in this regard. Vidmar writes:

> Declarations of independence change or intend to change the legal status of the territory whose independence they are declaring ... Where state creation is consensual, an entity may become a state at the moment of the declaration of independence ... In the moment when the declaration of independence is issued, the new state is not (yet) recognized. This is, however, not a problem where a declaration of independence is issued with an approval of the parent state.[109]

[106] See Lassa Oppenheim, *International Law: A Treatise, Volume I: Peace* (Longmans, Green and Co 1912) 120.

[107] Johann Caspar Bluntschli, *Das moderne Völkerrecht der civilisirten Staten als Rechtsbuch dargestellt* (Druck und Verlag der C H Beck'schen Buchhandlung 1872) 72.

[108] Border disputes between the new State and its parent are common and could lead to disastrous consequences, as shown by the 1998–2000 war between Eritrea and Ethiopia over the disputed territory of Badme.

[109] Jure Vidmar, 'Conceptualizing Declarations of Independence in International Law' (2012) 32(1) Oxford Journal of Legal Studies 153, 157. Consider also in this regard the Spanish position on Kosovo (which Spain does not recognise) in light of its recent decision to recognise Palestine. According to a Spanish foreign ministry spokeswoman, Kosovo and Palestine are two very different situations, as recognition of the latter does not affect Israel's territorial integrity—Palestinian territory 'never [having] been legally part of the state of Israel'. 'Spain Says Its Decision Not to Recognize Kosovo Unchanged

Thus, if the Parent State consents to the independence of a part of its own territory, recognition by third States would be declaratory insofar as no one else has a legitimate claim to it. Ultimately, while some of the new State's rights could possibly still be impaired by non-recognition, the lack of contestation would certainly have importance for others, especially regarding the rules governing the use of force in international relations. In this respect, it is reasonable to distinguish between situations where the Parent State is attempting to re-establish control over a secessionist entity, and those where an unrecognising third State, following consensual separation and in the absence of any other legitimate claims to the territory, attempts to seize it for itself.

7. Conclusion

State practice strongly supports the notion that statehood can sometimes become opposable even in the absence of individual recognition. Recognition, whether it exists or not, then becomes merely declaratory or political, although it may still retain importance under domestic law and for the establishment of diplomatic relations between the two States. However, this does not happen because the new State has become a State *de facto* but by virtue of other norms of international law applicable to the situation. This cannot be explained by declaratist doctrine.

Recognition doubtless becomes declaratory in case of common membership in the United Nations. As the Organisation is open to States, membership is both indicative and constitutive of statehood. This may also be the case with membership in some other international organisations.

It is somewhat less certain, but in my view still very likely that a similar effect may be produced by the existence of a right to external self-determination recognised by the United Nations General Assembly. According to the ICJ, colonial countries enjoy some of the rights of States even before achieving statehood, material independence, or recognition by other States. Certainly, the existence of external self-determination negates the requirement of material statehood when recognition is given by other States, although an authority speaking for its people should at least have a formal claim of statehood. Such entities are best regarded as States in the legal sense, their statehood flowing from a people's exercise of its right to self-determination.

It is also possible for an individual State to hold itself bound to more demanding standards under international law as required under the declaratory approach. States which publicly assert the link between statehood and effectivity may find it difficult to deny a demand for recognition by an entity that meets the requisite

After Deciding to Recognize Palestinian State' (*Radio Free Europe*, 28 May 2024) <https://www.rferl.org/a/spain-kosovo-serbia-recognition-palestine-israel/32967388.html> last accessed 11 June 2024.

criteria. In addition, a regional treaty—such as the Montevideo Convention—could bind its parties to declaratory standards.

Statehood established through consensual separation should also be regarded as opposable to third States regardless of their recognition because it involves the transfer of a title over territory once lawfully held by the Parent State. Such entities have typically joined the United Nations without delay. In my view, just as in situations where a people is acting in pursuit of a recognised claim of external self-determination, statehood thus established should be regarded as fully opposable to third States, meaning that the new State should enjoy all of the rights accorded to States under general international law.

10

When Recognition is Constitutive

1. Opposability Based on Recognition

In an ideal situation, recognition takes place between State A and new State B, with A accepting to treat B as a State. The establishment of B as a new State is not prohibited by any rule of international law and A's decision to recognise it only produces effects in its own relations with B. Accordingly, A's recognition of B allows B to exercise statehood rights towards A; I discuss in Chapter 11 whether B also needs to recognise A for the relationship to become two-sided. Recognition thus forms the basis of opposability and transforms an extra-legal relationship into a legal one.

Today, the above situation is very rare in practice. There exists no more *terra nullius* on the Earth where a new State may be formed and all new entities claiming statehood must arise within the territory of an existing State. The creation of statehood will therefore always have a direct impact on the rights and interests of one or more existing States. Third States need to take these into account before taking any steps towards recognition; the law limits their right to do so, but it does not exclude it, and it is conceivable that their recognition will create an opposability. Together with identifying situations where opposability stems from situation-specific rules of international law—discussed in the previous chapter—and answering the question of whether recognition can also make a new State opposable is the second essential task for my normative theory of recognition. Accordingly, the regime of constitutive recognition remains valid in at least two types of situation, namely in cases of (i) secession, which occurs without the consent of the Parent State, and (ii) the dissolution of an existing State, normally some type of federal entity.

As we have seen, there is a strain of thought in law, going back at least as far as Vattel, according to which every entity that meets the criteria of statehood is *ipso facto* sovereign and enjoys the rights flowing therefrom. This condition is of an *a priori* nature and imposes itself on the law. If it were true, then consent, or recognition, would not be required for opposability.[1] Recognition would always be declaratory and we would not need to search for any specific rule in State practice, treaties, or even general principles: this would rather be an inherent trait of international law, derived not from practice but from reason, similarly perhaps to the principle of good faith.[2]

[1] Of course, this is not so in reality, but the current analysis is hypothetical.

[2] See in particular Robert Kolb, *La bonne foi en droit international public: contribution à l'étude des principes généraux de droit* (Presses universitaires de France 2000).

Recognition of States in International Law. Pavle Kilibarda, Oxford University Press. © Pavle Kilibarda 2024.
DOI: 10.1093/oso/9780198905653.003.0010

In reality, statehood and sovereignty are not principles: they are concepts invoked to describe a complex phenomenon that consists of various factual and legal elements, and, by extension, to define a person or subject of law. Every legal system defines its own subjects and who or what shall be the bearer of the rights and duties it prescribes: to find them, we must look within this system of law, not outside it. An increasing number of States today are expanding the notion of legal personality in their domestic law to cover certain non-human animal species—notably the most intelligent species of primates—but it would be a frustrating and fruitless endeavour to imagine that such personality flows directly from these animals' intellectual capacity. Moral personality may be deduced from ethical principles in such a manner, but legal personality can only stem from positive law. So too must it be in international law, however arcane or obscure the relevant norms may be.

Modern international law is not a system that sprang into being from rational principles to be illuminated by clever lawyers. It is a system which has undergone a steady evolution over several centuries and which was initially created by a small number of States to deal with local matters that required legal regulation. These States did not regard all other States as participating in this normative system simply because they too were States: nineteenth-century legal literature is replete with explanations, either apologetic or shameless, of why international law could only apply to 'civilised' nations.[3] From this core of European powers, the system gradually expanded to include other States—like membership in a country club. The tool of this expansion was of course recognition in various forms. The process was not always consistent, it was not equal around the world, and it was certainly not always freely given, but the general practice, for good or ill, is hard to deny.[4] The content of international law expanded greatly and became more 'humanised' in the twentieth century, but not even the adoption of the League of Nations Covenant and later of the UN Charter have changed the fundamental aspects of the system. Sovereignty does not supervene on statehood, at least if the latter is imagined purely as an effectivity, which is typical of declaratist doctrine.

There are of course other views on the origins and evolution of recognition. Dugard and Raič find that '[a]s international law until recent times did not exalt respect for existing boundaries into a well-nigh absolute rule', recognition earlier served as little more than a means of validating secession or independence and was thus common, whereas today, with 'sacrosanct' borders, it is a rare phenomenon.[5]

[3] A convincing demonstration and explanation of how modern international law expanded from an initially much more limited community of European and Christian States to the global normative framework we know today is given in Alfred Verdross, 'Règles générales du droit international de la paix' (1929) 30 RCADI 271, 318ff.

[4] For a particularly compelling picture of pre-Second World War practice, see Hersch Lauterpacht, *Recognition in International Law* (CUP 2013) 7ff.

[5] John Dugard and David Raič, 'The Role of Recognition in the Law and Practice of Secession' in Marcelo G Kohen (ed), *Secession: International Law Perspectives* (CUP 2006) 94, 94–95.

It is suggested that recognition may be more important today than it was in previous decades. I disagree with this view, which is based purely on post-Second World War observations, whereas recognition is a much older practice. Whatever the case, it does not matter whether recognition is more or less important today than it was before, at least in terms of political practice: what matters is to ascertain its legal effects. Even if there are no rules directly governing the effects of recognition, these do not exist outside the law, and there are both abstract principles and identifiable rules that come into play.

2. Conditions of Lawful Recognition

I have already examined the material criteria of statehood, which are usually understood as the possession of a defined territory, a permanent population, and an effective, independent government. From a legal perspective, a State is better understood as a subject of international law possessing, in the words of the International Court of Justice (ICJ), a 'totality' of rights and duties foreseen in law.[6] It does not really matter whether international law defines States, or is even capable of doing so, as suggested by some authors;[7] all that matters is that it can set prerequisites for treating an entity as a State, and that means for its recognition.

In situations where there exists no norm of international law requiring that an entity be considered a State, recognition will only be lawful and lead to opposability if the recipient meets the two preconditions of effectivity and legality.

There are two fundamental reasons why such prerequisites are necessary. First, statehood does not merely entail rights under international law but also important duties, as States bear the primary responsibility for ensuring the safety and wellbeing of the population within their territory and must act in respect of the rights of their peers. It is doubtful whether an entity thoroughly incapable of preventing armed bands from forming within its borders and endangering neighbouring States deserves the label of a State, at least at the time it is proclaimed. Today, it would also be quite problematic to leave primary responsibility for the protection of human rights in a territory to an entity that does not possess the capacity to do so.

There is another, more cogent reason to insist on the effectivity of a territorial entity seeking recognition as a State. As discussed earlier, any new States arising today would have to be formed on territory belonging to an existing State; this may happen against, and despite, that State's will. To pre-empt the

[6] *Reparation for Injuries Suffered in the Service of the United Nations*, ICJ Reports 174, Advisory Opinion of 11 April 1949, 180.

[7] Arrigo Cavaglieri, 'Règles générales du droit de la paix' (1929) 26 RCADI 311, 340.

recognition of the secessionist entity by third States, the Parent State will unerringly invoke its right of territorial integrity. Indeed, States are bound to respect each other's territorial sovereignty, which includes respect for the principle of non-intervention in other States' internal affairs.[8] As the ICJ confirmed in the *Nicaragua* case, the principle of non-intervention does not merely cover intervention using armed force, but entails 'the right of every sovereign State to conduct its affairs without outside interference',[9] and that it 'forbids all States or groups of States to intervene directly or indirectly in internal or external affairs of other States ... on matters in which each State is permitted, by the principle of State sovereignty, to decide freely'.[10] Doctrine unanimously espouses the view that premature recognition in itself violates the territorial integrity of the Parent State, and Lauterpacht even finds that this 'tortious or delictual aspect of recognition' may be the only one certainly regulated by law.[11] Dugard adds to this the observation that '[t]here is no case in which a State asserted its freedom to recognize when it please'.[12]

If the secessionists manage to establish a polity with an effective government over a defined territory and population, and that polity ensures for itself sufficient stability, recognition by third States is authorised and will no longer be considered an undue interference in the Parent State's domestic affairs—although the latter is by no means obliged to change its position towards the secessionist entity or to accept its recognition by other States. Interestingly, although premature recognition would doubtless violate the parent's territorial integrity, the secession itself does not.[13] Of course, the creation of the new State must not stem from or involve such a serious breach of international law as would prevent it from being recognised.

Thus, for the lawful recognition of a new State, the criteria of effectivity and legality need first be met. The first are elements that must be present for recognition to be authorised; the latter require that certain breaches be absent, otherwise recognition will be prohibited.

[8] The principle is embodied in art 2(4) and 2(7) of the UN Charter and has been confirmed a number of times by the ICJ as a fundamental principle of international law; see eg *The Corfu Channel Case (United Kingdom v Albania)*, ICJ Reports 4, Judgment of 4 April 1949, 35 and *Case Concerning Military and Paramilitary Activities In and Against Nicaragua (Nicaragua v United States of America)*, ICJ Reports 14, Judgment of 27 June 1986 (hereafter *Nicaragua* case) 106ff.

[9] *Nicaragua* case (n 8), ibid 106.

[10] ibid 108.

[11] Hersch Lauterpacht, *Recognition in International Law* (CUP 2013) 7.

[12] John Dugard, 'The Secession of States and Their Recognition in the Wake of Kosovo' (2013) 357 RCADI 9, 29; this author recalls the premature recognition of Panama by the United States in 1903 that led the latter to pay reparations to Colombia. See page 38 of the work.

[13] As confirmed in *Accordance with International Law of the Unilateral Declaration of Independence in Respect of Kosovo*, ICJ Reports 403, Advisory Opinion of 22 July 2010 (hereafter *Kosovo* case) paras 79ff.

2.1 Effectivity

2.1.1 Classical and Extended Criteria

Although constitutivist and declaratist scholars differ in the value and consequences attached to the material elements of statehood, they largely agree on what they are and that they must be present for a State to exist. The common denominator are the three elements identified initially by Jellinek, namely the possession of a defined territory, a permanent population, and an effective government. The Montevideo Convention adds a fourth criterion, the capacity to enter relations with other States, but in my view this criterion is implicit in that of an effective government of a State, which is expected to represent that State not only internally, within its own territory, but also externally, towards its peers. It is of course extremely difficult to ascertain whether these criteria are universally and consistently present in State practice in all similar situations, but there exists in legal theory no credible alternative concept.

A self-proclaimed State that does not meet these criteria, unless it can rely on another rule of international law to substantiate its claim of statehood, cannot be lawfully recognised. This is why the 'Republic of Cabinda', claimed by a 'government-in-exile' sitting in Paris while the territory is fully administered by Angola, cannot be recognised without violating the latter's territorial integrity.[14] When Biafra, which functioned as an organised polity between 1967 and 1970, received recognition from several neighbouring States, this was justly regarded as premature and therefore a violation of the territorial integrity of Nigeria as its government was ultimately unable to achieve permanent independence from Lagos (this was made obvious when Nigerian forces finally overran remaining Biafran strongholds in 1970).[15] Therefore, effectivity—understood by reference to the three traditional elements combined with some prospect of permanency—is both legally and practically necessary for recognition.

Several authors, such as Crawford and Corten, suggest additional requirements as possible elements of statehood, and thus conditions of recognition. In my view, some of these are already implicit in the above definition, such as independence. Others, such as respect for *jus cogens*, should be evaluated as separate criteria of legality, and a third group ought to be discarded altogether as either material or legal prerequisites (eg democratic legitimacy). Such concerns may certainly inform a third State's decision to recognise the new State but they are not part of the

[14] The Front for the Liberation of the State of Cabinda, which claims to represent the Republic of Cabinda, argues that the people of Cabinda enjoy a right to external self-determination vis-à-vis Angola. In its decision regarding a communication under the African Charter of Human and Peoples' Rights, the African Commission on Human and People's Rights disagreed with this claim. See *Front for the Liberation of the State of Cabinda v Angola* (2013) Comm No 328/06, paras 125–126. On the status of Cabinda under international law more generally, see Catherine Maia and Robert Kolb, *Le statut international de la province angolaise du Cabinda à la lumière du droit international public* (Pedone 2015).

[15] See Jean J A Salmon, *La reconnaissance d'état* (Librairie Armand Colin 1971) 192ff.

legal equation making that decision either lawful or unlawful. Therefore, the three elements of statehood identified in doctrine since the nineteenth century are still exhaustive in situations of general or constitutive recognition.

2.1.2 The Claim Aspect

It is evident that some form of claim is a prerequisite for an entity to be considered a State and recognised by others. Such a claim will usually be expressed by the authority controlling a population within a defined territory, but the declaring authority need not be the same as the future governing authority: title over territory may also be passed by a Parent State to a part of its own territory undergoing the process of separation, as was the case many times in the decolonisation era. However, it is clear that a third State, being a party with no claim of its own to the territory in question, cannot recognise a State unless there exists a previous claim to statehood by an authority that either already exercises sovereignty over a territory and is bestowing it with independence, or one that has stable effective control over it and seeks to be accepted as a State by others. The claim need not be explicit, and even an implicit claim, as Ronen correctly deduces, could be sufficient to bridge the gap between effectivity and statehood.[16] Taiwan is an interesting example in this regard: this '*de facto* State' apparently satisfies all the material criteria of statehood,[17] but does not regard itself as a State—at least, not as a separate State from mainland China.[18] Until such time as Taiwan claims independent statehood, it is not reasonable to regard it as a State.[19]

2.1.3 The Question of Who Can Speak for the New State

From a recognising State's perspective, it is vital to know who can speak for the new entity, for example by declaring independence on its behalf. Clearly, if the entity on whose behalf independence is claimed meets the material conditions of statehood, then it must be represented by the body forming its effective government. Still, there exist uncertainties in some cases, although they are comparatively rare.

[16] Yaël Ronen, 'Entities that Can Be States but Do Not Claim to Be' in Duncan French (ed), *Statehood and Self-Determination: Reconciling Tradition and Modernity in International Law* (CUP 2013) 23, 28, and 47ff.

[17] See Parris Chang and Kok-ui Lim, 'Taiwan's Case for United Nations Membership' (1996–1997) 1(2) UCLA Journal of International Law and Foreign Affairs 393–430.

[18] For a long time, the Nationalist government in Taipei insisted on its claim to all Chinese territory, and while this has been downplayed in recent years, Taiwan still does not claim independence from China.

[19] At present, only a handful of United Nations members recognise the 'Republic of China' (ROC), and then only as the government of China; the Holy See, a UN observer, has consistently maintained its recognition of Taiwan as the government of China even after the People's Republic of China (PRC) took over the ROC's UN seat in 1971. As the PRC suspends diplomatic relations with States recognising the authority of Taipei in any capacity, it is practically impossible for States to maintain relations with both the PRC and ROC (although some, such as Saint Lucia, have expressed a desire for closer relations with the PRC when recognising the ROC). In the absence of a clear and unambiguous claim of independent statehood by Taiwan, any such act of recognition ought to be seen as erroneous.

A notable conundrum arose when a declaration of independence was proclaimed by the Kosovar authorities, which had formally been functioning under a UN mandate as Kosovo's 'Provisional Institutions of Self-Government' (PISG). These included the Assembly of Kosovo, where independence was ultimately proclaimed. At the time of the declaration, these bodies, composed largely of Kosovar Albanian staff and politicians, exercised control over most of the territory of Kosovo with the exception of Serbian-majority municipalities where Serbian State mechanisms persisted even after the Kosovo War. However, when the ICJ was called to render its advisory opinion on the declaration of independence, the authors of the declaration maintained that the declaration had not, in fact, been made by the PISG but rather the 'representatives of the people of Kosovo'; this was presumably done to avoid the constraints of Security Council Resolution 1244 (1999) which guarantees the territorial integrity of the Federal Republic of Yugoslavia (and therefore Serbia as its continuator) pending a final settlement of the status of Kosovo. The Court strangely accepted this argument,[20] which implied that although the territory was administered by the PISG, independence was proclaimed by a separate, unrelated entity—which, logically, could not also administer Kosovo. Vidmar explains, '[T]he ICJ did not see the declaration of independence as being issued by a random group of people but rather by those who are entitled to act on behalf of Kosovo and its people. Even if the authors of the Declaration, in the ICJ's controversial view, acted outside of the organs of self-government, they were occupying the posts in the effective government of Kosovo.'[21] This was evidently a sufficient explanation for the numerous States that recognised the independence of Kosovo, now represented by a government acting on behalf of a 'Republic of Kosovo'.

Regarding the authorship of a declaration of independence, Vidmar makes a clever argument by comparing the 'illegal' declaration of independence of the Smith government in Rhodesia and a hypothetical declaration in favour of Scotland made by himself: 'It is thus difficult to accept that international law was not concerned with [the Rhodesian] Declaration at all . . . The difference is that the Smith government of Southern Rhodesia was in effective control of that entity.' Conversely, 'it is very unlikely that the UN organs would ever deal with a hypothetical declaration of independence of Scotland, issued by the author of the present article, who is obviously not in effective control of Scotland. This "declaration of independence" would have no consequences, neither for the international community nor for the people of Scotland.'[22] We can regard in the same way the 2017 Catalan declaration of independence, as Spain never lost effective control over the

[20] *Kosovo* case (n 13) paras 107–109.

[21] Jure Vidmar, 'Conceptualizing Declarations of Independence in International Law' (2012) 32(1) Oxford Journal of Legal Studies 153–77, 160.

[22] ibid 158.

region of Catalonia. This declaration is thus not capable of producing any international legal effects as it is not made by an entity in effective control of the territory, wherefore it was ignored by other States.[23] This works well as the rule of thumb but there exist more nuanced cases, under the 'special regimes' of recognition discussed in the previous chapter; there, effectivity may be disregarded, chiefly to protect the interests of a people acting in pursuit of its right to self-determination. Where such a people does not possess its own authority exercising effective control over the territory it inhabits, it can be considerably more difficult to determine who is authorised to speak for it.

2.1.4 Secession and Dissolution

Doctrine tends to neglect the distinction between secession and the complete dissolution of a State, but it is both factually and legally important. In cases of secession, a new State arises while the Parent State continues to exist and disputes the validity or effectivity of the breakaway entity[24] (consensual 'secession', exemplified by cases such as the breakup of the Soviet Union and of Serbia and Montenegro, is usually referred to as separation). As the Parent State does not accept the act of secession, the territory in question is subjected to two competing claims. Dissolution means that the Parent State ceases to exist, and two or more units that had previously constituted it begin a separate life as new States. This usually happens in federal States with defined internal borders and jurisdictions among federal units which facilitate their transition into independent States. Dissolution may be peaceful and consensual when the new States agree on its modalities, as was the case in Czechoslovakia, but it can also be contested, as occurred in Yugoslavia. The latter situation may raise complex issues of international law. Finally, in some situations it may be difficult to distinguish between secession and dissolution. Although the Soviet Union is commonly said to have 'dissolved' (and this is certainly correct in political and historical terms), the former republics agreed that Russia would be the continuator of the legal personality of the former Union.[25] Therefore, from a legal perspective, Russia is the same State as the old Soviet Union, which never ceased to exist and from which other former republics merely separated.

Secession and dissolution are challenging for settling matters of succession to international treaties but also for resolving matters of ownership over movable

[23] On the question of Catalan independence, see Robert Kolb and Tarcisio Gazzini, 'The Autonomous Community of Catalonia and International Law' (2021) 31(1) Swiss Review of International and European Law 3–23.

[24] This is the meaning given to the term 'secession' by Marcelo Kohen and accepted by John Dugard; see Marcelo G Kohen (ed), *Secession: International Law Perspectives* (CUP 2006) 3 and Dugard, 'The Secession of States' (n 12) 25.

[25] See more on this matter in Rein Mullerson, 'The Continuity and Succession of States, by Reference to the Former USSR and Yugoslavia' (1993) 42(3) The International and Comparative Law Quarterly 473.

and immovable property (particularly abroad, when settling who 'inherits' possession over the old State's diplomatic and consular representations and residences), public debt, nationality, and many other matters. International law does not regulate this matter in significant detail, but the prevailing theory is that in case of secession, the new State starts with a 'clean slate' in terms of its treaty obligations: with some exceptions, such as regarding external borders, territorial regimes,[26] and, perhaps, multilateral human rights treaties,[27] the State is largely liberated from the treaties that its parent had ratified.[28] This is less clear in case of dissolution, and the Badinter Commission notably held that all of its former republics should be considered as successor States of the former Yugoslavia.[29] Most of these States proceeded to accede or declare their succession to many treaties that the old socialist federation had ratified, so the question of automatic succession was not raised in practice. It seems that even when the Parent State ceases to exist, its spectre continues to 'haunt' its successors as all its legal commitments do not simply dissipate along with it.

Whether a new State is created through secession or dissolution also has an impact on its recognition. Secession is the more common and simpler example and certainly the main reason for which there exist material conditions of statehood and recognition. If the seceding entity does not meet them, then its recognition as an independent State will violate the territorial integrity of the Parent State, insofar as that State opposes the secession. In case of dissolution, the Parent State no longer exists, meaning that there is no State whose territorial integrity would be interfered with through recognition. The material elements remain important (there must exist some degree of factual statehood to be recognised), but their application may be less stringent, as exemplified by the recognition of Bosnia by many States before its admission to the United Nations.

Practice presents other problems with dissolution. Where the breakup involves contesting claims, the Parent State seldom 'goes quietly'. From the outset of the

[26] See more in Andreas Zimmermann, *Staatennachfolge in völkerrechtliche Verträge: Zugleich ein Beitrag zu den Möglichkeiten und Grenzen völkerrechtlicher Kodifikation* (Springer 2000).

[27] See more in Menno T Kamminga, 'State Succession in Respect of Human Rights Treaties' (1996) 7 European Journal of International Law 469 and Andreas Zimmermann and James Devaney, 'State Succession in Treaties' in Anne Peters and Rüdiger Wolfrum (eds), *Max Planck Encyclopedias of International Law* (OUP 2019) <https://opil.ouplaw.com/display/10.1093/law:epil/9780199231690/law-9780199231690-e1109> last accessed 7 June 2024.

[28] See more in Diba B Majzub, 'Does Secession Mean Succession—The International Law of Treaty Succession and an Independent Quebec' (1999) 24(2) Queen's Law Journal 411–50; an attempt was made to regulate the issue through the Vienna Convention on Succession of States in Respect of Treaties, but very few instruments of ratification have been deposited so far; see Vienna Convention on Succession of States in Respect of Treaties Arts, 1946 UNTS 3 (signed 22 August 1978, entered into force 6 November 1996); see also in general Ivan Shearer, 'State Succession in Relation to Treaties: Looking Back and Looking Forward' in Tiyanjana Maluwa, Max du Plessis, and Dire Tladi (eds), *The Pursuit of a Brave New World in International Law: Essays in Honour of John Dugard* (Brill/Nijhoff 2017) 321–57.

[29] 'Conference on Yugoslavia Arbitration Commission: Opinions on Questions Arising from the Dissolution of Yugoslavia, 11 January and 4 July 1992' (1992) 31 ILM 1488, 1524–25.

breakup of Yugoslavia to the overthrow of the Milošević regime, the government in Belgrade maintained that it acted as the continuator of the legal personality of Yugoslavia. The Badinter Commission used a number of indicators to determine that Belgrade was no longer acting on behalf of the federation as a whole and rejected this argument (introducing the terms 'participation' and 'representativeness', unknown in previous doctrine).[30] The Security Council also decided to prevent the new Federal Republic of Yugoslavia (Serbia and Montenegro) from taking the seat of the Socialist Federal Republic of Yugoslavia at the United Nations.[31] The controversy was largely dismissed when the new democratic government in Belgrade applied for membership in 2000. The Yugoslav example nevertheless demonstrates the immense difficulties and dangers inherent in the dissolution of federal States, which practically makes this scenario resemble that of secession cases.[32]

Still, dissolution normally presents one advantage for third States observing it, which is due to the fact that federal States are typically constituted of units with well-defined internal borders. One reason why the Serbian and Croatian secessionist entities in Bosnia could not have been considered States were their undefined borders that constantly fluctuated with the front lines of combat during the war. It may come to pass that secessionist entities form within borders defined internally by the Parent State, such as Kosovo within Serbia or the pro-Russian separatist entities in the Donetsk and Lugansk Oblasts of Ukraine. But I do not find convincing the Badinter Commission's resort to the principle of *uti possidetis* in such cases—at least insofar as this principle validates a claim to territory (which it should, following its Roman origins).[33] It is true that the way the principle was espoused by the ICJ could be interpreted as having broader application, but it has to be understood that the colonial context in the *Frontier Dispute* case meant that *uti possidetis* was a limitative factor to self-determination, not an enfranchising one.[34] Otherwise, internal State borders are determined by domestic law and there is no reason why domestic law should also determine international law, although it may have indicative value when assessing whether the material conditions of statehood have been met.

To summarise, before any entity may be recognised as a State, it must first meet the three material conditions of statehood. This requirement may be less stringent in cases of State dissolution, although this is debatable. In addition, the entity must

[30] ibid 1496.

[31] UNSC Resolution 777 (1992).

[32] The matter was not helped by the Badinter Commission's initial finding that Yugoslavia was in a 'state' of dissolution, which was only deemed to have been finalised several months later; this begs the question of the status and position of the federation between the two sessions of the Commission.

[33] See more in Giuseppe Nesi, 'Uti Possidetis Doctrine' in Anne Peters and Rüdiger Wolfrum (eds), *Max Planck Encyclopedias of International Law* (OUP 2018) <https://opil.ouplaw.com/display/10.1093/law:epil/9780199231690/law-9780199231690-e1125> last accessed 13 June 2024.

[34] See *Case Concerning the Frontier Dispute (Burkina Faso/Mali)*, ICJ Reports 554, Judgment of 22 December 1986, paras 20ff.

first consider itself a State: this is today usually expressed through a declaration of independence, but such a declaration is not a necessary element as the requisite will may also be expressed in some other form.

2.2 Legality

The second major requirement for a new State to arise and subsequently be recognised is legality. This means that its creation must respect international law. Not just any rule of international law will be relevant, but the requirement is broader than simply respecting *jus cogens* (although the consequences of a *jus cogens* breach may be different from those of other norms). This principle is always limitative, in the sense that it prevents recognition; the opposite situation, where a rule of law would require recognition or render it declaratory, would take us outside the general regime on recognition of statehood and into one of the special regimes of declaratory recognition discussed in the previous chapter.

To flesh out the legality requirements, the first step must be to identify the rules that could either invalidate statehood altogether or prevent its recognition. The norms that come into play differ in terms of their strength, the consequences of their breach, as well as their scope *ratione personae*. Thus, the implications of a breach of *jus cogens* will be different from the implications of a violation of a Security Council resolution. I will not deal here with the consequences of premature recognition: even though such recognition would result in a violation of international law, it is intrinsically linked to the material conditions of statehood, whereas the norms analysed here are independent of them.

Before looking at the specific norms, it is necessary to consider the relationship between a factual situation and a legal violation preventing it from producing legal effects. The International Law Commission's Articles on the International Responsibility of States for Wrongful Acts foresee that States shall not recognise situations 'created' by a breach of a peremptory norm of international law[35] (in practical terms, only violations of the prohibition of aggression and the principle of self-determination seem to matter in the context of statehood). This suggests that statehood would be invalidated if it either results from such a breach or if it amounted to one. This recalls the establishment of an independent Rhodesian State, which was found to violate the right of self-determination by entailing apartheid and widespread and systematic racial discrimination,[36] or the invalidity of Russia's recognition of the independence of separatist entities in Eastern Ukraine, which stemmed from illegal use of force.[37]

[35] *Responsibility of States for Internationally Wrongful Acts* (28 January 2002) A/RES/56/83 [Annex] Article 41, arts 40–41.

[36] See L C Green, 'Rhodesian Independence—Legal or Illegal' (1968) 6 Alberta Law Review 37.

[37] See UNGA Resolution ES-11/1 of 2 March 2022.

Therefore whether a particular situation, including the creation of a State, 'involves' such a violation of international law as to be precluded by it can primarily be inferred from the reaction of other States and international organisations. Sometimes the response will be almost unanimous condemnation, as was the case with Rhodesia and Eastern Ukraine; sometimes there will be an overall lack of reaction of any sort, as with Somaliland; and sometimes the response will be mixed, and the matter unresolved, which is true of Kosovo. Nevertheless, while different States may have a different view of the situation and circumstances in each case, the underlying principles are the same and uncontroversial.

The two main situations where legality may come into play are when the creation of the State involves a breach of *jus cogens* or a Security Council resolution. There may also be other situations where international law prevents recognition.

2.2.1 *Jus Cogens*

The most widely accepted definition of a peremptory norm of international law is provided in the Vienna Convention on the Law of Treaties, which describes *jus cogens* as a 'norm accepted and recognized by the international community of States as a whole as a norm from which no derogation is permitted and which can be modified only by a subsequent norm of general international law having the same character'.[38] Such norms are few in number and a full list of *jus cogens* has not been definitively established, with significant controversies arising regarding the status of certain rules.[39] Doctrine commonly cites the prohibition of aggression, genocide, racial discrimination, torture, slavery, and piracy as examples of norms whose peremptory status is not controversial.[40] The right to self-determination is today also considered to form part of *jus cogens*.[41]

In extant practice, non-recognition of statehood for violations of *jus cogens* appears to be limited to the rules on aggression and self-determination; that other norms, such as the prohibition of genocide, could also come into play is not excluded—there is simply no precedent in this regard based on which to evaluate State practice.[42] This analysis is therefore limited to *de facto* States whose creation violates the prohibition of aggression or the principle of self-determination. Even

[38] Vienna Convention on the Law of Treaties, 1155 UNTS 331 (concluded 23 May 1969, entered into force 27 January 1980) (hereafter VCLT) art 53.

[39] A list of peremptory norms identified by the International Law Commission is available in *Report of the International Law Commission* (2019) A/74/10, 146–47.

[40] See eg James Crawford, *Brownlie's Principles of Public International Law* (OUP 2019) 564 and Stefan Talmon, 'The Duty Not to "Recognize as Lawful" a Situation Created by the Illegal Use of Force or Other Serious Breaches of a Jus Cogens Obligation: An Obligation without Real Substance?' in Christian Tomuschat and Jean-Marc Thouvenin (eds), *The Fundamental Rules of the International Legal Order* (Martinus Nijhoff Publishers 2006) 99–100.

[41] See *Report of the International Law Commission* (2019) A/74/10, 146–47; cf *Case Concerning East Timor (Portugal v Australia)*, ICJ Reports 90, Judgment of 30 June 1995, para 29.

[42] Thus, Dugard leaves the door open to a broader application of *jus cogens* in this regard, see Dugard (n 12) 32.

though Article 41 of the Articles on the Responsibility of States for Internationally Wrongful Acts implies the existence of an obligation of non-recognition in relation to all violations of *jus cogens*, in practical terms, only these two norms are relevant to non-recognition of States.

According to the Vienna Convention, a treaty that conflicts with *jus cogens* at the time it is concluded is absolutely void,[43] and the same is true of unilateral declarations.[44] Both treaties and unilateral declarations can be sources of international law, but a conflict with a peremptory norm precludes them from producing any legal effect. Insofar as recognition takes the form of one or the other, it is subjected to the same principles relevant to treaties and unilateral declarations in general. However, it is important to distinguish a breach of *jus cogens* inherent in a treaty or declaration from that involved in the creation of a State as their object of recognition. In practice, these largely coincide, as the validity of the act of recognition will surely depend on the validity of its object, the latter being a situation (legal fact) that prompts additional positive duties from the international community. To be precise, an act of recognition violating *jus cogens* will be void of effect, but a State created in violation thereof will be an illegal situation, which will additionally entail a duty of non-recognition of an *erga omnes* nature.[45]

Some authors, mainly belonging to the declaratory school, reject the notion that a State can be 'unlawful'.[46] According to them, a State is simply a fact and thus cannot be subjected to meaningful legal scrutiny.[47] The widespread non-recognition of *de facto* States, which includes a rejection of the opposability of their actions, speaks against this approach (Talmon attempts an interesting declaratist workaround for this problem but I do not ultimately find it successful).[48] Verily, accepting the legal effects of a State built on aggression would be tantamount to accepting the legal effects of aggression itself. Like the underlying act, such a State would have to be negated and diminished, with a view to restoring the *status quo ante* as far as possible.

There are numerous examples where the creation of a State was rejected on the grounds that it stemmed from or involved a violation of the prohibition of

[43] VCLT (n 38) art 53.

[44] 'Guiding Principles Applicable to Unilateral Declarations of States Capable of Creating Legal Obligations, with Commentaries Thereto' (2013) II(2) Yearbook of the International Law Commission 2006 160, Principle 8.

[45] See *Legal Consequences for States of the Continued Presence of South Africa in Namibia (South West Africa) Notwithstanding Security Council Resolution 276 (1970)*, ICJ Reports 16, Advisory Opinion of 21 June 1971.

[46] See eg Alphonse Rivier, *Principes du droit des gens: Tome premier* (Arthur Rousseau 1896) 55 and Stefan Talmon, 'The Constitutive Versus the Declaratory Theory of Recognition: *Tertium Non Datur*?' (2004) 75(1) British Yearbook of International Law 101–81, 125.

[47] '[T]he additional criteria of legality proposed are not criteria for statehood but merely conditions for recognition, *viz* reasons for not recognizing *existing States*'; Talmon, 'The Constitutive Versus the Declaratory Theory of Recognition (n 46).

[48] ibid 144ff.

aggression, such as Northern Cyprus or Abkhazia and South Ossetia in Georgia. Rhodesia and the South African Bantustans are commonly given as examples of States built on apartheid and violations of the right to self-determination.[49] Despite meeting the criterion of effectivity, the statehood of such entities cannot be accepted as opposable to any other State, and any acts of recognition were (or are) absolutely void.

2.2.2 Resolutions of the Security Council

In addition to certain norms of *jus cogens*, United Nations Security Council resolutions are sometimes taken as preventing a State from arising. As States are often created in the throes of armed conflict and thus linked to an ongoing threat to international peace and security, the Security Council has acted to protect the territorial integrity of the Parent State and prohibit their recognition. The Security Council has thus condemned the declarations of independence of Southern Rhodesia,[50] Northern Cyprus,[51] and Republika Srpska,[52] amongst others. In one of its resolution on Bosnia and Herzegovina, the Security Council thus called for respect for the territorial integrity of that State and declared that 'any entities unilaterally declared or arrangements imposed in contravention thereof will not be accepted'.[53]

The Security Council serves a dual role in this regard. First, its resolutions may be indicative that the creation of a particular State violates *jus cogens*, insofar as the violation corresponds with the Council's mandate to safeguard international peace and security. Second, as its resolutions are binding, it can act as a secondary legislator in its own right. Coupled with the precedence of Member States' obligations under Article 103 of the Charter over their other obligations, this suggests, in my view, that the Security Council can effectively block the creation of a State even when peremptory norms are otherwise respected. In the latter case, recognition of such a State would be a violation of the relevant Security Council resolutions, whereas in the former, it would be both a violation of the resolutions and of *jus cogens*.

There are of course some differences between the two situations, which are largely of theoretical value. Whereas violations of *jus cogens* have an *erga omnes* effect, resolutions of the Security Council function *erga omnes partes*, namely

[49] In relation to Transkei, Dugard notices that the main concern preventing recognition was the compulsory extension of Transkeian nationality to all persons 'connected' to Transkei: 'If Transkeian nationality had not been compulsorily extended to all persons connected with Transkei, however remotely, it might have been possible to view Transkeian independence as a simple achievement of statehood. But once South Africa set the denationalization of all persons ethnically or culturally linked with Transkei as the price for independence, the goal of recognition became impossible.' John Dugard, 'South Africa's "Independent" Homelands: An Exercise in Denationalization' (1980) 10 Denver Journal of International Law and Policy 11, 16. Ultimately, Transkei was only recognised by South Africa itself.

[50] See UNSC Resolutions 216 (1965) and 217 (1965).

[51] See UNSC Resolution 541 (1983).

[52] See UNSC Resolution 787 (1992).

[53] ibid para 3.

towards other United Nations members. In addition, peremptory norms entail the absolute voidness of acts conflicting with them and a duty of non-recognition towards violations; the consequences of violations of Security Council resolutions are such as the Council itself foresees. In practice, there does not seem to be a significant difference between these two situations. In most situations when the Security Council ordered non-recognition explicitly, such as in relation to Southern Rhodesia or Northern Cyprus, the Council first identified either aggression or a violation of self-determination.[54] This is however less evident in the case of Republika Srpska, whose declaration of independence was implicitly condemned in Resolution 787 (1992), but in much milder terms than had been used in earlier resolutions, and mostly in connection to 'threats' to the territorial integrity of Bosnia and Herzegovina and the practice of 'ethnic cleansing'. If the creation of Republika Srpska was not connected to unlawful use of force like Northern Cyprus, then the obligation of non-recognition could stem only from the relevant Security Council resolutions; this is also the case with Somaliland,[55] and perhaps with Nagorno-Karabakh prior to the reintegration of this territory into Azerbaijan in late 2023.[56] As recognition by Member States has not been forthcoming in these cases, it is only possible to conjecture about the legal implications of non-compliance with the UNSC decisions.

2.2.3 Other Relevant Rules

In addition to the above situations, the legal validity of an act of recognition could depend on other norms. The breadth of international law-making renders it difficult to anticipate all such cases, including their scope and effects. Recognition may feasibly be prohibited by a bilateral or multilateral treaty. For example, Croatia, Bosnia and Herzegovina, and Serbia are all States Parties to the Dayton Agreement, according to which the parties shall 'shall refrain from any action, by threat or use of force or otherwise, against the territorial integrity or political independence of Bosnia and Herzegovina or any other State'.[57] This could be understood to contain an obligation not to recognise the independence of any hypothetical entity that may arise within Bosnian territory even if it met the criterion of effectivity and recognition would normally be authorised within the general framework; clearly, legal regimes such as the one described in relation to Bosnia are not general but particular, but they could in principle be established in relation to any State or region in the world.

Of course, the effects of any such arrangements would be exclusively *inter partes*, and would influence only the act of recognition, not the statehood of the

[54] See UNSC Resolutions 216 (1965) and 217 (1965) on Rhodesia and 541 (1983) on Cyprus.

[55] See UNSC Resolution 897 (1994).

[56] See UNSC Resolution 853 (1993).

[57] See General Framework Agreement for Peace in Bosnia and Herzegovina with Annexes (signed and entered into force 14 December 1995) (1996) 35 ILM 89, art I.

entity in question, which could not be a party to the initial accords anyway. The implications of an act of recognition taking place in violation of such a norm would have to be determined on a case-by-case basis, and according to the rules and principles governing its source in law. In my view, the opposability of the statehood in question towards the recognising State would still be inhibited, although other outcomes are certainly possible.

3. The Effects of Recognition

If there exists an entity seeking recognition that meets both the requirements of effectivity and legality, international law authorises recognition. The workings of this process are difficult to pinpoint in abstract terms. For example, 'authorisation' is a word to be employed with great caution: it presumes the existence of a specific rule authorising conduct, yet even with great effort, we will be hard-pressed to find such a rule in the context of recognition. Authorisation might also imply a requirement on the part of non-recognising States to respect the decision of the granter of recognition regardless of their own views, which is not the case. Let us therefore say that, if the above are met, international law does not prohibit recognition (in line with the *Lotus* principle), and there will be no violation of the territorial integrity of the Parent State by the recognising third State. This much at least has been demonstrated by practice and doctrine.

However, to say that recognition is permitted or authorised says nothing about its effects. I have already discussed doctrinal views at length, and clearly there is no consensus about the general effects of recognition. The views of most contemporary doctrine tend to shy away from either constitutive or declaratory positions and commonly describe recognition as political or perfunctory, but 'sometimes' legally important, and therefore not quite declaratory.[58] Because these views often flow from a conflation of cases with little or no legal or factual similarities and frequently ignore the necessity of putting recognition in a broader framework, I find them neither satisfactory nor scientifically accurate.

It should be borne in mind that the act of recognition of States, in its most basic form, is a unilateral act or declaration of the granting State. Recognition may take place in a treaty or, if implicit, be inferred from a conclusive action. Both these forms are either fully derivative or sufficiently analogous to recognition as a unilateral act as to be considered from the same point of reference.

(1) The principle that limits to a State's sovereignty cannot be presumed was confirmed in the *Lotus* case and may still be described as a cornerstone of

[58] See eg Dugard and Raič, 'The Role of Recognition' (n 5) 94.

international law. The *Lotus* judgment sets up a presumption that the existence of a State obligation must be proven, but it also describes a broader notion of consent-based international law.[59] Unless a specific rule requiring States to modify their behaviour to accommodate for a new State may be identified, then no such obligation may be inferred. As we have seen above, a broad overview of the legal and judicial landscape does not support the conclusion that there exists a rule of international law linking material and legal statehood. The limited number of relevant sources saying otherwise—the Montevideo Convention comes to mind, but also the views of the Badinter Commission and some domestic jurisprudence—is inadequate proof of such a norm of general international law. In its absence, the opposability of one State to another must be established, as per the classical formula, through their consent *in casu*, which occurs when an existing State recognises a new one.

(2) Recognition signifies acceptance or consent to be bound by certain legal provisions, and in this respect, it may be the most meaningful of all usual unilateral acts. According to the International Law Commission, '[d]eclarations publicly made and manifesting the will to be bound may have the effect of creating legal obligations. When the conditions for this are met, the binding character of such declarations is based on good faith; States concerned may then take them into consideration and rely on them; such States are entitled to require that such obligations be respected.'[60] The principle of good faith provides a basis for the legally binding character of recognition and formalises the obligation undertaken by the recognising State to treat the recipient as a peer; this is also true if recognition takes place in a treaty. The State granting recognition thereby accepts the opposability of the recipient's statehood or 'sovereignty': this is a catch-all term for rights bestowed upon all States without distinction. The specific content of statehood may evolve in time, but the elements must be identifiable in either customary law or in general principles at any given moment, and thus cannot depend on treaty relations alone.[61] At the same time, recognition does not

[59] See on this matter George Wendell Berge, 'The Case of the S.S. "Lotus"' (1928) 26(4) Michigan Law Review 361; Photini Pazartsis, 'Judicial Activism and Judicial Self-Restraint: The PCIJ's *Lotus* Case' in Christian J Tams and Malgosia Fitzmaurice (eds), *Legacies of the Permanent Court of International Justice* (Martinus Nijhoff 2013) 319–35; and Stéphane Beaulac, 'The *Lotus* Case in Context: Sovereignty, Westphalia, Vattel, and Positivism' in Stephen Allen and others (eds), *The Oxford Handbook of Jurisdiction in International Law* (OUP 2019) 41–58; on the role of consent in the formation of customary law, see I M Lobo de Souza, 'The Role of State Consent in the Customary Process' (1995) 44(3) The International and Comparative Law Quarterly 521.

[60] 'Guiding Principles' (n 44) Principle 1.

[61] This idea is defended by Anzilotti; see Dionisio Anzilotti, *Cours de droit international, Premier volume; Introduction—Théories générales* (Librairie du Recueil Sirey 1929) 174 (for Anzilotti, the recognising State is free to choose what it wishes to accept vis-a-vis the recipient, but for practical purposes accepts whatever is understood by statehood rights at a given moment in history when it is recognising).

create any obligations for its recipient unless accepted, explicitly or implicitly, which usually happens by courteous diplomatic gratitude that simply confirms mutual recognition—although the new State's recognition, if any, of existing States may be purely declaratory, based on other criteria.

Recognition does not have the power to create a State or to explain why it exists within law. States cannot create legal obligations for third parties without their consent, and this of course applies to the new States they confirm through their unilateral acts. Recognition has no other power than to establish the opposability of the rights of statehood towards the granter: once recognised, the recipient may claim, under the law, respect for its sovereignty and territorial integrity; its State immunities, and those of its officials and diplomats; its standing to bring claims against its peer; and so on. The recipient may not be recognised by all other States and it may not recognise them in turn.

This demonstrates why the question of 'Is A a State?' is so misplaced in a legal context, at least when framed in such absolute terms. Namely, the question is polar, so A is either a State or it is not, and it makes very little sense to say that A is a State for B but not for C. Conversely, the matter would be very different if we asked, 'Is A entitled to treatment by B as a State?', where A's bilateral opposability does not imply its universal opposability, nor does it mean that A is otherwise deprived of duties under international law: because if A is not a State, it is not bound by the legal duties imposed on States; yet if it is simply not entitled to a certain level of treatment by B, its own legal existence remains independent of such bilateral relations.

(3) The question remains of what is specifically made opposable through recognition. There are legal obligations that are owed to the international community, and not to any other State individually: these include obligations *erga omnes,* but are not limited to them, and certainly extend to the customary provisions of human rights law which are not directly owed to any other State. Bilateral recognition cannot make these opposable in any way. A non-recognising State cannot attack the population of a State that it does not recognise, nor can a new State engage in torture or slavery simply because it has not been recognised. Some constitutivist writers believed that an unrecognised State has no legal existence at all, and that its territory and population are quite simply outside of the scope of the law.[62] This is both morally reprehensible and legally incorrect. Recognition can only influence the enjoyment of those rights to be exercised bilaterally, such as respect for territorial integrity, immunities, jurisdiction over territory, sovereign

[62] See eg Lassa Oppenheim, *International Law: A Treatise, Volume I: Peace* (Longmans, Green and Co 1912) 116ff and Arrigo Cavaglieri, 'Règles générales du droit de la paix' (1929) 26 RCADI 311, 348.

equality, and others. An unrecognised State may demand that a State that does not recognise it (usually the Parent State) respect its borders and sovereign rights, but the latter is under no obligation to do so; barring special circumstances such as the exercise of self-determination, the claim is a moral one and often simply wishful thinking. However, it is the State that is not recognised and that therefore cannot exercise its own rights: rights which are owed to individual human beings or minority groups, as well as those owed to the international community as a whole, are not bestowed upon that State and exist independently of it.

(4) An important point to be considered is whether recognition has retroactive effect. Regardless of the object of recognition—whether State or government—the little jurisprudence on the matter is divided. In *Oetjen v Central Leather Company*, the Supreme Court of the United States accepted that recognition of Carranza's rule in Mexico had retroactive effect and validated all acts of that government since it had come into existence, rather than from the moment of recognition.[63] The same principle was accepted by the House of Lords in *Lazard Bros v Midland Bank Ltd*,[64] whereas the bench in *Luther v Sagor* was more divided.[65] The Permanent Court of International Justice in *Upper Silesia* seems to deny the retroactive effects of recognition.[66] It is important not to confuse the effects of recognition of statehood with those of recognition of governments in this regard. Insofar as the government of an established State is effective, its representation of that State is opposable to other States regardless of recognition,[67] which means that an analysis of 'retroactive' effects is then superfluous; but this is not always the case, and recognition of governments may indeed have important repercussions in situations where a State has no effective government. It makes sense to discuss the retroactive effects of such recognition, similarly to that of statehood, where effectivity is not enough for opposability.

Recognition is said to have retroactive effects because it involves the taking of cognisance of a change in external circumstances and a reaction to it. Because the recognised element necessarily predates cognition and exists independently of it, it is reasonable to trace any effects to its object, rather than to the act of recognition. For declaratist scholars, this approach is theoretically sound (although it is then imprecise to discuss the retroactive effects of recognition, when we are really talking

[63] *Oetjen v Central Leather Co* (1918) 246 US 297, 298.

[64] *Lazard Bros v Midland Bank Ltd* (1933) AC 289, 297.

[65] *Luther v Sagor* (1921) 3 KB 532, 543ff.

[66] *Case Concerning Certain German Interests in Polish Upper Silesia (Germany v Poland)*, Judgment of 25 May 1926, Ser A, No 7, 28ff.

[67] *Tinoco Claims Arbitration (Great Britain v Costa Rica)* (1923) 1 RIAA 369, 381; *Luther v Sagor* (1921) 3 KB 532, 543–44; *The Arantzazu Mendi* (1939) AC 256, as reproduced in L C Green, *International Law Through the Cases* (Steven & Sons Ltd 1970) 136–38.

about the prospective effects of statehood). However, if recognition has the effect of creating opposability, to attribute retroactive effect to the object of recognition itself means to mix the proverbial apples and oranges.

To clarify: if the territorial integrity of A is opposable to B because B recognises the statehood of A, then the source of that opposability is not the statehood of A, but its recognition by B. The legal effects under scrutiny are not produced at the moment of statehood, but at recognition.

Let us imagine that A is a breakaway region of B that eventually succeeds in fulfilling the criteria of effectivity and proclaims independence, thus factually achieving statehood and acting as a State. For years, B refuses to recognise that independence, and commonly meddles in matters A considers its own internal affairs (and which B itself would agree to be impermissible towards a State it recognised). It also continuously refuses to extend any sort of immunities to the representatives of A, who (for the sake of the argument) agree to attend peace negotiations in the capital of B. B eventually recognises A and thereafter treats it as it does any other State. If recognition had retroactive effect, then all the above-mentioned indignities B had earlier inflicted upon A would now in hindsight be considered violations of international law, even though they were not such at the time they were committed. This view does not make sense and it is not at all realistic to expect that States would endure it.

This does not mean that relations post-recognition start from a blank slate. Although recognition would not have retroactive effects *strico sensu,* it may imply that certain acts of the recipient will from then on be considered as valid *ex tunc* by the bodies of the recognising State. For example, a court in B may refuse to consider a birth or marriage certificate produced by A before it is recognised, but accept even those documents that precede the act of recognition once the latter has been given. Whether or not domestic courts will do so is purely a matter of domestic law and judicial policy and is not at all determined by international law, although practice generally corresponds to the approach described here—it would not make any sense at all for a domestic court to refuse to apply the law of a foreign country simply because it was passed at a time recognition had not yet been given; perhaps this was the real reason behind the House of Lords' decision to attribute retroactive effects to recognition in the *Lazard Bros* case.

4. Conclusion

As a unilateral legal act grounded in the principle of good faith, recognition will lead to the opposability of statehood if it conforms to certain rules of international law. However, it may not be the only source of opposability in bilateral relations between two States. Effectivity alone is not enough in this regard, as it is currently impossible to demonstrate the existence of a rule of international law automatically linking effectivity to opposability. This is the main shortcoming of the declaratory approach.

Unless a rule of international law can be applied to establish opposability independently of recognition in an individual case, then this quality may be inferred exclusively from recognition. But not every act of recognition will lead to opposability, as the prerequisites of recognition are, to some extent, present in international law.

The recipient of recognition must first fulfil the criteria of effectivity and legality. 'Effectivity' here requires that the object possess material statehood by meeting the criteria of effective government, permanent population, and defined territory with a reasonable degree of permanence; it must also claim to be a State. 'Legality' means that the recipient State cannot be constituted in violation of certain *jus cogens* norms, specifically the principle and right of self-determination and the prohibition of aggression, or if non-recognition has been ordered by the United Nations Security Council. Recognition in violation of the principle of effectivity will be considered premature and violate the right to territorial integrity of the Parent State; recognition in violation of the principle of legality will normally have effects *erga omnes*; both should be seen as void. If both the requirements of effectivity and legality have been met, international law authorises recognition, but does not require it.

This regime where recognition is constitutive of legal statehood on a bilateral level is only applicable where there exists no other norm of international law establishing the opposability of the State seeking recognition. Where such norms may be identified, opposability will not depend on recognition, which becomes declaratory of legal statehood.

11
Statehood Beyond Recognition

1. The Theoretical and Practical Value of 'Self-Recognition'

Recognition may be required for a new State to become opposable to others, but it does not 'create' the recipient in any meaningful sense of the word. Contrary to widespread conviction, most constitutivist scholars do not maintain such a counterintuitive position. A State's legal existence may depend on recognition, but a State is not solely, nor indeed primarily, a legal fact: it exists as a material fact and persists or fails regardless of its lawfulness. Even as a person of law, a State may exist without recognition from any other State, as recognition by a third State is merely required to establish a legal relationship whereby statehood rights become opposable between the two States. Therefore, unrecognised States may still be held responsible for violations of international law, something that extreme forms of constitutivism fail adequately to explain.

History is replete with declarations of independence or statehood, whether successful or not. Such declarations are usually taken as the precise moment of the creation of a new State, even when statehood is contested. This is, of course, a legal fiction. When the Thirteen Colonies proclaimed independence from the British Crown in 1776, they had already been at war for a year; the contention that something miraculously came to pass on that 4 July that intrinsically altered the territories' status from colonies to independent States would hardly stand to scientific scrutiny. Nevertheless, declarations of independence are memorialised and venerated in much of the world as symbolic of statehood. They may even serve a legal function in domestic law, which might only apply from the moment of the declaration. It is not always required that the new State proliferate a formal instrument claiming statehood; when independence is granted by the Parent State, the formal moment of independence may trace back to an act of that State. Many British dominions became independent States by an act of the British parliament, namely the Statute of Westminster, which was passed in 1931.

A declaration of independence may have more than symbolic value. When Kosovo declared independence from Serbia in 2008, its representatives explicitly committed to respect international law, including obligations undertaken by Yugoslavia and the United Nations Mission in Kosovo. It is, in fact, common for a declaration of independence to be followed by some sort of commitment on behalf of the new State that it will abide by international law, as attested by the declarations of Montenegro and South Sudan. This is done to grant an aura of legitimacy

Recognition of States in International Law. Pavle Kilibarda, Oxford University Press.
DOI: 10.1093/oso/9780198905653.003.0011

to the newly independent State and potentially draw further recognition, but at a conceptual level, such a commitment allows us to explain why the new State is bound by international law regardless of recognition by others. In Kelsen's words:

> Such proclamation [of statehood] has only the effect that the community becomes a subject of international law for itself and not in relation to others. If a new community is formed in some territory and the organ representing this community declares itself a state as understood by international law, the effect of this declaration is analogous to the effect of the declaration made by another state that the new community is a state. The effect of the latter recognition is limited to the relation between the recognizing and the recognized state. In case a new community declares itself to be a state, both subjects are identical. The new state starts its legal existence with its declaration of statehood but it exists only for itself, not in relation to other states.[1]

Just as the grant of recognition by another State is a unilateral undertaking of obligations towards the recipient, so too is the actual or postulated declaration of statehood an assumption of duties reserved for States in international law. Such an act, as a 'manifestation of will aiming to produce legal effects' (*des manifestations de volonté visant à produire des effets de droit*),[2] does not create obligations for third parties but binds the proclaiming State to a core of international legal norms existing at the time of its 'self-recognition'. This notion is already present in the works of Strupp and Cavaglieri[3] and answers how unrecognised States are still bound by international law. This may be referred to as the theory of self-recognition. In line with Kelsen's postulate, with which I agree, that a State's legal existence is merely relative,[4] entity A proclaiming itself a State is in effect 'recognising' itself as such, unilaterally. In assuming statehood, it is also claiming a specific package of rights and committing to certain obligations in its relations with other States.

This theory enjoys some judicial support. During the proceedings in the *Croatia v Serbia* case at the International Court of Justice (ICJ), Serbia raised a preliminary objection against the Court's jurisdiction to consider acts taking place before 27 April 1992, this being the day when the new Constitution of the Federal Republic of Yugoslavia (FRY) was promulgated.[5] It was argued that Serbia was

[1] Hans Kelsen, 'Recognition in International Law: Theoretical Observations' (1941) 35(4) The American Journal of International Law 605, 609.

[2] Éric Wyler, *Théorie et pratique de la reconaissance d'état: Une approche épistemologique du droit international* (Bruylant 2013) 69.

[3] For Strupp, the new state is bound by international law from the moment it manifests its intention to become its subject; for Cavaglieri, it is bound to respect the principles of conduct common to the society of States. As quoted in ibid 140–41.

[4] Kelsen, 'Recognition in International Law' (n 1) 609.

[5] 'Serbia maintains that, in so far as Croatia's claim concerns acts said to have occurred before the FRY became party to the Convention on 27 April 1992 (and the great majority of Croatia's allegations concern events before that date), the Convention was not capable of applying to the FRY (and, therefore, any breaches of it cannot be attributable to Serbia).' *Application of the Convention on the*

not a continuator of Yugoslavia, wherefore conduct taking place before that date could not be attributed to it, but only to Yugoslavia. To a certain extent, the Court accepted this argument, finding that 'the FRY was not bound by the obligations contained in the Genocide Convention until it became party to that Convention' and that 'succession resulted from the declaration made by the FRY on 27 April 1992 and its Note of the same date ... The date on which the notification of succession was made coincided with the date on which the new State came into existence.'[6] It was similarly found that Croatian claims related to acts committed prior to 8 October 1991 (when the moratorium on its declaration of independence expired and Croatia 'became' a State) were admissible as they were 'pertinent to an evaluation of whether what took place after that date involved violations of the Genocide Convention'.[7] As subsequently the Court determined that no genocide had taken place in Croatia, it did not find it necessary to pronounce whether it would have been attributable to Yugoslavia or whether Serbia had 'inherited' Yugoslav responsibility.[8]

2. Conceptualising a New State's Legal Position

What, then, are the rights thereby claimed and the duties assumed by the entity claiming statehood? In Cavaglieri's conception, international law was initially of a contractual nature and only bound States to respect those rules to which they agreed in their dealings with other States. These were primarily rules concerning the delimitation of States' territorial jurisdiction and governing their mutual relations. However, the evolution of international law has long since overcome this contractual nature, leading to the creation of universal rules governing treaties, diplomatic law, the rights of foreigners, and so on; these rules are fundamental for international relations and it is through their acceptance that a State joins the 'international legal society'.[9] Cavaglieri refers to these rules as 'principles of conduct common to the society of States' (*principes de conduite communs à la société des États*).[10]

Under contemporary international law, the new State would therefore be bound to respect those rules which bind all States without distinction. These are the general rules of international law, including peremptory norms and universal

Prevention and Punishment of the Crime of Genocide (Croatia v Serbia), ICJ Reports 3, Judgment of 3 February 2015, para 91.

[6] ibid para 104.
[7] ibid para 119.
[8] ibid para 442.
[9] Arrigo Cavaglieri, 'Règles générales du droit de la paix' (1929) 26 RCADI 311, 326ff.
[10] ibid 355.

customary law, also known as 'general international law'; the State will not be bound by treaties until it becomes a party to them, with the possible exception of automatic succession with regard to certain treaties. In particular, these rules include the *erga omnes* prohibition of genocide, torture, slavery, and other fundamental rules of human rights law and international humanitarian law.[11] Because these obligations are not owed to specific States but to the 'international community as a whole', other States are bound to respect these in their dealings with the new State regardless of whether or not they recognise it, although the unrecognised State may not procedurally be able to enforce claims for practical lack of a forum where it could have legal standing. In addition, the new State will also be bound by customary law, such as the rules on the freedom of the seas, the obligation not to claim as its own the common heritage of mankind, and to respect the rights of foreigners. However, rules whose nature necessitates bilateral relations—such as the customary law of State and personal immunities—are owed to other States directly and cannot be applied if the beneficiary's statehood is not opposable to the other party concerned.

The prohibition of aggression deserves a more careful analysis in this section. There can be no doubt that aggression is prohibited by a norm of *jus cogens* and that it is in principle applicable to an unrecognised State. The mainstream view is that aggression may only be committed between States.[12] Recognition is doubtless important in this regard: when the United Nations General Assembly adopted a definition of aggression, it stated that the term 'State' was used 'without prejudice to questions of recognition or to whether a State is a member of the United Nations'.[13] This was certainly done to appease the fears of many States that their use of force against unrecognised States (as in the case of secession) could be deemed aggression. Thus, unless a broader definition of aggression were accepted—one that would include, for example, unlawful use of force in violation of a ceasefire or a UN-established administrative line—aggression requires that the statehood of the victim be opposable to the perpetrator. Declaratory doctrine often raises this as an argument against the constitutive theory. In my view, it is necessary for the statehood of one State to be opposable to another before the latter could be held responsible for aggression (although other views exist).[14] Following the successful

[11] *Report of the International Law Commission* (2019) A/74/10, 146–47.

[12] See UNGA Resolution 3314 (XXIX) of 14 December 1974, art 1.

[13] ibid art 1(a).

[14] In the Friendly Relations Declaration, the UNGA recalled that '[e]very State likewise has the duty to refrain from the threat or use of force to violate international lines of demarcation, such as armistice lines, established by or pursuant to an international agreement to which it is a party or which it is otherwise bound to respect. Nothing in the foregoing shall be construed as prejudicing the positions of the parties concerned with regard to the status and effects of such lines under their special regimes or as affecting their temporary character.' This means that the prohibition on the use of force does not only extend towards other States—a State violating an armistice line within its own territory could be seen as violating the rule. See *Declaration on Principles of International Law Concerning Friendly Relations and Cooperation Among States in Accordance with the Charter of the United Nations* (24 October 1970) A/

operations launched by the Azeri government to reintegrate Nagorno-Karabakh in 2020 and 2023 (the latter operation forcing the ethnic Armenian separatists to abandon their dreams of independence), criticism could be heard from the United States and the European Union—mostly regarding possible violations of human rights and humanitarian law, but not necessarily that the use of force by Azerbaijan within its own territory amounted to a violation of the prohibition on the use of force.[15] In practice, this could only be problematic in two types of situation: (i) if the Parent State (or a co-belligerent) uses force against secessionists, which is commonplace in international relations and cannot credibly be labelled aggression; or (ii) where a foreign State intervenes on behalf of a secessionist State that fulfils the prerequisites for lawful recognition. In the latter case, the conflicting legal 'realities' of the Parent State and the intervening State would lead to a normative clash that cannot be resolved by contemporary international law. Luckily, such situations are typically rare.[16]

Practice clearly demonstrates that States may consider accountable for violations of international law even those States that they do not recognise. It may feel awkward for some States to advance claims against States they do not recognise, because it may come across as an acceptance of the other's statehood, but there is no reason in law why this should be the case. It is perfectly legitimate, and even beneficial, for unrecognised States to be called to account if they violate the obligations they assumed by claiming statehood. States notably had such expectations of Israel

RES/2625(XXV). However, I am not aware that such violations have been treated in practice as a violation of international law, or at least not as aggression.

[15] See the discussion in Michael N Schmitt and Kevin S Coble, 'The Evolving Nagorno-Karabakh Conflict—An International Law Perspective—Part I' (Articles of War, 27 September 2023) <https://lieber.westpoint.edu/evolving-nagorno-karabakh-conflict-international-law-perspective-part-i/> last accessed 7 June 2024. Like many others, these authors consider Nagorno-Karabakh to have been occupied by Armenia and evaluate the lawfulness of the use of force by Azerbaijan to reclaim the territory as an instance of interstate use of force against Armenian forces (concluding that it was lawful under *jus ad bellum*). Of course, if Nagorno-Karabakh was indeed occupied by Armenia, this would render its statehood legally impossible and trigger obligations under the non-recognition regime discussed by the ICJ in the *Namibia* case. Schmitt and Coble conclude that, even if Nagorno-Karabakh had not been occupied, 'there would be no issue regarding the use of force prohibition ... Azerbaijan would be engaged in a lawful law enforcement operation subject to its domestic laws, international human rights law, and (perhaps) the law of non-international armed conflict, but not the *jus ad bellum*'. I fully agree with this perspective.

[16] This problem is partially illustrated by Russia's full-scale invasion of Ukraine since February 2022. Initially, Russia recognised the independence of two breakaway regions in Eastern Ukraine, the so-called republics of Donetsk and Lugansk; the subsequent use of force against Ukraine was then justified based on a purported right of collective self-defence. If Russia's recognition of the Donbas republics had been lawful, the situation discussed in this chapter might have materialised. However, the act of recognition was unlawful because the requirements of legality, and probably also of effectivity, had not been met, wherefore no separate 'normative plane' was thereby created. See Pavle Kilibarda, 'Was Russia's Recognition of the Separatist Republics in Ukraine "Manifestly" Unlawful?' (*EJIL:Talk!*, 2 March 2022) <https://www.ejiltalk.org/was-russias-recognition-of-the-separatist-republics-in-ukraine-manifestly-unlawful/> last accessed 7 June 2024.

after it had declared independence but before its recognition.[17] Frowein finds support for this position in the *Namibia* case, where the ICJ linked State liability to territorial control rather than sovereignty or legitimacy of title,[18] leading the author to conclude that '[t]his is true irrespective of non-recognition and means that States may claim compensation even in cases of non-recognition'.[19]

Of course, before asserting that the new State is bound by at least some rules of international law, we must first ascertain whether the entity claiming statehood possesses the capacity to comply with them. There is a significant difference between requiring that Kosovo or Taiwan respect international law and making the same demand of Sealand or Liberland. The entity in question must first fulfil the material requirements of statehood to be capable of complying with legal obligations. Therefore, the preconditions of recognition are also relevant for evaluating an entity's claim to statehood.[20]

2.1 Continuation and Succession

Transfer of sovereignty over a territory involves a number of complex legal issues, many of which are still the subject of significant controversy. State succession is particularly challenging, and Brownlie and Crawford are correct to find that 'it is possible … that not many settled legal rules have yet emerged'.[21] From the outset, two situations need to be distinguished, namely, when the new State acts as a continuator of an old State, and when it is a successor.

In cases of continuity, the new State inherits the legal person of its parent, and essentially remains the same State: it is bound by the same treaties and inherits the old State's membership in international organisations; this is how Russia continues the legal personality of the Soviet Union. In such situations, no question of the opposability of the 'new' State arises, for this will proceed automatically from the opposability of the former one. However, it may be exceedingly difficult

[17] See Thomas D Grant, *The Recognition of States: Law and Practice in Debate and Evolution* (Praeger Publishers 1999) 20–21 and Andrew Clapham, *Brierly's Law of Nations* (OUP 2012) 151, fn 16.

[18] 'The fact that South Africa no longer has any title to administer the Territory does not release it from its obligations and responsibilities under international law towards other States in respect of the exercise of its powers in relation to this Territory. Physical control of a territory, and not sovereignty or legitimacy of title, is the basis of State liability for acts affecting other States.' *Legal Consequences for States of the Continued Presence of South Africa in Namibia (South West Africa) Notwithstanding Security Council Resolution 276 (1970)*, ICJ Reports 16, Advisory Opinion of 21 June 1971, para 118. Of course, in this case the statehood of South Africa was not in dispute, but the principle is also relevant for States lacking recognition.

[19] Jochen A Frowein, 'Non-Recognition' in Anne Peters and Rüdiger Wolfrum (eds), *Max Planck Encyclopedias of International Law* (OUP 2011) para 4 <https://opil.ouplaw.com/display/10.1093/law:epil/9780199231690/law-9780199231690-e1073> last accessed 13 June 2024.

[20] See John Dugard, 'The Secession of States and Their Recognition in the Wake of Kosovo' (2013) 357 RCADI 9, 30.

[21] James Crawford, *Brownlie's Principles of Public International Law* (OUP 2019) 410.

to determine whether continuation has actually occurred, particularly if a federal State disintegrates into its constituent units, and no agreement is reached among them to delineate a single continuator. This was notably the case with Yugoslavia when the FRY's claim to continuity with the old socialist federation was denounced by the other republics and eventually the United Nations. Although the Badinter Commission relied on several indicators to determine that the FRY did not continue the legal personality of the Socialist Federal Republic of Yugoslavia, international law does not provide clear guidance on how to objectively determine a continuator in case of competing claims.[22] Under the circumstances, a continuator may likely only be established with the consent of all successor States.

Succession is more controversial. A successor State is a different person from its parent, with whom it still shares a 'genetic link' that influences its initial legal situation. Succession is important as it may broaden the scope of legal provisions by which the new State is bound (or rights to which it is entitled) by relying on some of the commitments of the Parent State. This is most often the case with treaties but it may also go beyond that, in the interest of safeguarding the acquired rights of third parties. When the International Law Commission started examining the matter in the 1960s, the decolonisation backdrop required that two opposing interests be carefully balanced: 'On the one hand was the concern for the continuity of international law and the rights of those states that had entered into agreements which covered the territories which were emerging as new states on the international scene. On the other hand, the principle of self-determination ... suggest[ed] that these "new states" should start life with a "clean slate" unencumbered by the international obligations assumed by the colonial powers.'[23]

The result was a compromise, integrated into the 1978 Vienna Convention on Succession of States in Respect of Treaties.[24] This compromise foresaw the distinction between new States arising in the colonial context, which would be entitled to a 'clean slate',[25] and non-colonial succession. In the latter case, the Convention requires that the new State generally succeed its predecessor's participation in treaties, unless otherwise agreed by the 'States concerned'.[26] However, the Vienna Convention has very few States Parties, and it is difficult to maintain that it reflects customary law, at least in the post-colonial context.

[22] See James Crawford, *The Creation of States in International Law* (OUP 2007) 705 *a contrario* regarding the dissolution of the Soviet Union (where the situation was only resolved through an agreement between the potential successor States) and Andreas Zimmermann, *Staatennachfolge in völkerrechtliche Verträge: Zugleich ein Beitrag zu den Möglichkeiten und Grenzen völkerrechtlicher Kodifikation* (Springer 2000) for an overview of practice in this regard.

[23] Clapham, *Brierly's Law of Nations* (n 17) 164.

[24] Vienna Convention on Succession of States in Respect of Treaties, 1946 UNTS 3 (signed 22 August 1978, entered into force 6 November 1996).

[25] ibid Article 16; cf Andrew Clapham, *Brierly's Law of Nations* (OUP 2012) 164–165.

[26] Vienna Convention on Succession of States in Respect of Treaties (n 24) Article 35.

Even if a secessionist entity does not inherit all its parent's treaty obligations, there are doubtless some duties that will continue for it. The principle of acquired rights, whereby 'a change of sovereignty has no effect on the acquired rights of foreign nationals', has achieved some judicial support. For example, the Permanent Court of International Justice in the *Lighthouses* case between France and Greece determined that the latter was bound by a concession agreement concluded between the Ottoman Empire and a French company concerning territory ceded to Greece after the Balkan Wars.[27] The underlying principle is that the lawfully acquired rights of a third party should not be affected by a change of territorial sovereignty. There is also some support for the view that new States succeed automatically to the human rights treaty obligations of their parent, although this remains controversial; the matter is discussed in the following section.

On the other hand, many States, upon declaring independence, voluntarily undertake to respect their predecessor's obligations, particularly those contained in multilateral treaties—and often some bilateral ones as well. Where succession is freely assumed, it is not necessary to ascertain whether it would have been required anyway. Only if a new State refuses such succession should the matter be examined with greater scrutiny. Ultimately, it is not presently necessary to determine all of the legal obligations of a new State: it is sufficient to conclude that a new State is bound by at least some rules of international law even if it does not receive recognition from any other State.

2.2 International Human Rights Law

Bearing in mind the growing attention paid to States' human rights obligations, it is important to consider the position of a new State in this regard. It is not controversial that even an unrecognised State will be bound by customary human rights law, along the modalities previously discussed, but it is more difficult to determine which specific rights and freedoms are of a customary nature. This also raises the question of succession to human rights treaties, both regarding their substantive and procedural provisions. The peculiarities of contemporary human rights could imply that succession to human rights conventions occurs in a different manner than with respect to 'ordinary' treaties.

When an entity secedes from its Parent State, the latter's human rights jurisdiction does not cease automatically, at least for so long as the secession may be credibly disputed. While it may serve the interest of the population of a secessionist State to continue to presume the existence of some degree of jurisdiction by the Parent State still claiming the territory, the fairness and the sheer realism of such a

[27] See *Lighthouses Case Between France and Greece*, Judgment of 17 March 1934, Ser A/B, No 62.

presumption must also be considered. In *Ilaşcu and Others v Moldova and Russia*, the European Court of Human Rights thus determined that Moldova continued to exercise partial jurisdiction in breakaway Transdniestria, a region it does not control.[28] In the Court's view, Moldova had positive obligations to engage with the authorities of Transdniestria to ensure that the human rights of persons deprived of liberty were respected. The question of whether the ruling was fair or even feasible has been greatly discussed in doctrine, and the Court's finding that Moldova had an 'obligation to re-establish control over Transdniestria'[29] to implement the European Convention on Human Rights has been justly criticised.[30]

The situation is more complex elsewhere. Serbia ratified the European Convention in 2004, but Kosovo has not, which raises the issue of the Convention's applicability to that territory. In 2013, the Court issued a decision in *Azemi v Serbia* finding the application of a Kosovar Albanian for lack of enforcement of a judgment by a Kosovo court in central Serbia inadmissible. Contrary to the *Ilaşcu* case, the Court held that the applicant was not under the jurisdiction of Serbia because 'there is no evidence that Serbia exercised any control over [the United Nations Mission in Kosovo], Kosovo's judiciary or other institutions that had been established by virtue of UNMIK regulations'[31] and because Kosovo's declaration of independence and recognition by a part of the international community meant that 'there existed objective limitations which prevented Serbia from securing the rights and freedoms in Kosovo'.[32] Applications at the European level have also targeted European contributors to NATO's Kosovo Force, but the Court refused to consider them, finding that ultimate authority over the mission resided with the United Nations, not individual States.[33] As Kosovo is not currently a Council of Europe member,[34] this means that claims under the European Convention are essentially unenforceable at the international level.

[28] *Ilaşcu and Others v Moldova and Russia* App no 48787/99 (8 July 2004) paras 310ff.

[29] ibid para 340.

[30] See eg Thomas D Grant, 'Ukraine v. Russian Federation in Light of Ilaşcu: Two Short Points' (*EJIL:Talk!*, 22 May 2014) <https://www.ejiltalk.org/ukraine-v-russian-federation-in-light-of-ilascu-two-short-points/> last accessed 13 June 2024.

[31] *Azemi v Serbia* App no 11209/09 (5 November 2013) para 45.

[32] ibid para 46.

[33] See *Behrami and Behrami v France and Saramati v France, Germany and Norway* App no 71412/01 and 78166/01 (5 February 2007).

[34] In April 2023, Kosovo's application for membership was accepted by a two-thirds majority in the Committee of Ministers, whereby the admission process was initiated. In April 2024, the Parliamentary Assembly accepted a report recommending a positive final decision on membership to the Committee of Ministers, but also requesting that a way be found to admit Kosovo that considers the 'unprecedented circumstances' that a part of Council of Europe members do not recognise it and that individual positions on status are not thereby prejudged. However, subsequent political developments led to a *de facto* suspension of the admission process, and as of June 2024, Kosovo is not currently a Council of Europe member. See 'PACE Recommends That Kosovo* Becomes a Member of the Council of Europe' (*COE Newsroom*, 17 April 2024) <https://www.coe.int/en/web/portal/-/pace-recommends-that-kosovo*-becomes-a-member-of-the-council-of-europe> last accessed 7 June 2024 and Perparim Isufi and Antigone Isufi, 'Germany Snubs Kosovo's Last Push for Council of Europe Membership' (*Balkan Insight*, 16 May 2024) <https://balkaninsight.com/2024/05/16/germany-snubs-kosovos-last-push-for-council-of-europe-membership/> last accessed 7 June 2024.

It is therefore more important to determine whether the seceding entity has human rights obligations of its own and whether and how these may be enforced. The idea of ensuring automatic treaty succession for human rights instruments has thus far enjoyed very limited success. Amidst the breakup of Yugoslavia and the Soviet Union, the United Nations Human Rights Committee adopted the position that 'all the peoples within the territory of a new State that constituted a part of the former Yugoslavia were entitled to the guarantees of the [International Covenant on Civil and Political Rights]' and that 'all the peoples within the territory of a former State party to the Covenant remained entitled to the guarantees of the Covenant, and that, in particular, Armenia, Georgia, Kazakhstan, Kyrgyzstan, Tajikistan, the former Yugoslav Republic of Macedonia, Turkmenistan and Uzbekistan were bound by the obligations under the Covenant as from the dates of their independence'.[35] However, as these countries quickly proceeded to ratify the Covenant anyway, whether the Human Rights Committee's views were accepted in practice is not easy to determine.[36] More recently, the Committee has reaffirmed the applicability of the Covenant in Kosovo in spite of the fact that Kosovo is not a party and Serbia is 'unable to monitor the application of the Covenant in Kosovo'.[37]

Nevertheless, the approach of human rights bodies, including at the United Nations level, has not been consistent. According to Kamminga, 'Croatia, Bosnia-Herzegovina and Slovenia have argued that the [Federal Republic of Yugoslavia] cannot be regarded as a party to treaties such as the International Covenant on Civil and Political Rights, the International Convention on the Elimination of All Forms of Racial Discrimination and the Convention on the Elimination of all Forms of Discrimination against Women ... Because this approach has prevailed at meetings of States parties of these treaties the FRY has been barred from attending them.'[38] It was, however, agreed that the FRY was still bound by the former Yugoslavia's human rights treaty obligations.[39]

Thus, automatic continuity or succession with respect to human rights treaties is hardly a settled point of law. A preliminary report on *Human Rights and State Succession* written by Kamminga for the Venice Commission found that 'the [Vienna Convention on Succession of States in Respect of Treaties] approach in this respect has attracted little support from states and does not appear to reflect customary international law'.[40] Although practice varies, most States seem to prefer the 'clean slate' doctrine.[41] The Commission on Human Rights in South Sudan has not held that either the International Covenant on Civil and Political Rights or the

[35] UN Doc A/49/40 (21 September 1994) paras 48–49.
[36] See Menno T Kamminga, 'State Succession in Respect of Human Rights Treaties' (1996) 7 European Journal of International Law 469, 475ff.
[37] CCPR Concluding Observations: Serbia (10 April 2017) CCPR/C/SRB/CO/3, para 3.
[38] Kamminga, 'State Succession in Respect of Human Rights Treaties' (n 36) 477.
[39] ibid 478.
[40] *Human Rights Treaties and State Succession* (7 September 2005) CDL-UD(2005)013rep, 2.
[41] ibid 2–5.

International Covenant on Economic, Social and Cultural Rights apply in South Sudan, even though Sudan had been a party since 1986.[42] On the other hand, the European Court found that both the Czech Republic and Slovakia were bound by the European Convention after its ratification by Czechoslovakia.[43]

Ultimately, whether a new State should be held to succeed to a human rights treaty may be as much a matter of political and practical considerations as of law. It would also appear to depend on practice related to a specific treaty, or, more realistically, the views of the treaty body in question: some treaties may therefore allow automatic succession, while others do not. Even if there existed sufficient proof of automatic State succession regarding human rights treaties, it will always be prudent, from a practical perspective, to allow the new State to ratify an instrument itself and thereby give it more 'ownership' in the treaty. Separate ratification or accession to a treaty may be necessary for procedural reasons—for example, to allow individual communications to treaty bodies—but substantive obligations are likely to continue automatically. Still, the persistent debate and controversy surrounding the matter suggest that it will always have to be resolved on a case-by-case basis.

2.3 International Humanitarian Law

The scope of application *ratione materiae* of international humanitarian law extends, beyond some rules already applicable in peacetime, to two types of situations: international armed conflicts, as may arise between States; and non-international armed conflicts, fought between States and non-state armed groups, or between such groups without the involvement of a State.

It is not uncommon for rebel groups to engage government forces with a view to carving out a piece of land and claiming independence. Should this come to pass, they may regard themselves as a State and the conflict an international one. At the same time, for the government the conflict remains non-international. Such differences between belligerent parties regarding conflict classification are common: during the Chechen Wars, Chechen insurgents considered the conflict international, whereas Russia described it as a counter-terrorism operation and thus not even an armed conflict.[44]

[42] *Report of the Commission on Human Rights in South Sudan* (21 February 2019) A/HRC/40/69, para 15.

[43] See eg *Matter v Slovakia* App no 31534/96 (5 July 1999) para 36; *Nemec and Others v Slovakia* App no 48672/99 (15 November 2001) para 30; and others.

[44] Marta Mísová, 'The legal character of the conflict in Chechnya' (*Prague Watchdog*, 18 May 2001) <https://reliefweb.int/report/russian-federation/legal-character-conflict-chechnya> last accessed 13 June 2024.

2.3.1 The Role of Common Article 2

According to Common Article 2 to the 1949 Geneva Conventions, in order for there to be an international armed conflict, there must be a case of 'declared war or of any other armed conflict ... between two or more of the High Contracting Parties', or a case of occupation of one party's territory.[45] Customary humanitarian law will treat a conflict between two States as international even if one of them is not a party to the Geneva Conventions.[46] But what role does recognition play in this regard?

The International Criminal Tribunal for the Former Yugoslavia insisted that recognition had no relevance for conflict classification. In *Milošević*, the Court classified the conflict between Croatian forces and the Yugoslav People's Army in 1991 as international because Croatia met, in the Court's view, the requirements of material statehood.[47] In the *Tadić* case, a Trial Chamber determined that there existed an international conflict between Bosnia and Herzegovina and the Federal Republic of Yugoslavia 'from the beginning of 1992 until 19 May 1992'[48] (which was the date of the official withdrawal of the Yugoslav People's Army from Bosnia and Herzegovina).[49] The Chamber took note of the fact that Bosnia and Herzegovina was admitted into the United Nations on 22 May 1992, becoming the '*de jure* State against which Bosnian Serb forces were in revolt', but also highlighting that 'even before that date, the Republic of Bosnia and Herzegovina was an organized political entity, as one of the republics of the Socialist Federal Republic of Yugoslavia, having its own republican secretariat for defence and its own TO [Territorial Defence]'.[50] Therefore, both Bosnia and Herzegovina and Croatia were treated as States from their declaration of independence and regardless of the reaction of the Parent State, or even the criteria of material statehood (at least in the case of Bosnia). This approach has been endorsed by the International Committee of the Red Cross (ICRC) in its new Commentary to the Geneva Conventions:

> One of the recurrent problems in determining the existence of an international armed conflict is whether one of the Parties thereto claiming statehood is

[45] Geneva Convention I for the Amelioration of the Condition of the Wounded and Sick in Armed Forces in the Field, 75 UNTS 31 (adopted 12 August 1949, entered into force 21 October 1950) art 2; Geneva Convention II for the Amelioration of the Condition of Wounded, Sick and Shipwrecked Members of Armed Forces at Sea, 75 UNTS 85 (adopted 12 August 1949, entered into force 21 October 1950) art 2; Geneva Convention III Relative to the Treatment of Prisoners of War, 75 UNTS 135 (adopted 12 August 1949, entered into force 21 October 1950) art 2; and Geneva Convention IV Relative to the Protection of Civilian Persons in Time of War, 75 UNTS 287 (adopted 12 August 1949, entered into force 21 October 1950) art 2.

[46] See *Partial Award, Prisoners of War, Ethiopia's Claim 4, between the Federal Democratic Republic of Ethiopia and the State of Eritrea* (1 July 2003) XXVI RIAA 73.

[47] *Prosecutor v Slobodan Milošević* IT-02-54-T (16 June 2004) [Decision] paras 83ff.

[48] *Prosecutor v Duško Tadić* IT-94-1-T (7 May 1997) [Trial Chamber Judgment] para 569.

[49] ibid paras 565–568.

[50] ibid para 563.

> effectively a State as defined under international law. This issue can be encountered notably at the occasion of a secessionist project or the disintegration of a State as a consequence of a non-international armed conflict. In this regard, it is possible that what started as a non-international armed conflict becomes international if the secessionist entity is successful in becoming a State by fulfilling the criteria for statehood under international law. The statehood of the belligerents, which determines the nature of the armed conflict as an international armed conflict, is ascertained by objective criteria under international law, which carry their own complexities. The fact that one of the Parties does not recognize the other as a State is irrelevant.[51]

This position appears to be a recent development, as the old Commentary of 1952 refrains from pronouncing itself on the matter.[52]

Doctrine otherwise does not deal with the matter at great length, with a few notable exceptions. In 1975, the Institute of International Law took the position that 'armed conflicts between political entities which are separated by an international demarcation line or which have existed de facto as States over a prolonged period of time, or conflicts between any such entity and a State' were not covered by the notion of 'civil war'.[53] At the time, the Institute was not examining conflict classification, but the exception they make to civil wars also comes across as relevant from the perspective of humanitarian law. Individual scholars remain divided: Djemila Carron[54] and Julia Grignon[55] have both taken a declaratory view of recognition in conflict classification, whereas Dapo Akande,[56] Kubo Mačák,[57] and Robert Kolb and Richard Hyde[58] are more cautious, although none of these authors embraces the constitutive theory explicitly.

[51] *Geneva Convention for the Amelioration of the Condition of the Wounded and Sick in Armed Forces in the Field of 12 August 1949: Commentary of 2016* (ICRC 2016) para 231.

[52] See *Geneva Convention for the Amelioration of the Condition of the Wounded and Sick in Armed Forces in the Field of 12 August 1949: Commentary of 1952* (ICRC 1952).

[53] 'The Principle of Non-Intervention in Civil Wars' (1975) 56 Annuaire de l'Institut de Droit International 544, 547.

[54] Interestingly, Carron accepts that recognition is required for opposability, thus she would be a constitutivist according to my classification, but she nevertheless suggests that recognition *should* be declaratory for the application of the law of international armed conflicts. See Djemila Carron, *L'acte déclencheur d'un conflit armé international* (Schulthess 2016) 121–22.

[55] '[I]t [is not] necessary for the parties to the armed conflict to recognize each other as States, mutually or even unilaterally.' Julia Grignon, 'The Beginning of Application of International Humanitarian Law: A Discussion of a Few Challenges' (2014) 96(893) International Review of the Red Cross 139, 145.

[56] Akande is sceptical about the idea that a non-state actor may become a State while the conflict with its Parent State is still ongoing; see Dapo Akande, 'Classification of Armed Conflicts: Relevant Legal Aspects' in Elizabeth Wilmshurst (ed), *International Law and the Classification of Conflicts* (OUP 2012) 50.

[57] Mačák recalls that no State has come into being during the conflict with its parent and that the international humanitarian law of non-international armed conflicts must be seen as applicable for the duration of the conflict. Kubo Mačák, *Internationalized Armed Conflicts in International Law* (OUP 2018) 61.

[58] 'If during a civil war a part of the territory manages to secede from its old mother-country, and if this new entity acquires international recognition, such as admission to the United Nations, the

States historically predicated the application of the laws of war in non-international conflicts on the recognition of the rebellious forces as a belligerent, which was famously done during the American Civil War.[59] This allowed the applicability of a singular body of law applicable to conflicts between States before a separate framework was adopted in 1949. If recognition is still necessary for the general opposability of a secessionist State in cases of constitutive recognition but not for the applicability of rules governing interstate conflicts, then the source of such partial opposability, which only exists for the purposes of humanitarian law, would need to be sought in that branch of law.

It is certainly conceivable that humanitarian law has developed in this direction. It may well be the case that a declaratory view of recognition must be accepted for conflict classification purposes. However, proving that such a rule of customary law emerged somewhere between 1945 or 1949 and the early 1990s is a daunting task. The authors who argue for the applicability of international armed conflict rules in such cases usually do not explain the basis for their findings (the case of Grignon) or do so explicitly *de lege ferenda* (the case of Carron). Many declaratist scholars insist on the new State's possession of a degree of permanence and stability before its statehood may be regarded as settled, which is precisely not the case in an ongoing war of secession. Even if a norm could be established to this effect, it does not seem very realistic that States involved in non-international armed conflicts that transform into international ones would agree to such an arrangement: States would be obliged to treat rebels and insurgents as prisoners of war and regard themselves as the Occupying Power in territories to which they have a lawful claim. Another crucial point is raised in this regard by Miloš Hrnjaz: the 'internationalisation' of a non-international armed conflict is usually determined *ex post facto*, after the end of the conflict; this does not help the belligerent parties to determine the applicable law, which must be done from the beginning of the conflict and for its duration.[60] Finally, not even the humanitarian reasons for asserting the theory of effectivity-based conflict transformation are clear: as Carron correctly remarks, human rights law could be the more protective branch,[61] and

belligerent relations it may continue to face with the old mother-country will no longer be the subject of the law of NIAC, but will be governed by the law concerning IAC.' Robert Kolb and Richard Hyde, *An Introduction to the International Law of Armed Conflicts* (Hart Publishing 2008) 81. Notice the emphasis on 'international recognition'.

[59] The recognition is said to have taken place on 19 April 1861 when President Lincoln ordered a blockade of the coastline of seceding States. Other States, such as the United Kingdom, quickly followed with declarations of neutrality. See Wyndham Legh Walker, 'Recognition of Belligerency and Grant of Belligerent Rights' (1937) 23 Problems of Peace and War 177, 186–87.

[60] Miloš Hrnjaz, *Raspad Jugoslavije pred sudom: Pravna kvalifikacija oružanih sukoba u Jugoslaviji u praksi sudova u Srbiji* (University of Belgrade, Faculty of Political Science 2021). Of course, conflict transformation may also be ascertained during an armed conflict; see Jérôme de Hemptinne, *Les conflits armés en mutation* (Pedone 2019).

[61] Carron, *L'acte déclencheur d'un conflit armé international* (n 54) 122.

it is the framework governing non-international armed conflicts that leaves more room in this regard—in part, because it is less well developed.

At the same time, even if claiming statehood, an insurgent party should not be held bound by the law of international armed conflicts if the Parent State itself is absolved from it. Humanitarian law simply does not conceive of such relativism: a conflict is either international or non-international; it cannot be international for one party and non-international for the other. In my view, it is much more credible to maintain, as Mačák does, that the conflict remains non-international until recognition has been given, or until another rule establishing opposability comes into play, rather than to insist on the very superficial notion that there can be such a thing as a State 'for the purposes of humanitarian law'. Historically, this was the approach to the Korean War, which was considered non-international before the involvement of UN forces and China.[62] Of course, the law of international armed conflicts can always be brought into effect through recognition of belligerency or by means of a special agreement under Common Article 3 to the Geneva Conventions.

2.3.2 The Role of Article 4(A)(3) of GC III

Article 4(A)(3) of the Third Geneva Convention foresees that '[m]embers of regular armed forces who profess allegiance to a government or an authority not recognized by the Detaining Power' shall be treated as prisoners of war, a status reserved for members of the armed forces who fall into the hands of the enemy in an international armed conflict. As this provision specifically mentions recognition, it may have some impact on the position of unrecognised States.

Article 4(A)(3) was introduced into the text of the Convention to account for the position of French forces professing allegiance to De Gaulle's National Liberation Committee after the 1940 French–German armistice.[63] The terms of the armistice foresaw that French nationals continuing the fight against Germany would be excluded from the application of the laws of war; however, at the behest of the ICRC, Germany eventually extended prisoner of war status to captured Free French forces, with the understanding that Free French forces were 'fighting for England'.[64] According to the old ICRC Commentary, the decision to introduce Article 4(A)(3) was controversial during preparatory work on the Conventions, as '[i]t was feared … that the proposal might be open to abusive interpretation, and the Conference therefore decided to add that such forces must, in order to benefit by the Convention, be fighting "in conjunction" with a State recognized as a belligerent State by the enemy'.[65] In the ICRC's view, '[i]t is also necessary

[62] See ICRC, *Inventaire D AO COREE1, Activités de la délégation en Corée et au Japon pendant la guerre de Corée 1950–1953* (Geneva 2006) 3.

[63] *Geneva Convention Relative to the Treatment of Prisoners of War of 12 August 1949: Commentary of 1960* (ICRC 1960) 61–62.

[64] ibid 63.

[65] ibid 62.

that this authority, which is not recognized by the adversary, should either consider itself as representing one of the High Contracting Parties, or declare that it accepts the obligations stipulated in the Convention and wishes to apply them.'[66] Thus, the 'authority' discussed by Article 4(A)(3) does *not* refer to a State but to a government-in-exile or to a part of the armed forces continuing to fight after the central authorities have surrendered or concluded peace, as in the case of a 'national redoubt'.[67]

The ICRC's updated Commentary takes a different view: 'Article 4 A (3) complements common Article 2. The failure by one State Party to recognize another is not a barrier to the classification of a conflict as an international armed conflict, nor to the recognition of prisoner-of-war status for members of the armed forces, other militias and other volunteer corps involved.'[68] The alleged link between Article 4(A)(3) and Common Article 2, which was not identified by the old Commentary, is strenuous at best, and the former does not in any event concern conflict classification; however, the extension of the regime of Article 4(A)(3) to unrecognised States does enjoy some support in doctrine.[69] In my view, Article 4(A)(3) may be relevant for the relations between non-recognising belligerents that are High Contracting Parties or to situations where recognition is not necessary for opposability, as discussed in Chapter 9.

3. The Opposability of Existing States to New States

An important matter to be examined, beyond a new State's obligations under general international law, is the opposability of other States towards it, regardless of whether it has received recognition from them. Recognition by another State is a unilateral act by that State and as such it cannot bind its own recipient; this is why Anzilotti's theory of mutual constitutive recognition fails to explain practice, although he is correct in identifying the problem of the new State's relationship with its environment.

After a new State is declared, it does not always recognise the same third States as its parent did, nor does it even recognise all entities that purport to recognise it. The former Yugoslavia recognised the State of Palestine soon after it had been

[66] ibid 63.

[67] ibid 63–64.

[68] *Geneva Convention Relative to the Treatment of Prisoners of War of 12 August 1949: Commentary of 2020* (ICRC 2020) para 1043.

[69] 'The non-recognition of one belligerent by another has no effect on combatant status. Thus, if state A, as a matter of politics, does not recognise state B and both states become involved in an armed conflict on opposing sides, the non-recognition has no influence on the combatant status of the soldiers of either party, and hence it has no influence on the duty to grant POW status to the combatants of the other party who are captured.' Kolb and Hyde, *An Introduction to the International Law of Armed Conflicts* (n 58) 198.

declared in 1988, but several of its successors later refused to do so (specifically, Croatia, North Macedonia, and, until June 2024, Slovenia). Similarly, Taiwan recognised Kosovo after its declaration of independence, but it is not regarded as either an independent State or the Chinese government by the authorities in Priština. This raises the question of 'succession' of recognition and its reciprocity.

(1) An analogy with principles governing treaty succession may provide a means to explain this process. Accordingly, if a new State arises with a 'clean slate' regarding its treaty obligations, it would also make sense to entrust it with the discretion of choosing whom it wishes to recognise. If this comes across as giving the new State too wide a margin of appreciation to choose whom to treat as a State, I ask the reader to bear in mind that all States whose statehood is unconstested are currently members of the United Nations, depriving bilateral recognition of much legal and practical value. Otherwise, if the State may be said to succeed its parent's treaty obligations, there is no reason why the same could not be said of bilateral succession by the Parent State. Certainly, this second possibility must be true in cases of consensual separation, as any other conclusion would harm the legitimate interests of third States in a way that neither the Parent State nor the new State are entitled to do. An analogy could be made with the doctrine of acquired rights to the effect that a third country's status ought not to be impacted by the creation of a new territorial sovereign. Even in cases of secession, a strong argument can be made for automatic sucession of recognition (and regardless of treaty succession). At the very least, there must exist a presumption in favour of continuing recognition, unless the new State clarifies its contrary view in a timely and appropriate fashion.

(2) The fact that a State receives recognition from another does not mean that recognition is reciprocal. The new State must recognise existing States in turn if it does not agree to succeed its parent's obligations. In practice, this problem rarely occurs, as following a declaration of independence, the new State normally invites others to recognise it and responds courteously to notifications of recognition. Such acceptance of recognition must be understood as an act of reciprocity with retroactive effects.

More problematic is the opposability of non-recognising States, including the Parent State. A secessionist movement always functions in the territory of an existing State, and should its struggle be rewarded with statehood, it would be counterintuitive for this new State to deny the existence or opposability of the State from which it was forged. Of course, this does not really happen in practice but there have been some statements to the contrary. For example, following its declaration of independence, Kosovo never questioned the statehood of Serbia, but in recent years began to insist on 'mutual recognition' as a desired outcome of its negotiations with Serbia (as though Kosovo did not regard Serbia as a State, which is ridiculous). Reciprocity is not required in case of unilateral secession and it is perfectly reasonable for Serbia not to regard Kosovo as a State while expecting to be treated as a State by the latter.

What has been said of the Parent State will also be true of other non-recognising States. Continuing with the same example, Kosovo has been calling for years on those members of the European Union that do not recognise it to change their position—to no avail. Spain has been particularly adamant about its stance of non-recognition. Evidently, from a Kosovar perspective, Spanish statehood is not in doubt. Strictly speaking, its opposability may be inferred either from earlier relations between Serbia and Spain, its own call for recognition, or both. The fact of the matter is that new States do not enter the world as equals with existing ones and must rely on recognition in a way which is not required of established States.

4. Conclusion

Recognition does not create a State: it merely confers upon it the legal personality of States in bilateral relations with other States if another rule leading to opposability cannot be identified. Thus, when a new State is proclaimed, its authorities can be held to the rules of international law at least insofar as these do not require the existence of a bilateral legal relationship. Because the entity is claiming statehood, it is subjecting itself to the rule of international law and may be held responsible for violating it.

An unrecognised State will be bound to respect the peremptory norms of international law because these are not owed to individual States but to the international community as a whole. This is also true of universal customary law, but not of any treaty obligations. The new State will only be bound by those treaties it ratifies or to which it accedes and, possibly, in case of treaty succession.

There is a growing body of doctrine arguing that unrecognised States are bound by the substantive rules of human rights law. If it is exercising effective control over a territory and claiming the same status as any other State, there is no reason why an unrecognised State should not have human rights obligations. Such obligations would most likely flow from customary human rights law, although the argument has also been made that new States succeed their parent's obligations under human rights treaties.

It is also not controversial that international humanitarian law applies to unrecognised States; the only challenge would be to determine whether it is the body of law governing international or non-international armed conflicts that applies. Doctrine, including the ICRC, currently favours the declaratory view, namely that a non-international armed conflict may become international if an insurrectional movement achieves effective independent statehood. However, this view is by no means universal. In my opinion, the classification of a conflict involving an unrecognised State ought to depend on the general matter of opposability as discussed in previous chapters. Thus, if the statehood of A is not opposable to B under general international law, it should also not be opposable to it under international humanitarian law, wherefore any conflict between them ought to be seen as non-international in the absence of a special agreement, as was initially the case during the Korean War. At any rate, even if the humanitarian law of international armed conflicts were to apply, this alone would not make the unrecognised State opposable to the other belligerent parties under other branches of international law.

12
Withdrawal of Recognition

1. Conceptualising Derecognition

In rare cases, States decide to withdraw their recognition of other States, whereupon they refuse to further accord them the treatment befitting a State. Previously regarded by some lawyers as a purely theoretical matter, the practice of withdrawal of *de jure* recognition is actually a recent development.[1] Accordingly, the subject of 'derecognition' is poorly understood: many writers on recognition do not mention it or merely discuss it in summary terms. Tatjana Papić remarks that 'the literature on derecognition ... is measured not in books, but in paragraphs'.[2] The reason for this is most likely to be the limited practice on derecognition.

Both declaratist and constitutivist scholars have espoused negative views of the possibility of withdrawing recognition, the latter perhaps more so because of the importance they attach to the act. From a declaratist perspective, withdrawal of recognition cannot have any legal effects, as recognition is a merely political act. It may entail a rupture of diplomatic relations between the two States, but it cannot negate the statehood of the entity whose recognition has been withdrawn, for that fact never depended on recognition in the first place.[3] The matter is more complicated for constitutivist scholars. If statehood is generated or becomes opposable through recognition, then withdrawal surely stems from the desire to negate the legal situation resulting from recognition: a derecognised State would no longer be a State, legally speaking, for the State withdrawing recognition. Constitutivist scholarship therefore tried to negate this possibility.[4] Thus, Anzilotti argued that in the 'purely theoretical' situation of a withdrawal of recognition, or of a treaty cancelling the applicability of all legal norms between two or more subjects, the end

[1] A rare example of derecognition before the Second World War is the US withdrawal of recognition of Armenia in 1920.

[2] Tatjana Papić, 'Derecognition of States: The Case of Kosovo' (2022) 53 Cornell International Law Journal 683–729, 683.

[3] See eg James-Leslie Brierly, 'Règles générales du droit de la paix' (1936) 58 RCADI 1, 59ff and Gerald Fitzmaurice, 'The General Principles of International Law Considered from the Standpoint of the Rule of Law' (1957) 92 RCADI 1, 28.

[4] See in particular Hersch Lauterpacht, '*De Facto* Recognition, Withdrawal of Recognition, and Conditional Recognition' (1945) 22 British Yearbook of International Law 164–90, 179ff.

Recognition of States in International Law. Pavle Kilibarda, Oxford University Press. © Pavle Kilibarda 2024.
DOI: 10.1093/oso/9780198905653.003.0012

of legal personality could only be inferred from a factual extinction of the entity thereby personified.[5]

I agree in principle that lawful recognition cannot be withdrawn and that derecognition cannot produce effects in international law, although it may be otherwise under municipal law. However, this may not be so simple in situations of contested statehood. A 'withdrawal' of recognition may also be possible in situations where recognition was only given provisionally or conditionally. Finally, if derecognition is ever possible, then we must determine its effects, and especially whether it could produce retroactive effects. I will consider these matters in light of recent practice related to Kosovo.

1.1 Of Derecognition in General

To understand the practice of withdrawal of recognition, it is first necessary to properly contextualise it and to differentiate it from the *extinction* of statehood. Although it is today rare for a State to simply 'die out', the consensus is that such an end of legal personality arises a matter of fact. Should this happen, it is not up to third States to 'recognise' the new situation; this is a sentiment shared by both constitutivist and declaratist writers. Thus, Kelsen writes that '[w]e have only to recall that any state is entitled ... at any time to establish the fact that a community which has been a state in an international law sense, has ceased to be such, because it no longer fulfills the condition prescribed by general international law. The establishment of such a fact is not a withdrawal of recognition.'[6] Brierly agreed with this logic, writing that statehood would only be extinguished if the State itself ceased to exist as a matter of fact, and could therefore no longer be recognised to exist, but this cannot be referred to as withdrawal of recognition.[7]

Regardless of the state of international law on the matter, derecognition has become a much more widespread phenomenon in recent years, particularly in relation to Western Sahara and Kosovo. If both constitutivists and declaratists negate the possibility of withdrawal of recognition, then what is to be made of this increasingly popular practice?

Tatjana Papić recently argued for a different perspective on the possibility of derecognition outside of the context of State extinction. Her argument may be summarised as follows: as a political act, recognition is not a legal transaction,

[5] Dionisio Anzilotti, *Cours de droit international, Premier volume; Introduction—Théories générales* (Librairie du Recueil Sirey 1929) 178; cf Brierly, 'Règles générales du droit de la paix' (n 3) 59 ('La question n'est guère d'ordre pratique').

[6] Hans Kelsen, 'Recognition in International Law: Theoretical Observations' (1941) 35(4) The American Journal of International Law 605, 613 (note however that Kelsen writes here in the context of the difference between *de jure* and *de facto* recognition).

[7] Brierly (n 3) 59.

nor is there any concrete legal obligation to recognise a new State. The application of the *Lotus* principle dictates that an obligation *not* to derecognise would have to be demonstrated in positive law in order to preclude States from engaging in such acts, and no norm can be identified in this regard.[8] She further clarifies that international law cannot be expected to manage 'controversial social realities' such as contested statehood, wherefore it is prudent to distinguish between situations where statehood is uncontested (and the law properly regulates the new situation) and those where it is contested by competing claims (where the law simply cannot provide a way out). She recalls: '[V]iewing state recognition as revocable—based on the absence of any legal rule to the contrary—recognizes the limits of international law and the fact that it is not about specific outcomes that should be reached, but about which tools should be used to reach them.'[9] Papić concludes that derecognition is possible but that it cannot affect the derecognised State's existence or status or its rights under international law, although it may affect the derecognised State's rights under the (de)recognising State's domestic law.[10]

Papić is correct to identify that derecognition is possible in situations of contested statehood and, more broadly, to recognise the inadequacies inherent in law to resolve such controversial matters. Her approach is nevertheless based on a declaratory notion of recognition and thus suffers, in my view, from the same deficiencies that she finds with those arguing against the possibility of withdrawal of recognition, such as the lack of proof of a link between effectivity and opposability. Certainly, there exist situations where statehood is opposable regardless of recognition, rendering recognition political: in such situations, her analysis stands. However, where recognition creates legal obligations but the recipient's statehood is still contested, this is no longer the case.

This point is illustrated by the contemporary practice, mentioned earlier, in relation to Western Sahara and Kosovo. Both entities have received a number of acts of recognition that were subsequently withdrawn, even though factually nothing had changed suggesting that material statehood, if it ever existed, had disappeared. To the contrary, withdrawal of recognition was undertaken specifically in favour of and with respect to the arguments of a party with a competing claim to the territory in question, namely Morocco in Western Sahara and Serbia in Kosovo.

It must be assumed that the derecognising States had previously recognised Western Sahara or Kosovo because either (i) they found that these entities met the conditions for statehood or (ii) they believed that they were entitled to statehood regardless of effectivity, for example, based on the right of self-determination. This was a necessary basis to regard their claims as expressing a lawful and legitimate

[8] Papić. 'Derecognition of States' (n 2) 722–23.

[9] ibid 723.

[10] ibid 724ff. These include the right to property in its territory, legal standing in domestic courts, and other similar matters.

territorial title. Just as the recognition of their independence had meant an acceptance of such title at the expense of the other parties with concurrent claims, derecognition achieved the opposite effect.[11] This makes recent derecognition cases much more complex than it may appear at first sight.

I have argued that a distinction must be made between situations where the opposability of statehood rests primarily on recognition and those where it may be inferred from another rule of international law. In the latter case, recognition is declaratory, which implies that international law is neutral towards its withdrawal, but that 'constitutive derecognition' is impossible. The matter is very different in the comparatively rare situations where recognition produces a constitutive effect. Such recognition, which is either a unilateral legal act or contained in a treaty, cannot be revoked arbitrarily.[12]

The form in which recognition is given may also determine whether it may be withdrawn. *De facto* recognition is usually regarded as provisional and the issuing State may withdraw it if the recipient fails to stabilise as a State. Some writers, notably Kelsen,[13] deny that withdrawal of *de facto* recognition amounts to derecognition, as the 'withdrawing' State is simply taking cognisance of the fact that effective statehood never materialised, and thus recognition never really took place.

Assuming that *de facto* recognition produces the same effects as *de jure* recognition—albeit provisionally—the principal question is whether it was lawful: if it was not lawful, it could not produce legal effects, and therefore cannot truly be withdrawn; if it was lawful, it must have produced legal effects, meaning that the normative situation would change if withdrawal were successful. In the latter case, the author of recognition may choose to withdraw it is unconvinced of the recipient's capacity to survive as a State: withdrawal of such recognition is possible as it was foreseen in the act itself and it must be assumed that the issuing State, being sovereign, would not have proceeded with recognition without such an important limitation. This is also true if recognition were made conditional upon the fulfilment of certain criteria other than those already present in law and whose fulfilment is subject to the issuing State's appreciation of the relevant facts. If the act of conditional recognition is otherwise lawful but the author becomes convinced that the additional requirements have not been met, recognition will have taken place for a time, and cease to produce effects from the moment of withdrawal.

But States do not normally recognise other States *de facto* nowadays, and conditional recognition seems to have been performed in a very limited context, namely

[11] Lauterpacht wrote that States do not disappear into a legal vacuum and in case of a State's extinction, withdrawal of recognition really signifies the recognition of another's claim. See Lauterpacht, '*De Facto* Recognition' (n 4) 180–81.

[12] 'Guiding Principles Applicable to Unilateral Declarations of States Capable of Creating Legal Obligations, with Commentaries Thereto' (2013) II(2) Yearbook of the International Law Commission 2006 160–66, Principle 10.

[13] Kelsen, 'Recognition in International Law' (n 6) 613.

in relation to the former Yugoslavia and the Soviet Union. In most situations where a new State arises and is recognised, the recognition given is full, *de jure* recognition. Such recognition is sometimes explicitly described as 'irrevocable'[14] and the issuing State clearly cannot later rely on its terms to find a legal possibility of withdrawal. There must also be a presumption that the recipient State will rely on the act of recognition from the moment it is given, as the matter concerns its own existence vis-à-vis the other State. Derecognition could thus only be possible in the purely hypothetical case where the recipient consents to it: as this would amount to legal suicide, it will never happen in practice. Therefore, unless the State genuinely ceases to exist, it cannot be derecognised.[15]

States may also try to withdraw recognition of certain non-state entities whose legal personality resembles that of States. Such entities may be treated as possessing the rights and duties normally incumbent only upon States even though their own lack of statehood is a well-known and acknowledged fact; such is the case of the Order of Malta and the Holy See. In 2012, the President of Ecuador declared that his State withdrew recognition of the Order of Malta, and relations were only restored in 2019 under a new Head of State.[16] As the Order is not a State, it is dubious whether the same standards may be applied to its recognition or derecognition as would be applied to States: the principles developed by the International Law Commission (ILC) on unilateral declarations refer to obligations undertaken by States towards other States, the 'international community as a whole', or to 'other entities'.[17] This speaks in favour of revocation being impossible. However, as the preconditions of recognition are only valid for new States and not for non-state entities, the law is more difficult to navigate in this regard, and I do not believe it is necessary to take a firm position on this matter at present.

1.2 'Quasi-Derecognition'

My conclusion above assumes that the act of recognition was authorised by international law and that the prerequisites of effectivity and legality were met at the time of recognition. If this were not the case, the situation would be different. In particular, the requirement of legality may serve to invalidate an act of

[14] This is the wording used by France for its recognition of Kosovo; see *Accordance with International Law of the Unilateral Declaration of Independence in Respect of Kosovo*, Written Submission by the French Republic, 18 April 2009, para 9.

[15] See also Papić (n 2) 711ff.

[16] See José Ayala Lasso, 'La Orden Soberana de Malta' (*El Comercio*, 10 March 2012) <https://www.elcomercio.com/opinion/orden-soberana-malta.html> last accessed 6 June 2024, as well as a later statement by the Order of Malta on renewal of relations, 'Se renueva la amistad entre Ecuador y la Orden de Malta' (24 September 2019) <https://www.orderofmalta.int/es/noticias/se-renueva-la-amistad-entre-ecuador-y-la-orden-de-malta/> last accessed 6 June 2024.

[17] 'Guiding Principles' (n 12) Principle 6.

recognition, usually because the creation of the State contravened *jus cogens* provisions. Recognition of a State created in violation of peremptory norms will be void *ab initio* and cannot produce any legal effects. It is certainly conceivable that a recognising State might later change its approach, take notice of the illegality of its recognition, and subsequently withdraw it. Such revocation may resemble a withdrawal of recognition—indeed, it may have the same consequences politically—but it does not amount to legal withdrawal because of its non-existent object: the revoked recognition did not produce legal effects and therefore did not really exist in the first place. The withdrawal might at least signify that the formerly recognising State is now refraining from an ongoing violation of international law, as the initial recognition itself amounted to an internationally wrongful act. In addition to *jus cogens*, other rules may also come into play, and formerly recognising States may refer to them when withdrawing recognition. As we will see further below, some of the acts derecognising Kosovo fall within this category.

If recognition was given before the entity had effectively achieved statehood, there may be no violation of *erga omnes* provisions but the premature nature of the act will amount to a violation of the territorial integrity of the Parent State. In my view, this negates the validity of the act of recognition altogether, because if it did not, the doctrine of premature recognition would be so deprived of usefulness that it might as well be discarded from legal theory altogether. Therefore, recognition given in the absence of effectivity should not be regarded as producing legal effects (apart from violating another State's territorial integrity, which is a separate issue), and cannot truly be withdrawn.

The two situations given above only superficially come within the scope of derecognition as in both cases the act of recognition is invalid. As a result, they may only be considered instances of quasi-derecognition. This points to the conclusion that constitutive derecognition is not possible, and certainly this will be the case where recognition is given to an entity whose statehood is not contested. But as mentioned before, the situation may be different in situations of contested statehood.

To conclude, derecognition is in many ways a 'mirror image' of recognition: just as it is not possible to recognise a State if the criteria of effectivity and legality are not met, so too is it not possible to derecognise it if they are still present—especially in the more limited situation of contested statehood, where effectivity ought to be considered in light of contesting territorial claims. It is of course difficult to imagine that a State could be derecognised because, subsequently to its inception, it no longer meets the criterion of legality (this recalls the position of Schwarzenberger and some others towards Nazi Germany during the Second World War).[18] I cannot think of a scenario where this could be the case in reality. Effectivity thus remains

[18] See Georg Schwarzenberger, 'The Standard of Civilisation in International Law' (1955) 8(1) Current Legal Problems 212.

the key criterion in this recognition–derecognition dichotomy. Similarly, in situations where opposability does not stem from recognition, it cannot be negated through derecognition.

2. Constitutive Derecognition and Contested Statehood

Contestation of statehood is important, as in some cases of secession, the seceding entity X may fulfil the criteria of effectiveness in spite of the persistent refusal by Parent State A to acknowledge its independence. *Ceteris paribus*, third State B would be authorised to recognise X without violating the integrity of A. Normally, we would assume that derecognition is then impossible. However, the fact that the Parent State also maintains a claim which is both permissible under international law and usually politically legitimate must somehow come into play here; it would be naïve to assume otherwise. For example, if B recognised X as independent, and A at some point was to fully re-establish control over the territory of X, would B thenceforth be obliged to regard X as an occupied territory, and A as an Occupying Power in a part of its territory whose statehood had never become opposable to it? Or could it withdraw recognition of X and acknowledge A's claim? This was arguably the case with Biafra, which was recognised by several States before being forcefully reintegrated into Nigeria (these States did not subsequently dispute the validity of Nigeria's claim to Biafran territory).[19]

This scenario precisely demonstrates the inadequacy of international law to resolve such controversial matters as contested statehood—it is a mistake to look to law for solutions. Rather, our task should be to illuminate the legal aspects of the solution, while noting that the conundrum can only be resolved through political means. The law provides a framework for a political resolution without dictating it.

Accordingly, there are two avenues for dealing with derecognition in situations of contested statehood.

(1) 'Constitutive derecognition' may be impossible. This is because recognition does not only make the seceding entity opposable to the recognising State, but also necessarily and inherently recognises its claim to the territory in question (this aspect may be more complex in reality as the proper delineation of a new State's territory could itself be controversial while its statehood is not).[20] According to Schwarzenberger, 'However weak a title may be, and irrespective of any other criterion, recognition estops the state which has

[19] See Jean J A Salmon, *La reconnaissance d'état* (Librairie Armand Colin 1971) 192ff and John Dugard, 'The Secession of States and Their Recognition in the Wake of Kosovo' (2013) 357 RCADI 9, 135ff.

[20] See eg *Case Concerning the Frontier Dispute (Burkina Faso/Mali)*, ICJ Reports 554, Judgment of 22 December 1986.

recognized the title from contesting its validity at any future time.'[21] If such an analogy can be made, then withdrawal is off the table and a third State's choice will from then on shape its legal outlook on the relationship between the seceding State and its parent. This position is legally sound but practically inflexible.

(2) In the alternative, derecognition may be possible to a limited extent. For example, if recognition were authorised and undertaken, a State would be bound by its own act, however it should also be mindful that the Parent State has a different legal perspective from its own (and is moreover entitled to it). Thus, if the Parent State were to re-establish control over the seceding entity against its will—for example, by military force—then the recognising third State should not regard this as belligerent occupation or a violation of the rules on the use of force in international relations. Rather, it should consider that, bearing in mind the Parent State's legitimate claim, there came into being a fundamental change of circumstances allowing it to withdraw recognition of the seceding entity and reconfirm the parent's claim, restoring its legal relationship with the victorious Parent State to the *status quo ante* (this would not be possible if the statehood of the conquered entity had become opposable to the Parent State). Admittedly, it does not appear that the third State would be required to acknowledge the parent's reassertion of control over the breakaway territory—but if a State which had not earlier recognised its independence would now be precluded from doing so for lack of effectivity, it may be assumed that recognising States too ought to at least reconsider their position vis-à-vis the situation. This seems to me the better view, because it is more pragmatic, allows for a broader range of resolutions of a case of contested statehood, and mitigates the relativism flowing from constitutive recognition. Withdrawal of recognition under the circumstances would amount to true derecognition, unlike cases where revocation is made because of a violation of international law, and where recognition itself had been impossible.

If this last point is true, then we may once again call into question the practical importance of effectivity, and with it the simplistic conclusions of the declaratory approach. Withdrawal would be possible in situations where the recognised State no longer effectively exists, but only if its statehood had been contested: otherwise, there would be a continued presumption that the State exists legally. A State's authorities may be effectively wiped out by foreign aggression, but we could not conclude that that the State has ceased to exist, as fundamental rules of the contemporary legal order prohibit the acquisition of territory through conquest. This

[21] Georg Schwarzenberger, 'Title to Territory: Response to a Challenge' (1957) 51(2) The American Journal of International Law 308, 316–17.

would not be the case if a breakaway territory were reintegrated into its Parent State, unless that State had previously given up its own claims to the seceding territory. The practical issue, once again, is how to determine that the seceding entity no longer fulfils the criterion of effectivity. Would negotiations between the Parent State and the secessionists on the latter's status be sufficient to bring their statehood into question? As we will see, this seems to be the understanding of some States that have withdrawn recognition of Kosovo. Whatever the case, it is just as difficult to determine whether in practice the requirements of effectivity have disappeared as it is to ascertain whether they have been met in the first place.

If we accept the possibility of true derecognition, then we must also examine its effects. Obviously, derecognition would have the opposite result of recognition and negate opposability. Like recognition, it would produce effects *ex nunc*, which is to say, from the moment of derecognition: any legal transactions concluded between the States prior to derecognition should be regarded as valid. Conversely, the 'effects' of quasi-derecognition (where recognition itself was invalid) would superficially come across as *ex tunc* (from recognition), whereas it is really the act of recognition that was void *ab initio*.

3. Recent Practice Related to Kosovo

The recent 'wave' of States derecognising Kosovo provides a rare opportunity to scrutinise the legal aspects of withdrawal of recognition in practice. By mid-2020, the Serbian government maintained that sixteen States had withdrawn recognition of Kosovo, starting with Suriname in 2016. Other derecognising States included Burundi, the Central African Republic, the Comoros, Dominica, Ghana, Grenada, Lesotho, Madagascar, Nauru, Palau, Papua New Guinea, Sierra Leone, the Solomon Islands, and Togo.[22] The Serbian Foreign Ministry also maintained that São Tomé and Príncipe had revoked recognition,[23] but the question regarding the São Toméan recognition is whether it was ever issued in the first place. In January 2023, the Serbian president claimed that a further nine countries had withdrawn recognition,[24] but as any diplomatic correspondence to that effect has neither been made public nor available to the author of this work, these alleged withdrawals will not be discussed here. Priština initially dismissed news of derecognition as 'fake

[22] The relevant *notes verbales* notifying the Serbian government of the derecognition decision of each of these States except for Sierra Leone were provided to the author of this book by the Serbian Foreign Ministry in December 2019 following a request under the Freedom of Information Act; the Leonian note was made publicly available after its reception in March 2020.

[23] The Ministry provided a communication issued by the then-President of São Tomé and Príncipe on 7 January 2013 denying that Kosovo had been recognised.

[24] Milica Stojanovic, 'Serbian President Claims "Nine More Kosovo Recognition Withdrawals"' (*Balkan Insight*, 5 January 2023) <https://balkaninsight.com/2023/01/05/serbian-president-claims-nine-more-kosovo-recognition-withdrawals/> last accessed 6 June 2024.

news' spread by the administration in Belgrade, but eventually acknowledged the trend, faulting Serbia for its 'illegitimate' derecognition campaign and dismissing any legal effects of withdrawal of recognition.[25]

Recognition and derecognition of Kosovo have led to much political bickering between the Serbian and Kosovar Albanian sides, and Priština accused Belgrade of 'shopping' for derecognition through bribery and arms sales—in much the same way Serbia had earlier accused Kosovo and its Western allies of 'purchasing' recognition from smaller members of the United Nations. But the politics of the debate camouflages its legal relevance, and any possible foul play involved (if 'purchasing' recognition or derecognition could really be deemed morally inappropriate) cannot be established with any credibility. The motives of a State to grant or withdraw recognition may be important to establish whether it is acting in good faith and in the genuine belief that it is behaving in accordance with international law—but their true nature is usually impossible for casual observers to determine. I will therefore take these acts of derecognition at face value and examine them under their own terms.

Some of the diplomatic correspondence considered here does not explain the choice to derecognise; other notes invoke Security Council resolutions, premature recognition, or both as the reason for the revocation.

3.1 Derecognition in Light of Legality

Most of the *notes verbales* notifying Belgrade or Priština (there is some divergence as to *who* is notified of derecognition)[26] clearly refer to general rules of international law, or to specific United Nations instruments (such as Security Council Resolution 1244), as a basis for derecognising Kosovo. Derecognition in these cases clearly refers to an initial breach of the principle of legality by the act of recognition and therefore may be regarded as 'quasi-recognition': the States concerned are really admitting that their recognition was void at the time it was made. Statements to this effect have been made by Burundi, the Comoros, Ghana, Dominica, Lesotho, Madagascar, Nauru, and Papua New Guinea.

Several States use identical or nearly identical wording in their *notes verbales*, suggesting at least some level of coordination between them and, probably, Belgrade in the preparation of the acts of withdrawal. This is notably the case with

[25] See eg Filip Rudic and Die Morina, 'Kosovo Slams Serbia's "False Recognition" Claims' (*Balkan Insight*, 27 November 2017) <https://balkaninsight.com/2017/11/27/kosovo-deputy-pm-slams-serbia-s-false-recognition-claims-11-27-2017/> last accessed 6 June 2024.

[26] The documents were provided by the Serbian Ministry of Foreign Affairs, so it would appear that Serbia as the Parent State has been notified of all of them; however, separate documents were also sent to Kosovo in some cases (eg Suriname) and in others the act was addressed directly at Priština while Belgrade apparently received a copy (as in the case of Guinea-Bissau).

Burundi, the Comoros, and Togo. All three States remarked that the unilateral declaration of independence of Kosovo had been in contradiction with Principles 3 and 4 of the Helsinki Final Act and, more fundamentally, Resolution 1244.[27] The same arguments were raised (using different wording) by Ghana[28] and Lesotho,[29] the latter of which revoked 'all previous statements made with regards to the status of Kosovo, especially those that could be interpreted in any way as the recognition of Kosovo'. Nauru[30] and Madagascar[31] only referred to Resolution 1244, the latter addressing its letter at the authorities in Priština rather than Belgrade. Papua New Guinea explained that its decision to recognise Kosovo in 2012 was made because of Belgrade's apparent unwillingness to engage in negotiations on its status as required under Resolution 1244, but that since negotiations were now taking place with the mediation of the European Union, it would adopt a 'neutral' stance and terminate 'any letters/communications issued by [Papua New Guinea] in 2012 recognising Kosovo's independence ... until both parties complete the negotiation process and agree on the final status of Kosovo' in line with the Resolution.[32] Finally, Dominica made its decision simply upon considering 'recommendations of the UN General Assembly and of the International Court of Justice and in the interest of comity'.[33]

Interestingly, several States that clearly referred to legality also mentioned that their recognition had been premature. 'Prematurity' usually relates to effectivity and means that the material elements of statehood were not met at the time of recognition; it is unusual to describe as premature the recognition of an entity that is illegal (in the sense that it involves or stems from a very serious violation of international law, such as *jus cogens*) as illegality typically cannot be overcome with the passage of time. As this correspondence usually speaks of a Security Council resolution which does not prejudge the outcome of status negotiations in relation to Kosovo, it is likely that the derecognising States felt that independence could become legally possible at a later moment, namely if it were foreseen by a

[27] '[L]a déclaration unilatérale d'indépendance du Kosovo de février 2008 est en contradiction avec l'Acte Final d'Helsinki, entre autres en ses principes 3 et 4 et, plus fondamentalement, s'oppose à la Résolution 1244 (1999) du Conseil de Sécurité de l'ONU, adoptée sous le chapitre VII de la Charte de l'ONU.' *Note verbale* of 15 February 2018 from the Republic of Burundi to the Serbian Foreign Ministry. The *notes verbales* of the Union of the Comoros of 1 November 2018 and of the Republic of Togo of 28 June 2019 use identical wording.

[28] *Note verbale* of the Ministry of Foreign Affairs and Regional Integration of the Republic of Ghana to the Ministry of Foreign Affairs of the Republic of Serbia of 7 November 2019.

[29] *Note verbale* of the Ministry of Foreign Affairs of the Kingdom of Lesotho to the Ministry of Foreign Affairs of the Republic of Serbia of 16 October 2018.

[30] *Note verbale* of the Ministry of Foreign Affairs of the Republic of Nauru to the Ministry of Foreign Affairs of the Republic of Serbia of 13 November 2019.

[31] *Note verbale* of the Ministry of Foreign Affairs of the Republic of Madagascar to the Ministry of Foreign Affairs of Kosovo of 5 December 2018.

[32] *Note verbale* of the Ministry of Foreign Affairs and Trade of Papua New Guinea to the Ministry of Foreign Affairs of the Republic of Serbia of 27 June 2018.

[33] *Note verbale* of the Ministry of Foreign and CARICOM Affairs of the Commonwealth of Dominica to the Ministry of Foreign Affairs of the Republic of Serbia of 30 October 2018.

settlement between Serbia and Kosovo. The unusual predicament wherein recognition is premature because of norms rather than material factors is thus very context-specific and would not be applicable to other situations where no such secondary legislation exists (unless, of course, States individually believe that the Parent State's consent is one of the determining factors of the legality of a declaration of independence).

3.2 Derecognition in Light of Effectivity

As stated above, the use of the word 'premature' in several notes could be a reference to effectivity, but this does not seem to be the case—the States in question are stating that their recognition was premature because of renewed negotiations. As negotiations of this sort, which would presumably also extend to status matters at some point, *prima facie* bring into question the very existence of a breakaway entity as an independent State (for if it is already independent, why negotiate?), it is also possible to regard all references to negotiations as reflecting a lack of effectivity as well.

None of the acts of withdrawal issued so far mention any of the material criteria of statehood. However, a few—specifically those of Grenada and Palau—may be interpreted as referring to material rather than legal elements of Kosovo's self-proclaimed statehood. The government of Grenada decided to review its position on the matter because 'support for the solution of the future status of Kosovo arrived at through dialogue between Belgrade and Pristina is paramount' and added that 'once the two parties reach an agreement, the Government of Grenada will steadfastly support the position reached by the parties'.[34] Palau expressed the same views and stated that the outcome of the dialogue should not be prejudged.[35] Both notes share many contours with those invoking legality, however, the focus seems to be rather on the fact that there are ongoing status negotiations, rather than that recognition is prohibited by international law.

Whether or not this is the case with Kosovo, the importance of status negotiations for recognition and derecognition should not be underestimated. Consent by the Parent State is not required for effectivity to arise and a breakaway State to be formed and enjoy recognition. However, the material aspects of statehood must be achieved with a degree of stability: ongoing negotiations with the Parent State that still does not recognise the statehood of its interlocutor may cast doubt

[34] *Note verbale* of the Ministry of Foreign Affairs of Grenada to the Ministry of Foreign Affairs of the Republic of Serbia of 30 October 2018.

[35] *Note verbale* of the Ministry of State of the Republic of Palau to the Ministry of Foreign Affairs of the Republic of Serbia of 17 January 2019.

on whether such stability exists. The fear of being perceived in such a light could dissuade breakaway States from entering into negotiations with their Parent State.

3.3 Derecognition Without Explanation or For Reasons Other than Legality or Effectivity

The first act of derecognition sent to the Serbian Foreign Ministry, that of Suriname, does not provide any explanation for the decision. Aside from the usual diplomatic pleasantries in the *note verbale*, the Permanent Mission of Suriname to the United Nations conveyed to its Serbian counterpart in New York 'the decision of the Government of the Republic of Suriname of its revocation of the recognition of Kosovo and Metohija as an independent and sovereign State' and that '[a] diplomatic note has been sent to the Ministry of Foreign Affairs of Kosovo ... informing of said decision'.[36] Guinea-Bissau, which followed soon after with its withdrawal, also gave no reasons for its decision, but addressed its note directly to the 'Ministry of Foreign Affairs of the Republic of Kosovo', presumably sending a copy to the Serbian Foreign Ministry[37] (according to the Kosovar Ministry of Foreign Affairs, it soon thereafter received another note from Guinea-Bissau re-affirming recognition).[38]

The Liberian note, dispatched in 2018, should also be added to the category of acts of derecognition that do not provide reasoning under the traditional criteria of statehood. The Minister of Foreign Affairs wrote that 'Liberia recognized the independence of Kosovo based on its realization that Belgrade was not prepared to negotiate a solution with its Southern Province Kosovo' but also that '[t]oday, the dialogue between Belgrade and Pristina is taking place under umbrella of European Union' and that therefore 'it is only appropriate for Liberia to take a stance, which allows for a sustainable solution for citizens of Serbia and Province of Kosovo, as is being done through current negotiations'.[39] Accordingly, Liberia 'annulled' its letter of recognition until the end of the negotiations under the auspices of the European Union.

[36] *Note verbale* of the Permanent Mission of the Republic of Suriname to the United Nations to the Permanent Mission of the Republic of Serbia to the United Nations of 30 October 2017. 'Kosovo and Metohija' is the formal designation of the autonomous province under the Serbian Constitution.

[37] *Note verbale* of the Ministry of Foreign Affairs of the Republic of Guinea-Bissau to the Ministry of Foreign Affairs of Kosovo of 21 November 2017 (the decision was taken after 'careful consideration', according to then note).

[38] *Note verbale* of the Ministry of Foreign Affairs of the Republic of Guinea-Bissau to the Ministry of Foreign Affairs of Kosovo of 25 January 2018.

[39] *Note verbale* of the Ministry of Foreign Affairs of the Republic of Liberia to the Ministry of Foreign Affairs of the Republic of Serbia of 20 June 2018. Although its arguments recall those of the Papua New Guinean *note verbale*, it makes no mention of Security Council Resolution 1244, which is why I decided not to classify the two documents in the same category.

This note is interesting as Liberia does not refer to its recognition as either premature or having violated relevant instruments of international law: like the reasons for recognition, the derecognition seems to be based on political concerns (the willingness of the parties to find a 'sustainable solution'). But this does not imply that its effects were intended as purely political. Indeed, in situations where recognition is authorised, the decision whether to pursue it may be based on a variety of political motivations. There are thus two possibilities for the interpretation of this withdrawal: (i) Liberia is in fact saying that its initial decision was premature (in light of the ongoing negotiations between the parties), which would displace it to the category invoking effectivity; or (ii) Liberia believes that it has the sovereign right to derecognise another State.

3.4 Denial of Previous Recognition

Two documents received by the Serbian Foreign Ministry cannot be described as withdrawal of recognition, although practically—if not legally—they may still be relevant and are illustrative of the political controversies surrounding recognition. In both cases, the issuing State is not withdrawing recognition but is denying that recognition has ever happened, and for different reasons in both cases.

The Central African Republic issued a very simple factual denial of recognition: the Minister of Foreign Affairs assured his Serbian counterpart that there was no proof that recognition had ever taken place. According to the *note verbale*, the government could find no written proof of ever having recognised Kosovo:

> Lors de notre audience, et du tout dernier échange avec votre Conseiller Spécial, j'ai pris note de votre préoccupation quant à une lettre écrite par un de mes prédécesseurs en reconnaissance de l'État du Kosovo … [L]es autorités de la République Centrafricaine n'ont retrouvé aucune lettre dans laquelle l'État Centrafricain prenait une position relative à l'État du Kosovo.[40]

The Minister goes on to reaffirm the Central African Republic's commitment to sovereignty and the rule of law for all States in general and the Republic of Serbia in particular, as well as its support for a peaceful and mutually acceptable agreement in the Serbia-Kosovo dialogue.

More complicated is the note provided by São Tomé and Príncipe, whose head of government adopted a resolution recognising Kosovo in 2012. The President later issued a communication (which was apparently also shared with the Serbian Foreign Ministry) that the recognition had been invalid as, according to the

[40] *Note verbale* of the Ministry of Foreign Affairs of the Central African Republic to the Ministry of Foreign Affairs of the Republic of Serbia of 24 July 2019.

Constitution, such a decision could only be made in consultation with the head of State. According to the President, São Tomé and Príncipe had in fact never recognised Kosovo,[41] wherefore the communication did not amount to a revocation of recognition.

3.5 Outstanding Issues

Both the São Toméan and Central African examples demonstrate seemingly incidental issues which can become crucial points in the recognition and derecognition discussion, and, by implication, in relation to the opposability of statehood. The statement coming from the Central African Republic could be easy to disprove factually (eg by producing the requisite letter).[42] If recognition could be proven as a matter of fact, then the question still remains, separately, of whether it may be withdrawn. What if the issuing of an act of recognition is not in dispute factually but is contested as a matter of domestic law? What if it is not communicated to the recipient through diplomatic channels but is simply a decision adopted by the government, possibly without much pomp or even without the domestic or foreign public being aware of it?

These questions concern form as much as effects and recognition as much as derecognition, and it can be very difficult to make any sense of them. A few points may be made in this regard. (i) Recognition and derecognition have either taken place or they have not—there can be no grey zone in between. It may be difficult to ascertain from the given declarations and concluding acts whether either has come to pass, but every State will have to be placed within a binary function offering either recognition or non-recognition. (ii) If recognition or derecognition have been established, they will produce effects solely according to the rules of international law, irrespective of domestic legality. However, the relevance of domestic law cannot be entirely disregarded in this domain. Domestic legislation and constitutional considerations may play a crucial role in establishing whether recognition has occurred as a matter of fact, even if they do not serve to either validate or invalidate the act from the perspective of international law. Heads of State, government, and foreign ministers in general, as well as other persons representing the State in specific areas, are competent to formulate declarations undertaking obligations on behalf of the State, even if they are acting *ultra vires* under domestic law. This principle has been confirmed by the International Court of Justice with seemingly no exceptions[43] (although the ILC maintains that domestic legality as a requirement

[41] Communication of the President of São Tomé and Príncipe of 7 January 2013.

[42] I am not aware that his has occurred since the 2019 note of the Central African Republic.

[43] *Case concerning Armed Activities on the Territory of the Congo (New Application: 2002) (Democratic Republic of the Congo v Rwanda)*, ICJ Reports 6, Judgment of 3 February 2006, para 46.

for the binding force of unilateral declarations is not entirely ruled out)[44] and, as such, it was adopted for the Vienna Convention on the Law of Treaties.[45] But even if the principle were truly absolute, the São Toméan case still demonstrates why it can be difficult to establish whether a governmental decision made in violation of domestic legislation amounts to an act of recognition (or derecognition, *mutatis mutandis*). (iii) More generally, regardless of whether recognition can be proven in cases where it is disputed, and regardless of the legal effects of derecognition, its practical consequences cannot be ignored. Based on the statements coming from derecognising States, it does not seem likely that they would be prepared to treat Kosovo as a State in any sense of the word after withdrawing recognition. Even if bilateral legal opposability could be established, the political fallout for contested States could be much more concerning: for example, they would likely lose the derecognising States' support for membership in international organisations, a key mechanism for demonstrating one's own statehood. Thus, (de)recognition plays a role of special importance in cases of contested statehood.

4. Conclusion

Contemporary lawyers typically treat derecognition as legally impossible: recognition, once given, is final and irrevocable. Nevertheless, States continue to withdraw recognition in practice, and sometimes in significant numbers, as exemplified by recent practice.

If the statehood of the recipient of recognition is uncontested then there is clearly no room for derecognition, and at least full (*de jure* and unconditional) recognition cannot be withdrawn. However, this is not true of situations where the initial act of recognition violated international law or where the statehood of the recipient remains subject to competing legitimate claims (specifically, that of its parent).

If the recipient of recognition was created in violation of the principles of legality or effectivity, then the act of recognition violated international law, and the issuing State may choose to 'withdraw' it subsequently. At least as far as recognition violating legality is concerned, this is not possible: if the recipient State was created in violation of *jus cogens* norms, its recognition must be regarded as null and void under international law and thus logically cannot be withdrawn ('quasi-derecognition'). Quasi-derecognition may still have legal effects under domestic law depending on the nature of the national legal system. True derecognition entails the revocation (with effects *ex nunc*) of an act otherwise producing legal

[44] See 'Guiding Principles' (n 12) Principle 4 with related commentary.

[45] Vienna Convention on the Law of Treaties, 1155 UNTS 331 (concluded 23 May 1969, entered into force 27 January 1980) arts 46–47.

consequences. If opposability does not flow from recognition, then derecognition cannot negate it, meaning that derecognition is then merely political. However, if opposability was established through recognition, then actual withdrawal may be possible in cases where the recipient's statehood is still contested ('constitutive derecognition'). This is not a majority or mainstream view, but I believe it is justified under certain circumstances as a matter of positive law. Outside of the limited context of contested statehood, constitutive derecognition is indeed impossible.

13
Concluding Remarks

This book has attempted to address and resolve some of the persistent controversies surrounding statehood and recognition in international law. Bearing in mind the fundamental importance of these matters, it is only natural that they been scrutinised across countless pages of tomes, volumes, and textbooks, and by some of the most brilliant scholarship in our field. It would be hubris to think that this work has resolved them in a manner that would be to everyone's satisfaction. Nevertheless, it is the author's hope that the book might at least achieve the more modest goal of demonstrating a new perspective on these issues and perhaps illuminate the path for future scholars who may finally crack recognition.

As it stands, studying recognition has come to be regarded by many of my more illustrious colleagues as a fruitless endeavour, for they will either regard the matter as settled, or as a one that is altogether impossible to resolve; either way, the labour is Sisyphean, and any time and effort spent on it must surely be wasted. I cannot agree with this notion. Although recognition is becoming something of an undesirable word in the vocabulary of more practical or high-minded lawyers, its legal role is hardly diminished in the twenty-first century. The fact remains that entities that do not meet the Montevideo criteria are treated as States by other States and that some entities that fulfil them are not. Sooner or later, the question of recognition unerringly arises when discussing such entities, wherefore the matter should still be studied and analysed.

Regardless of what mixture of law and politics is thrown into a specific act of recognition, it must be regarded as a legal act. The author of recognition—a State—is thereby expressing cognisance of a certain situation, confirming its existence as a legal fact, and accepting its legal implications.

For decades, scholars have tended to think of recognition as an act of singular value: if it is declaratory in one case, then it must be declaratory in another; the same may be said of most constitutivist authors. I have tried to demonstrate throughout this book that such a narrow approach is neither practical nor legally justified. In reality, recognition is sometimes constitutive, and sometimes declaratory, depending on how the rules of positive law interact in a given situation.

Contemporary law still revolves around States and largely concerns itself with their relations and the peculiarities of their engagement at the international plane. In this regard, law has been doing perfectly well without ever dictating what a State is or what it should be. Is it truly so important to settle the question of an entity's statehood by reference to law? Is it even appropriate for law, the product of States,

Recognition of States in International Law. Pavle Kilibarda, Oxford University Press. © Pavle Kilibarda 2024.
DOI: 10.1093/oso/9780198905653.003.0013

to make such an attempt? These matters are surely better left to the more discerning methods of political and social scientists; for law, it suffices to determine what a State is in the legal sense, and that means nothing else than to say how it is to behave towards others, and how others must treat it in turn. It is much more useful not to insist on using legal tools to divine the thing-in-itself, but rather its normative manifestations as reflected in human behaviour. Therefore, a State only makes sense *legally* as an opposability, reflected in various ways across the spiderweb of bilateral relations that we call international law.

Opposability is always a normative term: a rule is opposable to a subject because it is bound to respect it; a fact is opposable because a norm bestows it with legal significance. To identify opposability in any given context, we must first identify the relevant norm.

It cannot be denied that there has been an evolution in doctrine and jurisprudence favouring the declaratory view in recent decades, but these are auxiliary sources of law. As such, they can only serve as proof of a rule or provision existing in a primary source, typically customary law. Yet, despite the best efforts of some scholars, the hypothesis according to which there exists a customary rule linking effective, *de facto* statehood to opposability is very difficult to demonstrate. Apart from some jurisprudence at the domestic level which doubtless accepts the declaratory view—as in Switzerland, where this book was written—and some international case law that deals with the matter indirectly, no convincing evidence of the existence of a rule of customary law rendering recognition declaratory has ever been presented. Even if we took the Badinter Commission as the point of reference, we would realise that even the practice of those same European States that had convoked it would not later fully reflect its views (as recognition was given to entities that did not yet meet the criteria of statehood). That the declaratists have won the day has become something of a dogma: it is restated from one textbook to another, with a multitude of authors quoting each other in a cycle that begins and ends in doctrine and legal theory (and sometimes in error, such as when indubitably constitutivist authors are quoted as favouring declaratism),[1] but the belief otherwise enjoys little support in State practice.

The author of this book nevertheless hopes that the reader will not conclude that he has the proverbial axe to grind with the declaratory theory. Both constitutivist and declaratist approaches chiefly suffer from defects that are not of their own making and that all ultimately boil down to the inconsistency and opaqueness of State practice. Indeed, whether recognition is constitutive or declaratory according to most States may be impossible to discern, as a single situation may have elements

[1] For example, Megiddo and Nevo conclude that '[r]ecognition is today predominantly considered declaratory and not constitutive' while referring to Lauterpacht's work in the relevant footnote; see Tamar Meggido and Zohar Nevo, 'Revisiting Lessons on the New Law of Statehood: Palestinian Independence in a Post-Kosovo World' in Duncan French, *Statehood and Self-Determination: Reconciling Tradition and Modernity in International Law* (CUP 2013) 187, 188, fn 16.

of both, or be interpreted from different angles; the same is often true of judicial practice. Under the circumstances, one should not expect there to be adequate or sufficiently unambiguous practice to infer the existence of a rule of customary law. Because the declaratory theory predicates the existence of such a rule, it is susceptible to greater scrutiny and may be more easily challenged.

An advantage of the approach I suggest—which I call the normative theory of recognition—is that it does not require the existence of such a specific provision. If there is no rule of international law stating that 'Recognition is constitutive' or 'Recognition is declaratory' (or making some other determination to the same effect), that does not mean that a rule cannot be found in a given context making that particular case one of declaratory recognition. If such a rule cannot be found, then we must draw upon the general principles of law, namely, that of good faith, and bind States to their own undertakings, grounding opposability in recognition itself. To summarise:

(1) Regardless of whether it is a unilateral, bilateral, or multilateral act in a given case, recognition always signifies the author's cognisance that a certain legally relevant situation has arisen, and their acceptance to treat it in a manner governed by international law. If law is not thereby violated, then such an act will naturally create an opposability. Of course, recognition may not be the only basis for opposability in the case at hand, and opposability may arise even in the absence of recognition, when there exist separate grounds for it. One does not employ the word 'recognition' in international law without the expectation that others will rely on it.

(2) There are as many objects of recognition as there are situations that could be opposable to legal persons. This includes States, governments, belligerency, and territorial claims. When a new State is the object of recognition, the criteria of material statehood (as prerequisites of lawful recognition) will be crucial unless a rule of international law can be found requiring that the entity be treated as a State regardless of such considerations.

(3) The effects of recognition are to produce an opposability. This is true even if recognition is said to only have a declaratory effect: opposability will then come from a different source, which does not diminish the power of the act of recognition to produce legal effects. I fundamentally disagree with Charpentier's finding that there exists no necessary link between recognition and the opposability of statehood.[2] It is a fact that many domestic courts will give preponderant weight to recognition, or lack thereof, by their own executive when ascertaining the opposability of new States. It is true that such practice is not universal, but the absence of universality in domestic

[2] See Jean Charpentier, *La reconnaissance internationale et l'évolution du droit des gens* (Pedone 1956) 5.

jurisprudence does not disprove the notion that recognition can create an opposability according to the rules governing the sources of international law. Finally, even in situations where recognition is declaratory under international law, it may still be required for the domestic law opposability of at least some rights of States, such as the possibility of enjoying legal standing in the local judiciary.

(4) Opposability does not only stem from recognition. When a new State arises and seeks recognition, a step-by-step normative analysis ought to be undertaken to determine whether it is opposable to existing ones. If a norm can be identified that leads to opposability separately of recognition, then the act is declaratory and the new State will be opposable to others. This is usually the case when the new State joins the United Nations or another similar organisation, is entitled to external self-determination, or, perhaps, secedes with the consent of its parent. If no such rule exists, then recognition conforming to effectivity and legality can create an opposability, and thus have a constitutive effect.

(5) An entity whose statehood is not opposable to one or more States does not exist in a legal vacuum: both practice and reason disprove Oppenheim's idea that international law 'takes no notice' of unrecognised States.[3] In claiming statehood, the new State is committing itself to a certain legal regime, and is thereby bound to its rules; State-like entities that from the outset refuse to 'play by the rules' of international law, such as the jihadist 'Islamic State' that briefly rose to prominence as a quasi-state formed in Iraq and Syria in 2014, are universally shunned and cannot achieve the status of States in the legal sense even if they otherwise fulfil the requirements of material statehood. However, if an entity's statehood is not opposable to another State, then no bilateral legal relationship will exist between the two, and the non-recognising State will not be required to treat it as a peer.

Recognition is but one tool for establishing opposability—there may well exist others to render it declaratory and superfluous. However, there will certainly exist situations where recognition will be necessary for the creation of legal statehood. The normative theory of recognition requires a situational approach, and is thus perhaps deserving of the label of a 'mixed' theory should the reader insist on categorising it.

Finally, my focus throughout this work has been to determine the State of positive international law regarding recognition: the decision to neglect the surrounding politics was deliberate. In truth, the politics of recognition may be as important as the law surrounding the act and warrants serious analysis. Sometimes, the decision

[3] Lassa Oppenheim, *International Law: A Treatise, Volume I: Peace* (Longmans, Green and Co 1912) 116ff.

to recognise a new State, even when international law allows it, may have serious political ramifications—for example, by creating expectations of recognition elsewhere, or encouraging separatist tendencies at home or abroad: strictly speaking, it is within this political domain, and not in law, that recognition may create a precedent.[4] Any decision to recognise a new State should only be made following a rigorous legal and political analysis, and the onus to demonstrate the justification or benefits of such a decision rests with the party calling for it.

[4] States typically raise that their decisions to recognise a new State created through secession are *sui generis* cases and do not constitute precedent, whether legally or politically; for a cogent criticism of this idea, see John Dugard, 'The Secession of States and Their Recognition in the Wake of Kosovo' (2013) 357 RCADI 9, 35, 43ff, and 195ff.

Select Bibliography

Abi-Saab G, 'Cours general de droit international public' (1987) 207 RCADI 9

Ago R, 'Positive Law and International Law' (1957) 51(4) American Journal of International Law 691

Alfaro RJ, 'Rights and Duties of States' (1969) 97 RCADI 91

Anderson G, 'Secession in International Law and Relations: What Are We Talking About?' (2013) 35 Loyola of Los Angeles International & Comparative Law Review 343

Akande D, 'Classification of Armed Conflicts: Relevant Legal Aspects' in Elizabeth Wilmshurst (ed), *International Law and the Classification of Conflicts* (OUP 2012)

Aloupi N, 'The Right to Non-intervention and Non-interference' (2015) 4(3) Cambridge Journal of International and Comparative Law 566

Anzilotti D, *Cours de droit international, Premier volume; Introduction—Théories générales* (Librairie du Recueil Sirey 1929)

Barber R, 'Could the General Assembly Exclude Myanmar from the UN by Refusing to Recognise the Credentials of its Ruling Military Junta?' (*EJIL:Talk!*, 26 February 2021) <https://www.ejiltalk.org/could-the-general-assembly-exclude-myanmar-from-the-un-by-refusing-to-recognise-the-credentials-of-its-ruling-military-junta/> last accessed 13 June 2024

Barber R, 'Will the Taliban Represent Afghanistan at the UN General Assembly?' (*EJIL:Talk!*, 1 September 2021) <https://www.ejiltalk.org/will-the-taliban-represent-afghanistan-at-the-un-general-assembly/> last accessed 13 June 2024

Bartolini G, 'Italian Legal Scholarship of International Law in the Early Decades of the Twentieth Century' in Giulio Bartolini (ed), *A History of International Law in Italy* (OUP 2020)

Baty T, 'So-Called "De Facto" Recognition' (1922) 31(5) The Yale Law Journal 469

Beaulac S, 'The *Lotus* Case in Context: Sovereignty, Westphalia, Vattel, and Positivism' in Stephen Allen and others (eds), *The Oxford Handbook of Jurisdiction in International Law* (OUP 2019)

Bellows TJ, 'Taiwan's Foreign Policy in the 1970s: A Case Study of Adaptation and Viability' (1976) 16(7) Asian Survey 593

Berat L, 'John Dugard's Recognition and the United Nations' (1989) 24 Texas International Law Journal 501

Berge GW, 'The Case of the S.S. "Lotus" ' (1928) 26(4) Michigan Law Review 361

Besson S, 'Sovereignty' in Anne Peters and Rüdiger Wolfrum (eds), *Max Planck Enyclopedias of International Law* (OUP 2013) <https://opil.ouplaw.com/display/10.1093/law:epil/9780199231690/law-9780199231690-e1472?prd=EPIL> last accessed 13 June 2024

Besson S 'International Courts and the Jurisprudence of Statehood' (2019) 10(1) Transnational Legal Theory 30

Birnbaum KE, *East and West Germany: A Modus Vivendi* (Lexington Books 1973)

Bluntschli JC, *Das moderne Völkerrecht der civilisirten Staten als Rechtsbuch dargestellt* (Druck und Verlag der C H Beck'schen Buchhandlung 1872)

Bodin J, *Six livres de la république* (Librairie générale française 1993)

Bonfils H, *Manuel de droit international public* (Arthur Rousseau 1894)

Borchard E, 'Recognition and Non-Recognition' (1942) 36(1) The American Journal of International Law 108

Bowman MJ and Dino Kritsiotis D (eds), *Conceptual and Contextual Perspectives on the Modern Law of Treaties* (CUP 2018)

Brett A, 'The Subject of Sovereignty: Law, Politics and Moral Reasoning in Hugo Grotius' (2020) 17(3) Modern Intellectual History 619–45

Brierly JL, 'Règles générales du droit de la paix' (1936) 58 RCADI 1

Brownlie I, *Principles of Public International Law* (OUP 1998)

Caddell R, 'Treaties, Secret' in Anne Peters and Rüdiger Wolfrum (eds), *Max Planck Encyclopedias of International Law* (OUP 2006) <https://opil.ouplaw.com/display/10.1093/law:epil/9780199231690/law-9780199231690-e1489?prd=EPIL> last accessed 13 June 2024

Cahin G, 'Reconstruction et construction de l'état en droit international' (2020) 411 RCADI 9

Cançado Trindade AA, 'The Domestic Jurisdiction of States in the Practice of the United Nations and Regional Organisations' (1976) 25(4) The International and Comparative Law Quarterly 715

Canizzaro E, *The Law of Treaties Beyond the Vienna Convention* (OUP 2011)

Carron D, *L'acte déclencheur d'un conflit armé international* (Schulthess 2016)

Cavaglieri A, 'Règles générales du droit de la paix' (1929) 26 RCADI 311

Chang P and Lim K, 'Taiwan's Case for United Nations Membership' (1996–1997) 1(2) UCLA Journal of International Law and Foreign Affairs 393–430

Charpentier J, *La reconnaissance internationale et l'évolution du droit des gens* (Pedone 1956)

Chen FT, 'The Meaning of "States" in the Membership Provisions of the United Nations Charter' (2001) 12(1) Indiana International & Comparative Law Review 25

Chen TC, *The International Law of Recognition* (Stevens & Sons Ltd 1951)

Clapham A, *Human Rights Obligations of Non-State Actors* (OUP 2006)

Clapham A, *Brierly's Law of Nations* (OUP 2012)

Cochran CL, 'De Facto and De Jure Recognition: Is there a Difference?' (1968) 62(2) The American Journal of International Law 457

Cohen (Higgins) R, 'The Concept of Statehood in United Nations Practice' (1961) 109(8) University of Pennsylvania Law Review 1127

Corten O, 'La résolution 940 du Conseil de sécurité autorisant une intervention militaire en Haïti: L'émergence d'un principe de légitimité démocratique en droit international?' (1995) 6(1) European Journal of International Law 116

Corten O and Klein P, 'Are Agreements between States and Non-State Entities Rooted in the International Legal Order?' in Enzo Canizzaro (ed), *The Law of Treaties Beyond the Vienna Convention* (OUP 2011)

Cosnard M, 'Rapport introductif' in Société française pour le droit international, *Colloque du Mans: Le sujet en droit international* (Pedone 2005)

Cottier T and Müller JP, 'Estoppel' in Anne Peters and Rüdiger Wolfrum (eds), *Max Planck Encyclopedias of International Law* (OUP 2021) <https://opil.ouplaw.com/display/10.1093/law:epil/9780199231690/law-9780199231690-e1401?prd=EPIL> last accessed 13 June 2024

Craven MCR, 'The European Community Arbitration Commission on Yugoslavia' (1996) 66(1) British Yearbook of International Law 333

Crawford J, *The Creation of States in International Law* (OUP 2007)

Crawford J, 'Chance, Order, Change: The Course of International Law: General Course on Public International Law' (2014) 365 RCADI 9

Crawford J, *Brownlie's Principles of Public International Law* (OUP 2019)

Cremona M (ed), *The Enlargement of the European Union* (OUP 2003)

Cullen A and Wheatley S, 'The Human Rights of Individuals in *De Facto* Regimes under the European Convention on Human Rights' (2013) 13(4) Human Rights Law Review 691

Daillier P, Forteau F, and Pellet A, *Droit international public* (LGDJ—Léxtenso éditions 2009)

Damm J and Lim P (eds), *European Perspectives on Taiwan* (Springer 2012)

De Hemptinne J, *Les conflits armés en mutation* (Pedone 2019)

De la Rasilla I, *International Law and History* (CUP 2021)

De Vattel E, *The Law of Nations* (Liberty Fund, Inc 2008)

De Visscher C, *Problèmes d'interprétation judiciaire en droit international public* (Pedone 1963)

De Visscher C, 'Cours Général de principles de droit international public' (1972) 86 RCADI 445

Decaux E and De Frouville O, *Droit international public* (Dalloz 2018)

Del Mar K, 'The Myth of Remedial Secession' in Duncan French (ed), *Statehood and Self-Determination* (CUP 2013)

Denza E, *Diplomatic Law: Commentary on the Vienna Convention on Diplomatic Relations* (OUP 2016)

Derek Croxton D, 'The Peace of Westphalia of 1648 and the Origins of Sovereignty' (1999) 21(3) The International History Review 569
Dimitrijević V and others, *Osnovi međunarodnog javnog prava* (Belgrade Centre for Human Rights 2007)
Dimitrijević V and others, *Contemporary Right of Self-Determination of Peoples* (Belgrade Centre for Human Rights 2011)
Divac Öberg M, 'The Legal Effects of Resolutions of the UN Security Council and General Assembly in the Jurisprudence of the ICJ' (2006) 16(5) The European Journal of International Law 879–906
Dixon MJ, 'Recent Developments in United Kingdom Practice Concerning the Recognition of States and Governments' (1988) 22(2) The International Lawyer 555
Dugard J, 'South Africa's "Independent" Homelands: An Exercise in Denationalization' (1980) 10 Denver Journal of International Law and Policy 11
Dugard J, *Recognition and the United Nations* (Grotius Publications Limited 1987)
Dugard J, 'Secession: Is the Case of Yugoslavia a Precedent for Africa?' (1993) 5 African Journal of International and Comparative Law 63
Dugard J and Raič D, 'The Role of Recognition in the Law and Practice of Secession' in Marcelo G Kohen (ed), *Secession: International Law Perspectives* (CUP 2006)
Dugard J, 'The Secession of States and Their Recognition in the Wake of Kosovo' (2013) 357 RCADI 9
Dugard J, Du Plessis M, Maluwa T, and Tladi D, *Dugard's International Law: A South African Perspective* (Juta 2019)
Dugard J, 'What Is a State in International Law? How Is This to Be Determined?' in Niels M Blokker, Daniëlla Dam-de Jong, and Vid Prislan (eds), *Furthering the Frontiers of International Law: Sovereignty, Human Rights, Sustainable Development: Liber Amicorum Nico Schrijver* (Brill/Nijhoff 2021)
Dunning WA, 'The Politics of Aristotle' (1900) 15(2) Political Science Quarterly 273
Eckart C, *Promises of States under International Law* (Hart Publishing 2012)
Egerton GW, 'Britain and the "Great Betrayal": Anglo-American Relations and the Struggle for United States Ratification of the Treaty of Versailles, 1919–1920' (1978) 21(4) The Historical Journal 885
Eisenmann PM and Koskenniemi M (eds), *State Succession: Codification Tested against the Facts* (Brill/Nijhoff 2000)
Elias O, 'Persistent Objector' in Anne Peters and Rüdiger Wolfrum (eds), *Max Planck Encyclopedias of International Law* (OUP 2006) <https://opil.ouplaw.com/display/10.1093/law:epil/9780199231690/law-9780199231690-e1455?prd=EPIL> last accessed 13 June 2024
Erasmus G, 'Criteria for Determining Statehood: John Dugard's Recognition and the United Nations' (1988) 4(2) South African Journal on Human Rights 207
Evans M (ed), *International Law* (OUP 2006)
Fassbender B and Anne Peters A (eds), *The Oxford Handbook of the History of International Law* (OUP 2012)
Fauchille P, *Traité de droit international public: Tome 1er, Première partie: Paix* (Arthur Rousseau 1922)
Fenwick CG, *Cases on International Law* (Callaghan and Company 1935)
Finck F, 'The State Between Fact and Law: The Role of Recognition and the Conditions Under Which it is Granted in the Creation of New States' (2016) XXXVI Polish Yearbook of International Law 51
Fiore P, *Le droit international codifié* (Paris 1890)
Fitzmaurice G, 'The General Principles of International Law Considered from the Standpoint of the Rule of Law' (1957) 92 RCADI 1
Fortin K, *The Accountability of Armed Groups Under Human Rights Law* (OUP 2017)
Franck TM, 'The Emerging Right to Democratic Governance' (1992) 86(1) American Journal of International Law 46
François JPA, 'Règles générales du droit de la paix' (1938) 66 RCADI 1

French D (ed), *Statehood and Self-Determination: Reconciling Tradition and Modernity in International Law* (CUP 2013)

Frowein JA, 'Non-Recognition' in Anne Peters and Rüdiger Wolfrum (eds), *Max Planck Encyclopedias of International Law* (OUP 2011) <https://opil.ouplaw.com/display/10.1093/law:epil/9780199231690/law-9780199231690-e1073> last accessed 7 June 2024

Frowein JA, 'De Facto Regime' in Anne Peters and Rüdiger Wolfrum (eds), *Max Planck Encyclopedias of International Law* (OUP 2013) <https://opil.ouplaw.com/display/10.1093/law:epil/9780199231690/law-9780199231690-e1395> last accessed 13 June 2024

Garner JW, 'Recognition of Belligerency' (1938) 32(1) The American Journal of International Law 106

Graham MW, *The League of Nations and the Recognition of States* (University of California Press 1933)

Grant JP, *International Law Essentials* (Edinburgh University Press 2010)

Grant TD, 'Defining Statehood: The Montevideo Convention and its Discontents' (1998–1999) 37(2) Columbia Journal of Transnational Law 403

Grant TD, *The Recognition of States: Law and Practice in Debate and Evolution* (Praeger Publishers 1999)

Grant TD, 'Ukraine v. Russian Federation in Light of Ilaşcu: Two Short Points' (*EJIL:Talk!*, 22 May 2014) <https://www.ejiltalk.org/ukraine-v-russian-federation-in-light-of-ilascu-two-short-points/> last accessed 13 June 2024

Green JA, *The Persistent Objector Rule in International Law* (OUP 2016)

Green LC, 'Rhodesian Independence—Legal or Illegal' (1968) 6 Alberta Law Review 37

Green LC, *International Law Through the Cases* (Steven & Sons Ltd 1970)

Gregory H Fox and Brad R Roth (eds), *Democratic Governance and International Law* (CUP 2000)

Grignon J, 'The Beginning of Application of International Humanitarian Law: A Discussion of a Few Challenges' (2014) 96(893) International Review of the Red Cross 139

Gross L, 'The Charter of the United Nations and the Lodge Reservations' (1947) 41(3) The American Journal of International Law 531

Grotius H, *The Rights of War and Peace, Book I* (Liberty Fund 2005)

Hall JC, 'International Law–Power of Government-in-Exile to Enact Valid Legislation' (1954) 52(5) Michigan Law Review 753–56

Hammer L, 'The 2015 Comprehensive Agreement Between the Holy See and the Palestinian Authority: Discerning the Holy See's Approach to International Relations in the Holy Land' (2017) 6(1) Oxford Journal of Law and Religion 162

Hannum H, 'Rethinking Self-Determination' (1993) 34(1) Virginia Journal of International Law 1

Hannum H, 'The Advisory Opinion on Kosovo: An Opportunity Lost, or a Poisoned Chalice Refused?' (2011) 24(1) Leiden Journal of International Law 155

Hart HLA, *The Concept of Law* (OUP 2012)

Heffter AW, *Das europäische Völkerrecht der Gegenwart* (E H Schroeder 1844)

Heintze HJ, 'Are De Facto Regimes Bound by Human Rights?' (2010) 15 OSCE Yearbook 2009 267

Herdegen M, 'Clerget v Banque commerciale pour l'Europe du Nord Case' in Anne Peters and Rüdiger Wolfrum (eds), *Max Planck Encyclopedias of International Law* (OUP 2007) <https://opil.ouplaw.com/display/10.1093/law:epil/9780199231690/law-9780199231690-e1077> last accessed 13 June 2024

Hershey AS, 'Notes on the Recognition of De Facto Governments by European States' (1920) 14(4) The American Journal of International Law 499

Hewes JE, 'Henry Cabot Lodge and the League of Nations' (1970) 114(4) Proceedings of the American Philosophical Society 245

Hobbes T, *Leviathan: Or, The Matter, Forme, & Power of a Common-wealth Ecclesiasticall and Civill* (McMaster University 1999)

Hrnjaz M, *Raspad Jugoslavije pred sudom: Pravna kvalifikacija oružanih sukoba u Jugoslaviji u praksi sudova u Srbiji* (University of Belgrade, Faculty of Political Science 2021)

Hubatsch W, *Die deutsche Frage* (A G Pleotz 1964)

Jamnejad M and Michael Wood M, 'The Principle of Non-intervention' (2009) 22(2) Leiden Journal of International Law 345

Janis MW, 'Sovereignty and International Law: Hobbes and Grotius' in Reginald St John Macdonald (ed), *Essays in Honour of Wang Tieya* (Martinus Nijhoff 1993)

Jean d'Aspremont, 'The Rise and Fall of Democracy Governance in International Law: A Reply to Susan Marks' (2011) 22(2) European Journal of International Law 549

Jellinek G, *Die Lehre von den Staatenverbindungen* (Alfred Hölder 1882)

Jellinek G, *Allgemeine Staatslehre* (Verlag von O Häring 1914)

Jessup PC, *A Modern Law of Nations: An Introduction* (Macmillan 1948)

Johnson LD, 'What's Wrong With This Picture? The UN Human Rights Council Hears the Military Junta as the Legitimate Government of Myanmar' (*EJIL:Talk!*, 31 March 2021) <https://www.ejiltalk.org/whats-wrong-with-this-picture-the-un-human-rights-council-hears-the-military-junta-as-the-legitimate-government-of-myanmar/> last accessed 13 June 2024

Johnson LD, 'Expert Backgrounder: How Can the Taliban be Prevented from Representing Afghanistan in the United Nations?' (Just Security, 18 August 2021) <https://www.justsecurity.org/77806/expert-backgrounder-how-can-the-taliban-be-prevented-from-representing-afghanistan-in-the-united-nations/> last accessed 13 June 2024

Jovanović S, *Država: Knjiga prva* (Belgrade 1936)

Kalvoda J, 'Masaryk in America in 1918' (1979) 27(1) Jahrbuch für Geschichte Osteuropas 85

Kamminga MT, 'State Succession in Respect of Human Rights Treaties' (1996) 7 European Journal of International Law 469

Kelsen H, 'Théorie générale du droit international public: Problèmes choisis' (1932) 42 RCADI 117

Kelsen H, 'Recognition in International Law: Theoretical Observations' (1941) 35(4) The American Journal of International Law 605

Kelsen H, 'The Principle of Sovereign Equality of States as a Basis for International Organization' (1944) 53(2) The Yale Law Journal 207

Kelsen H, *The Law of the United Nations: A Critical Analysis of Fundamental Problems* (Steven & Sons 1951)

Kelsen H, 'Théorie du droit international public' (1953) 84 RCADI 1

Kelsen H, *Reine Rechtslehre* (Mohr Siebeck 2008)

Ker-Lindsay J, 'Engagement Without Recognition: The Limits of Diplomatic Interaction with Contested States' (2015) 91(2) International Affairs 1

Kilibarda P and Kolb R, 'The International Court of Justice, International Humanitarian Law and Human Rights' in Robert Kolb, Gloria Gaggioli, and Pavle Kilibarda (eds), *Research Handbook on Human Rights and Humanitarian Law* (Edward Elgar 2022)

Kilibarda P, 'Was Russia's Recognition of the Separatist Republics in Ukraine "Manifestly" Unlawful?' (*EJIL:Talk!*, 2 March 2022) <https://www.ejiltalk.org/was-russias-recognition-of-the-separatist-republics-in-ukraine-manifestly-unlawful/> last accessed 13 June 2024

Klabbers J, *International Law* (CUP 2017)

Klein E, 'Self-Contained Regime' in Anne Peters and Rüdiger Wolfrum (eds), *Max Planck Encyclopedias of International Law* (OUP 2006) <https://opil.ouplaw.com/display/10.1093/law:epil/9780199231690/law-9780199231690-e1467?prd=EPIL> last accessed 13 June 2024

Klüber JL, *Europäisches Völkerrecht, Erster Band* (J G Cotta'sche Buchhandlung 1821)

Kolb R, *La bonne foi en droit international public: contribution à l'étude des principes généraux de droit* (Presses universitaires de France 2000)

Kolb R, 'La maxime "*Nemo ex propria turpitudine commodum capere potest*" (nul ne peut profiter de son propre tort) en droit international public' (2000) 1/2000 Revue belge de droit international 84–136

Kolb R, 'Nouvelle observation sur la détermination de la personnalité juridique internationale' (2002) 57 Zeitschrift für Öffentliches Recht 229

Kolb R and Hyde R, *An Introduction to the International Law of Armed Conflicts* (Hart Publishing 2008)

Kolb R, *Ius contra bellum: Le droit international relatif au maintien de la paix: précis* (Helbing & Lichtenhahn 2009)
Kolb R, 'Autodétermination et "sécession remède" en droit international public' in M Cherif Bassiouni and others (eds), *Yearbook of International Law and Jurisprudence: Global Trends: Law, Policy & Justice* (Oceana 2013)
Kolb R, *Théorie du droit international* (Bruylant 2013)
Kolb R, *Good Faith in International Law* (Hart Publishing 2017)
Kolb R, *International Law on the Maintenance of Peace: Jus Contra Bellum* (Edward Elgar 2018)
Kolb R and Gazzini T, 'The Autonomous Community of Catalonia and International Law' (2021) 31(1) Swiss Review of International and European Law 3–23
Kolb R, 'Le droit international comme corps de droit privé et de droit public: Cours général de droit international public' (2021) 419 RCADI 9
Koskenniemi M, 'Lauterpacht: The Victorian Tradition in International Law' (1997) 2 European Journal of International Law 215
Koskenniemi M, 'Imagining the Rule of Law: Rereading the Grotian "Tradition"' (2019) 30(1) European Journal of International Law 17
Kunz JL, 'Individual and Collective Self-Defense in Article 51 of the Charter of the United Nations' (1947) 41(4) The American Journal of International Law 872
Kunz JL, 'Critical Remarks on Lauterpacht's "Recognition in International Law"' (1950) 44(4) The American Journal of international Law 713
Kwiecień R, 'Sir Hersch Lauterpacht's Idea of State Sovereignty—Is It Still Alive?' (2011) 13 International Community Law Review 23
Langhorne R, 'The Regulation of Diplomatic Practice: The Beginnings to the Vienna Convention on Diplomatic Relations, 1961' (1992) 18(1) Review of International Studies 3
Langhorne R, The Diplomacy of Non-State Actors' (2005) 16 Diplomacy and Statecraft 331
Lauterpacht H, 'Règles générales du droit de la paix' (1937) 62 RCADI 95
Lauterpacht H, 'Recognition of States in International Law' (1944) 53(3) The Yale Law Journal 385
Lauterpacht H, '*De Facto* Recognition, Withdrawal of Recognition, and Conditional Recognition' (1945) 22 British Yearbook of International Law 164
Lauterpacht H, 'The Subjects of International Law' in Elihu Lauterpacht (ed), *International Law: Being the Collected Papers of Hersch Lauterpacht, Volume I: The General Works* (CUP 1970)
Lauterpacht H, 'Recognition of Governments' in Elihu Lauterpacht (ed), *International Law: Being the Collected Papers of Hersch Lauterpacht QC, LLD, FBA, Volume 3* (CUP 1977)
Lauterpacht H, *Recognition in International Law* (CUP 2013)
Lim P and Winkler S, 'The European Union's Relations with the Republic of China (Taiwan)' in Jens Damm and Paul Lim (eds), *European Perspectives on Taiwan* (Springer 2012)
Lobo de Souza IM, 'The Role of State Consent in the Customary Process' (1995) 44(3) The International and Comparative Law Quarterly 521
Lowe V, *International Law* (OUP 2007)
Mačák K, *Internationalized Armed Conflicts in International Law* (OUP 2018)
Maia C and Kolb R, *Le statut international de la province angolaise du Cabinda à la lumière du droit international public* (Pedone 2015)
Majzub DB, 'Does Secession Mean Succession—The International Law of Treaty Succession and an Independent Quebec' (1999) 24(2) Queen's Law Journal 41
Malanczuk P, *Akehurst's Modern Introduction to International Law* (Routledge 1997)
Maluwa T, Du Plessis M, and Tladi D (eds), *The Pursuit of a Brave New World in International Law: Essays in Honour of John Dugard* (Brill/Nijhoff 2017)
Marmor A, 'Legal Positivism: Still Descriptive and Morally Neutral' (2006) 26(4) Oxford Journal of Legal Studies 683
Marston G, 'The Personality of the Foreign State in English Law' (1997) 56(2) The Cambridge Law Journal 374
Martens FF, *Современное международное право цивилизованных народов, Том I* (A Benke 1904)

Maryan Green NA, *International Law* (Pitman Publishing 1987)
McBeth A, Nolan J, and Rice S, *The International Law of Human Rights* (OUP 2017)
McCorquodale R, 'Group Rights' in Daniel Moeckli, Sangeeta Shah, and Sandesh Sivakumaran (eds), *International Human Rights Law* (OUP 2018)
Meggido T and Nevo Z, 'Revisiting Lessons on the New Law of Statehood: Palestinian Independence in a Post-Kosovo World' in Duncan French (ed), *Statehood and Self-Determination: Reconciling Tradition and Modernity in International Law* (CUP 2013)
Meron T, *Human Rights and Humanitarian Norms as Customary Law* (OUP 1989)
Mervin D, 'Henry Cabot Lodge and the League of Nations' (1971) 4(2) Journal of American Studies 201
Milanović M and Wood M (eds), *The Law and Politics of the Kosovo Advisory Opinion* (OUP 2015)
Miltner B, 'Territory and its Relationship to Treaties' in Michael J Bowman and Dino Kritsiotis (eds), *Conceptual and Contextual Perspectives on the Modern Law of Treaties* (CUP 2018)
Mintz SI, 'Leviathan as a Metaphor' (1989) II Hobbes Studies 3
Miron A, 'La reconnaissance du statut d'État à des entités contestées au regard des autorités juridictionnelles françaises' in Thierry Garcia (ed), *La reconnaissance du statut d'Etat à des entités contestées: approches de droits international, régional et interne* (Pedone 2018)
Mísová M, 'The legal character of the conflict in Chechnya' (Prague Watchdog, 18 May 2001) <https://reliefweb.int/report/russian-federation/legal-character-conflict-chechnya> last accessed 13 June 2024
Moeckli D, Sangeeta Shah S, and Sandesh Sivakumaran S (eds), *International Human Rights Law* (OUP 2018)
Momtaz D, 'Le droit international humanitaire applicable aux conflits armés non internationaux' (2001) 292 RCADI 9
Morgenthau HJ, 'Positivism, Functionalism, and International Law' (1940) 34(2) American Journal of International Law 260
Morrow GR, 'Plato and the Rule of Law' (1941) 50(2) The Philosophical Review 105
Mullerson R, 'The Continuity and Succession of States, by Reference to the Former USSR and Yugoslavia' (1993) 42(3) The International and Comparative Law Quarterly 473
Murphy SD, 'Democratic Legitimacy and the Recognition of States and Governments' (1999) 48(3) The International and Comparative Law Quarterly 545
Neff SC, *War and the Law of Nations* (CUP 2005)
Nesi G, 'Uti Possidetis Doctrine' in Anne Peters and Rüdiger Wolfrum (eds), *Max Planck Encyclopedias of International Law* (OUP 2018) <https://opil.ouplaw.com/display/10.1093/law:epil/9780199231690/law-9780199231690-e1125> last accessed 13 June 2024
Nolte G, 'Faktizität und Subjektivität im Völkerrecht: Anmerkungen zu Jochen Froweins "Das de facto-Regime im Völkerrecht" im Licht aktueller Entwicklungen' (2015) 75 Zeitschrift für ausländisches öffentliches Recht und Völkerrecht 715
O'Connell DP, *State Succession in Municipal and International Law, Volume I* (CUP 1967)
O'Hudson M, 'Recognition and Multipartite Treaties' (1929) 23(1) The American Journal of International Law 126
Okeke EC, *Jurisdictional Immunities of States and International Organizations* (OUP 2018)
Oppenheim LFL, *International Law: A Treatise, Volume I: Peace* (Longmans, Green and Co 1912)
Oppenheimer FE, 'Governments and Authorities in Exile' (1942) 36(4) The American Journal of International Law 568
Osiander A, 'Sovereignty, International Relations, and the Westphalian Myth' (2001) 55(2) International Organization 251
Padelford NJ and Andersson KGA, 'The Aaland Islands Question' (1939) 33(3) The American Journal of International Law 465
Pajtinka E, 'Between Diplomacy and Paradiplomacy: Taiwan´s Foreign Relations in Current Practice' (2017) 11(1) Journal of Nationalism, Memory & Language Politics 39
Papić T, 'On Hezbollah, Huawei, Homosexuality, Sharon Stone and a Chainsaw: The Economic Normalization Agreement between Serbia and Kosovo' (*EJIL:Talk!*, 8 September 2020)

<https://www.ejiltalk.org/on-hezbollah-huawei-homosexuality-sharon-stone-and-a-chain saw-the-economic-normalization-agreement-between-serbia-and-kosovo/> last accessed 13 June 2024

Papić T, 'Derecognition of States: The Case of Kosovo' (2022) 53 Cornell International Law Journal 683–729

Pauer-Studer H, 'Kelsen's Legal Positivism and the Challenge of Nazi Law' in Maria Carla Galavotti, Elisabeth Nemeth, and Friedrich Stadler (eds), *European Philosophy of Science – Philosophy of Science in Europe and the Viennese Heritage* (Springer 2014)

Payn BR, 'French Legislation in Exile' (1946) 28(3–4) Journal of Comparative Legislation and International Law 44–53

Pazartsis P, 'Judicial Activism and Judicial Self-Restraint: The PCIJ's *Lotus* Case' in Christian J Tams and Malgosia Fitzmaurice (eds), *Legacies of the Permanent Court of International Justice* (Martinus Nijhoff 2013)

Petersen N, 'The International Court of Justice and the Judicial Politics of Identifying Customary International Law' (2017) 28(2) The European Journal of International Law 357–85

Phillipson C, *Wheaton's Elements of International Law* (Steven and Sons Ltd 1916)

Piédelièvre R, *Précis du droit international public ou droit des gens: Des Etats et de leurs relations en temps de paix* (Pichon 1894)

Pinto R, 'Les règles du droit international concernant la guerre civile' (1965) 114 RCADI 451

Portmann R, *Legal Personality in International Law* (CUP 2010)

Pradier-Fodéré P, *Cours de Droit Diplomatique: A l'Usage des Agents Politiques du Ministère des Affaires Étrangères des États Européens et Américains* (Paris 1899)

Price PP, 'The Impact of Constitutive Recognition on the Right to Self-Determination: An Analysis of United States Recognition Practices Utilizing the Chinese Question as a Guide' (1979) 14(1) Valparaiso University Law Review 123

Raič D, *Statehood and the Law of Self-Determination* (Kluwer Law International 2002)

Rawnsley GD, *Taiwan's Informal Diplomacy and Propaganda* (Palgrave Macmillan 2000)

Reuter P, *Institutions internationales* (Presses universitaires de France 1969)

Rivier A, *Principes du droit des gens: Tome premier* (Arthur Rousseau 1896)

Robertson WS, 'The First Legations of the United States in Latin America' (1915) 2(2) The Mississippi Valley Historical Review 183

Robertson WS, 'The Recognition of the Hispanic American Nations by the United States' (1918) 1(3) The Hispanic American Historical Review 239

Robertson WS, 'The United States and Spain in 1822' (1915) 20(4) The American Historical Review 781

Romero M, 'The United States and the Liberation of the Spanish-American Colonies' (1897) 165(488) The North American Review 70

Ronen Y, 'Recognition of Divorce without Recognition of Statehood' (2004) 63(2) The Cambridge Journal of International Law 268

Ronen Y, 'Entities that Can Be States but Do Not Claim to Be' in Duncan French (ed), *Statehood and Self-Determination: Reconciling Tradition and Modernity in International Law* (CUP 2013)

Rousseau JJ, *Du contrat social, Ou principes du droit politique* (Athena 2023)

Ruffert M, 'Recognition of Foreign Legislative and Administrative Acts' in Anne Peters and Professor Rüdiger Wolfrum (eds), *Max Planck Encyclopedias of International Law* (OUP 2021) <https://opil.ouplaw.com/display/10.1093/law:epil/9780199231690/law-9780199231690-e1087> last accessed 13 June 2024

Ruys T, *'Armed Attack' and Article 51 of the UN Charter* (CUP 2010)

Ruys T, Corten O, and Hofer A, *The Use of Force in International Law: A Case-Based Approach* (OUP 2016)

Ruys T, Nicolas Angelet N, and Luca Ferro L (eds), *The Cambridge Handbook of Immunities and International Law* (CUP 2019)

Sakran, S and Hayashi M, 'Palestine's Accession to Multilateral Treaties: Effective Circumvention of the Statehood Question and its Consequences' (2017) 25(1) Journal of International Cooperation Studies 81–99

Salmon J, *La reconnaissance d'état* (Librairie Armand Colin 1971)
Sassòli M, *International Humanitarian Law: Rules, Controversies, and Solutions to Problems Arising in Warfare* (Edward Elgar 2019)
Sastroamidjojo A and Delson R, 'The Status of the Republic of Indonesia in International Law' (1949) 49(3) Columbia Law Review 344
Scelle G, 'Règles générales du droit de la paix' (1933) 46 RCADI 327
Schmitt BE, 'The Peace Treaties of 1919–1920' (1960) 104(1) Proceedings of the American Philosophical Society 101
Schmitt MN, 'Ukraine Symposium—Territorial Acquisition and Armed Conflict' (Articles of War, 29 August 2023) <https://lieber.westpoint.edu/territorial-acquisition-armed-conflict/> last accessed 13 June 2024
Schmitt MN and Coble KS, 'The Evolving Nagorno-Karabakh Conflict—An International Law Perspective—Part I' (Articles of War, 27 September 2023) <https://lieber.westpoint.edu/evolving-nagorno-karabakh-conflict-international-law-perspective-part-i/> last accessed 13 June 2024
Schwarzenberger G, 'Title to Territory: Response to a Challenge' (1957) 51(2) American Journal of International Law 308
Sebok AJ, 'Misunderstanding Positivism' (1995) 93(7) Michigan Law Review 2054
Shaw MN, *International Law* (CUP 2017)
Shearer I, 'State Succession in Relation to Treaties: Looking Back and Looking Forward' in Tiyanjana Maluwa, Max du Plessis, and Dire Tladi (eds), *The Pursuit of a Brave New World in International Law: Essays in Honour of John Dugard* (Brill/Nijhoff 2017)
Simma B, 'Legal Aspects of East-West German Relations' (1985) 9(1) Maryland Journal of International Law 97
Stansifer CL, 'Application of the Tobar Doctrine to Central America' (1967) 23(2) The Americas 251–72
Steadman JM, 'Leviathan and Renaissance Etymology' (1967) 28 Journal of the History of Ideas 575
Stern WB, 'Kelsen's Theory of International Law' (1936) 30(4) The American Political Science Review 736
Strydom H (ed), *International Law* (OUP 2016)
Suganami H, 'Understanding Sovereignty through Kelsen/Schmitt' (2007) 33(3) Review of International Studies 511
Susan Marks, *The Riddle of All Constitutions: International Law, Democracy, and the Critique of Ideology* (OUP 2000)
Suy E, *Les actes juridiques unilatéraux en droit international public* (R Pichon & R Durand-Auzias 1962)
Šahović M, 'Codification des principes du droit international des relations amicales et de la coopération entre les états' (1972) 137 RCADI 242
Talmon S, 'The Constitutive Versus the Declaratory Theory of Recognition: *Tertium Non Datur*?' (2004) 75(1) British Yearbook of International Law 101
Talmon S, 'The Duty Not to "Recognize as Lawful" a Situation Created by the Illegal Use of Force or Other Serious Breaches of a Jus Cogens Obligation: An Obligation without Real Substance?' in Christian Tomuschat and Jean-Marc Thouvenin (eds), *The Fundamental Rules of the International Legal Order* (Martinus Nijhoff Publishers 2006)
Talmon S, 'New Zealand's Policy of Implied Recognition of States: One Step Ahead or Falling Behind?' (2009) 7 New Zealand Yearbook of International Law 3
Tennant JS, 'Recognition Cases in American Courts, 1923–1930' (1931) 29(6) Michigan Law Review 708
Tesson S, 'La doctrine Hallstein, entre rigueur et pragmatisme (1955–1969)' (2002) 110 Relations internationales 219–34
Thirlway H, *The Sources of International Law* (OUP 2019)
Thormodsgard OH and Moore RD, 'Recognition in International Law' (1927) 12(2) Washington University Law Review 108

Tierney B, '"The Prince is Not Bound by the Laws." Accursius and the Origins of the Modern State' (1963) 5(4) Comparative Studies in Society and History 378

Tomuschat C, 'Secession and Self-Determination' in Marcelo G Kohen (ed), *Secession: International Law Perspectives* (CUP 2006)

Tomuschat C, 'The Status of the "Islamic State" Under International Law' (2015) 90(3/4) Die Friedens-Warte 223

Triepel H, *Völkerrecht und Landesrecht* (Verlag von C L Hirschfeld 1899)

Turns D, 'The Stimson Doctrine of Non-Recognition: Its Historical Genesis and Influence on Contemporary International Law' (2003) 2(1) Chinese Journal of International Law 105–43

Türk D, 'Recognition of States: A Comment' (1993) 4 European Journal of International Law 66

Van den Wyngaert C and Stessens G, 'The International Non Bis In Idem Principle: Resolving Some of the Unanswered Questions' (1999) 48(4) The International and Comparative Law Quarterly 779–804

Verdross A, 'Règles générales du droit international de la paix' (1929) 30 RCADI 271

Verdross A, 'The Plea of Domestic jurisdiction before an International Tribunal and a Political Organ of the United Nations' (1968) 28(1) Zeitschrift für Öffentliches Recht und Völkerrecht 33

Verhoeven J, *La reconnaissance internationale dans la pratique contemporaine* (Pedone 1975)

Vidmar J, 'Remedial Secession in International Law: Theory and (Lack of) Practice' (2010) 6(1) St Antony's International Review 37

Vidmar J, 'The *Kosovo* Advisory Opinion Scrutinized' (2011) 24(2) Leiden Journal of International Law 355

Vidmar J, 'Conceptualizing Declarations of Independence in International Law' (2012) 32(1) Oxford Journal of Legal Studies 153

Vidmar J, 'Remarks' (2013) 107 ASIL Proceedings 215

Vidmar J, 'The Importance of Legal Criteria for Statehood: A Rejoinder to Dapo Akande' (*EJIL:Talk!*, 9 August 2013) <https://www.ejiltalk.org/the-importance-of-legal-criteria-for-statehood-a-rejoinder-to-dapo-akande/> last accessed 13 June 2024

Vink M, 'The Competition for Self-Determination in Czechoslovakia, 1918–1919' (2012) 46 New Zealand Slavonic Journal 41

Vinx L, 'Austin, Kelsen, and the Model of Sovereignty' (2011) 24 Canadian Journal of Law & Jurisprudence 47

Visoka G, Doyle J, and Newman E (eds), *Routledge Handbook of State Recognition* (Routledge 2020)

Wagnon H, 'La personnalité du Saint-Siège en droit international: Les faits – les doctrines' (1977) 30(4) Studia Diplomatica 321

Walker WL, 'Recognition of Belligerency and Grant of Belligerent Rights' (1937) 23 Transactions of the Grotius Society 177

Warbrick C, 'The New British Policy on Recognition of Governments' (1981) 30(3) The International and Comparative Law Quarterly 568

Warbrick C, 'Recognition of States' (1992) 41(2) The International and Comparative Law Quarterly 473

Warbrick C, 'Recognition of Governments' (1993) 56 The Modern Law Review 9

Warbrick C, 'States and Recognition in International Law' in Malcolm Evans (ed), *International Law* (OUP 2006)

Warbrick C, 'Kosovo: The Declaration of Independence' (2008) 57(3) The International and Comparative Law Quarterly 675

Wehberg H, 'La guerre civile et le droit international' (1938) 63 RCADI 1

Wilk K, 'Federal Republic of Germany Case Note' (1976) 70(1) The American Journal of International Law 147

Williams JF, 'Some Thoughts on the Doctrine of Recognition in International Law' (1934) 47(5) Harvard Law Review 776

Wong KT, 'Changing Taiwan's Foreign Policy: From One China to Two States' (2000) 24(1) Asian Perspective 5

Wood M, 'The *Caroline* Incident–1837' in Tom Ruys, Olivier Corten, and Alexandra Hofer, *The Use of Force in International Law: A Case-Based Approach* (OUP 2016)

Wright H, 'The Montevideo Conference and Organization for Peace' (1934) 97(2) World Affairs 100

Wright Q, 'Some Thoughts About Recognition' (1950) 44(3) The American Journal of International Law 548

Wyler É, *Théorie et pratique de la reconaissance d'état: Une approche épistemologique du droit international* (Bruylant 2013)

Yang X, *State Immunity in International Law* (CUP 2012)

Yefes JM, 'Les problèmes fondamentaux du droit des gens en Amérique' (1934) 28 RCADI 1

Zemanek K, 'The Legal Foundations of the International System: General Course on Public International Law' (1997) 266 RCADI 229

Zimmermann A, 'State Succession and the Nationality of Natural Persons' in PM Eisenmann and M Koskenniemi (eds), *State Succession: Codification Tested against the Facts* (Brill/Nijhoff 2000)

Zimmermann A, *Staatennachfolge in völkerrechtliche Verträge: Zugleich ein Beitrag zu den Möglichkeiten und Grenzen völkerrechtlicher Kodifikation* (Springer 2000)

Zyberi G, 'The International Court of Justice and the Recognition of States' in Gëzim Visoka, John Doyle, and Edward Newman (eds), *Routledge Handbook of State Recognition* (Routledge 2020)

Index

For the benefit of digital users, indexed terms that span two pages (e.g., 52–53) may, on occasion, appear on only one of those pages.

The manufacturer's authorised representative in the EU for product safety is Oxford University Press España S.A. of el Parque Empresarial San Fernando de Henares, Avenida de Castilla, 2 – 28830 Madrid (www.oup.es/en or product.safety@oup.com). OUP España S.A. also acts as importer into Spain of products made by the manufacturer.

www.ingramcontent.com/pod-product-compliance
Lightning Source LLC
Chambersburg PA
CBHW061054080726
47757CB00027B/68
9780198905653

sole limitation may be found in the *Lotus* dictum against presuming limitations on State sovereignty, which the ILC recognised by recalling that, '[i]n the case of doubt as to the scope of the obligations resulting from such a declaration, such obligations must be interpreted in a restrictive manner'.[52] An additional limitation is that the declaration or act must be made by 'an authority vested with the power to do so',[53] namely individuals or organs capable of 'speaking' for the State as an abstract entity.

3.1.4 Diplomatic Recognition as a Unilateral Act in Particular

As mentioned earlier, the majority view in doctrine is that diplomatic recognition belongs to the category of unilateral acts. This view has been expressed by lawyers coming from a plethora of different conceptions of international law, including Cavaglieri,[54] Kelsen,[55] Hersch Lauterpacht,[56] Verhoeven,[57] Crawford,[58] Shaw,[59] and Special Rapporteur Rodríguez Cedeño,[60] to name a few. Brierly describes it as a unilateral political act,[61] but that comes across as a position on the effects, rather than nature, of recognition.

Throughout history, recognition of statehood has been expressed in a formal declaration issued by an existing State to a new one. Illustrative of this practice is the US recognition of South Sudan, taking the form of a presidential statement whereby 'the US formally recognizes the Republic of South Sudan as a sovereign and independent state ... After so much struggle by the people of South Sudan, the

Anne Peters and Rüdiger Wolfrum (eds), *Max Planck Encyclopedias of International Law* (OUP 2006) <https://opil.ouplaw.com/display/10.1093/law:epil/9780199231690/law-9780199231690-e1455?prd=EPIL> last accessed 13 June 2024 and James A Green, *The Persistent Objector Rule in International Law* (OUP 2016).

[52] Guiding Principles on Unilateral Declarations (n 28) Principle 7.

[53] ibid Principle 4.

[54] 'Des nombreux exemples historiques de reconnaissance solennelle d'un nouvel État se dégage, à notre avis, la conviction qu'il s'agit d'un acte unilatéral, d'une manifestation des États anciens adressée à l'État nouveau'. Cavaglieri (n 5) 352.

[55] 'The legal act of recognition is, as the establishment of a fact, a unilateral act'. Kelsen (n 2) 609.

[56] 'The practice of States shows that recognition is as a rule a unilateral act ....' Lauterpacht (n 5) 57.

[57] Joe Verhoeven, *La reconnaissance internationale dans la pratique contemporaine* (Pedone 1975) 2.

[58] 'Plainly recognition is a political process interposed by unilateral assessment by a State deciding whether or not it will recognize another as a State and thereby engage in normal political and legal relations with that other State.' James Crawford, 'Chance, Order, Change: The Course of International Law: General Course on Public International Law' (2014) 365 RCADI 9, 148.

[59] Shaw (n 10) 90.

[60] 'Acts of recognition in general could represent a specific category of ... acts whereby States assume unilateral obligations.' *Sixth report on unilateral acts of States, by Mr Victor Rodríguez Cedeño, Special Rapporteur* (30 May 2003) A/CN.4/534, 55–56.

[61] 'Nous pouvons donc conclure que la reconnaissance, en droit international, a toujours une portée simplement déclaratoire, et non constitutive. C'est un acte de politique et non pas de droit et l'on y chercherait donc en vain des effets juridiques.' James-Leslie Brierly, 'Règles générales du droit de la paix' (1936) 58 RCADI 1, 59.